CONTEMPORARY READINGS IN

AMERICAN GOVERNMENT

EDITED BY MARK J. ROZELL
AND
JOHN KENNETH WHITE

THE CATHOLIC UNIVERSITY OF AMERICA

Prentice
Hall

Upper Saddle River, New Jersey 07458

Library of Congress Cataloging-in-Publication

Contemporary readings in American government/edited by Mark Rozell and John Kenneth White.
    p. cm.
    Includes index.
    ISBN 0-13-040645-7
    1. United States—Politics and government—1993–2001. I. Rozell, Mark J. II. White, John Kenneth.

    JK271.C732 2002
    320.473—dc21

                      2001050047

Sr. Acquisitions Editor: Heather Shelstad
Editorial Assistant: Jessica Drew
Exec. Managing Editor: Ann Marie McCarthy
Production Liaison: Fran Russello
Project Manager: Marty Sopher/Lithokraft II
Prepress and Manufacturing Buyer: Ben Smith
Interior Design: Lithokraft II
Art Director: Jayne Conte
Cover Designer: Bruce Kenselaar
Cover Art: Anthony Edgeworth/Corbis Stock Market
Marketing Manager: Claire Rehwinkel

This book was set in 10/12 Meridien by Lithokraft II and was printed and bound
by Courier Companies, Inc. The cover was printed by Phoenix Color Corp.

©2002 by Pearson Education, Inc.
Upper Saddle River, New Jersey 07458

Printed in the United States of America
10 9 8 7 6 5 4 3 2 1

ISBN 0-13-040645-7

Pearson Education LTD, *London*
Pearson Education Australia Pte, Limited, *Sydney*
Pearson Education *Singapore,* Pte. Ltd.
Pearson Education North Asia Ltd., *Hong Kong*
Pearson Education Canada, Ltd., *Toronto*
Pearson Educación de Mexico, S.A. de C.V.
Pearson Education—*Japan, Tokyo*
Pearson Education *Malaysia,* Pte. Ltd.
Pearson Education Upper Saddle River, *New Jersey*

CONTENTS

PREFACE

The purpose of this volume is to offer faculty and students a unique reader for introductory American government courses. There are many fine introductary-level readers providing substantial numbers of classical and contemporary essays. Typically these readers have as many as 50 or more articles. This volume is the outcome of our long-standing desire for a reader that provides one or two substantial essays on each of the major topics usually covered in an introduction to American government textbook. Since the standard textbooks nicely cover the foundational material, we like to have students also read contemporary essays to establish the relevance of text material to the current political world.

The readings we have chosen are highly contemporary—for example, articles that create a "buzz" among those in the academy—yet speak to a wider audience. As we begin a new century, our politics are in transition. A post-industrial/Information Age economy is taking shape, creating a new kind of politics and new means of linking voters to government. Old party coalitions have disappeared, and new ones are forming. Our institutions of government have had to adapt to new situations. Witness, for example, first the downsizing of a Cold War-based presidency into one focused on domestic issues, and then the sudden shift to combating international terrorism. Republican control of the Congress in the mid-late 1990s reshaped that institution and now a divided Congress seeks to maintain its authority during a period of crisis and pleas for a much strengthened presidency. The Supreme Court has had to cope with new cases that arise out of the Information Age—much in the same way that the Court at the turn of the 20th century had to deal with cases stemming from the new industrial era. The readings we have selected each speak to the dizzying array of change that has swept the American political landscape.

Several persons provided us with assistance for which we are grateful. We thank Steven Brust, La Toya Bennet, and Nina Weiss for their help with a number of library and administrative tasks. Beth Gillett Meja was the initial editor of this project who assisted in the formulation stage and Jennifer Bryant ably assumed editing duties as the project developed. Marty Sopher provided very helpful editing of the selections. Finally, we thank our colleagues in the Department of Politics at The Catholic University of America for providing a supportive environment in which to pursue our teaching and writing.

Mark J. Rozell
John Kenneth White

ABOUT THE EDITORS

Mark J. Rozell is a Professor of Politics at The Catholic University of America. His previous books include *Executive Privilege; Second Coming: The New Christian Right in Virginia Politics* (co-written with Clyde Wilcox); *Interest Groups in American Campaigns* (also co-written with Clyde Wilcox); and *The Bush Presidency* (co-written with Ryan Barrileaux).

John Kenneth White is a Professor of Politics at The Catholic University of America. His latest book is entitled *The Values Divide: American Politics and Culture in Transition.* Among his previous books are *The Politics of Ideas* (co-edited with John C. Green); *Political Parties in the Information Age* (co-written with Daniel M. Shea); *Still Seeing Red: How the Cold War Shapes the New American Politics; The New Politics of Old Values;* and *The Fractured Electorate: Political Parties and Social Change in Southern New England.*

INTRODUCTION

WHAT MAKES THE AMERICAN POLITY UNIQUE?

John Kenneth White
Catholic University of America

"*I want a house!*" Those were the last words Yelena Bonner spoke upon leaving the United States in 1986 to return to her native Soviet Union. Her dream was the quintessential American dream: to be oneself in one's private dwelling place. "A house," said Bonner, "is a symbol of independence, spiritual and physical." At age sixty-three the Soviet dissident and wife of the Soviet inventor of the atom bomb, Andre Sakarov, mourned, "I've never had a house . . . [not even] a corner I could call my own." She sadly concluded, "My dream, my own house, is unattainable for my husband and myself, as unattainable as heaven on earth."[1]

Yelena Bonner's "dream" is not so much about home ownership as it is a longing for freedom. Observers frequently describe American values by using metaphorical devices. "The Star Spangled Banner" proclaims the United States to be the "*land* of the free" and the "*home* of the brave." Most countries, including the United States, pour considerable quantities of mortar and brick into mausoleums that immortalize national heroes. However, the United States has also devoted nearly equal amounts to erect monuments to ideas: on Ellis Island, the Statue of Liberty; in Philadelphia, the Liberty Bell and Independence Hall; in Boston, the Freedom Trail. In addition, New Hampshire license plates bear the motto, "Live free or die." These symbols are not mere icons passed from generation to generation, but meaningful symbols of American values. A second-generation citizen told of his immigrant forebears' reverence for the

---

[1] Yelena Bonner, "A Quirky Farewell to America," *Newsweek,* 2 June 1986, p. 45.

Statue of Liberty: "She was America to my parents. They talked about her like she was alive. To them, I guess, she was."[2]

As these symbols demonstrate, the American polity is not a structure of government, but a contract between the government and its people whose clauses contain shared values. Among the most cherished of these is freedom. A blue-collar worker in the early 1960's said:

> My God, I work where I want to work. I spend my money where I want to spend it. I buy what I want to buy. I go where I want to go. I read what I want to read. My kids go to the school that they want to go to, or where I want to send them. We bring them up in the religion we want to bring them up in. What else—what else could you have?[3]

For many Americans, love of country means more than love of the area it occupies. In his 1997 State of the Union Address, Bill Clinton said: "America is far more than a place. It is an idea, the most powerful idea in the history of nations. And all of us in this chamber, we are now bearers of that idea, leading a great people into a new world."[4] Most Americans believe that freedom is at the core of the American idea. According to a 1986 poll, 88 percent believed that "freedom and liberty were two ideas that make America great."[5] A 2000 poll found 91 percent agreed with the statement, "Being an American is a big part of who I am."[6] And, once here, Americans don't want to leave: one survey found just 11 percent saying they would like to emigrate elsewhere—a sharp contrast with the one-third of Britons and Germans, and one-fifth of the French and Canadians who prefer living somewhere else.[7]

Freedom and liberty are values closely associated with the United States. Cherishing freedom began with the first settlers. William Pitt captured this aspect of the colonists when he told the British House of Lords in 1770: "I love Americans because they love liberty."[8] Six years later Thomas Jefferson elaborated on this

---

[2]Quoted in Lee Iacocca, "What Liberty Means to Me," *Newsweek,* 7 July 1986, p. 18.

[3]Robert Lane, *Political Ideology: Why the Common Man Believes What He Does* (New York: Free Press, 1962), p. 24.

[4]Bill Clinton, State of the Union Address, Washington, D.C., February 3, 1997.

[5]"Foreign Roots on Native Soil," *U.S. News and World Reports,* 7 July 1986, p. 18.

[6]Blum and Weprin Associates, poll, March 13-16, 2000. Text of question: "Do you agree or disagree with this statement: "Being an American is a big part of who I am?" Agree, 91 percent; disagree, 8 percent; not sure/refused to answer, 1 percent.

[7]Cited in Alan Wolfe, *One Nation After All* (New York: Viking, 1998), p. 133.

[8]Quoted in ABC News, "Liberty Weekend Preview," July 2, 1986.

theme in the Declaration of Independence: "We hold these truths to be self-evident, that all men are created equal, that they are endowed by their Creator with certain unalienable rights, that among these are Life, Liberty and the pursuit of Happiness."

As the years passed, an ideology that was uniquely American and based on freedom took hold. One British writer after visiting the United States in the 1920s, concluded, "America is the only nation in the world that is founded on a creed."[9] That creed is this: A belief in the malleability of the future by the individual. Most often, however, the phrase "American dream" is the expression commonly used to express this idea. The American dream is as old, and as young, as the United States itself. Regarding the presidency of John Quincy Adams, one historian wrote that Adams believed his country stood for opportunity, "the chance to grow into something bigger and finer, as bigger and finer appealed to him."[10] At the turn of the twenty-first century, little has changed. Like the sixth president, people everywhere continue to hope that their lives and their children's lives will be better.

Today, Americans of every political stripe extol the American dream. Accepting the Republican presidential nomination in 1960, Richard Nixon told the delegates: "I believe in the American dream because I have seen it come true in my own life."[11] Perhaps the most eloquent testimonials to the American dream come from ordinary Americans themselves. A steelworker captured the sentiments expressed by Nixon more forcefully: "If my kid wants to work in a factory, I'm gonna kick the hell out of him. I want my kid to be an effete snot. I want him to be able to quote Walt Whitman, to be proud of it. If you can't improve yourself, you improve your posterity. Otherwise life isn't worth nothing."[12] When asked what the American dream means to them, respondents often mention a strong family life and financial security: 25 percent said it is having a good family life and taking care of one's family; 20 percent said it is the freedom to choose; 19 percent said it was having financial stability and making a good living; 16 percent thought it lies in achieving success and reaching one's goals; 16 percent said it was enjoying life

---

[9]Gilbert G. Chesterton, *What I Saw in America* (New York: Dodd, Mead, 1922), p. 8.

[10]The phrase "the American dream" was coined by James Trunslow Adams during the Great Depression in James Trunslow Adams, *The Epic of America,* (Boston: Little, Brown, 1935), p. 174.

[11]Richard Nixon, Acceptance Speech, Republican National Convention, Chicago, July 28, 1960.

[12]Quoted in Terry W. Hartle, "Dream Jobs?" *Public Opinion* (September/October 1986): II.

and achieving happiness; 11 percent said it was owning a home; 10 percent said it was having a good job and being happy with your work.[13]

The freedom to excel is an important component of the American dream. But another value is also inherent in the concept: equality of opportunity. Americans have been nearly fanatical in their devotion to this particular value. Max Berger wrote that the most indelible impression nineteenth-century British travelers had of their former colonies was "the aggressive equalitarianism of the people."[14] Faith in aggressive equalitarianism has made the American dream especially appealing to the ordinary citizen. Indeed, it is the common man and woman who figure most prominently in the dream's persistence. They gave birth to it; they sustain it. Richard Nixon realized this. Accepting the Republican presidential nomination for a second time in 1968, he told the delegates that it was the "great majority of Americans, the forgotten Americans" who "give lift to the American dream."[15] Today, the "forgotten Americans" still believe that with enough diligence and energy they can, like Nixon, see the American dream come true—if not in their lives, then in the lives of their children.

This conviction has a long history. In his 1782 essay "What Is an American?" Jean de Crevecoeur found the answer in the American penchant for hard work:

> Here the rewards of his industry follow with equal steps the progress of his labour; his labour is founded on the basis of *self-interest*; can it want a stronger allurement? Wives and children, who before in vain demanded of him a morsel of bread, now, fat and frolicsome, gladly help their father to clear those fields whence exuberant crops are to arise to feed and to clothe them all; without any part being claimed, either by a despotic prince, a rich abbot, or a mighty lord."[16]

Glorification of the work ethic has endured. A 1997 survey finds that 77 percent of Americans believe that the United States is

---

[13]Hart and Teeter Research Companies, poll, October 29-30, 1997. Text of question: "What does the term 'the American dream' mean to you? What would you say are the major characteristics of the American dream?"

[14]Max Berger, *The British Traveler in America, 1836-1860,* (New York: Columbia University Press, 1943), pp. 54-55.

[15]Richard Nixon, Acceptance Speech, Republican National Convention, Miami, 8 August 1968. *New York Times,* 9 August 1968, 20.

[16]Michel-Guillaume-Jean de Crevecoeur, *Letters from an American Farmer, 1782* in Henry Steele Commager, ed., *Living Ideas in America,* (New York: Harper and Brothers, 1951), p. 21.

unique among all other countries in that it offers the opportunity for a poor person to get ahead by working hard. Seventy-six percent say they are satisfied with their opportunities to get ahead thanks to hard work.[17] No wonder that civil rights leader Martin Luther King, like so many before him, seized on the American commitment to equalitarianism to woo supporters to the civil rights cause. Addressing thousands gathered at the Lincoln Memorial in 1963, King said in his speech, "I have a dream that my four little children will one day live in a nation where they will not be judged by the color of their skin but by the content of their character."[18]

THE AMERICAN CONSENSUS

The values of freedom, liberty, and equality of opportunity are dominant themes in U.S. history. They explain, for example, why so many Americans admire successful entrepreneurs. In the nineteenth century, Horatio Alger created a role model for many. By the late twentieth century, Microsoft Chairman Bill Gates had become a folk hero, much admired for his ingenuity and dedication to hard work.[19] Gates, whose worth is an estimated *$90 billion*, consistently appears on Gallup's "most admired man list," and two-thirds view him favorably, despite the recent attempts of the U.S. government to break up Microsoft. Americans see Gates as the premier business leader of the twentieth century, and one-third name Gates as the greatest

---

[17]Princeton Survey Research Associates, poll, July 31-August 17, 1997. Text of question: "We'd like to know in what ways, if any, you think the United States is different from all other countries. As I read you a list of possible ways the U.S. is unique, tell me which ones you think make this country different. What about this . . . the opportunity for a poor person to get ahead by working hard? Does this make the U.S. different from all other countries, or not?" Yes, makes different; 77 percent; no, does not; 21 percent; don't know/refused, 3 percent. Gallup poll, January 10-14, 2001. Text of question: "Next, I'm going to read some aspects of life in America today. For each one, please say whether you are very satisfied, somewhat satisfied, somewhat dissatisfied, or very dissatisfied. . . . The opportunity for a person in this nation to get ahead by working hard." Very satisfied, 36 percent; somewhat satisfied, 40 percent; somewhat dissatisfied, 14 percent; very dissatisfied, 8 percent; no opinion, 2 percent.

[18]Martin Luther King, "I Have a Dream," Address at the Lincoln Memorial, August 28, 1963.

[19]Gallup poll, January 25-26, 2000. Text of question: "Just off the top of your head, would you happen to know the name of the chairman of Microsoft?" Bill Gates (correct), 62 percent; any other response, 3 percent; no opinion, 35 percent.

business figure in the last *thousand years*.[20] As these polls indicate, Gates's success is universally celebrated, not derided.

Business people are celebrated principally because they embody the American dream. Not surprisingly, Americans are obsessed with property (and property rights), largely because they are the tangible products of a triumphant political creed. Political scientist James Q. Wilson described the tendency of Southern Californians to display the fruits of their labors: "Each family had a house; there it was for all to see and inspect. With a practiced glance, one could tell how much it cost, how well it was cared for, how good a lawn had been coaxed into uncertain life, and how tastefully plants and shrubs had been set out."[21] The reverence for property is especially strong, even if not everyone has much to show off. In 1972 Democratic presidential candidate George McGovern made what he thought would be a surefire, popular promise to blue-collar rubber factory workers: as president he would seek to increase inheritance taxes so that the rich

---

[20]Gallup/CNN/*USA Today*, poll, December 15-17, 2000. Text of question: "What man that you have heard or read about, living today in any part of the world, do you admire most? Who is your second choice?" Bill Clinton, 6 percent; Pope John Paul II, 6 percent; Colin Powell, 5 percent; George W. Bush, 5 percent; Al Gore, 5 percent; Reverend Billy Graham, 4 percent; Ronald Reagan, 3 percent; Nelson Mandela, 3 percent; Jimmy Carter, 1 percent; Bill Gates, 1 percent; former president George Bush, 1 percent; Jesse Jackson, 1 percent; Tiger Woods, 1 percent; Gordon Hinckley, 1 percent; Dalai Lama, 1 percent; Michael Jordan, 1 percent; friend/relative, 5 percent; other, 26 percent; none/no opinion, 33 percent. Gallup/CNN/*USA Today*, poll, May 5-7, 2000. Text of question: "Thinking about Bill Gates—the founder and CEO (Chief Executive Officer) of Microsoft—do you have a favorable or unfavorable opinion of Bill Gates?" Favorable, 69 percent; unfavorable, 16 percent; never heard of (volunteered), 3 percent; no opinion, 12 percent. NBC News/*Wall Street Journal*, poll, September 9-12, 1999. Text of question: "Which one of the following do you consider to be the most important American business leader of the 20th century? Bill Gates, founder of Microsoft; Henry Ford, founder of Ford Motor Company; Andrew Carnegie, founder of US (United States) Steel; John D. Rockefeller, founder of Standard Oil; Thomas Watson, founder of IBM (International Business Machines); Sam Walton, founder of Wal-Mart; Ray Kroc, founder of McDonald's?" Bill Gates, 32 percent; Henry Ford, 28 percent; Andrew Carnegie, 8 percent; John D. Rockefeller, 7 percent; Thomas Watson, 6 percent; Sam Walton, 6 percent; Ray Kroc, 3 percent; all (volunteered), 6 percent; none/other (volunteered), 1 percent. ABC News, poll, August 16-22, 1999. Text of question: "Who do you feel is the greatest figure in the last thousand years, from anywhere in the world, specifically in the field of business?" Bill Gates, 33 percent; Henry Ford, 6 percent; John D. Rockefeller, 6 percent; Donald Trump, 5 percent; Lee Iacocca, 2 percent; Andrew Carnegie, 2 percent; specific businesses, 2 percent; Steve Forbes, 1 percent; Adam Smith, 1 percent; Warren Buffett, 1 percent; Allan Greenspan, 1 percent; Ross Perot, 1 percent; Howard Hughes, 1 percent; Joseph Kennedy, 1 percent; other business, 11 percent; no opinion, 27 percent.

[21]James Q. Wilson, "A Guide to Reagan Country: The Political Culture of Southern California," *Commentary* (May 1967): 40.

could bequeath less to their families and more to the government. To McGovern's amazement, he was roundly booed.[22]

Not every American attains the success promised by the American dream. During a period of high unemployment in the 1980s, singer-songwriter Bruce Springsteen in a song entitled "The River," wondered aloud whether the American dream is a lie if not fulfilled or whether it represented something worse. Throughout history, Americans have consistently refused to confront Springsteen's haunting question, preferring to shoulder the blame themselves for having failed to live up to expectations. A quarter of a century ago a mechanic said:

> I could have been a lot better off but through my own foolishness, I'm not. What causes poverty? Foolishness. When I came out of the service, my wife had saved a few dollars and I had a few bucks. I wanted to have a good time, I'm throwing money away like water. Believe me, had I used my head right, I could have had a house. I don't feel sorry for myself—what happened, happened, you know. Of course you pay for it.[23]

Any attempt to limit the American dream meets with considerable resistance. Opportunity without constraints has been a recurrent pattern in our political thought. A 1940 Fortune poll found 74 percent rejected the idea that there "should be a law limiting the amount of money an individual is allowed to earn in a year."[24] Forty-one years later, the consensus held: 79 percent did not think that "there should be a top limit on incomes so that no one can earn more than $100,000 a year." Even those who earned less than $5,000 held that opinion.[25]

Beneath such opinions is a faith that approaches fanaticism. Historian Garry Wills wrote in 1978 that in the United States one must adopt the American dream "wholeheartedly, proclaim it, prove one's devotion to it."[26] He may have had in mind the House Committee on Un-American Activities, which was established during the hysteria about worldwide communist expansionism in 1945. For three decades the committee inquired into the public and private lives of suspected communists. Perhaps the most notable

---

[22] Cited in Lance Morrow, "Freedom First," *Time,* 16 June 1986, p. 29.

[23] Quoted in Lane, *Political Ideology,* p. 69.

[24] Cited in Everett Carll Ladd, *The American Polity,* (New York: Norton, 1987), 67.

[25] Survey by Civic Service, 5-18 March 1981.

[26] Gary Wills, *Inventing America* (New York: Vintage Books, 1978), p. xxii.

among the committee's many investigations was one led by freshman congressman Richard M. Nixon in 1946. Nixon doggedly pursued the suspected ties of a State Department official, Alger Hiss, to the U.S. Communist party—an inquiry that eventually resulted in Hiss's indictment and conviction for perjury. However, the committee's injudicious blacklisting of other Americans formed a stain on the witnesses and the committee itself that could not be removed. In 1975 the Committee on Un-American Activities was abolished on the grounds that it, too, was un-American.

The Committee on Un-American Activities illustrates the rigid enforcement of political orthodoxy in the United States. Former Library of Congress director Daniel Boorstin rhetorically asks, "Who would think of using the word 'unItalian' or 'unFrench' as we use the word un-American?"[27] Over the years, our advancement of the "American Way of Life" has taken on missionary proportions. In the nineteenth century Herman Melville compared Americans to the biblical tribes of Israel, calling them "the peculiar chosen people . . . the Israel of our time."[28] A century later Ronald Reagan subscribed to a similar creationist view: "Think for a moment how special it is to be an American. Can we doubt that only a Divine Providence placed this land, this island of freedom, here as a refuge for all those people in the world who yearn to breathe free?"[29] While Americans remain highly pluralistic regarding public expressions of unpopular views, their ideological zealotry about "the American way" places limits upon such speech. A 1996 National Opinion Research Center (NORC) poll found large majorities wanting classroom history lessons to include the following themes:

- "With hard work and perseverance, anyone can succeed in America." (83 percent)
- "American democracy is only as strong as the virtue of its citizens." (83 percent)
- "America's contribution is one of expanding freedom for more and more people." (71 percent)
- "From its start, America had a destiny to set an example for other nations." (65 percent)
- "Our nation was founded on biblical principles." (58 percent)

---

[27]Daniel J. Boorstin, *The Genius of American Politics* (Chicago: University of Chicago Press, 1953), p. 14.

[28]Quoted in Thomas E. Cronin, *The State of the Presidency* (Boston: Little, Brown, 1980), p. 161.

[29]Remarks by the president and first lady in a national television address on drug abuse and prevention, Washington, D.C., 14 September 1986.

◆ "America has a special place in God's plan for history." (50 percent)[30]

These figures reflect an enduring pattern. Through the years, Americans have been extremely reluctant to have public schools used as a platform for opposing ideologies. More than six decades ago a conference on immigrant education held the academic process responsible for ensuring the longevity of the American creed: "We believe in an Americanization which has for its end the making of good American citizens by developing in the mind of everyone who inhabits American soil an appreciation of the principles and practices of good American citizenship."[31] In 1987, the American Federation of Teachers reaffirmed this view, urging educators to abandon a "morally neutral" approach to teaching and affirm that "democracy is the worthiest form of human government ever conceived."[32]

A PUERILE CONFLICT?

After traveling the breadth of the United States in 1831 and 1832, and having spoken to notables and ordinary citizens, the Frenchman Alexis de Tocqueville remarked, "All the domestic controversies of the Americans at first appear to a stranger to be incomprehensible or puerile, and he is at a loss whether to pity a people who take such arrant trifles in good earnest or to envy that happiness which enables a community to discuss them."[33] Tocqueville's observation was inspired by the relative ideological homogeneity in the United States—especially when compared to his native land. No wonder that he found the young nation's political disputes almost quaint, even charming.

But as Tocqueville also noted, political scraps in the former British colonies were earnestly fought. Most were the result of an insufficient ideological underpinning. The Founding Fathers realized that freedom and liberty, the two ideas that "make America great," were not enough to build a nation. Writing in *The Federalist Papers,*

---

[30]National Opinion Research Center, General Social Surveys, 1996 poll. Reported in *The Public Perspective,* February/March 1997, p. 9. Text of question: "In teaching the American story to children, how important is the following theme?"

[31]"Proceedings of the State Conference on Immigration in Massachusetts Industries," *Bulletin of the Department of Education* (5 November 1920).

[32]Cited in Edward B. Fiske, "With Old Values and New Titles, Civics Courses Make a Comeback," *New York Times,* June 7, 1987, p. 1.

[33]Alexis de Tocqueville, *Democracy in America,* Richard D. Heffner, ed. (New York: New American Library, 1956), p. 90.

James Madison observed, "Liberty is to faction what air is to fire."[34] He labeled the cacophony of interests (or to use his term "factions") as the source of all "instability, injustice, and confusion" introduced into public forums, which have been "the mortal diseases under which popular governments have everywhere perished."[35] Liberty, in Madison's view, must have a suitable companion value to restrain its inevitable excesses. But which value? The Pledge of Allegiance speaks of "liberty and justice." Tocqueville himself paired liberty with several values: morality, law, the common good, and civic responsibility. Each of liberty's potential mates seeks to restrain it. To pair liberty and morality, for example, implies that sexual mores must be confined to what constitutes "common decency." The marriage of liberty and civic responsibility also suggests that behavior must be circumscribed. The lawlessness depicted in the ancient political philosopher Thomas Hobbes's "state of nature," wherein life was "solitary, poor, nasty, brutish, and short," suggested what could happen if there was liberty without civic responsibility.[36] Even a staunch democrat like Andrew Jackson acknowledged that "individuals must give up a share of liberty to preserve the rest."[37] The late *New York Times* columnist James Reston once compared liberty without restraint to a "river without banks. . . . It must be limited to be possessed."[38]

The question Americans have always faced is how do you limit liberty and still possess it? This is what divided Alexander Hamilton and Thomas Jefferson. Hamilton wanted liberty to be coupled with authority, so that economic interests (including his own) could be protected. Jefferson preferred that liberty be paired with local civic responsibility. It was on this basis that the enduring struggle between Hamiltonian Nationalism and Jeffersonian Democracy began.

Hamiltonian Nationalism envisions the United States as one "family," with a strong central government—especially an energetic executive—acting on its behalf. In 1791 Hamilton proclaimed:

> Ideas of a contrariety of interests between the Northern and Southern regions of the Union, are in the main as unfounded as they are

---

[34]James Madison, "Federalist Number Ten," in Alexander Hamilton, John Jay, and James Madison, *The Federalist,* Edward Mead Earle, ed. (New York: Modern Library, 1937), p. 55.

[35]Ibid., 53-54.

[36]Thomas Hobbes, *Leviathan* (New York: Collier Books, 1962), p. 100.

[37]Quoted in Arthur M. Schlesinger, *A Thousand Days* (New York: Greenwich House, 1983), pp. 105-106.

[38]James Reston, "Liberty and Authority," *New York Times,* June 29, 1986, p. E-23.

mischievous . . . Mutual wants constitute one of the strongest links of political connection . . . Suggestions of an opposite complexion are ever to be deplored, as unfriendly to the steady pursuit of one great common cause, and to the perfect harmony of all parts.[39]

Thomas Jefferson was wary of Hamilton's motives. Unlike Hamilton, Jefferson had a nearly limitless faith in the ordinary citizen. To a nation largely composed of farmers, he declared, "Those who labor in the earth are the chosen people of God, if ever He had a chosen people, whose breasts He has made the peculiar deposit for substantial and genuine virtue."[40] Jefferson's devotion to liberty made him distrust most attempts to restrain it, particularly those of government: "Were we directed from Washington when to sow, and when to reap, we should soon want bread."[41] In 1825, Jefferson warned of the expanding power of state government and wrote that the "salvation of the republic" rested on the regeneration and spread of the New England town meeting.[42] The best guarantee of liberty in Jefferson's view was the exclusion of the "invisible hand" of government. Americans, he said, would "surmount every difficulty by resolution and contrivance. Remote from all other aid we are obliged to invent and execute; to find means within ourselves and not lean on others."[43] Given the unique character of his compatriots, it was not surprising that Jefferson won the presidency in 1800.

By the time of Tocqueville's visit almost six decades after the revolt against King George III, most citizens remained suspicious of central government. Tocqueville described them as having "acquired or retained sufficient education and fortune to satisfy their own wants. They owe nothing to any man, they expect nothing from any man, they acquire the habit of always considering themselves as standing alone, and they are apt to imagine that their whole destiny is in their own hands."[44]

For nearly two centuries the debate between Hamiltonian Nationalism and Jeffersonian Democracy has dominated U.S. politics. Republicans and Democrats have argued both sides of the issue, not always adhering to the same one. During the Civil War and the

[39]Morton J. Frisch, ed., *Selected Writings and Speeches of Alexander Hamilton* (Washington, D.C.: American Enterprise Institute, 1985), p. 316.

[40]Quoted in Ted Morgan, *FDR: A Biography* (New York: Simon & Schuster, 1985), p. 38.

[41]Quoted in Richard Reeves, *The Reagan Detour* (New York: Simon & Schuster, 1985), p. 19.

[42]Quoted in Robert Kennedy, *To Seek a Newer World* (New York: Doubleday, 1967), p. 56.

[43]Morgan, FDR, p. 365.

[44]Tocqueville, *Democracy in America*, p. 194.

industrial era that followed, Republicans stood with Hamilton; Democrats claimed Jefferson as their own and promoted "states rights." Since the days of Franklin D. Roosevelt, Democrats have consistently aligned themselves with Hamilton, preferring to view the nation as a family. Republicans, meanwhile, have sought to reinvigorate Jeffersonian Democracy. Listen to Ronald Reagan: "Through lower taxes and smaller government, government has its ways of freeing people's spirits."[45] Reagan and his partisans view the country not as a family but as a collection of diverse communities for whom liberty means "the right to be let alone."[46]

Historian Henry Steele Commager believes that since the nation's founding, the character of the American people has not changed greatly nor has the "nature of the principles of conduct, public and private, to which they subscribe."[47] Our values may be constant, but the circumstances in which they are applied are not. The whiff of civil war, the onset of a depression, or the ravages of inflation inevitably cause Americans to take stock of the situation, their expectations of government, and settle upon a course of action in a manner consistent with the American creed.

At critical junctures, Americans have oscillated from Hamiltonian Nationalism to Jeffersonian Democracy. The shift in public attitudes has usually been influenced by a dominant personality. Abraham Lincoln reasserted Hamilton's vision of a national family so as to save the Union. Three score and ten years later, Franklin Roosevelt chose Hamiltonian Nationalism to meet the Great Depression head on: "We have been extending to our national life the old principle of the community . . . [The] neighbors [now] are the people of the United States as a whole."[48] At other times Jeffersonian Democracy has been preferred. Ronald Reagan promised to restore the concept of neighborhood in 1980 by taking "government off the backs of the great people of this country" and turning "you loose again to do those things that I know you can do so well."[49] George W. Bush echoed Reagan in 2000 with his call for a tax cut and more responsibility given to the states.

Usually, however, citizens do not choose between Hamiltonian Nationalism and Jeffersonian Democracy but enjoy the fruits of both

---

[45]Ronald Reagan, State of the Union Address, Washington, D.C., January 27, 1987.

[46]*Olmstead v. U.S.,* 279 U.S. 849 (1925): 476. Justice Brandeis wrote a dissenting opinion in this case.

[47]Henry Steele Commager, ed., *Living Ideas in America* (New York: Harper & Brothers, 1951), p. xviii.

[48]Quoted in Reeves, *The Reagan Detour,* p. 43.

[49]Ronald Reagan-Jimmy Carter Presidential Debate, Cleveland, October 29, 1980.

simultaneously. Newspaper columnist Walter Lippmann put it this way: "To be partisan . . . as between Jefferson and Hamilton is like arguing whether men or women are more necessary to the procreation of the race. Neither can live alone. Alone—that is, without the other—each is excessive and soon intolerable."[50] Nevertheless, Americans have tried at various intervals to live with one and not the other. The results have been less than satisfactory. One writer maintains that Hamilton "perverted that national idea as much as Jefferson perverted the American democratic idea, and the proper relation of these two fundamental conceptions one to another cannot be completely understood until this double perversion is corrected."[51]

It is the inevitable perversion of Hamiltonian Nationalism and Jeffersonian Democracy that insures periodic swings from one to the other. As each prevails at one juncture or another, Americans experience a sense of return when the old battles start up again on new but seemingly familiar territory. Hamilton would be astonished to learn that his concept of a national family is being used to promote the interests of the have-nots, especially women and minorities. And Ronald Reagan's espousal of Jeffersonian Democracy is premised on a welfare state first erected by Roosevelt's New Deal. The circumstances may change, but the arguments always have a familiar ring. Meanwhile, the distinctive qualities that make the United States unique persist. The fights that continue between the successors of Hamilton and Jefferson have, ironically, only further enhanced the American devotion to the ideas of freedom, individualism, and equality of opportunity.

---

[50]Quoted in Reston, "Liberty and Authority."

[51]Herbert Croly, *The Promise of American Life* (New York: Archon Books reprint, 1963), p. 29.

P A R T 1

INSTITUTIONS

No president of the modern era has left office in such a controversial manner as Bill Clinton. His use of the pardon power on his last day in office especially created a groundswell of criticism that he had abused the office of the president. Of course, Bill Clinton was no stranger to controversy during his two terms as president. He was both a powerfully transforming political leader as well as a lightning rod for conflict. Supporters and detractors alike had intense feelings about him.

One thing that all Clinton observers could agree on toward the end of his presidency was that he cared deeply about history's ultimate judgment of his leadership. Clinton's controversial pardons appear all the more difficult to comprehend if we accept the widespread judgment that he was motivated by a desire to be viewed favorably in history. *Washington Post* White House correspondent John Harris observed the Clinton presidency from up close and wrote a thoughtful reflection on the former president's quest for admiration in history. Harris's essay tells much about how Clinton's activities in his last year in office derived from this quest for "redemption" and also provides a lesson on the opportunities and frustrations of presidents as their terms expire and powers wane.

A key to Clinton's legacy was the possible election of his two-term vice president Al Gore as president. That did not happen and the former president realized that much of his agenda would be undone by the GOP administration of George W. Bush. Few vice presidents have had the fortune to be elected to the presidency directly from the office of vice president. In fact, only once has that happened since the beginning of the twentieth century: George Bush in

1988. Presidential scholar Richard Neustadt is Gore's former professor at Harvard University. During the 2000 campaign Neustadt wrote an essay analyzing the value of the vice presidential experience to serving as president. History suggests that being vice president is not necessarily a predictor of presidential success.

In the 1994 elections the Republican Party shocked political observers by taking control of the U.S. Congress. That election gave the GOP control of the House of Representatives for the first time in forty years. Since then, the party has retained control of the House, but its legislative majority has slipped considerably. In addition, the party's agenda for dramatic policy change fizzled in the face of some intense opposition. What happened to the "Republican Revolution?" Congressional scholar Richard Fenno explains that understanding the GOP disappointments requires knowledge of the realities of the legislative process. His critique of the GOP revolution provides important lessons for those who believe that policy and legislative procedures can be fundamentally altered in the short term given that the constitutional framers created Congress as a slow and deliberative body.

Although many Americans look to the courts for non-partisan resolution of cases and some issues, the reality is that the judicial process is deeply mired in politics. Consequently, the politically active in our society care deeply about appointments to the Supreme Court. Recent Court decisions, most notably the *Bush v. Gore* case that settled the controversial 2000 presidential election, have been decided by narrow margins revealing the deep divide over matters of constitutional interpretation. One issue that concerns many Court watchers is the "representativeness" of the Court's membership. That is, are the Court's members a sufficient cross-section of the U.S. population? Are all perspectives adequately represented on the Court? Judicial scholars Barbara Perry and Henry Abraham analyze the historical importance of a representative Court and the continued symbolic emphasis given to that factor in the modern era.

The *Bush v. Gore* case displayed deep divisions on the current Supreme Court. As the selections here show, some of the justices were very blunt in their opinions of their colleagues' votes. The high profile of this landmark case made it abundantly clear to the public that the Court is both a constitutional and a political body and that it is not so far removed from the daily partisan strife of our nation as many once believed.

THE LAST CHANCE PRESIDENCY

John F. Harris

STILL HIS AIRPLANE

The indignities of commercial travel, or hustling jets from rich friends, were still a few months away. So Bill Clinton made himself comfortable aboard Air Force One on a Saturday night in June as the great plane streaked across the continent—away from the gaggle of entertainment moguls and celebrities who had loudly cheered him during a sprint of fundraising appearances in Los Angeles, to the empty, spouseless, second-story apartment otherwise known as the White House living quarters.

His shoes were off, his feet were on the couch. One hand held a Diet Coke, leaving the other free to point, wave and chop the air. The mood and moment were perfect for lecturing his way from one coast to the other.

And he had an appreciative audience. Sharing the ride was Commerce Secretary Bill Daley, who just days before had been tapped by Vice President Gore to be the latest head of his campaign. For a year, the operating assumption of Gore and his campaign had been that the disgraced incumbent was a terrible burden to be overcome. Daley's view, as he had expressed it privately to friends, was, "Anyone who thinks that is an idiot." Why not reap the benefits of association with—and advice from—the most successful Democratic politician of this generation?

Why not indeed, is Clinton's view. His airborne discourse that night was an especially spirited rendition of a performance he has delivered hundreds of times this year—usually in private with friends or aides, but occasionally blurted out publicly in some after-dinner speech or interview when his certitude got the better of him. It is Clinton's new self-appointed role: consultant in chief.

The president ran down the list of names then in play to be the vice presidential nominees for both Gore and George W. Bush, clinically dissecting the merits and problems' of each. He told Daley: Here's the argument you need to make against Bush, unfolding the attack line by line, phrase by phrase. And here's the argument Gore needs to make for himself, line by line, phrase by phrase.

Then Clinton turned to his own role. Come autumn, Clinton said, he would be in the thick of battle against congressional Republicans over the budget. Normally, when vice presidents run for the top job it's best for the sitting president to recede into the shadows. But by the particular logic of this year—happy coincidence!—the best thing for Gore would be for Clinton to keep a high profile as a fully engaged president, activist to the end, framing the debate on behalf of Democrats.

"I can help here," Clinton said.

I can help here. It says much about Bill Clinton's drive for self-justification that a president who never commanded a majority in a presidential election, who endured a succession of personal scandals that culminated in impeachment, whose character is disapproved of by a large majority of Americans—even by those who say they support his presidency—finds it perfectly reasonable to presume that he would be a splendid asset to any other politician fortunate enough to be associated with him.

It says something about America on the brink of the post Clinton era that he may well be right.

Bill Clinton has outlasted everyone. Those who despise him, no less than those who adore him, now operate in a political landscape in which Clinton methods and Clinton values reign. This is a place where judgments are never final, and reality is always pliable, where it really does depend on what the meaning of *is* is. A great president or a disgraced one? A peacemaking statesman or a perjurer whose home state authorities are seeking to have disbarred? A tempered idealist or a money-chasing, poll-obsessed cynic? There is no right answer, only an argument that goes on and on—rest assured it will not end on January 20, 2001 and that Clinton devoutly believes he is winning bit by bit.

Which may be more than wishful thinking. Almost exactly two years after Clinton's survival looked to be in doubt—on that September morning when he told a White House prayer breakfast that he had reached "rock bottom truth" and announced that he was beginning spiritual counseling—he is on his way to arguably the most successful and energetic final year in the history of the modern presidency.

Truman left office despised. Eisenhower left beloved, but in slumber. Kennedy was killed, Johnson crushed, Nixon evicted, Ford and Carter both defeated. Reagan at the end was drifting into senescence, and Bush was staggering from forces he neither anticipated nor understood. Now comes Clinton, whose ordeals were more searingly personal than those of his predecessors. And he is not slumping to the finish line but sprinting.

"In terms of personal credit," Clinton said in an interview for this story, "you know, presidencies go through several incarnations, many of which occur after they're long gone. I have had the opportunity just in my service as president to read about administrations, including administrations that most Americans don't know much about. And I see all the time there is this sort of constant process of reassessment about every period in our history. So I'll leave that to history."

But not just yet. For now, he's a man in a hurry. The finish line isn't a goal to be reached so much as an enemy to be defied. "I'll make a little confession," he said. "The only thing that I am feeling about this last year is that I just want to keep working, I never want to sleep."

He didn't get much sleep, in any event, on the day of our conversation early last month. It began at 6 a.m. when he left the White House for a day trip to tour forest fires in Idaho. After a four-hour flight, he found himself on a small helicopter receiving an airborne tour of the fire zone.

Clinton began the helicopter ride in a lively spirit. His manner was at once more imperial, and more colloquial, than he shows in public. "I'm cold. Are you cold? It's cold in here," he honked, his Southern accent a bit thicker than I'm used to hearing. "Let's do something about the temperature!" It was like he was doing a Lyndon Johnson impersonation. By his feet was a garment bag with a change of clothes, but Clinton said he didn't care if the clothes he was wearing got a little wrinkled. "What the heck is this doing here? Let's get that out of here." He munched on a bagel and a banana, and listened as Forest Service Chief Mike Dombeck gave a tour. Clinton had many questions: How fast do the fires move? Isn't it true that more logging would do nothing to curb fires? Dombeck remarked on the enormous energy contained in the lightning bolts that start many fires. "That's a good argument," the president cracked, "for getting off the golf course" in a storm.

Within minutes, though, the chatter trailed off. While Dombeck was still talking, the president's eyes closed behind the sunglasses he was wearing. He was asleep.

He woke up a few minutes later and picked up right where he left off with more questions and comments about the burned expanse below.

Air Force One landed back in Washington 14 hours after taking off. But Clinton wasn't going home. Instead, another helicopter was waiting to take him on an hour flight to a fundraiser in Charlottesville. He didn't return to the White House until nearly 1 a.m., 19 hours after the day began.

This day was noteworthy only because it was routine. While his aides circulate their résumés, Clinton circulates himself. His days are a comic juxtaposition of the grand and the trivial. Ennobling moments come hard up against embarrassing ones. He jets overseas for international summits (seven trips and 13 countries so far this year), then jets back home to raise money for obscure members of Congress (some $75 million at 115 events for various Democrats between the first of the year and the end of the Democratic convention). He phones Jerusalem to talk with Prime Minister Ehud Barak about Mideast peace, then dials his lawyer, David Kendall, to talk about the Little Rock proceedings to strip his law license. One day brings a searching sermon on education, and what America will be like a hundred years from now. Another brings a reminder from the world's most powerful man that Americans should be sure to handle their food safely this holiday weekend to avoid salmonella.

With just four months left in his presidency, he remains the Jupiter of our national space. He dominates any appearance as effortlessly as on the day he arrived. He is so dominant, in fact, that even his wife, Hillary Rodham Clinton, now running for the Senate from New York, has had to weigh carefully how often he should be allowed to appear on her behalf.

Both of his would-be successors labor in his shadow. Al Gore thought his problem would be that voters would assume he is another Bill Clinton. It turns out his more likely problem is that many voters have appraised his clumsy reinventions—the tinny, artificial voice he brings to the artifices of politics—and concluded: This guy is no Bill Clinton; now *there* is someone sincerely good at artifice. George W. Bush, meanwhile, is running a campaign that amounts to a daily salute to the incumbent. While the Republican promises to restore the lost honor of the presidency, he crafts a centrist strategy that is lifted expressly from Clinton's book on how to command the middle ground in American politics.

Part of the mythology about Clinton is that he is the Great Compartmentalizer, capable of putting unpleasant subjects out of mind while he concentrates on the business at hand. This was always fiction, "pure bunk," in the words of a former aide who once helped promote it. He and many colleagues now acknowledge that during the Monica Lewinsky scandal Clinton often seemed utterly lost to the world, overcome by a combination of rage toward his opponents and recrimination toward his own weak self.

It turns out the real compartmentalizer is the public itself. The Clinton years have enveloped all America in one dysfunctional family. Things that once seemed extravagantly weird—a president who goes to pastoral therapy sessions once a week to recover from his sex addiction; a first lady who moves out of the White to run for office in a state where she never lived—now seem routine. And everyone has learned to avert their gaze from those sides of Clinton they prefer not to see.

Those who hate Clinton can't bear it. Not only has he survived, he has mastered the office of the presidency as thoroughly as any occupant since Franklin D. Roosevelt. Never mind if you agree with his ends. Think only of sheer competence. The public can see part of it: the casual fluency he shows at news conferences, or the ease with which he trumps congressional Republicans in public relations battles over legislation. There is much that remains unseen: the way Clinton has merged his polling and policy operations, so that he almost never gets caught flat-footed by an emerging issue or controversy. Or the way that Clinton, no matter how controversial at home, moves nimbly among foreign heads of state, clearly the dominant figure at any summit. It strains memory now to think of the first-term Clinton, how callow he seemed, how often his fumbling White House was swamped by Washington and left timid and confused by events overseas.

Set aside, if you prefer, sheer competence. Think only of appearance. Clinton's hair is full gray now, and his weight still goes up and down. But the combined visual effect is one of maturity and command. Alone among modern presidents, he actually looks better at the end of his term than he did at the beginning. The conclusion is inescapable: This is a man with an endless capacity for recovery and growth—by far his most appealing characteristic—and he is in tangible ways a better president than he was before.

But those ready to glorify Clinton can't face another truth: In maddening ways, he is unchanged, a recidivist to the end. His sense of selfish grievance—by far his most unappealing characteristic— still erupts with dreary frequency. Clinton is the Old Faithful of whining. In late July, shortly after a new poll showed Hillary Clinton running behind her GOP opponent in New York, Clinton moaned in an interview with a Miami Fox TV affiliate, "Everybody that always hated me all those years and were so mean to me, they've all transferred all their anger to her now. It's almost as if they've got one last chance to beat me."

And there is the familiar flight from reality over Lewinsky. He has apologized for the affair ad infinitum but to understand how Clinton really feels you must listen to the apologies very carefully. What he did was a "personal mistake," he concedes, but as events recede he becomes more defiant than ever that he does not bear responsibility for its public consequences. He paid a judge's $90,000 fine for providing false testimony under oath, he says, to get the matter over with, not because he lied. He settled the Paula Jones case, he said at an April news conference, because the appeals court that would have heard the matter was politically biased against him. And then there was his interview in May with WAMU's Diane Rehm, when she asked what effect the White House years had had on his marriage: "Oh, I think it's been good for ours, because I got to live above the store." His own aides rolled their eyes: What planet is he on? Of course, it was this penchant for denial that some friends believe led to the scandal in the first place.

And the scandal led to the imperative Of 2000: to try to cleanse the stain by having the most hyperkinetic final year in office that any president has ever had. Clinton may not have exorcised his demons—the vanity or the compulsiveness—but he does seem to have harnessed them to a higher purpose. He wants to negotiate Mideast peace, elect Hillary, beat Republicans on the budget, solve Northern Ireland, elect Gore, travel to Vietnam, raise money for his library, win back the Congress.

Bill Clinton, as ever, wants it all.

The news was bad, and it was greeted by an explosion of presidential profanity and indignation. "They're trying to destroy my last year in office," he hissed.

This thunder was provoked when an adviser reported back to Clinton on a conversation with a man who under other circumstances has been an important administration ally: AFL-CIO President John Sweeney. The labor leader told the Clinton emissary that union political strategists believed that they now had the votes to defeat the president on his most important legislative priority of the year, and one of the most important of his presidency: a vote on whether to extend permanent normal trading status to China. Labor's vehemence was well understood; the vote cut straight to the fissure in the Democratic Party over trade. But Clinton was feeling unappreciated. Think of all he had done for working Americans, he railed, and think of how much he had riding on this vote over China. And he was being killed by his friends.

As it happened, Sweeney's optimism was premature. Clinton won the May trade vote, and by a surprisingly wide margin. The presidential outburst was noteworthy, though, in several ways. It was a reminder that the stereotype about Clinton—that he is a risk-averse leader who allows politics to trump all—can be unfair. His first instinct is to avoid conflict. But in this case, as in several previous episodes in his presidency, Clinton defied the most expedient course and took on a fight with a powerful constituency in his own party. And Clinton's line about the union wrecking the last year of his presidency underscores something else: He is in the midst of what surely counts as one of the most methodically, and self-consciously, organized closing acts in White House history.

"Legacy" is a word chat Chief of Staff John Podesta has banned from the Clinton White House, lest Clinton be perceived as a lame duck trying to score last-minute points on some historical ledger. Even so, several current and former White House aides say Clinton has approached the year with an acute sense of history and of the fact that the window is swiftly closing on the chance to make it.

What was once perhaps a chaotic and random White House operation has become among the most controlled. So in late 1999, White House senior adviser Douglas Sosnik (who has since departed for a job with the National Basketball Association) began at Clinton's instruction to prepare a detailed final year road map. The process began with a question for the boss: What was important?

Clinton had a long list of legislative proposals, from HMO reform to gun control to increasing the minimum wage, but most of these fell in a second-tier category: It would be fine if they passed, but hardly a disaster if they didn't. The China trade vote was the paramount exception, a must-win issue. For once, a Clinton legislative effort was not conducted with the equivalent an end-of-semester all-nighter. For weeks, Clinton worked over wavering House members of his own party, lecturing them in small groups in the Yellow Oval Room of the White House, bending their ears in phone calls.

Several foreign affairs issues—sketched in a memo from national security adviser Sandy Berger—likewise fell in the no-nonsense category. A president who was once uncomfortable with foreign policy, aides say, has developed over time—like many of his predecessors—a preference for this part of the job. And foremost among his ambitions is the Middle East. Clinton, according to several people close to him, sees the intractable rivalries and hatreds of the region as filled with redemptive possibilities, a noble use for his powers of seduction and persuasion. He once made this point publicly, during the height of the Lewinsky scandal, when he said that laboring to close the gaps between Israel and Palestinians was part of his "personal journey of atonement." In the months before July's Camp David summit, which brought the two sides closer than ever but ended without agreement, Clinton worked the issue assiduously, usually without publicity. There were 30 presidential phone calls between January and July to Barak and Palestinian Authority Chairman Yasser Arafat.

"I think he believes all things are doable," says former senator Dale Bumpers, who has been friendly with Clinton since their days as Arkansas pols. "I think he thinks he is a great facilitator, and that he can use that for good, and I agree with him . . . Most of us at the end of our political careers start to realize, this is history-making time, and I think he's afflicted with that."

There were other questions as Clinton and his team planned out how they wanted this chapter of history to read. Where did Clinton want to travel? (A planned November trip to Vietnam was a priority.) What could he do to help Gore, Hillary and congressional Democrats? (Raise money, lots of it.) How much time would Clinton need for legal battles, including the fight over disbarment and an ongoing probe into 1996 fundraising? (One adviser says that while legal matters don't require vast amounts of time, they do take "far more psychic energy" from Clinton than he lets on; aides have learned to cushion his schedule accordingly.)

All this planning took place with an awareness that the natural cycles of politics were working against an eighth-year incumbent. Aides carefully looked at the calendar for dates when all eyes would not be on the presidential candidates, when Clinton would be able to "break through" and attract news coverage. The planning also took into account a more personal factor: Perhaps no president has ever sought the office more intensely, or savored the emotional rewards that come with it more exquisitely.

"We wanted to plan a year that would allow him to inhale the job," recalls Sosnik.

Some old advisers marvel that he is still so interested in inhaling. Few people have endured more during Washington's war over Clinton these past eight years than former White House deputy chief of staff Harold Ickes. He has been called to testify under oath 35 times before sundry congressional panels and in grand jury proceedings and depositions. Weary himself, Ickes notes of his former boss: "He doesn't seem tired, he doesn't seem worn out, there's no sense of ennui."

One person who has worked for the administration offers this guide to understanding Clinton's presidency: Think of this not as year eight but rather as year two of the fourth consecutive presidency Clinton has occupied. There was the first presidency, when he was surrounded by Arkansas loyalists and young campaign aides still swooning from their first political crush. This was the presidency of the successful 1993 budget bill and, disastrously, health care reform. That led to the repudiation of the 1994 elections, which led in turn to the second Clinton presidency, the one in which Republican consultant Dick Morris held sway, refashioning Clinton for reelection. This led logically to the reign of Chief of Staff Erskine Bowles, a conservative businessman, who trekked regularly to Capitol Hill to strike deals with Republicans. Then came scandal, and the third Clinton presidency, sending Clinton back into the embrace of congressional Democrats as survival became the all-consuming goal. Now Clinton is in stage four, the Last Chance Presidency.

At times, while his aides juggle job interviews and goodbye parties, Clinton appears to be the only person in this White House not coasting. "There's nothing, when you put it in front of him, that he doesn't want to do," says Jim Steinberg, who recently departed as deputy national security adviser. As Clinton himself told me, "I can rest starting at noon on January 20th."

It is revealing to look at the people around Clinton now. The star-struck young aides, like George Stephanopoulos before his disillusionment, or the longtime associates, like Morris or Mack McLarty, or the personal friends, like Bowles—those sorts of people are nearly all gone. Overwhelmingly, the senior White House is made up of Washington operatives, like Chief of Staff Podesta, or his deputy, Steve Ricchetti, both veteran lobbyists. The anonymous Sosnik spent far more intimate time around Clinton than the famous Stephanopoulos ever did. But he was never under any illusion about his real role, basically that of a lawyer to a client. In year eight, romance has been replaced by professionalism.

Also realism. In their clinical detachment some aides wonder if his admirable energy is approaching a worrisome frenzy. In June, Clinton was preparing with aides for a news conference later that day. Usually, Clinton nibbles a healthful raisin bagel during such sessions. But this time he was shoveling down food, a full meal in moments. Perhaps he was just hungry. But here is how you have learned to think if you are a veteran of the Clinton White House: *Uh-oh. He eats like that when he's out of control. And when he's out of control, bad things happen.* So as the meeting broke up, one aide confessed to wondering: *What new surprise is hurtling toward us now?*

Hillary Clinton, the new Senate nominee, had just finished her acceptance speech at the New York Democratic Party convention in Albany this past May when she and her husband met with supporters at a reception. His presence in Albany was a last-minute surprise. His aides told reporters he had decided only that morning that he simply could not miss this occasion. And now Clinton told the crowd that the thing that had been holding him back before was a previous commitment he had made to the Mexican American Legal Defense Fund. "So I told that group, 'I've been with you a long time, and if you let me go hear my wife give a speech, I'll do any event you want, anywhere in America,'" Clinton said.

Here is a fine specimen of Clinton phraseology. Words are for him the currency in a negotiation with reality, in which a statement can qualify as true so long as it is not demonstrably false. In fact, he had been waiting for more than a week for word on whether he would be allowed to go to Albany. Hillary Clinton's two most important advisers, Mark Penn and Mandy Grunwald, had been against it, sources familiar with the deliberations say, feeling that his presence would send a not-so-subliminal message that her campaign is really about him. Other aides, including press secretary Howard Wolfson, felt just as strongly: It looks weird when a candidate's spouse does not show up at an event that most normal couples would attend together. The candidate sided first with the stay-away side, brooded some more, then reversed herself.

The very existence of such a debate underscores the transcendent weirdness of the New York campaign. The paradox is that even as she has moved physically apart from the president, the campaign has underscored, and strengthened, their closeness.

To the astonishment of many who work with both of them, the relationship is by all appearances as strong as it has ever been. They talk constantly, aides say, often several times a day. He is informed about and often the decisive adviser on every aspect of her Senate campaign. One old Arkansas friend of his isn't surprised that the relationship has seemingly rebounded so swiftly from the Lewinsky catastrophe. "This is a relationship that thrives on distance," says the friend. With Hillary in New York, this theory goes, the president can nurture the idealized portrait that he has always had of her virtues. And now that she is immersed in a project that is truly her own, say people close to her, she more than ever appreciates and benefits from the extraordinary political mind that first attracted her to him.

For her major speeches, he sometimes takes hours out of his schedule to help with her presentation. Drafts of the text, an adviser recalls, go back and forth between New York and Washington. "B, what do you think of this?" she asks. He scribbles up the page with notations, then adds, "I love you, B."

"I'm not kidding," the adviser who told me this added hastily.

It is true, however, that the Senate campaign's origins lie emphatically in the year of scandal. The story line Hillary Clinton has promoted is that she was taken aback when New York Democrats in early 1999 began talking her up as a possible candidate. But this notion of her being drafted into service is contradicted by a White House adviser, who recalls the Clintons in the fall of 1998 talking in dead earnest about her running. It was plain then that her heart was set on it from the moment incumbent Daniel Patrick Moynihan made clear he was retiring—and well before even a murmur of public speculation had been heard.

The president offered only encouragement. In the wake of the scandal, the scales in the marriage were weighted heavily in her favor. "His view was that whatever she wanted, he was going to give her," says a former White House aide. "This was a project for them to work on together."

The project has shown something else: In a way that unsettles some of her admirers, Hillary is more like Bill than many people imagined. Her approach toward even longtime Clinton loyalists has become frankly utilitarian; several of these people say that when they told her they thought running for Senate was a bad idea, she turned cold before their eyes. Even her chief of staff, Melanne Verveer, was cast into a secondary orbit, sources, say, after arguing that Hillary had nothing to gain by making the race.

If there is a compartmentalizer in this marriage, it is her, not him. One White House aide recalls conversations with her in the thick of the sex scandal, in which she analyzed defense strategies with the incisive detachment of a lawyer discussing a client. Diane Blair, the Arkansas political scientist who was Hillary's best friend before her death from cancer this summer, once told a White House aide that the first lady had never discussed Clinton's adultery with her during countless conversations in the year of Lewinsky.

There is a popular view, which many of her advisers once endorsed, that Bill and Hillary represent two distinct poles in the Clinton Enterprise. She is the ideologue, eager to win but motivated principally by the higher cause; he is the compromiser, eager to do good but motivated principally by the imperative of victory. But it is Bill Clinton's brand of politics that is the animating force of her campaign.

Nothing illustrates this more than a tense episode early this year when she was deciding who to hire as her media adviser. The job had been all but offered, several sources say, to a veteran Chicago political consultant named David Axelrod. The president himself then weighed in with another idea: Hire Mark Penn. He was already signed on as pollster for both Hillary's campaign and the White House. Clinton believed he should take on an additional role in shaping her campaign's message.

"That was her decision," Clinton said, in our conversation, acknowledging that he had been thoroughly familiar with it. "She's got the best of both worlds because [Axelrod] is working for the state party."

The significance of Penn is that he, more than any other adviser, is the architect of the president's successful effort to define and occupy the political center. Penn believes that swing voters are moved not so much by a candidate's inspiring rhetoric or compelling personal biography, but by concrete issues whose popularity is scientifically ascertained through exhaustive polling. It is a data-driven approach to politics, wonderfully suited to a president who inhales data, and over the years the smooth pol and the rumpled pollster have established a remarkable communion.

But whether that communion can be transferred successfully to Hillary is another matter. The May convention speech was a perfect example of why her Senate campaign has left some longtime supporters despondent. It was a collection of issue slogans—I support a patients' bill of rights, I support a prescription drug benefit for Medicare. I support targeted tax cuts for education—delivered in a voice raised to a shout. It was as if someone had called the Democratic National Committee and said, "I can't tell you the name of the candidate, but fax me a stump speech right away!" There was scarcely a word about her biography, her values, her personal reasons for running.

"We have lost the real Hillary in this campaign, says one campaign adviser.

The president emphatically rejects this, constantly professing admiration at her emergence as a politician in her own right. He confesses that he sometimes bobbles his own role as supportive spouse. In July, an old Arkansas colleague turned adversary leveled a lurid allegation that Hillary Clinton had hurled antisemitic slurs at him 26 years ago. Clinton called the *New York Daily News* to defend her. "It may not have even been the right thing to do," he said in our interview, "because all it did was sort of give more visibility to a charge that was hokum."

His old aide Harold Ickes, who is informally advising her campaign, says the occasionally awkward reversal of roles between Bill and Hillary has led to a new dimension in the relationship. "There's a deeper appreciation," he says. "She understands now how good he is, and how difficult it is to do what he does.

If the 2000 campaign has strengthened Bill Clinton's relations with Hillary, it has grievously strained his relationship with his other partner, Vice President Gore. Episodically over the past year there have been reports from anonymous Clinton sympathizers describing the president's anger at Gore's attempts to distance himself from Clinton's scandals by ostentatiously volunteering how upset he was by the Lewinsky affair.

Bur Clinton's predominant emotion, several White House aides say, is one of bewilderment. He is genuinely confused by Gore's clumsy efforts at disassociation, and he is baffled by Gore's deficiencies in the theater of politics. "I think Clinton is just incredibly frustrated," says one longtime political adviser. "He's thinking, 'Why doesn't he say it like this? Here's what the ads should say.'"

Clinton and his team are also irritated by what, from their vantage point, looks like an effort to prematurely end the Clinton presidency. The one consistent theme of the Gore team's complaints is that Clinton, with his ability to command the spotlight, is stepping on the vice president's message. "They think that we're getting the eight seconds on the evening news that they should be getting," said a senior White House official before Gore's nomination. "They don't realize they're not getting the eight seconds anyway."

From the Gore camp's vantage point, Clinton's performance epitomizes the selfishness of the man. But if anything, this year Clinton has shown a concern for others that some doubted he had. He has willingly shared his political talents—for endorsements, fundraising or behind-the-scenes advice with any Democrat who has asked (and with some who didn't).

"He is fully conversant with every race," says Sen. Robert Torricelli of New Jersey, who heads the Democratic Senatorial Campaign Committee and has traveled extensively with Clinton this year. "He knows the polls, he knows the issues. There is almost no level of detail with which he's not familiar." Torricelli recalls flying recently on Air Force One to raise money for Democratic Sen. Ron Wyden of Oregon. Clinton spent the flight giving Wyden a discourse on how to win his own campaign.

As for Hillary Clinton, she acknowledged her own debt to her husband in her speech in Albany. In a line that aides insist she added to the speech spontaneously—and which left some of them aghast—Hillary turned to her husband and said, "I would not be standing here tonight if it were not for Bill."

At a commencement speech at Carleton College in June, an aide slipped the president a note saying that Syria's Hafez Assad had died. Clinton rubbed his eyes, deep in thought. For that moment he was leader of the world. Ten minutes later he was something else: a politician so repellent that one young woman walked straight past the outstretched hand he extended to each graduate. The woman said later she cannot abide Clinton. The president, confidants say, especially hates it when young people reject him (a year before when several graduates at the University of Chicago would not shake his hand, aides say, he stewed for days).

These jarring contrasts come all the time. One Monday afternoon came news that a legal ethics panel in Arkansas had announced it would seek to have Clinton disbarred for his misleading testimony under oath in the Paula Jones case. On Wednesday came triumph: Clinton had succeeded in his top legislative priority of the year, when the House of Representatives deferred to his request to give permanent trading status to China. And that night came eulogy: 13,000 Democrats gathered at MCI Center for a massive fundraiser and a celebration of his legacy.

If everyone could agree that Clinton is a talented, and lucky, rascal who screwed some things up and did pretty damn well with others, we probably could agree to end our national argument over him. The Clintons believe it is the right wing that won't let the argument die. But the hagiographic video tribute at MCI Center made clear how incapable Clinton himself is of calling a truce. The president can't be a decent guy, he must be a saintly one. His achievements can't be scattershot and satisfactory; they must be epochal. So the debate drones on, and Clinton wears a halo one moment and horns the next.

These days, the prospect of being stripped of his law license horrifies him. For several days before the judicial ethics committee's decision to pursue disbarment came down, Clinton had been predicting the very action the panel took (its recommendation has forced a trial scheduled in Little Rock for later this year). The panel was biased, he told aides, since everyone on the panel who knew or had supported him had been hectored into recusing themselves from the vote. "This is a setup deal," Clinton insisted, according to a friend who talked with him.

On the day the ethics panel's decision came, Clinton was set to talk with NBC's Tom Brokaw. In the space of just one answer, Clinton displayed the full rainbow of his self-justifying strategies. First came denial, as Clinton reiterated that he never lied in the Paula Jones case. Then selflessness: He knew he would "always be at a severe disadvantage" defending himself "because I will not personally involve myself in any of this until I'm no longer president." In fact, "the only reason I agreed even to have papers filed" by lawyers was to uphold precedent. Finally, victimhood: Other cases involving "more significant kinds of conduct" than he engaged in had led to "nowhere near this kind of decision."

He came into office as the Man From Hope, and Clinton plainly hopes to leave that way as well. But there is one theme that has snaked darkly around and under the optimistic image Clinton seeks to project to the world. It is grievance.

In September two years ago, Clinton summoned his Cabinet to apologize for the Lewinsky affair, and he made a startling admission: He had been angry nearly every day of his presidency.

I told him in our interview that I was astonished to learn that he had harbored this much resentment, and asked him if he did still. "I'm not by nature an angry person," he said, adding, "I work on it all the time."

Then he launched into the second unprompted discourse on the Whitewater scandal in the interview. "I think that this whole Whitewater business will be looked upon by any rational observer in history as an absurd episode in American history which didn't amount to a hill of beans," he said. "And that the coverage of it as if it were serious required people essentially to suspend all ordinary notions of proof and common sense . . . And now we know, after all this time, that Whitewater thing was a total sham."

The specificity with which loyal Arkansas friends detail years-old resentments suggests something of Clinton's view. In an interview, Jim Blair, the Clinton friend who got unwanted fame as the person who helped Hillary with her commodities trades, dissected New York Times articles that ran more than eight years ago.

White House aides say Clinton himself still engages in similar exercises. Earlier this year he knew all the best nuggets in a book by Jeffrey Toobin that was critical of Ken Starr. And when *The Washington Post* assigned a writer from the anti-Clinton American Spectator to review the book, he howled indignantly in conversations with his press secretary, Joe Lockhart, and political consultant James Carville. "What more do you need to know?" said Clinton, who with Hillary has long believed this newspaper has a vendetta against them over Whitewater.

One former aide who remains on good terms with Clinton says it is nearly impossible to overstate the sense of victimhood he feels. He loved the revelations about Newt Gingrich's affair, not out of any special animus toward the fallen speaker, but as proof of the vast hypocrisy he sees all around him in Washington.

"I think it still bothers him," says Paul David Leopoulos, an old Arkansas friend. "He was not allowed to be president. They changed all the rules for him."

His eruptions, however, come with less vehemence than before. Every aide and confidant interviewed for this article said Clinton seems far more at peace.

"I think he believes people are starting to understand him more and give him credit," says Rahm Emanuel, a former aide still in steady touch with Clinton.

Clinton said his sense of grievance is abating, in part because of the spiritual counseling sessions he attends. And he is becoming philosophical about one of the abiding mysteries of his career: Why should a centrist politician, whose first instinct is to try to get along with everyone, inspire such hostility? "It's not the dislike, it's the intensity factor," says Blair, recalling the pattern established when Clinton was first elected in Arkansas. "He does not understand it, and it has always bothered him."

Clinton's usual answer is that conservatives are envious of his success. "They railed against entitlements, but they thought they had an entitlement to govern," he said. I've heard him give this explanation dozens of times, but in our interview he offered other theories that showed I more detachment. Some of the criticism of him is "based on a certain critique of the '60s . . . I think a lot of them genuinely felt that I represented a lot of things in the culture that they didn't like." He can joke about it now, saying he sometimes feels like the guy who slips and falls off the edge of the Grand Canyon, goes to Heaven and asks God, "Why me?" And God replies: "Son, there's just something about you I don't like," Clinton laughed. "So you've got to allow for that."

Clinton can allow for it, friends say, because there is something liberating about full exposure. After all, what can people say about him now? That he's having sex with an intern? What can they do about it? Impeach him?

Clinton acknowledged as much. "I think part of it is—when you go through any difficult period it either breaks you or makes you better," he said. "I just wake up every day with this enormous feeling of gratitude. I'm grateful—I'm grateful to my wife and to my daughter. I've got my family back. I'm grateful to the people who work with me, who stuck with me. And I'm enormously grateful to the American people for continuing to support what I was trying to do for them. To me, everyday is a gift now."

When White House aides bring family and friends to tour the West Wing—which they are allowed to do after 8 p.m.—it is not uncommon for the president to still be there, shaking hands with some aide's aunt from Moline, or some intern's college roommate from Durham. When Clinton is not there, it usually means he is out. Several times a week, his motorcade cruises through Washington on its way to some fundraiser; often there are two or three fundraisers on a single night.

Still, a former close White House aide to Clinton, contemplating the empty house that greets the president at the end of each workday now that his wife is in New York, surmises, "I think he's really lonely."

If so, it is not the loneliness of solitude, or of Nixonian confessions to the portraits in the White House hallways. In his determination to squeeze all out of this final year, Clinton has apparently resolved to never be by himself.

Many close friends and loyal aides are gone, no longer close or no longer loyal. But Clinton is surrounded by new friends and aides, a great many of whom, like fundraiser Terry McAuliffe, he did not even know when he became president. "I really don't think Bill Clinton has any true friends," says one person who has known and, worked with Clinton for two decades. Instead, by this reckoning, he has a constantly shifting universe of companions. Even those who have remained, like his Arkansas chum Leopoulos—who on a White House visit this spring stayed up talking with Clinton until 5 a.m.— say he can be marvelous company, but almost never shares what is really going on inside his head.

The ebullient McAuliffe, one of the world's most upbeat men, is perhaps Clinton's most frequent companion these days. He may talk to the president more than any person save Hillary. They stay up late watching movies, or talking until 2 a.m., as they did one night in July, about plans for the Democratic National Convention in Los Angeles, for which McAuliffe was the chairman.

And even when he is alone he is not. There is still the phone. He tracked down Skip Rutherford, an Arkansas crony helping organize the Clinton library, on his cell phone while Rutherford was driving to a Little Rock mall. He tracked down Rahm Emanuel on the beach—by calling his wife's cell phone. No explanation of how the operators got the number. When the phone rings at 11 p.m. or midnight, or later, Clinton's friends know who it will be. Bill Daley, Gore's campaign chief and all early-to-bed type, says that when Clinton wakes him up at 11 p.m., "I can't remember the next day what I said."

The fact that Clinton is never alone, however, does not demolish a theory held by many of the friends and aides: They believe he is in many ways a solitary man.

"All the activity is his way of coming back" from the shame of scandal, says a longtime aide. "It's his way of getting back up in his head, where he's happiest, and not having to confront the way he feels."

"He's always been like that," says Leopoulos. Though he was constantly in Clinton's home growing up, it was not until he read a magazine article in 1992 that he learned that Clinton's adoptive father was an alcoholic who sometimes turned violent. Why didn't you ever say anything, he asked Clinton. "This is for me to deal with," Clinton replied.

Other people point to the fluidity of his inner circle. Why is it that someone like McAuliffe, who never knew Clinton before he became president, should be his best friend? Why is it that there are so many people to whom Clinton was once close, whether George Stephanopoulos or Dick Morris, who now have no relationship with him at all?

In fact, it is rare for someone to drop out of Clinton's universe completely. But people move constantly between inner and outer orbits. Bruce Lindsey, the Arkansas aide who was the keeper of all secrets during the early days, is still at the White House but less frequently by Clinton's side. The Lewinsky scandal changed many dynamics. Vernon Jordan, while still friendly with Clinton, is hardly the omnipresent figure he used to be, say White House officials. Erskine Bowles, the former chief of staff who was deeply shaken by Clinton's lie to him about Lewinsky, fell a notch or two last year when he told the Clintons he would not help them finance their new house in Westchester County. Instead, McAuliffe stepped in with last-minute help to secure the loan.

All the motion of Clinton's last year, some believe, masks a certain sorrow. "There's clearly a sense of melancholy about leaving" the White House, says Sen. Christopher Dodd of Connecticut, who is among the senators closest to Clinton. "He's counting the days, not because he's looking forward to the end." Dodd recalls watching Clinton nervously at an Irish American dinner Dodd hosted a couple months ago, not wanting the president to get trapped for long at an obligatory event. Then it became clear: "He did not want to leave," Dodd says. "He stayed for three hours."

"History," said the historian Pieter Geyl, "is an argument without end." If so, the argument over Bill Clinton will be continued for many years on the banks of the Arkansas River in Little Rock. It is there that Clinton intends to build the Clinton Center, the library with his presidential papers. And there will also be an apartment where he says he plans to spend perhaps a third to half his time. There will be programs to stimulate debate and new ideas about issues Clinton cares about, from race relations to peacemaking to youth service. The place is expected to cost $150 million to build, a large chunk of which has already been raised in undisclosed large pledges collected by Clinton and McAuliffe from wealthy donors. Not surprisingly, perhaps, the people Clinton has recruited for work on the center are the die-hard defenders—secret-keepers and loyalists like McAuliffe and Lindsey and Cheryl Mills, the young African American lawyer who argued Clinton's case against conviction on the Senate floor.

Mostly, though, the Clinton Center is the place from which Bill Clinton will launch his next campaign, the one to win the ex-presidency. Skip Rutherford, the Little Rock public relations man who is serving as a principal organizer for the center, predicts Clinton will begin the next phase of his career just as he began his terms as governor and president: by overdoing it. "He will travel, he will write, he will speak, he will campaign for people," Rutherford says. "Forget prioritizing—he'll try to do it all."

As he has studied the ex-presidency, aides say, Clinton has tried to become closer to a man with whom his relations for a variety of reasons have long been tense, Jimmy Carter. Carter, Clinton now believes, has had the most worthy post-presidential career. Last winter, Clinton invited the Carters, to a private dinner at the White House.

But as a younger and more vigorous man than the other living ex-presidents, Rutherford contends, "he will dominate the group."

It is appropriate that the Clinton Center will take root on a patch of land sorely in need of reinvention. Right now the site is a litter-strewn lot adjacent to some dingy warehouses. But it is only a quarter mile or so down the street from the old Capitol building where Clinton twice claimed election-night victories for the presidency. While the center is being built, Clinton's papers will be stored in a former Oldsmobile dealership nearby.

It is appropriate, too, that the Clinton Center be in Arkansas. It is the place where all roads, smooth and rocky, seem to lead in Clinton's life. The place of sentimental homecomings—like the kind the Clintons had in July, when they returned to Fayetteville, the first place they lived after their marriage, for an emotional memorial service for Diane Blair. And the place of constant indignities, where the disbarment trial looms and where some dimly remembered name can spring forth to accuse Hillary of antisemitism or Bill of sexual assault. Friends like Jim Blair and Leopoulos, outraged at how Arkansas is treating its native son, say they've encouraged Clinton to say the hell with it and move his presidential papers to Georgetown University. But he says he's not interested in such payback.

In the meantime, there is a race underway—not Gore against Bush, but Clinton against the clock. Air Force One was on the tarmac, and aides were hovering for the interview to end. I asked Clinton a last question: Did he think a successful close could cleanse the stains of 1998?

"No," he answered. "I think that the only thing that can cleanse a mistake ever is an apology and an atonement." Clear enough. But then he added: "To the extent that the promise I made to the American people to work like crazy for them every day I was president is a part of that, I think that the answer to your question may be, yes."

ARTICLE 2

TRAINING TIME: DOES IT HELP TO HAVE BEEN THE VICE PRESIDENT?

Richard E. Neustadt
Harvard University

D oes it help to have been vice president? With respect to sharing in government and later becoming president, the answer to that question would have been strongly "no" as recently as 50 years ago. Until the 1950s, American vice presidents had been in the position of crown princes in most monarchies: confined to asking daily, as one of ours once said, about the ruler's health and otherwise excluded form the real business of government. But nowadays the answer would be "yes." From being a pathetic appendage of Congress with but two constitutional functions—to preside over the Senate and to break tie votes—our vice presidency has become for most incumbents a functioning, high-level element in executive decision-making and also in implementation, to varying degrees, as each president sees fit.

The change owes its beginnings to the shock of Harry Truman's takeover from Franklin Roosevelt without any preparation. Truman's vice presidential successor, Alben Barkeley, was the first to be a statutory member of the then-new National Security Council (although, as a "legislative officer," which is what he thought he was, he declined to attend most meetings). In the next administration, Dwight Eisenhower's, Richard Nixon was the first vice president to have a suite of lofty rooms, complete with personal staff, in the Old Executive Office Building. His predecessors had possessed only a relatively modest office at the Capitol. Jimmy Carter's vice president, Walter Mondale, was the first to gain an office in the West Wing of the White House itself. Mondale also was the first to be assured a weekly luncheon, agenda open, with the president in private. Once granted, these perquisites all stuck to the vice presidency, helping to transform it.

And Al Gore has been the first vice president, at least in modern times, to be invited into every sort of presidential meeting (assignations aside), free to argue with the president in front of others present—albeit not in public—whenever and on whatever topic the V.P. chose. Mondale once told me that he carefully abided by a rule he'd learned from Hubert Humphrey, who in turn apparently had drawn it from observing Lyndon Johnson as vice president and then living under him when he succeeded JFK: "Never be seen by anyone else to differ from the president, except by prearrangement and with his assent." This rule, it seems, evaporated in the (special?) case of Gore, in part, perhaps, because he and Bill Clinton had campaigned together from the same wing of the party and the same section of the country and in part, for sure, because of Clinton's unexampled generosity toward his own choice of successor.

Since Nixon's time in the vice presidency, all save Spiro Agnew seem to have amassed a working knowledge, though in variable depth, of policies and politics across the board at the presidential level. This was bound to stand them in good stead if they took on the presidency in their own right—as George Bush actually did, along with Nixon on his second try, and LBJ as well as Gerald Ford by succession. But Nelson Rockefeller, Walter Mondale, and Dan Quayle were stopped short. The vice presidency, plainly, is of less use in campaigning for the top stop than in settling down to it after election.

If Gore is nominated and elected president next year—a strong possibility, though not, of course, assured—he will be sworn into office after eight years as vice president, ranking in that status with Bush and Nixon in the twentieth century, and with Martin Van Buren on a four-year basis in the nineteenth. What might that mean should Gore take office? Are the comparisons worthwhile? The questions may sound academic, but I think they're worth posing (and not just because, as readers should know, I was Gore's college instructor and have kept up with him since).

Gore will have been a new-style veep: eight years of an office in the West Wing of the White House, eight years of weekly lunches with the president alone, eight years of active participation in the NSC and other Cabinet-level groups, and eight years of managing a staff as large as the whole White House's during Truman's presidency. These do not necessarily make Gore different from Van Buren, who compensated for the lack of all these modern perquisites by having been a central member of Andrew Jackson's kitchen cabinet. But it makes them at least equals in White House experience and presidential-level observation, equal to each other and to Bush and Nixon.

Does this give Gore an advantage if and when he starts to govern on January 20, 2001? Three swallows do not make a summer, nor are Van Buren, Bush, and Nixon good predictors of the course of a Gore presidency. Still, perhaps they tell us something, not sure but at least suggestive.

Van Buren's presidency, from 1837 to 1841, suggests that Gore had better beware the next recession if its onset is delayed until after he takes office, especially if it is long and severe. Not only did the long-lived depression of 1837 cloud Van Buren's entire presidency and haunt him through his unsuccessful campaign for reelection, but also the severity of the public's reactions drew upon well-founded perceptions that Andrew Jackson's polices had set the stage for economic crisis—and that "Little Van" had been at Jackson's side throughout. Clinton's record may be harder to besmirch than Jackson's in that regard, but, if severe recession comes soon after he goes, I wouldn't bet on it.

Bush's presidency suggests at least two things about Gore's, should there be a Gore administration: first, in the spheres of policy and management that he cares most about, has most enjoyed so far and most relishes in prospect, the new president would be poised to proceed in both appointments and policy directions with an assuredness, a flexibility, a deftness of touch almost unknown to new administrations led by inexperienced chiefs—inexperienced, that is, in mysteries of "the" executive—and a minimum of the appalling hubris that has characterized most new administrations since JFK breezed in and fell on his face over the Bay of Pigs.

With Bush, there were no such early disasters; foreign affairs was his specialty, as his well-chosen team, unusually compatible, faced a world about to be transformed. I refer not to the Gulf war, which came later, but to German reunification and, more generally, to the Soviet retreat from East Central Europe. Bush and his associates accomplished major policy shifts in their first year, accommodating to these great changes.

But, where Bush's personal experience was relatively thin, his interest relatively low, his instincts relatively insecure, or his mind fixed elsewhere, he could and did produce mistakes aplenty, especially in domestic affairs, sometimes even in appointments, and not only at the start but during the whole course of his administration: for example, his second chief of staff, to say nothing of that huge nomination night blunder, "Read my lips. . . ."

A disastrous lurch in climate, or nuclear arming by potential terrorists, or an unexpected speedup in high-tech development further unsettling the communications world would undoubtedly leave a new President Gore well positioned to play Bush, or to outdo him, by responding on familiar ground. Gore didn't invent the Internet, but surely he understands its uses and potential better than most newsmen or politicians of his generation (to say nothing of their elders!). He has dealt seriously with arms control since entering the Senate almost a generation ago. And, while his views on global warming are still controversial in some quarters, he assuredly is interested, grounded, and well-informed.

What of Richard Nixon, the third "swallow" in this series and, indeed, a special sort for purposes of comparison? Nixon, although the first of modern vice presidents, never had a relationship with Eisenhower remotely as supportive as Gore's with Clinton or even Mondale's with Carter. Moreover, instead of succeeding Ike, Nixon narrowly lost to JFK, only becoming president himself eight years later after defeating Hubert Humphrey just as narrowly. Nixon then took office with a smoothness and a deftness—and a show of humility in just the right degree to suit his circumstances—that would have outshone Bush, except in one particular area. Nixon and national security assistant Henry Kissinger, for reasons never adequately explained, assumed that, while as patriots they could not repudiate Lyndon Johnson's war, dumping it on the Democrats, they were so much superior to Johnson and his people in toughness, ingenuity, imagination, and whatever else that, with newness and the valuable uncertainty it brings, they could gain an agreement with the North Vietnamese in just a year, an agreement that would keep South Vietnam going for a "decent interval." On this assumption Nixon and Kissinger based all their early tactics. In fact, it took them more than three and a half years.

That mistaken estimate was not a product of hubris in the Kennedy sense. Nor was it consequent on sheer inexperience combined with ebullience, like Clinton's early remarks on gays in the military. Rather, it seems to have welled up from within those two men, Nixon and Kissinger, expressive of their intellectual self-confidence—some would say arrogance—combined with close, critical, but only marginally involved views of Johnson's experience and resources (he a Democrat, they Republicans).

Had Nixon been elected in 1960 and made that sort of judgment with respect to something he inherited from Ike, no doubt there would have been in it more realism and less arrogance, as well as less reliance on the uses of newness. So Gore should escape that particular hazard. He is liable, however, to its opposite: misplaced defense of outworn positions with which he feels identified because his predecessors had pursued them (whatever Gore may privately have thought of them at the time). This is what cost Humphrey his election in 1968, clinging too long to Johnson's policy on North Vietnam, thus paving the way for Nixon.

Besides, there is the possibility that, despite Clinton's present standing in the polls, once his term nears its close, his retrospective popularity may sag as citizens mull over what they've come to know about him. The sag might be sufficient to relieve Gore of concern about supporting the outworn. To the contrary, it might make him, personally, seem vulnerable by association—which would place him in worse circumstances than even Nixon's successor. "What sort of man are you to have had him as a buddy for so long?" No one could hurl that at Gerald Ford.

What is there in the record of Gore's own vice presidency to suggest its uses should he gain the top spot for himself next year? Lacking answers myself, I'm intrigued by further questions.

The first intriguing question is where, if anywhere, in the whole spectrum of policy, both foreign and domestic, his experience lags, his interest flags, his knowledge is thin, and his attention wavers. The one time I saw President Bush in the White House (to discuss a wholly nonpolitical subject), I had the temerity to ask how he was finding it—this after he'd spent about a year in office. "Oh," he replied, "the foreign problems are fascinating . . . just fascinating. But that domestic stuff. . . ." He grimaced and trailed off. What, for Gore, is the equivalent "stuff"?

From afar, there is no means of knowing. The vice presidency itself affords no clue. For Gore has not merely been possessed of its modern perquisites all these years, but also he has exercised them, thanks to Clinton, with an intimate involvement in the president's official business and a freedom to speak up within the official family quite unparalleled, at least back to Van Buren. The memoirs so far published all agree on this. George Stephanopoulos even writes unselfconsciously, without quotation marks, of Gore as one of the three "Principals" in the White House, a term I first heard used by David Gergen—in wonder and disbelief—when he rejoined the White House staff for the fourth time and discovered that in this administration, unlike those in which he'd served before, there were more "Principals" than one, the president.

No president can wall off any area of policy for long. If issues are serious enough, and controversial enough, they'll eventually reach him in some form or fashion. In the Clinton administration, that holds true for the vice president as well. Since Clinton reportedly prefers to mull things over, not decide them fast, and since the V.P. is a principal participant in mulling, regularly free to speak his mind and push his views, Gore, if he is nominated, will come to the election with seven and a half years of experience—in everything. What facets of it he yearns to put on the back burner should but probably won't become the focus of intense press inquiry during the campaign. As journalism, I fear, it is boring.

A second intriguing question concerns differences between Clinton and Gore. Differences there certainly have been in this administration, evidently plenty of them, up to the point of Clinton's decision, for instance, at the outset, about intervening in Bosnia—Gore for, Clinton against. That was widely reported. The memoirs testify to this and other differences as well, but, for the most part, only in general terms. In a notably leaky regime, how the specifics have been kept relatively private, at least for those of us who live beyond the Beltway, is a wonder—particularly since so many differences must have been aired in sessions with assorted aides or Cabinet members present. But such is the case, it seems, or perhaps the differences were fewer than is usually the case, or possibly the press corps has become so used to these as to regard them as no longer news. If the last, that's a pity, thinking of what voters have to do next year.

I once asked one of Gore's former aides—he's been vice president so long that there are many such—how she could tell when he and the president came down on different sides of the same question. "He never says," she answered. "He won't give us a clue. We have to watch his eyebrows. But then," she sighed, "they usually don't tell us anything." "Woodenness" thus has its uses.

A third intriguing question is about the level of frustration Gore, along with all his predecessors, has encountered in the second slot, and what, if any, are the scars left on his mind? In the modern vice presidency, all the preceding Democrats led deeply frustrating, greatly constrained lives. They were constrained by their presidents, who owned their schedules, vetted their speeches, sanctioned their travels, and never let them forget who was the boss. In Lyndon Johnson's case, to be sure, it was not the president but rather his brother Robert who decreed the humiliations and eked out the punishments. But when LBJ succeeded Kennedy, he left no one but himself be equally mean to Humphrey, who was treated worse than all the others put together. As for Mondale, Carter's V.P., who venerated Humphrey and was briefed by him beforehand, there was no recorded presidential roughing-up, perhaps because the so-well-briefed vice president left no occasion for it. But there evidently was, for Mondale, the same cold politeness and ignored advice that Carter characteristically gave most of those around him. Mondale sometimes may have envied LBJ: Jack Kennedy (never mind Bobby) often paid attention when his V.P. spoke.

By comparison, Gore's experience appears to have been idyllic, energizing, creative—at least in its early years—and far from frustrating, except in the accumulation of advice not taken, arguments lost—which, over seven years, are bound to mount up—and also for the sheer embarrassment of close association with a grown man whose sex life more befitted early adolescence—and who lied about it even to his close associates, presumably including Gore. On the positive side, suffice it to say that their work relationship does Gore great credit, and Clinton still more. Powers and opportunities are so unequal in their offices that only a president can make the vice presidency a good experience, as Gore's has obviously been for the most part, at least up to Monica. Two cheers for Clinton.

But what of the lasting impact of the vice presidency on Gore's psyche? Humphrey and Mondale never got the chance to show what their experiences had done for them, except in the campaigns that they both lost. Nixon, and Johnson before him, may have suffered severely. Almost certainly their paranoia levels rose while they endured the second spot, and effects lingered. Why else did LBJ so humiliate Humphrey? And when Nixon was trying to resist mounting pressure to fire Chief of Staff H. R. Haldeman, he famously invoked the treatment Eisenhower had meted out to his chief of staff, Sherman Adams, whom Eisenhower had forced to resign when it was discovered that he had accepted minor, but improper, gifts from a businessman. To Nixon, this seemed an ignoble sacrifice of a loyal aide, something he, Nixon, would never do. (Ultimately, of course, Nixon did offer up Haldeman.)

There is nothing in the record to suggest that such resentments have been driven deep into Gore by the frustrations of his veepship. Monica presents a possibility. In foreign affairs there are others. But Gore is too reserved to let any such things show. As a practical matter, the question seems unanswerable—at least for now.

My fourth intriguing question, and by far the most important, has to do with the relevance, or lack thereof, of Gore's vice presidential experience to what history has in store for American policymakers during the decade ahead. Continuing dilemmas, perhaps deepening but on familiar themes, are what I foresee after the millennium year. Along with these come aftereffects of present happenings, as they will then appear in retrospect, posing the perhaps insistent questions: "What did the vice president know, and when did he know it?" as well as, "What did he say, and when did he say it?" Kosovo and Chinese espionage now seem to be case in point. Before Inauguration Day, 2001, there will be others.

The relevance of Gore's experience goes beyond policy problems into varieties of politics. He may lack Clinton's spontaneity and ease with people, as is often written, but he and Clinton are associates politically as well as governmentally, in the full sense of campaigning for public offices and laws alike. More than any of his predecessors, Gore was a central participant in the campaign of 1992, and again in 1996. With Congress, Gore appears to have been more observer and fixer, and occasionally strategist, than actual coprincipal, but that is a judgment from afar. Yet, in the crucial confrontation on the budget with Republican majorities, during the fall and winter of 1995–96, the time of government closings, Gore by all accounts was a coprincipal indeed. At least he was at every meeting—present in voice as well as body—that Stephanopoulos and his arch-rival, Dick Morris, choose to recall—a serious indication.

So Gore participated in one of the most significant departures of the modern presidency, "going public" to endeavor to bring pressure upon Congress, not by making speeches, not by holding fireside chats, not by dominating network news, not by delivering weekend radio addresses aimed at local outlets, and not by sending special messages to Congress itself—all tried-and-true techniques applied with great success as recently as Ronald Reagan's legislative fights of 1981—but rather by (or, more accurately, in addition to) using paid television ads in critical market areas across the country. I never saw those ads, being in England at the time, but Morris and Stephanopoulos alike credit them with creating the favorable public background against which then-Speaker Gingrich and his troops forced the government to close—and took the rap for it. What Reagan got for free, along with presidents before him as far back as FDR, Clinton had to pay for. And this is a harbinger of things to come for the next president, whoever he or she may be.

Gore's breadth of experience is virtually unprecedented. But his analytic strengths and weaknesses across the policy spectrum, foreign, defense, and domestic, have been shared with the press, and by the press with the public, only in a fragmentary way. His administrative strengths and weaknesses, his knowledge and imagination also have not been plumbed. Nor has his sense of history. Rather, more has been made, to date, of his stiffness in some public situations, his discomfort in spontaneous exchanges when he lacks the facts, his necessitous deference to Clinton, and his occasional verbal bloopers. Of these we shall hear and learn much more as the campaign season advances. I wish I were equally confident that journalists would press his colleagues on those other fronts and that the colleagues would respond to the fullest extent they conscientiously can. Otherwise, the man will run for office with this huge and relevant experience behind him, yet, outside of certain offices in Washington and overseas, no one will be the wiser about what it really means and what it may foreshadow if he gets the top job.

Not having served in Washington for more than three decades, nor having worked with Gore since he first became a congressman, I'm of no help in those respects. But I did teach him when he was in college, longer ago than I care to recall, and I do remember well the human qualities that made him a good student—and a good person. He was curious, imaginative, and indefatigable when aroused, with a nose for news, respect for facts, a sharp sense of humor, and a great girlfriend he had the wit to marry.

Before he left the United States to be a soldier in Vietnam, he and Tipper came to say goodbye to me and my wife. He was in Army private's uniform, belt and shoes shiny, pants creased, his usual wry humor much subdued, we thought, perhaps by boot camp—which must have been quite an experience for a St. Albans boy, fresh out of Harvard—but more probably by his imminent destination. When Gore reached Vietnam, the Army made him a correspondent for *Stars and Stripes*. So, although he had brushes with enemy fire, he was not steadily engaged in combat like some fellow infantrymen. No fools the Army, when posting senators' sons. But Al evidently did not know that when we saw him.

To Tipper and my wife and me—and him—Al was in a tough spot, headed for a brutal war of which we all had come to disapprove. Yet he was in that spot by choice. Unlike our son and many of Al's other classmates, similarly liable to be drafted, he had chosen not to wangle an officer-candidate's place in the Air Force or Navy. Rather, as he told me, he felt obligated to serve where most of his father's Tennessee constituents had to serve—in the ranks. That's what he was doing when he rose from our sofa to say goodbye and face Vietnam. He was very, very serious and stood up very straight. So did Tipper.

That's the picture in my head when I consider that this man has now become a candidate for president. Others will have other pictures. Mine is old but not, I think, irrelevant. Policies and politics take place in the context of character.

ARTICLE 3

LEARNING TO GOVERN: AN INSTITUTIONAL VIEW OF THE 104TH CONGRESS

Richard F. Fenno, Jr.

ONE

Forty Years

I am a Congress watcher. And for any Congress watcher the 104th Congress surely stands out as one of the most fascinating of recent times. For me the fascination grows out of one simple historical fact: the 104th was the first Congress in forty years in which the Republican party controlled the House of Representatives. Every account of the 104th Congress mentions it. But none of them makes anything of it. I want to tell a story that *does* make something out of it.

Certainly, there is nothing in our history to match this forty-year stretch—from 1955 to 1995—without an alternation in party control of the House. In the one hundred years from 1855 to 1955, the longest previous span of one-party dominance was sixteen years. The Republicans did it twice, from 1859 to 1875 and from 1895 to 1911, and the Democrats did it once, from 1931 to 1947 Indeed, forty years is an extraordinarily long time for one-party control of any democratically elected national legislature. During the same four decades that one party controlled our House of Representatives, for example, majority-party control of the British House of Commons changed hands four times, and the least victorious party ran the institution for nearly one-quarter of the period.

Forty years of unchanging partisan dominance may be very idiosyncratic. But it is enough of a phenomenon to have had some effect on the Congress that finally broke the mold, the 104th. Certainly, it was enough of a phenomenon to have had an effect on political scientists. For all those years we Congress watchers simply assumed that politics in the House of Representatives meant Democratic politics. We wrote extensively about the House Democrats, and we became the victims of our Democratic diet. We were quite unprepared to answer the question posed for us by the events of 1994—the question of long-term one-party dominance and the effects of its sudden reversal.

For students of Congress the question is "What effect did twenty consecutive Democratic Congresses have on the activity of the first Republican Congress that followed?"

For me the question has been stimulated by the counterfactual hunch that had we experienced even some minimal alternation in party control during the forty preceding years, the politics of the 104th Congress would have been different from what it was. My hunch is that those years of one-party control of the House helped produce some serious consequences, among which were the confrontational leadership behavior of Newt Gingrich, the deterioration in cross-party civility in the House, the Republican-led movement for term limits, and the accelerated decline of public confidence in Congress as an institution. Whatever the validity of these hunches, they have reinforced my idea that forty years without a change of party control had a major impact on the activities of the House of Representatives in the 104th Congress. And the House, let us not forget, is the institutional centerpiece of our system of representative democracy.

The argument I want to make is that forty consecutive years as the minority party in the House left the Republicans, as of November 1994, totally without first-hand political experience of two essential sorts: first, experience in *interpreting* electoral victory and, second, experience in *governing* the country. In both respects, the relevant experience had been available only to the Democratic majority. The Republicans' lack of relevant experience, together with their accumulated frustrations, I shall argue, led the new majority to make serious mistakes, first of interpretation and then of governance. Because of their inexperience and their mistakes, the House Republicans missed their golden governing opportunity and made possible the rehabilitation, resurgence, and reelection of Bill Clinton.

This argument is deliberately more developmental and more institutional than the accounts produced by observers who were close to the day-to-day action in Washington and who focused their analysis on the three leading players—Newt Gingrich, Bob Dole, and Bill Clinton. Elizabeth Drew, author of *Showdown,* a book about the first fifteen months of the 104th Congress, concluded her analysis this way:

> A great deal—no less than the role of the federal government—was at stake last year and is again this year. The histories of these battles cannot be understood in abstraction from the nature, and the interplay among, the three major *personalities* who commanded them.[1]

Similarly, Michael Weisskopf and David Maraniss, authors of *"Tell Newt to Shut Up!,"* their book about the 104th, concluded,

> This winter's historic struggle over the role of government has turned on a number of intertwined factors: the clear clash of ideologies, the 1996 presidential campaign, the battle of political message. But in the midst of those larger forces were three men . . . whose goals and *personalities* played *the determining role* in shaping events.[2]

My story of the House of Representatives in the 104th Congress is perfectly compatible with accounts that center on personalities. And I shall rely heavily on such on-the-scene reports.[3] But my perspective is more institutional, more long term, and more generalizable than that of the journalists on the beat. Or so, as a practicing political scientist, I should like to think.

TWO

Electoral Interpretation and the Majority-Minority Relationship

The period following an election is a critical time for every victorious political party. It is the time during which the winners decide for themselves what their victory meant and how it will shape their future activity. It is for them to interpret the election results; and it is their electoral interpretation that becomes the essential link between the business of campaigning and the business of governing. Everything that follows in the new Congress will be affected by the postelection interpretation of the winners. Political scientists will, of course, decide after many years and many Ph.D. dissertations what the voters' message *really* was. But the winning party cannot wait. It must choose its own working approximation early and will soon face the consequences.

The Republicans of 1994 had never faced this interpretive problem before. For twenty consecutive elections they had faced a very different problem: interpreting their defeat. And their interpretation had usually focused inward to a rash of blaming and bloodletting and to the cannibalizing of their leadership. This time, by contrast, their 1994 electoral interpretation would be their guide to governing the country. And this time their electoral interpretation was faulty. It set them off on the wrong course and was most unhelpful to them over the crucial year and a half that followed.

They chose to interpret their victory as an electoral mandate to undertake wholesale change, a mandate for what they called a Republican revolution. The election, they decided, had ratified their call for a *more responsive* government, by way of such constitutional changes as term limits, a balanced budget amendment, and a line-item veto, and their call for a *smaller* government, by way of legislative reductions in spending for a huge array of government programs.

So long as they described their mandate in the general language of change to a smaller, more responsive government and with an open-ended timetable, they retained some necessary flexibility in implementation. But the Republicans also decided in very concrete terms that the electorate had given its approval to their campaign document, the Contract with America. The document contained a lengthy list of policy proposals and a one-hundred-day timetable for completing House action on all of them. This more detailed electoral interpretation held that the public had voted support for a fairly specific program and for quick action to get it all under way. This refined reading of the election returns had two problems. There was scant evidence to support it. And, more important, it did not serve the party's long-term interest.

In the aftermath of the 1994 election, all available evidence told us that the election had been more a repudiation of the Democrats than an endorsement of the Republicans. Every incumbent House member, senator, and governor who lost was a Democrat. Every poll, plus the larger-than-normal midterm loss of Democratic seats, suggested an unusual degree of dissatisfaction with the Democratic president. Besides which, a large majority of voters had never heard of the Contract with America.

The voters had thrown out the Democrats and given the Republicans the opportunity to govern. But they had put the Republicans very much on trial and on a very short leash. Given their total lack of experience with Republican House majorities, the voters could hardly have done anything more than that. An accurate reading of the election results, therefore, would have been more provisional and more modest than the revolutionary ten-point mandate interpretation the Republicans adopted.

The accuracy of an electoral interpretation may not, however, be the only measure of its usefulness to a victorious party. Something we might call strategic wisdom matters, too. If the victors adopt an empirically unsupportable electoral interpretation but can still make it work for them strategically—that is, if they can use it to help them achieve their most important goals—accuracy may not matter. Ronald Reagan's interpretation of a mandate in 1980 would be a case in point. In strategy as well as accuracy, however, the Republican postelection interpretation of 1994 was faulty.

If, as I think was the case, the party's most important long-run goal was to bring about a *unified Republican government,* the Republicans should have interpreted the election as an invitation to take some carefully selected first steps toward the accomplishment of that goal.

Since 1980 the Republican–conservative movement had held an intellectual advantage in the national policy debate over the performance of big government; and it had capitalized on that intellectual advantage to capture, for varying lengths of time, both the presidency and the Senate. But never the House. Viewed strategically, therefore, the Republicans' 1994 capture of the House was a long-awaited and necessary step toward the eventual achievement of a unified conservative government of the sort that Margaret Thatcher enjoyed for twelve years in Great Britain. But the 1994 election hardly signaled the completion of that journey. In which case the overriding task of the Republican 104th Congress was to keep building toward the capture of the 105th Congress and, most important, the presidency in 1996. To contemplate, much less proclaim, a revolution without having captured the presidency as well was pure fantasy.

An electoral interpretation that emphasized the incremental and instrumental nature of their own governing opportunity would have constrained them to be cautious and selective in setting their legislative agenda. In the longer run what they most needed to accomplish was to retain their control over the terms of the national policy debate while also convincing an uncertain electorate that the country would function safely and smoothly in their hands. There was, in short, a huge difference between passing the Contract through the House in one hundred days and governing the country. A more modest, more provisional electoral interpretation would have encouraged the new majority to appreciate that difference and to subordinate the Contract to governing.

It is perfectly understandable, however, why the Republicans did not see the difference and why they chose the Contract-centered electoral interpretation they did. For one thing, they had never before had to interpret an election victory, and the absence of relevant past decisions created uncertainty. For another thing, forty years out of power had left them with a short fuse and a short time horizon. They had built up a massive backlog of frustration and energy. They had waited long enough. Understandably, patience and accommodation were not uppermost in their minds. They were anxious to seize the day and press their case as it was expressed in the Contract.

Their inexperience plus their impatience blinded them to the government-wide stakes and to the long-run governing opportunities that had flowed from their electoral victory.

Which brings us to the majority-minority relationship in the House. What does the relationship mean? What is it like to be in the minority in the House? Political scientists who study the two parties inside the legislature have found a great deal of structure and predictability in the majority-minority relationship. Based on the rules and practices of the House, certain recognizable and stable patterns of expectation, strategy, and behavior have developed. And they, as a bundle, define the relationship. Forty years of one-party rule in the House produced a recognizable, institutionally supported Democratic-Republican relationship. An equilibrium had been established, one unfavorable to the Republicans, but stable nonetheless. During four decades House Democrats learned only how to be a majority party, and House Republicans learned only how to be a minority party.

The two crucial structural features of the majority-minority relationship are first that *the majority party organizes* and runs the House and second that *the minority party adapts* to the governing majority. When the outgoing Democratic majority leader, Dick Gephardt, handed the gavel to the incoming Speaker, Newt Gingrich, on opening day January 1995, he said, "I hereby end 40 years of Democratic rule of this House."[1] *Rule* was the correct word. All our research tells us that the majority-party Democrats had long dominated the House floor and the House committees.

With respect to majority-party control of the House floor, consider these observations from Barbara Sinclair's authoritative studies of Democratic rule. "Consultation between the minority-majority parties on scheduling is rare in the House."[2] "The majority party leadership will structure [floor] rules so as to advantage the outcome its party members favor rather than that favored by the opposition party." "On major legislation meaningful participation in shaping the legislation and amassing support takes place . . . in the majority party."[3]

The majority party also controls committee activity—selecting leaders, shaping jurisdictions, assigning bills, setting committee size and majority-minority membership ratios, allocating staff resources, and establishing internal procedures. In a book that describes the majority party as "a legislative cartel," Gary Cox and Matt McCubbins conclude that "the legislative process in general—and *the committee system in particular*—is stacked in favor of majority party interests."[4] For forty years, whenever the House worked to reform its committee system, reforms were enacted by the majority party for the majority party, as repeated partisan struggles over minority staff resources and proxy voting attest.[5]

In short, the Republicans had little doubt about who organized and ran the House for forty years and who did not. A former member of the minority leadership compared his legislative influence with that of a majority party leader.

> As a Democrat, [he] set agendas; as a Republican, I reacted to them. As a Democrat, [he] helped to set the terms for debate, deciding what, if any, amendments would be considered when legislation reached the House floor; as a Republican, I pleaded with the Rules Committee for a chance to offer alternatives. As Democrats, [he] and his party's committee chairmen decided who would be allowed to testify before congressional committees and on what bills; as a Republican, I had to fight to get conservative views heard.

And he concluded, "Congress belonged to the Democrats and they acted like it."[6]

More than that, the Democrats acted as if Congress would belong to them for as far into the future as anyone could see. And indeed, that was the commonly held expectation throughout the period—that there was no alternation in power in sight. Political science studies of incumbency advantages, retirement ratios, and the career ambitions and strategic behavior of politicians all pointed to continued Democratic hegemony.[7] National surveys repeatedly showed that a majority of voters preferred Democrats to Republicans when voting for Congress.[8] And twenty consecutive election defeats kept ratifying these assumptions.

Accordingly, students of Republican party politics became increasingly pessimistic about the chances of a takeover. In his studies during the 1960s and 1970s Charles Jones found that many Republicans were adopting a minority mentality, "accepting minority status as a fact of life and accommodating themselves to their fate."[9] And he maintained that their chances of becoming a majority "do not appear very bright."[10] In their 1994 book, *Congress' Permanent Minority?*, William Connelly and John Pitney concluded that "as of the early 1990's, serious thoughts of a GOP Speakership are premature."[11] Many safe and talented minority-party members accepted this growing judgment and, despairing of their chances for attaining majority status, left the House.[12]

The widely shared expectation of continued Democratic party control affected the structure of incentives inside the chamber. The idea here is that when both parties expect to alternate in power, the party temporarily in the majority has an incentive to consult, cooperate with, and compromise with the party temporarily in the minority. A majority that expects one day to be in the minority is most likely to temper majority rule with a prudent respect for minority opinion. Under these circumstances, a sense of reciprocity develops between the two parties. But, goes the argument, when the majority party has not experienced minority status for decades and does not expect to be in the minority any day soon, the incentive for taking the minority into account is substantially reduced and a sense of reciprocity or comity is less likely to develop and persist. And that is what happened during forty years without any partisan alternation in power.

We can sense Democratic arrogance in such comments as these: from the majority leader, "Republicans are just going to have to get it through their heads that they are not going to write legislation."[13] From the majority whip, "What difference does it make what the Republicans think?"[14] From the Rules Committee chairman, "Hey, we've got the votes. Let's vote. Screw you."[15] From a top Education Committee staffer, "We rolled the Republicans every time. We had no fairness. We just screwed them."[16]

Webster's defines *frustration* as "a rendering vain or ineffectual all efforts however feeble or vigorous." And we can sense minority-party frustration in such comments as these: from the chairman of the Republican Policy Committee,

> [The Speaker] will do anything he can to win at any price, including ignoring the rules, bending the rules, writing rules, denying the House to work its will. It brings disrespect to the House itself. There's no sense of comity left. Why should you, if you are a Republican and given the way Republicans are treated, think of a Democrat as a colleague? They aren't colleagues.[17]

Or from the minority leader,

> Thirty-five years of uninterrupted power can act like a corrosive acid on the restraints of civility and comity. Those who have been kings of the hill for so long, may forget that majority status is not a divine right—and that minority status is not a permanent condition.[18]

Forty years of one-party rule—past, present, and projected—fostered a pattern of arrogance on one side and frustration on the other side of the majority-minority relationship in the House.

If, as I have said, the first feature of the majority-minority relationship is that the majority governs, the second feature is that the minority adapts. As William Connelly and John Pitney put it, "while majority party members must debate how to govern the country, minority members must debate how to cope with their lowly place in the House."[19] From 1955 to 1995 the Republicans carried on an internal debate about the appropriate strategy of adaptation to the majority.

On one side were the *institutional partisans* who advocated accommodation and cooperation with the majority, who worked within the existing rules of the House to get whatever they could by way of bipartisan or cross-partisan policy adjustment. On the other side were the *confrontational partisans* who advocated aggressive in-your-face treatment of the majority, who cared little about legislative responsibility, and whose only goal was to drive the Democrats from power. As one of the party's future leaders said in 1993, "We're having a struggle right now within the Republican party . . . [between] those who think they're here to govern and those who think they're here to take over a majority. I am not among those here to govern. I am here to take over a majority from the Democrats."[20] In the beginning the institutional partisans, working in cross-party coalition with defecting conservative Democrats, won some legislative battles, and they prevailed inside the party. But the forty-year trend in the adaptation debate moved gradually with each influx of Republican newcomers away from a preferred strategy of institutional partisanship and toward a preferred strategy of confrontational partisanship.

The central theme among political scientists studying recent Congresses has been the steady increase in partisanship inside the House, "the resurgence of partisanship" in David Rohde's words.[21] If we study this resurgence from the majority party's perspective, the increase in partisanship is explained by a gradually more cohesive, more ideologically homogeneous, better organized, and more decisively led Democratic party. Those conditions influenced Republican partisanship, too, as conservative southern Democrats joined the Republican ranks. But if we write the forty-year story from the minority party's perspective, the increase in partisanship must also be explained in terms of the gradual change in Republican adaptation strategy as institutional partisans were replaced by confrontational partisans. The shift in the internal balance was finally completed when the leader of the confrontational partisans was elected as both the leader of his party and Speaker of the House.[22]

Which brings us to the one personality we cannot avoid: Newt Gingrich. For he was the architect, the leader, the articulator, and the symbol of the minority party's confrontational adaptation strategy in coping with the majority. In my story his ideas and his activities are *not* personality matters.[23] They are institutional matters. From the time he came to Congress in 1978 he thought about the House in institutional terms, that is, in terms of the majority party-minority party relationship. His overriding goal was to make the Republicans the majority party in the House. His instrumental goal was to change the party's adaptation strategy from accommodation to confrontation.

Six months into his House career he began criticizing his party's strategy of accommodation. "For a great part of its minority life," he said, "the Republican party has allowed itself to become co-opted as an arm of the government. Too often, it has allowed itself to be cajoled into providing the necessary votes for the majority party to win."[24] "When I first came here," he later recalled, "the majority of the Republican caucus preferred passively accepting Democratic dominance and fighting them within a framework which Democrats and the establishment created."[25] "Democrats would go on the floor," he said, "to kick Republicans and show their contempt. The ranking Republicans would say how grateful they were to work with the chairman, when he had 70 staff people and the Republicans had three. It was the whole psychology of master and servant."[26] "I am interested," he said, "in breaking up the Democratic monopoly of power . . . the current one-sided rigging of the Rules Committee, the current rigging of the rules, the current liberal domination of scheduling and the current one-sided stamping on behalf of the Democrats."[27] And he vowed, "I will do almost anything to win a Republican majority in Congress."[28] From 1978 to 1994 he fought that battle. And its rationale was more institutional than personal.

He battled first by working to undermine two successive minority leaders, because he deemed them insufficiently confrontational. He and his soul mates pressured John Rhodes and then Bob Michel to be more aggressive in fighting Democrats than they wanted to be.[29] And that pressure contributed mightily both to the premature resignation of Rhodes and the premature retirement of Michel from their position as minority leader.[30]

Second, he battled by leading a sweeping attack on House Democrats. He attacked and humiliated Speaker Tip O'Neill for overstepping his bounds as presiding officer of the House.[31] He attacked Speaker Jim Wright for using his public position to enrich himself; and, in his greatest, triumph, drove Wright from the House. "I am engaged in a long-term struggle," he explained. "The House is sick and Wright is the symbol."[32]

Third, he battled by attacking the House as an institution. When criticized for his personal attacks on Democratic leaders, he replied that his target was the institution itself. "This is about systemic, institutional corruption, not personality," he declared."[33] And he charged that "the Democrats have run the House for 30 years. They've gotten sloppy. The House is a corrupt institution in the Lord Acton sense."[34] By which he meant that "Power corrupts and absolute power corrupts absolutely."

In November 1994 the pursuit of this confrontational strategy produced the Republican majority he had so single-mindedly sought. It was an incredible success story. But success carried with it some serious costs as the new majority took up its governing tasks.

First, by attacking a generation of his own party's institutional partisans, he was attacking, in effect, the established interparty relationships that had given definition and stability to the House as an institution for four decades. More than that, he seemed to be ruling out accommodation as an acceptable mode of cross-party behavior. If so, he left very unclear what new kind of majority-minority equilibrium he intended to put in its place. He said vaguely that he wanted to bring about "a big, long-term cultural change" from a "collegial" institution to a "professional" one.[35] If what he wanted was less collegiality in the 104th Congress, he surely got it. "In all my years in Congress," said one twenty-four-year House Democrat in 1996, "I have never seen such bitter feelings between the minority and the majority."[36] The Republicans, he said later, "don't know how to run the place."[37]

Second, the scope and severity of Gingrich's partisan attacks earned him personally an implacable legacy of ill will from a large number of Democrats. In 1991 he admitted to being "the most hated man on Capitol Hill."[38] And as one of his soul mates in the Conservative Opportunity Society said, "it is not good or useful to be hated in this institution."[39] When asked to explain the "polarized and embittered" House in 1995, respected Republican veteran Henry Hyde cited "the absolutely pathological hatred of Newt Gingrich" by the Democrats.[40] Their persistent payback harassment of Speaker Gingrich continues to this day to inhibit cross-party cooperation.

Finally, by couching his attacks in the language of institutional corruption and the personal abuse of power, Gingrich deliberately manipulated made worse an existing public cynicism and lack of confidence in the nation's most important representative institution. In attacking majority party arrogance, he was right on target. But it was impossible to hear or read his yearly litany of indictments and to come away thinking well of the Congress as an institution. In working to take control of the House, he had also undermined and weakened it in the public eye.

Newt Gingrich and his confrontational style, I believe, were the predictable results of forty years in the minority. If it had not been him it would have been another confrontational partisan very much like him. Had there been an occasional alternation in power, and had the Republicans of the 104th Congress been able to know and to reap the rewards and responsibilities of running the institution earlier, they would, I think, have settled on a more accommodationist leadership style. The act of trading places occasionally would necessarily have introduced constraints on their partisanship. Alternation would also have produced a strong incentive to protect the existing institutional framework, placing greater emphasis on cross-party comity and reciprocity. The explanation for Newt Gingrichs'

rise to party leadership and for his subsequent leadership performance depends heavily on the extraordinary length of time his party
had had to endure the deprivations and frustrations of an out-party
minority.[41]

THREE

Governing: The Contract, the Freshmen, the Speaker

What about the governing performance of the 104th Congress? The
good news was that the Republican party had been given a once-in-
a-lifetime opportunity. The bad news was that the Republican party
had been given a once-in-a-lifetime opportunity. It was forty years
since they had been in a position to govern. They were, arguably, the
least experienced House majority in one hundred years. And it
showed.

The party's new leader produced a torrent of rhetoric about governing. "This is a genuine revolution," said Gingrich. "We're going
to rethink every element of the federal government. We're going to
close down several federal departments."[1] But he had no idea how
to do any of it. He was, after all, just a smart, articulate, visionary
college professor. Governing was going to be a totally experimental
adventure for him.

Again, there is nothing surprising about this state of affairs.
The governing expertise the Republicans lacked was precisely the
kind that can only be acquired through trial and error by those who
have held power. The governing expertise of which I speak is not
subject matter expertise, which minority members can acquire in
their committees. It is expertise about the business of legislating.
That business involves a practical grasp of lawmaking as a lengthy,
incremental, multilevel, coalition-building process. And it involves
a seasoned strategic sense in matters such as establishing priorities,
negotiating outcomes across the separated institutions of government, and calculating feasibilities, trade-offs, and timing at every
decisionmaking juncture. In short, successful governing takes a lot
of practice, and the Republicans hadn't had any.

When the victorious Republicans huddled after the election—
under the influence of their we-won-it-and-we-got-a-sweeping-
mandate interpretation of the election results—they decided to take
the document they had crafted for *electioneering* purposes, the Contract with America, and adopt it wholesale as their *legislative* agenda.
The decision had the virtue of giving instant focus, organization, and
work to a new, inexperienced, and impatient majority. But its conception of the governing process was every bit as faulty as the faulty
electoral interpretation on which it rested.

First, because it had been packaged with the help of polls and
focus groups for electoral purposes, the Contract lacked any sense

for legislative priorities. It was a laundry list of ten vote-getting proposals, each placed on the same footing as every other by the promise that all would be brought to a vote in the House within one
hundred days. Yet they were a very mixed bag. Some were broadly
institutional, even constitutional, in their content and impact; others
were more narrowly programmatic. They commanded varying patterns of support inside the party. Some drew support from the
Democrats; others served to mobilize the minority party in opposition. Their future prospects were, therefore, very uneven.

By prescribing an equality of effort and an identical time line for
all Republicans substituted inflexibility for subtlety. They deprived
themselves of a chance to think about their legislative agenda in
terms of trade-offs, or to make distinctions between what they
would *like* to get and what they *had* to get. Participants in the legislative process typically have to settle for less than they might want.
It is very important to know when to declare victory, when to take
something for now and return for more later. The animating spirit of
the one hundred days was, in the words of Policy Chairman Christopher Cox, that "revolutions have a very short half life. If you don't
ask for it, you don't get it."[2] That spirit was inadequate preparation
for life in the legislative lane. Indeed, when they discovered, late in
the day, that the Contract left many priorities untouched, they
started piling lots of normal legislation directly onto their appropriations bills, a hasty improvisation that misused the appropriations
process, bogged down the flow of money bills, opened up jurisdic-
tional battles inside the party, and brought embarrassing defeats on
the House floor.[3]

In the second place the Contract conveyed no sense of a long-run
strategy for actually enacting any of its proposals into law. It focused
only on action inside the House. It took no account of the broader
legislative context that lay beyond, a context of separated institutions, sharing responsibility and power. It took no cognizance of the
Senate with its distinctive procedures and its different ideological
makeup, nor did it comprehend the president with his veto power
and his bully pulpit. This neglect of the larger context helped blind
House Republicans to certain structural limitations on their power,
for example, their very slim working majority of fourteen votes, a
majority that would become vulnerable under external pressure and
was not even close to being veto proof.

To be sure, the party did bring all ten Contract items to a vote in
the House and they did pass nine of them there. They displayed an
extraordinary diligence and discipline in doing so. When it was
over, however, they talked and acted as if they had mastered the legislative process. Not only had they not understood the difference between passing the Contract and governing the country, but what
was worse, they had mistaken one for the other. They took the view

that they had passed the crucial performance test and were now ready for public judgment. "We did what we said we would do," they said. And they tirelessly repeated their slogan, "promises made, promises kept." It conveyed a far broader sense of accomplishment than was warranted.

Their performance on the Contract had, in fact, been a short-run, narrowly focused, inward-looking legislative performance. It had been at best a preliminary test of their governing ability at the beginning of a more complicated and longer-lasting legislative effort.

It is not possible to understand the interpretive and the governing failures of the new majority party in the 104th Congress without paying attention to *the freshman class* that made the majority possible. The seventy-three newcomers are important to this analysis for at least two reasons. First, they enjoyed an unusually large potential for intraparty influence. Second, if inexperience was a problem for the new majority, the freshman class would most likely exemplify the problem.

When political scientists estimate the influence potential of legislative parties or party groupings, we pay special attention to their size and to their cohesion on policy matters. In both respects the freshman Republicans had a great potential for influence. They were the second largest group of newcomers in either party since World War II, and they made up one-third of their party's majority. They wore buttons that said, "Majority Maker," and they relished the prospect of their pivotal decision-making power inside the Republican caucus. They were not only an unusually large group, they were an unusually cohesive group. As some long-time observers noted, "They arrived on Capitol Hill with a sense of common purpose that has rarely been seen in any incoming class of congressmen."[4] And they "developed an unusually strong sense of class cohesion."[5] They shared a short-run commitment to the Contract with America; and they shared a long-run determination to transform their conservative policy preferences into a new pattern of government. Conservative commentators exulted in their presence. "When and if the leadership blinks, the freshman class will go on point," predicted Kate O'Bierne of the Heritage Foundation."[6]

Any large turnover in House membership is likely to be a source of new ideas, and the 1994 turnover certainly qualified as large. Even more relevant to their potential for policy influence was that sixty-five of the seventy-three newcomers—90 percent of them—came from constituencies that had been represented by Democrats in the 103d Congress. Students of the linkage between elections and public policy have found that these switched-seat newcomers, fresh from a victory over the opposing party, are the most potent carriers of new policy ideas. Historically, when there is an extra large influx of switched-seat newcomers into the majority party in Congress, major policy changes follow.[7] Sixty-five switched-seat Republican freshmen certainly qualified as an extra large influx. And they certainly had a missionary spirit when it came to changes in policy direction. As they frequently explained their zeal for change, "That's what I came here for."[8]

There were, of course, plenty of differences within the group. And we should not forget that. But because of their unusual potential for influence, they quickly came to be viewed by others as a collectivity. The media paid them an inordinate amount of attention. Headlines read: "A Class of New Warriors," "The GOP's Young Turks," "73 Mr. Smiths, of the GOP, Go To Washington," "The Transformers," "Freshmen: New Powerful Voice."[9] All seventy-three were lumped together and described variously as the "shock troops," "revolutionaries," "ideological firebrands," "giant killers," "red guards" of the new majority, and as "the 800 pound gorilla of Washington politics."[10]

They were not at all bashful about accepting these descriptions, since they, too, thought of themselves as a collective force. "[I am] not meaningful," said one member, "but the word 'freshman' is meaningful."[11] Accordingly, they spoke of themselves regularly as the freshman class. Listen to some of their self-characterizations, each from a different member.

> The freshman class is the best representation of an absolute commitment to change.[12]
>
> The difference between the freshmen and the people who have been here for a while is that we're closer to the people. We're more responsive to what they want to do.[13]
>
> The freshman class is prepared to go to the wall for what we believe in.[14]
>
> This freshman class has shown that we have the courage to stand up to this institution, even to our own leadership.[15]
>
> We're solid as a rock. There's no quit in this freshman class. We're going to keep pushing.[16]

Self-consciously and self-confidently they thought of themselves as a force to be reckoned with in the 104th Congress. As one freshman said to me, "The freshman class is a real thing."

As a group, therefore, the freshmen were long on size and cohesion. They were also long on conviction and confidence. But they were short on another major attribute of legislative influence—experience. Fewer than half (thirty-five) had previous electoral experience. Of that group, only seventeen had any experience in a state legislature; and of that group, just seven had any experience as a

member of the majority party in a state legislature. All told, therefore, only seven of the seventy-three Republican newcomers had
any governing experience as a member of a legislative majority,
which was, of course, the situation that faced them in the 104th
Congress. In an inexperienced majority party, they were the least experienced of all.

As far as I can tell, however, they did not think their lack of governing experience diminished their potential for influence. Some
even wore this deficiency as a badge of distinction. "Our class symbol should be the bumble bee," said one. "Aeronautical engineers
say the bumble bee can't fly because there's not enough wing size to
carry its weight. But the bumble bee flies because he never studied
aeronautical engineering."[17] Many of his classmates shared that cav-
alier attitude toward political experience.

They thought of themselves, instead, as citizen legislators, for
whom it was precisely their nonpolitical experience that would be
their most important contribution to the business of governing.
Because they were coming from the nonpolitical, workaday world,
they saw themselves as bringing the real life experiences of ordinary people to bear on the work of an insulated Congress. They
associated extended governing experience with a corrupting, self-
aggrandizing careerism that produced professional politicians who
were out of touch with everyday reality. Central to their self-image
was a devotion to term limits. And that special Republican devotion, I believe, was yet another product of forty years as the minority
party in the House.

As citizen legislators, many of them had put a limit on their tem-
porary assignment in Washington and had promised to return in a
foreseeable future to the daily life of the country from which they
had come. They were prepared to get their legislative experience on
the job. But because they had short-run career horizons, they were
not prepared to wait to get their experience before they tried to
make a difference. Their newcomers' enthusiasm, coupled with
their short-run career horizons, fueled an attitude of "let's get it all,
and get it all now."

The first decisions on which the freshman class had the chance
to make a difference were those involving the interpretation of their
electoral victory. Because only seven had ever been involved in this
kind of decision before, they had little independent judgment to
offer. Not surprisingly, they totally embraced the interpretation of a
sweeping mandate, the one that assumed voter approval of a Republican revolution. Because, as candidates, they had introduced themselves most recently *to* the electorate and now, as House members,
had come most recently *from* the electorate, they were confident that
they understood the electoral mandate better than most. If they

added anything independently to the interpretive process, therefore, it was a heightened sense of urgency about the party's mission and a desire for a quickened legislative pace. As one of them put it, "The freshman class is not a do-nothing class. This is a do-something-and-do-it-all-right-now freshman class."[18]

They quickly seized on the Contract with America as the authentic expression of their electoral mandate. Most had signed it; many were familiar with it from their campaigns. "The three most important issues for the freshman class," said one member, "are the Contract, the Contract, and the Contract."[19] Some wore their laminated copies around their necks. Others kept it with them always, in a coat pocket. Some called it "my Bible."[20] Even the few who had not signed the Contract gave it top priority. As one such member said, "I think the Contract, for the vast majority of the freshmen, is their Bible. We've got to sell it and pass it before we do anything else."[21] Although all of them acknowledged Newt Gingrich as their leader, they were prepared to hold his feet to the fire when the Contract was involved. As their class president said, "We intend to keep the pressure on the leadership not to deviate from the Contract."[22]

The freshmen became the proprietary guardians of the Contract. As each important item passed, they basked in media attention. Wearing buttons that read "Keeping Promises," and amid signs proclaiming "Promises Made, Promises Kept," they celebrated ceremoniously by putting check marks in the appropriate boxes on wall-sized charts and in their personal copies. When it was completed, they held a grand celebratory reprise on the Capitol steps.

Several times during the 104th Congress, I journeyed to the districts of two members of the freshman class. My conversations with them can add some insight into the dynamics of the 104th, first on interpreting the election, later on governing the country. They were in no sense representative of the class. From different parts of the country, from different backgrounds, and with differing ambitions, they were nonetheless typical of the class in some essential respects. They were deep-dyed conservatives, enthusiastic reformers, committed citizen legislators, and 100 percent supporters of the Contract. Neither man ever seemed the least bit jaded or cynical about the politics they were engaged in. Neither one was a shrinking violet within the class.

Both men subscribed to the idea that their victory was an electoral mandate and that the Contract with America was of crucial importance. It may be indicative of the very strong hold the Contract had on the group that both men embraced it so wholeheartedly, even though it played virtually no part in either of their election campaigns. Both men campaigned almost exclusively against Bill Clinton.

One campaigned by attacking his 1994 opponent as "a Clinton clone." His TV ads "morphed" his opponent's face into Clinton's face. Yet he eagerly signed the Contract and fully embraced it afterward. His action was based, he said, on "the ethics of campaigning." When he signed the Contract, in his view he made a promise; and once elected he was committed to fulfill that promise. That is what the voters expected him to do: pass the Contract, come home, and campaign on that basis.

It was a lofty embrace. If politicians hoped to retain public trust, he believed, they must maintain this link between campaigning and governing. As he explained in 1995,

> George Bush's idea was that the two were separate, that you campaigned on a platform and then governed without regard to it. That view bred cynicism. The new cohort of Republicans is saying, "hold us accountable." That puts us on the right path. And I can see a changed ethic in Washington.

For him, there was simply no other intellectual basis for an electoral interpretation than the Contract and its promises. His 1996 reelection campaign headquarters was dominated by a huge sign, "Promises Made, Promises Kept." All of his 1996 campaign brochures and his TV ads carried the slogan, "He did what he said he would do," or "he kept his word." If this freshman ever saw any problems with the Contract, he never mentioned it. Indeed, toward the end of the 104th he began to advocate a second Contract.

When I first met the second freshman, shortly after the one hundred days, he volunteered,

> By far the biggest factor in my election was Bill Clinton. People here were against everything he did. . . . When I first heard about the Contract, I was reluctant [to sign]. I was not real enthusiastic. I was happy running against Bill Clinton. . . . [But] the Contract gave me an agenda to talk about . . . [it] nationalized the election. That was its biggest contribution.

If, therefore, the Contract had a nationalizing effect, what better vehicle to serve as their defining electoral mandate? His attitude after the election was, "If we're going to make the voters feel good about giving Republicans all these seats, the first thing we need to do is implement the Contract." Unlike his colleague, however, he did show signs of second-guessing his early electoral interpretation.

In April 1996 I had no sooner climbed into his car than he asked me, "What happened in 1994? Did we win or did they lose?" "I think they lost," I said. "So, did we blow it?" he asked. "Yes," I said. "I think you blew it." It was the right question. But the answer had come too late. Six months later, he returned to his party's crucial interpretative mistake.

> When the Republicans held their very first conference after the election, there was a question I was dying to ask. And I've been kicking myself in the butt ever since for not asking it. I wanted to ask, "Did we win or did they lose?" If you think we won, give me five things you think we ought to do. If you think they lost, give me five things you think they should do. You can't figure out where you want to go until you take an inventory of what it was that got you there. The other question I wanted to ask was, "If you were in their place, what would you do?" We acted like we won. We never asked ourselves what the Democrats would do.

Whether or not his reconstruction was accurate, he was coming to understand the costs of his party's inexperienced rush to electoral interpretation.

The passage in the House of all but one Contract item in one hundred days was, indeed, a remarkable achievement, one worth celebrating—but with one cheer, not three. It was, I have argued, a self-contained, narrowly focused, inward-looking, short-run achievement. Its highly acclaimed workload statistics—time in session, pages of debate, measures reported, number of roll calls—reflected the ability to organize majority party power inside the House. But that achievement rested on a mistaken electoral interpretation, and a mistaken understanding of the overall governing process in the American political system. To the extent, therefore, that the freshman class enshrined and enforced the Contract with America, and it surely did, their guardianship only made the inadequacies of that document worse. Their attachment to the Contract introduced a big dose of rigidity into the legislative process, helping to set the party on a governing path that would be difficult to change.

The organization of majority party power inside the House was one thing Newt Gingrich *had* been planning well in advance of the 1994 election. His goal was to further centralize power. And his plans focused on the increased subordination of committee power to the power of majority party leadership.[23] But the underlying institutional condition that made further party centralization possible was this: the party had been out of power for so many years. As his predecessor, Speaker Tom Foley, explained, "I don't think any Democratic Speaker would be in quite the same situation as Speaker Gingrich. . . . There have been no Republican committee chairmen for over 40 years. . . . So he's had a *blank slate* on which to write and that has given him a great deal of influence.[24]

Seizing this opportunity, the new Speaker abolished some committees and subcommittees, appointed the committee chairmen,

extracted loyalty pledges from committee leaders, controlled committee staff, selected committee members, created and staffed ad hoc
task forces to circumvent committees, established committee priorities and time lines, and monitored committee compliance. The end
product was an American version of a prime minister in a system of
party government and a legislative process with a lot less of the deliberative and incremental pacing that a committee-centered system
can provide. Political scientists have produced a number of fascinating studies of the new Speaker's effort to centralize majority party
power.[25]

He carried out these changes with the approval of the Republican caucus, but he did it with such efficient dispatch—in concert
with a small advisory group—that there were few opportunities for
dissent. Where the freshman class was concerned, of course, he had
the advantage of forethought and experience. But in any case, the incoming group was strongly predisposed to follow his lead. Ideologically, they considered themselves his children and politically his
beneficiaries. The conservatism they brought increased the homogeneity of preferences within the party that analysts of "conditional
party government" associate with an increased willingness to cede
power to party leaders.[26]

To gain some perspective on the governing opportunities of the
1994 freshman class, it is helpful to compare it with the 1974 class of
freshman Democrats, the seventy-five so-called Watergate babies.
The two groups, the largest of the past half century, were equally big
and equally self-conscious of themselves as a class. The Class of '74,
too, had captured a very large number of seats from the other party:
forty-nine of the seventy-five, or 65 percent. As switched-seat occu-
pants they, like their 1994 cousins, were aggressive advocates of institutional and policy change. And in the end, both groups had a
measurable impact on the governing activities of their respective
partisan majorities. But the instructive difference between them was
that the liberal freshman Democrats of 1974 were joining a long-
standing, well-organized majority party that had been running the
House for twenty years, whereas the conservative freshman Republicans of 1994 were joining a brand new majority party. One group
was constrained by entrenched power; the other group was not.

Because their party was already enjoying power in the House,
the 1974 freshman Democrats were prepared to govern within the
constraints of established power relationships. The Speaker they
had to deal with, Carl Albert, was strongly attached to the organizational status quo. He was, Ronald Peters has written, "closely tied to
the committee system and the barons who ran it. . . . [He] and the
freshman Democrats talked past each other as if they were speaking
different dialects."[27] And Albert had a seventy-three-vote majority.

The freshmen, therefore, were constrained to adopt an incremental reform strategy, one designed to free the ordinary member from the constraints of hierarchy and seniority, or as they put it, to give rank and file members "a piece of the action." Most visibly, they spearheaded the unprecedented unseating of three veteran committee chairmen. The 1974 freshman class became the essential catalyst in accelerating the gradual decentralization of decision structures and the gradual diffusion of member influence that came to characterize "the post-reform Congress."[28]

The 1994 class, by contrast, faced few settled partisan routines and established party hierarchies. The Speaker they dealt with was openly and deeply in their debt. "When I see a freshman," said Newt Gingrich, "I see the majority. They had a huge influence. I wouldn't be Speaker if they weren't here."[29] The freshman Republicans, therefore, came to Capitol Hill with an expansive, almost open-ended, sense for the possibilities of change and for their own participatory opportunities. The diminution of committee power that the Democratic Speaker had resisted in 1974 the Republican Speaker engineered on his own in 1994. The freshmen accepted the view that if the Republicans were to change Washington, party power in the House would have to be centralized. They were a lot less concerned about getting a piece of the action than they were about facilitating the revolution. They accepted, therefore, a non-incremental reform strategy, precisely the opposite course from their 1974 counterparts. And in the beginning at least, they fully acquiesced in the largest concentration of majority-party power in a century.

The freshmen's willingness to support radical internal change was further buttressed by their strong anti-institutional preferences, as expressed in the Contract. Those sentiments, too, were different from those in the 1970s. Whether they actually campaigned on the Contract or not, the 1994 freshmen overwhelmingly campaigned in favor of its central institutional elements: term limits, the balanced budget amendment, and the line item veto. Singly or in combination, these items represented an attack on the performance of Congress as a political institution.

In one sense this attack was nothing new. During research travels in the 1970s I found most incumbent House members "running *for* Congress by running *against* Congress."[30] But they did so in a retail fashion, as a backdrop for personal self-congratulation and with language customized by individual members to fit their individual constituencies. Their criticisms did not cumulate in a way that would generate new governing programs or strategies.

In 1994, however, the anti-institutional message of the freshman candidates was the same nearly everywhere in the country. It was a coordinated, wholesale, frontal attack on the institution, promising three major changes in the power of Congress within the American political system. That was something new. The 1974 Democratic freshmen—perhaps because their party was in power—campaigned without broadside attacks on Congress. In 1994 a large group of legislators came to power having made a broad institutional argument. Further, theirs was an argument that dovetailed nicely with the institutional argument that their leader had been making for sixteen years. Their platform had attacked to an unprecedented degree the power and prerogatives of the very institution through which they proposed to govern. At the very least the freshmen were without any strong attachment to existing organizational forms in the House.

The new Speaker faced the unusual task of organizing a new system of party government and at the same time absorbing seventy-three inexperienced newcomers into the governing party. Experience had taught him a lot about freshmen. Every two years for fourteen years he had welcomed, socialized, organized, and energized each incoming Republican class. They became the building blocks of his new confrontational majority. "My strategy," he said, "was always [that] you would capture 70 to 80% of the incoming freshmen every two years and at some point, you would have transformed the whole structure."[31] That is what finally happened in 1994.

He dealt with his final freshman building block generously. He gave them an unprecedented number of assignments—twenty-four—to the five blue-ribbon House committees.[32] He involved them in the unusually important work of the task forces that he used to bypass committees. He met with them in weekly luncheons; he talked with them constantly; and he kept their noses to the grindstone.[33] In this latter respect the Contract was a success, a huge success. For one hundred days it focused, harnessed, preempted, and preoccupied the time and energies of a very ideological, very impatient freshman class. Who knows how they might have busied themselves otherwise?

As the Speaker quickly learned, however, governing with the freshmen would be a dicey enterprise. With a slim, fourteen-vote partisan margin, he needed all of them. A dozen or so recalcitrant freshmen (or any others) meant big trouble. They signalled as much early on when they fought him on the balanced budget amendment over a provision requiring a three-fifths vote to raise taxes.[34] Most of the time they were his allies. Freshman support for the leadership on roll call votes outpaced that of the rest of the Republicans.[35] Still, the relationship was one of mutual dependence. It required fairly constant monitoring and bargaining, especially on amendments. As he described it, "I am the leader of a broad coalition. I'm not a dictator. We have 73 freshmen. You don't get them marching in a line. You get them sort of saying, 'Maybe I'll be with you. Call back in an hour'."[36] As freshman members described the relationship, "Some of the time Gingrich uses us because he agrees with us. And some of the time he doesn't have a choice."[37] Or, "On some issues, we run him and on other issues, he runs us."[38] Of all the groups he had to deal with in the majority, the freshmen were the biggest and most consequential. The complexity and the uncertainty of their bargaining relationship would become amply evident during the fateful conflict over the budget.

NOTES

Chapter One

Forty Years

[1] Elizabeth Drew, "Can This Leadership Be Saved?" *Washington Post Weekly,* April 15–21, 1996.

[2] Michael Weiskopf and David Maraniss, "Endgame: The Revolution Stalls," *Washington Post Weekly,* January 29–February 4, 1996.

[3] A third very helpful book for understanding the ideological, antigovernment underpinnings of the Republican party, but again without an analysis of the institutional setting in Congress, is Dan Balz and Ronald Brownstein, *Storming the Gates* (Little, Brown, 1996).

Chapter Two

Electoral Interpretation and the Majority-Minority Relationship

[1] *Congressional Record,* daily ed., January 4, 1995, p. H4.

[2] Barbara Sinclair, *Majority Party Leadership in the U.S. House* (Johns Hopkins University Press, 1983), p. 110.

[3] Barbara Sinclair, *Legislators, Leaders and Lawmaking: The House of Representatives in the Post-Reform Era* (Johns Hopkins University Press, 1995), pp. 147, 304. See also Charles O. Jones, *Party and Policy Making: The House Republican Policy Committee* (Rutgers University Press, 1964), p. 136; and David Rohde, *Parties and Leaders in the Post-Reform House* (University of Chicago Press, 1991), p. 137.

[4] Gary Cox and Matthew McCubbins, *Legislative Leviathan* (University of California Press, 1993), p. 2.

[5] Roger Davidson and Walter Oleszek, *Congress against Itself* (Indiana University Press, 1977), pp. 67, 88, 137, 195, 208, 211, 240, 241, 251, 267; and David Rohde, "Electoral Forces, Political Agendas and Partisanship in the House and Senate," in Roger Davidson, ed., *The Post-Reform Congress* (St. Martins, 1992), pp. 27-47. On the Democratic culture permeating the

committee system, see Ronald Peters, "The Republican Speakership," paper prepared for the 1996 annual meeting of the American Political Science Association.

<u>6</u> Mickey Edwards, "A Tale of Two Reps: Study in Contrasts," *Boston Herald,* January 10, 1995. The Democrat was Dick Gephardt. The finest treatment, theoretically and historically, of these relationships between partisanship and procedure in Congress is Sarah Binder, *Minority Rights, Majority Rule* (Cambridge University Press, 1997).

<u>7</u> See David Mayhew, "Congressional Elections: The Case of the Vanishing Marginals," *Polity,* vol. 6 (1974), pp. 295–318; Richard Born, "Generational Replacement and the Growth of Incumbent Reelection Margins in the U.S. House," *American Political Science Review,* vol. 73 (1979), pp. 811–17; Gary Jacobson, *The Electoral Origins of Divided Party Government* (Boulder, Colo.: Westview, 1990); Alan Ehrenhalt, *The United States of Ambition* (Random House, 1991); and John Gilmour and Paul Rothstein, "Early Republican Retirement: A Cause of Democratic Dominance in the House of Representatives," *Legislative Studies Quarterly,* vol. 18 (August 1993), pp. 345–65.

<u>8</u> Juliana Greenwald and Deborah Kalb, "Poll Results Boost Hopes of Democrats," *Congressional Quarterly,* April 27, 1996.

<u>9</u> Charles O. Jones, *The Minority Party in Congress* (Little, Brown, 1970), p. 170.

<u>10</u> Jones, *Party and Policy Making,* p. 152. See also Burdett Looms, *The New American Politicians* (Basic Books, 1988), p. 221.

<u>11</u> William Connelly and John Pitney, *Congress' Permanent Minority? Republicans in the U.S. House* (Lanham, Md.: Littlefield, Adams, 1994), p. 64.

<u>12</u> Ibid., chap. 6; Richard Cohen, "Frustrated House Republicans Seek More Aggressive Strategy for 1984 and Beyond," *National Journal,* March 3, 1984; and Jeffrey Birnbaum, "House Republicans Frustrated in Minority Role Often Ask Themselves Whether It's Time to Leave," *Wall Street Journal,* June 5, 1987.

<u>13</u> Richard Cohen, quoted in John Rhodes, "The Business of Being Minority Leader," *National Journal Quarterly,* November 29, 1977.

<u>14</u> John Barry, *The Ambition and the Power* (Viking, 1989), p. 480.

<u>15</u> Connelly and Pitney, *Congress' Permanent Minority?,* p. 69. See also Lloyd Grove, "An Elephant Never Forgets," *Washington Post,* November 28, 1994.

<u>16</u> David Maraniss and Michael Weiskopf, *"Tell Newt To Shut Up!"* (Simon and Shuster, 1996), p. 31.

<u>17</u> Quoted in Barry, *Ambition and the Power,* p. 482.

<u>18</u> Quoted in Connelly and Pitney, *Congress' Permanent Minority?,* p. 86.

<u>19</u> Ibid., p. 19.

<u>20</u> Ibid., p. 62. The speaker was Tom DeLay, now majority whip.

21 Rohde, *Parties and Leaders,* chap. 1.

22 The struggles and the changes can be traced in Connelly and Pitney, *Congress' Permanent Minority?*; Jones, *Party and Policy Making*; Rohde, *Parties and Leaders*; Sinclair, *Legislators, Leaders and Lawmaking*; and in the running record of Newt Gingrich's public comments.

23 A thoughtful discussion of Gingrich in both institutional and personal terms is Randall Strahan, "Leadership in Institutional and Political Time: The Case of Newt Gingrich and the 104th Congress," paper prepared for the 1996 annual meeting of the American Political Science Association.

24 Irwin Arieff, "House Freshmen Republicans Seek Role as Power Brokers," *Congressional Quarterly,* July 7, 1979.

25 Connelly and Pitney, *Congress' Permanent Minority?*, p. 155.

26 Michael Barone, "Who Is This Newt Gingrich?", *Washington Post,* August 26, 1984.

27 Connelly and Pitney, *Congress' Permanent Minority?*, p. 27.

28 Peter Osterlund, "A Capitol Chameleon: What Will Newt Gingrich Do Next?", *Los Angeles Times,* August 25, 1991.

29 On Rhodes, see, for example, Richard Cohen, "House Republicans under Rhodes—Divided They Stand and Fret," *National Journal,* November 29, 1977; Arieff, "House Freshmen Republicans Seek Role as Power Brokers"; Mary Russell, "Low-Key Rhodes Woos Fired Up Freshmen and Conservatives," *Washington Post,* November 22, 1979; Mary Russell, "Rhodes Will Step Down as GOP Leader after Next Year," *Washington Post,* December 13, 1979; John Brummett, "Friend of Newt, Ex-Congressman Ed Bethune is 'Really Wired' Into The New GOP Power Loop," *Arkansas Democrat Gazette,* March 10, 1995; John Kolbe, "A Kinder, Gentler Congress: Rhodes Recounts More Civilized Age of DC Politics," *Arizona Republic,* December 17, 1995; and Michael Murphy and Kris Mayes, "Rhodes Lauds Gingrich Goals, But Finds Tactics Distasteful," *Arizona Republic,* October 14, 1995.
   On Michel, see, for example, Martin Tolchin, "GOP Campaign: For House Leader," *New York Times,* September 28, 1980; Margot Hornblower, "Reps. Michel and VanderJagt Battling Fiercely to Lead House GOP," December 8, 1980; Margot Hornblower, "House GOP Picks Michel as Leader," *Washington Post,* December 9, 1980; Margot Hornblower, "The Master of Gentle Persuasion," *Washington Post,* August 10, 1981; David Broder, "Michel's Departure End of an Era," *Times Picayune,* October 12, 1993; Norman Ornstein, "Michel Exit Ends Era of Cooperative Republican Leaders," *Roll Call,* October 11, 1993; Robert Michel, remarks in *Congressional Record,* daily ed., November 29, 1994; and Janet Hook, "House Hones a Sharper Edge as Michel Turns in His Sword," *Congressional Quarterly,* October 9, 1993.

30 He even applied the same debilitating pressure to his party's leader, President George Bush. "You are killing us, you are just killing us," Bush told Gingrich when he fought Bush's budget compromise in 1990.

Dan Balz and Serge Kovaleski, "Dividing the GOP, Conquering the Agenda," *Washington Post Weekly,* January 9–15, 1996.

<u>31</u> Barry, *Ambition and the Power,* pp. 165–66.

<u>32</u> Ibid., p. 688.

<u>33</u> Connelly and Pitney, *Congress' Permanent Minority?,* p. 160.

<u>34</u> Barry, *Ambition and the Power,* p. 366. See also p. 242.

<u>35</u> David Rogers, "General Newt: GOP's Rare Year Owes Much to How Gingrich Disciplined the House," *Wall Street Journal,* December 18, 1995.

<u>36</u> Representative Joseph Moakley, quoted in Jennifer Bradley and Ed Henry, "Members Bid Adieu to Historic 104th Congress," *Roll Call,* September 30, 1996.

<u>37</u> Guy Gugliotta, "Which Way Did the Revolution Go?," *Washington Post Weekly,* March 10, 1997.

<u>38</u> Osterlund, "Capitol Chameleon." See also Rohde, *Parties and Leaders,* p. 129.

<u>39</u> Connelly and Pitney, *Congress' Permanent Minority?,* p. 160.

<u>40</u> Jackie Koszczuk, "Gingrich Struggling to Control Revolts among the Troops," *Congressional Quarterly,* December 23, 1995, p. 3865.

<u>41</u> A different, more extensively developed, and very helpful view of Gingrich is Ronald Peters, "The Republican Speakership," paper prepared for the 1996 annual meeting of the American Political Science Association.

Chapter Three

Governing: The Contract, the Freshmen, and the Speaker

<u>1</u> Karen Hosler, "GOP Gets a Glimpse of the Promised Land," *Baltimore Sun,* May 14, 1995.

<u>2</u> John Harwood, "Reagan-Era Veterans Are Now Determined to Revive '80s Policies," *Wall Street Journal,* January 4, 1995.

<u>3</u> George Hager and Eric Pianin, *Mirage* (Random House, 1997), pp. 255–58; John Aldrich and David Rohde, "The Republican Revolution and the House Appropriations Committee," paper prepared for the 1996 annual meeting of the Southern Political Science Association; and David Cloud and Jackie Koszcuk, "GOP's All-or-Nothing Approach Hangs on a Balanced Budget," *Congressional Quarterly,* December 9, 1995.

<u>4</u> Jeff Shear, "Force Majeure?," *National Journal,* March 11, 1995.

<u>5</u> Paul Taylor and Helen Dewar, "Outsiders on the Inside," *Washington Post Weekly,* July 17–23, 1995.

<u>6</u> Robin Toner, "73 Mr. Smiths, of the GOP, Go to Washington," *New York Times,* January 7, 1995.

7 David Brady and Naomi Lynn, "Switched Seat Congressional Districts: Their Effects on Party Voting and Public Policy," *American Journal of Political Science,* vol. 17 (August 1973); Patricia Hurley, David Brady, and Joseph Cooper, "Measuring Legislative Potential for Policy Change," *Legislative Studies Quarterly,* vol. 11 (November 1977); David Brady, "Critical Elections, Congressional Parties and Clusters of Policy Change," *British Journal of Political Science,* vol. 8 (January 1978). For an argument that the size of the freshman class in the majority party brings rules changes, see Scott Ainsworth, Patrick Fett, and Itai Sened, "The Implications of Turnover and Term Limits on Institutional Stability," *American Journal of Political Science,* forthcoming.

8 Shear, "Force Majeure?"

9 Toner, "73 Mr. Smiths"; Kevin Merida and Kenneth Cooper, "A Class of Young Warriors," *Washington Post Weekly,* December 12–25, 1994; Graeme Browning, "The GOP's Young Turks," *National Journal,* February 25, 1995; Jackie Koszczuk, "Freshmen: New Powerful Voice," *Congressional Quarterly,* October 28, 1995; and Cohen, "The Transformers," *National Journal,* March 4, 1995.

10 Shear, "Force Majeure?"; Guy Gugliotta, "They Flat Do Not Care," *Washington Post Weekly,* January 1–7, 1996; Rhodes Cook, "Republican Freshmen Voting Support . . ."; and Karen Hosler, "Humbled House Freshmen Regroup," *Baltimore Sun,* January 26, 1996.

11 Susan Feeney, "GOP Presidential Candidates Prize Nod from House Freshmen," *Dallas Morning News,* January 17, 1996.

12 Toner, "73 Mr. Smiths."

13 Jim Mann, "Mission to Balkans; House Freshmen Cut Foreign Policy Class," *Los Angeles Times,* December 2, 1995.

14 Jill Zuckman, "GOP Freshmen Drive Debate in Washington," *Boston Globe,* October 22, 1995.

15 Jerry Gray, "Grading GOP Freshmen: High in Ambition, Low in Humility," *New York Times,* April 11, 1995.

16 Gugliotta, "They Flat Do Not Care."

17 Rhodes Cook, "Can GOP Freshmen Make Comeback?," *Congressional Quarterly,* June 29, 1996.

18 Gray, "Grading GOP Freshmen."

19 Browning, "GOP's Young Turks."

20 Toner, "73 Mr. Smiths"; and Merida and Cooper, "Class of Young Warriors."

21 Merida and Cooper, "Class of Young Warriors."

22 Browning, "GOP's Young Turks."

23 Randall Strahan, "Leadership in Institutional and Political Time: The Case of Newt Gingrich and the 104th Congress," paper prepared for the

1996 annual meeting of the American Political Science Association; and Rogers, "General Newt."

24 John Owens, "The Return of Party Government in the U.S. House of Representatives: Central Leadership-Committee Relations in the 104th Congress," *British Journal of Political Science*, vol. 27 (April 1997), pp. 247–72.

25 Roger Davidson, "Building a Republican Regime on Capitol Hill," in Lawrence C. Dodd, ed., *Extension of Remarks*, Legislative Studies section, American Political Science Association, December 1995; John Aldrich and David Rohde, "Conditional Party Government Revisited: Majority Party Leadership and the Committee System in the 104th Congress," in Dodd, ed., *Extension of Remarks*; Strahan, "Leadership in Institutional and Political Time"; Owens, "Return of Party Government"; Peters, "Republican Speakership"; C. Lawrence Evans and Walter J. Oleszek, "Partisan Leadership and Committee Reform," papers prepared for the 1996 annual meeting of the American Political Science Association; John H. Aldrich and David W. Rohde, "The Republican Revolution and the House Appropriations Committee," working paper 96–08, Institute for Public Policy and Social Research, Michigan State University, 1996. See also David S. Cloud, "Speaker Wants His Platform to Rival the Presidency," *Congressional Quarterly*, February 4, 1995; and David Rogers and Phil Funtz, "How Gingrich Grabbed Power and Attention—and His New Risks," *Wall Street Journal*, January 1, 1995.

26 David Rohde, *Parties and Leaders in the Post-Reform House* (University of Chicago Press, 1991); and Aldrich and Rohde, "Republican Revolution."

27 Ronald Peters, *The American Speakership* (Johns Hopkins University Press, 1990), pp. 201, 207.

28 Burdett Loomis, *The New American Politicians* (Basic Books, 1988); and Roger Davidson, ed., *The Post-Reform Congress* (St. Martins, 1992).

29 Jill Zuckman, "Freshmen Keep House on Course to the Right," *Boston Globe*, February 26, 1995.

30 Richard Fenno, *Home Style: House Members in Their Districts* (Little, Brown, 1978), pp. 162–69.

31 Dan Balz and Serge Kovaleski, "Dividing the GOP, Conquering the Agenda," *Washington Post Weekly*, January 9–15, 1996.

32 Tim Barnett and Burdett Loomis, "The 104th Republicans: of Classes and Cannon Fodder," in Burdett Loomis, ed., *Extension of Remarks*, Legislative Studies section, American Political Science Association, January 1997.

33 David Broder, "Keeping the GOP Juggernaut on Track," *Washington Post Weekly*, July 24–30, 1995.

34 James Gimpel, *Fulfilling the Contract: The First 100 Days* (Boston: Allyn and Bacon, 1996), pp. 46–47.

35 Jessica Lee, "New Course for GOP Freshmen," *USA Today*, January 30, 1995.

36 David Rogers, "Congress and White House Agree to Buy Time, But Gingrich Says, Budget Pact Must Come Soon," *Wall Street Journal,* October 2, 1995.

37 Zuckman, "GOP Freshmen Drive Debate."

38 Morton Kondracke, *Roll Call,* December 18, 1995. See also David Rogers, "In Budget Impasse, Gingrich's Control over GOP Rank and File is Never Clear," *Wall Street Journal,* November 16, 1995; and Koszcuk, "Freshmen: New, Powerful Voice."

A 'REPRESENTATIVE' SUPREME COURT?

THE THOMAS, GINSBERG, AND BREYER APPOINTMENTS

Barbara A. Perry
Sweet Briar College

Henry J. Abraham
University of Virginia

In a memorable segment of his eloquent, passionate dissent from the Supreme Court's 1943 majority opinion in *West Virginia State Board of Education v. Barnette,* Justice Felix Frankfurter declared, "[A]s judges we are neither Jew nor Gentile, neither Catholic nor agnostic." Similarly, upon nominating Tom Clark, a Protestant, to fill the seat vacated by Justice Frank Murphy, a Roman Catholic, President Harry Truman exclaimed with characteristic pugnacity, "I do not believe religions have anything to do with the Supreme Bench. If an individual has the qualifications, I do not care if he is a Protestant, Catholic, or Jew." On the subject of race as a factor in Supreme Court appointments, Justice William Brennan Jr. predicted in 1985 that the high bench would have a seat reserved for African-Americans in the foreseeable future, but that "fifty years from now, we won't even notice the color of a fellow's skin. And that's how it should be."

Judicial and presidential injunctions to the contrary, presidents of the United States have often included so-called "representative" characteristics in their criteria for selecting Supreme Court justices. Historically, such characteristics as geography, religion, race, and gender were rarely the overriding consideration for presidents, but they have long played a role. Indeed, Ronald Reagan stated in his 1980 campaign that he would fill one of his first Supreme Court vacancies with "the most qualified woman he could find." Recognition of a "Jewish seat" on the Court dates from at least 1939. President Franklin Roosevelt assumed that when Louis Brandeis left the bench

Judicature, The Journal of the American Judicature Society he would appoint Frankfurter (whom he actually nominated to succeed another Jewish justice, Benjamin Cardozo). After Frankfurter retired, that seat went to Arthur Goldberg, and then Abe Fortas.

The term "representative" is demonstrably more nuanced when applied to the Supreme Court than to the legislative or executive branches. Some justices have represented their respective groups actively and substantively (Thurgood Marshall and African-Americans), others do so only symbolically (Antonin Scalia and Italian-Americans), and still others actually voted against the interests or predominant views of their presumed "constituencies" (William Brennan and Catholics).

The last three nominations to the Supreme Court provide another opportunity to examine what role, if any, representative factors play. Justices Clarence Thomas, Ruth Bader Ginsburg, and Stephen Breyer illustrate the complexity of applying the concept of representation to a judicial body. President George Bush, notwithstanding his statements to the contrary, unquestionably chose Thomas primarily because of his race to fill the seat vacated by Thurgood Marshall. Yet while Justice Marshall had been a champion of African-American causes both on and off the bench, Thomas has questioned the very premises of many of the public policies that resulted from the civil rights movement. Conversely, Ginsburg has implemented on the high bench the gender rights initiatives that she fought for so tenaciously and successfully as a young litigator. Her majority opinion in the 1996 Virginia Military Institute (VMI) decision clearly embodied her understanding and championship of equal treatment for women.

Both Breyer and Ginsburg are Jewish and have occasionally spoken publicly and movingly about the influence of religion on their lives. Although no Jewish justice had served on the Court since Fortas resigned in 1969, gone are the days when anyone would speak of a "Jewish seat."

Likewise, Thomas's recent reconversion to Roman Catholicism barely caused a ripple in the media. Thomas had been raised as a Catholic by his grandparents, attended Catholic elementary and high schools, studied to be a priest, but left the seminary to enroll in the College of the Holy Cross. Later, he and his second wife became members of an Episcopal congregation in Northern Virginia. In 1996, however, Thomas announced at a Holy Cross class reunion that he had rejoined the Catholic Church. Moreover, commentators no longer refer to a "Catholic seat" on the high tribunal as they were wont to do in a previous era. Indeed, with Thomas's reconversion, three Catholics now sit on the Supreme Court, and few observers have remarked that they now constitute one-third of the Court's membership. Thomas's reconversion also marked a historic milestone for the Court, where Anglo-Saxon Protestants now for the first time constitute a minority of the justices.

This article explores representative characteristics of the most recent Supreme Court appointments within the context of the following considerations: the criteria used by, and the motivations of, appointing presidents; reactions of the pertinent racial, gender, and religious "constituent" groups to the nominations; and the votes of Thomas, Ginsburg, and Breyer in cases that seemed to have direct or indirect impact on these same groups. It concludes that although use of representativeness as a criterion in appointments has evolved away from geography and religion, race and gender will continue to play prominent roles in Supreme Court appointments as long as they are paramount on the nation's political agenda. In addition, other groups (Hispanics, Asians, gays, and the disabled, among them) may well clamor for representation on the Supreme Court so that it at least "mirrors" the diversity of 21st century American society. Distinctions between symbolic and substantive representation once appointees reach the Court will continue to depend on the other pervasive criterion in Supreme Court appointment history—namely, ideology or "real" politics. In the final analysis, justices' jurisprudential postures will determine whether they actively represent the groups from which they hail.

CLARENCE THOMAS

President George Bush's second opportunity to appoint a Supreme Court justice came in June 1991 with the retirement of Thurgood Marshall. In replacing the Court's first black member, the president faced a prickly political dilemma. On the one hand, he did not want to be seen as denying African-Americans a seat on the high bench. On the other hand, because Bush was on the record as opposing racial quotas, he could hardly nominate someone solely because of race. Moreover, always in trouble with the conservative wing of his party, he could not afford to nominate an objectively well-qualified, but politically moderate (let alone a liberal) minority.

Bush had the advantage of a detailed list of possible nominees that had been produced over the preceding year on the expectation that at least one of the Court's two remaining octogenarians would soon step down. Upon Marshall's retirement, the president's top advisers, the most influential of whom were White House Counsel C. Boyden Gray, Attorney General Richard Thornburgh, Vice President Dan Quayle, and Chief of Staff John Sununu, prepared the final list. Placing a heavy emphasis on finding a minority or female candidate, the list included four Hispanics: federal judges Richardo Hinojosa, Emilio Garza, Ferdinand Fernandez, and Jose Cabranes;

two women: judges Edith H. Jones and Pamela A. Rymer; and one African-American: Judge Clarence Thomas, a young, conservative jurist on the U.S. Court of Appeals for the District of Columbia. At the urging of Quayle and Gray, Bush chose Thomas.

In selecting Thomas, Bush stated implausibly at a press conference announcing his decision that "the fact that he is black and a minority has nothing to do with the sense that he is the best qualified at this time." Throughout the confirmation process, the president would repeat this claim. Yet very few believed that Thomas, with his limited experience, would have been chosen had he been white. Clearly, Bush's primary consideration was his desire to perpetuate the so-called "black seat" on the Court. In addition, his other main concern was finding a young conservative (Thomas was just 43) who could have years of influence on the Supreme Court, something that would placate the Republican party's rebellious right wing. Thus, race, ideology, and age (in that order) were the primary considerations for Bush in nominating Thomas. Bush could also make the case for a modicum of merit on Thomas's part, given his graduation with honors from Holy Cross and his Yale law degree.

Thomas had gained admission to Yale through its affirmative action program. Ironically, Thomas subsequently turned against such race-based preferential treatment programs. His position, along with the balance of his voiced conservative agenda, presented a dilemma for civil rights groups, who had also opposed his policies when he served as chair of the Equal Employment Opportunity Commission (EEOC) and assistant secretary for civil rights in the U.S. Department of Education. Nevertheless, as Professor Dianne Pinderhughes argued in a 1992 *PS: Political Science and Politics* article, "many [blacks] found race more significant than policy." In other words, they were willing to forego active representation of their interests on the Court in favor of symbolic representation of their race on the high bench.

Civil rights groups had varied reactions to the Thomas nomination. The NAACP, for example, opposed it, with a 49–1 vote by its board. The organization simply could not accept what it perceived as Thomas's stubborn refusal to comprehend or appreciate the history and vestiges of institutional racism in the United States. Among the major civil rights organizations, only the Southern Christian leadership conference supported him.

The Senate Judiciary Committee tied 7–7 in its vote on the nominee, and his nomination was headed to the full Senate without the endorsement of the committee. The now-familiar detour that Thomas's nomination took via Anita Hill's sexual harassment charges, with the resulting media circus surrounding a second round of Senate. hearings, only served to divide the black community further by adding the even more volatile factor of gender to the mix. Nevertheless, Thomas and his defenders were able to convince enough senators of his merits so as to win confirmation by the razor-thin margin of 52–48. Clarence Thomas became the 106th justice of the United States Supreme Court by the closest vote in this century, and with the most negative votes ever cast for a successful nominee.

In general, the civil rights community was correct in predicting that Thomas would often oppose its interests. His unwillingness to interpret broadly the Constitution or statutes clearly applies to matters of race. For instance, in a 1992 case, *Presly v. Etowah County Commission,* he joined the majority in holding that the Voting Rights Act of 1965 did not forbid two Alabama counties to change their systems of road management in such a way that they reduced the effective power of newly elected black commissioners. Similarly, he joined the Court in 1993's *Shaw v. Reno* to hold that state officials must present a "compelling" reason to justify "bizarre" congressional districts drawn to contain a majority of blacks or Hispanics. One year later, concurring in *Holder v. Hall,* he urged passionately that the Voting Rights Act does not require, nor could it constitutionally, that race be considered affirmatively in districting.

Thomas's most controversial opinions to date in race cases came at the end of the 1994–95 term. In *Missouri v. Jenkins II* the justices ruled 5–4 that a federal judge had improperly attempted to integrate the public schools of Kansas City, Missouri, by ordering massive expenditures in order to attract students from surrounding suburbs. Thomas's stunningly passionate concurring opinion, which was widely reported in the press, declared, "It never ceases to amaze me that the courts are so willing to assume that anything that is predominantly black must be inferior."

On the same day as *Jenkins,* the Court announced its opinion in *Adarand v. Peña,* which determined that judges must apply "strict scrutiny" to federal affirmative action programs, thus jeopardizing all such plans. Not surprisingly, given his previous record against affirmative action as a remedial public policy, Thomas voted with the narrow 5–4 majority. He also joined conservative soulmate Justice Scalia's concurrence, which went beyond Justice Sandra Day O'Connor's more moderate controlling opinion, to declare that the government can never constitutionally justify racial discrimination against whites as a remedy for past discrimination against minorities. Syndicated columnist William Raspberry pointed out the irony of Justices O'Connor and Thomas voting against affirmative action when they both had benefited from it in their elevation to the nation's highest tribunal, and Thomas had advanced throughout his academic and professional career because of racial preference policies. In the aftermath of Adarand, an emotional Carl Rowen described Thomas as "close to a pariah in black America."

Earlier in the 1994–95 term Thomas had obviously tried to stem the tide of unflattering media portrayals of him. As yet another uncomplimentary book on him produced more unfavorable publicity in the fall of 1995, Thomas held an extraordinary meeting at the Supreme Court, where he gathered with invited black journalists and other African-American opinion leaders. According to the *Washington Post,* Thomas responded to questions about his controversial votes in race cases by declaring, "I am not an Uncle Tom."

This most unusual convocation may have won over some of the invitees even if they continued to disagree with Thomas's votes. One self-described liberal admitted that the meeting was her first trip to the Court and she "was very moved" by some of Thomas's statements.

Little evidence exists, however, that Thomas has garnered support from more than a tiny minority of the African-American population. Although some civil rights groups were willing to settle for mere symbolic representation of blacks on the Supreme Court when Thurgood Marshall retired, what they have evidently reaped is a genuine conservative who, in their minds, has voted against the interests of blacks throughout the nation.

RUTH BADER GINSBURG

When asked if her career had gone as she planned, Justice Ruth Bader Ginsburg once responded bemusedly that she did not plan her career at all because women had so few professional opportunities when she was growing up in the 1930s and '40s. Indeed, despite her stellar academic career, which included an undergraduate degree from Cornell with election to Phi Beta Kappa, two years at Harvard Law School, and graduation first in her class from Columbia Law School, Ginsburg found the doors of private law firms closed to her. As one friend described it (as quoted in Ginsburg's entry in the *Encyclopedia of American Biography*): "A woman, a mother, a Jew—the kiss of death." Although there has never been a "mother's seat" on the Supreme Court, places have been "reserved" for women and Jewish justices in the past. What attributes played a role in Ginsburg's appointment to the highest court in the land?

Before his election in 1992, Bill Clinton stressed the following criteria for his future nominees to the federal judiciary: "I would appoint to the federal bench only men and women of unquestioned intellect, judicial temperament, broad experience. . . . I believe that public confidence in our federal judiciary is furthered by the presence of more women lawyers and more minority lawyers on the bench, and the judicial system and country benefit from having judges who are excellent lawyers with diverse experience."

Although he never memorialized the "respresentativeness" criteria in executive orders, as his Democratic predecessor Jimmy Carter had done, the federal bench shaped by Clinton's appointments is remarkably more diverse in terms of race and gender.

In fact, because of the criticism he was receiving regarding his commitments to diversity (displayed most pointedly in his aborted nomination of law Professor Lani Guinier to head the Justice Department's Civil Rights Division), Clinton reportedly searched for a white male in his first opportunity to nominate a member of the Supreme Court after Justice Byron White announced his retirement in March 1993. White House Counsel Bernard Nussbaum provided the president with an initial list of 42 candidates, replete with 8–10 page legal and personal profiles. Clinton had specified that he wanted someone with unquestionable qualifications and a "big heart." To this end, he announced that he would prefer a politician, rather than a sitting judge, in hopes that such a person would be a natural leader who could encourage the Court's then emerging center (O'Connor, Kennedy, and Souter) to move further to the left. Ideally, he wanted a reincarnation of Earl Warren.

After New York Governor Mario Cuomo and Secretary of Education Richard Riley (a former governor of South Carolina) took themselves out of consideration, and western politicians and environmental groups demanded Interior Secretary Bruce that position, Clinton apparently lost hope of finding a politician for the Court. He then turned to Stephen Breyer, a former Senate Judiciary Committee counsel and chief judge of the U.S. Court of Appeals for the First Circuit in Boston. Breyer, who possessed a superb academic and professional record (including a clerkship for Supreme Court Justice Arthur Goldberg), had the advantage of being relatively moderate and was popular among both Republicans and Democrats in the Senate because of his previous service with the Senate Judiciary Committee. He would also be the first Jewish justice to serve on the Court since Abe Fortas resigned in 1969. Yet Breyer had a minor "Zoe Baird problem" (a reference to Clinton's first choice as attorney general who had hired illegal aliens and had not paid social security taxes for them; neither had Breyer for his maid). Perhaps most damning for his candidacy, Breyer, who had just been released from the hospital after a cycling accident, had an apparently rather awkward lunch with the president. According to one account (Drew's *On the Edge: The Clinton Presidency*), Clinton reportedly later told aides that he thought Breyer was selling himself too hard, that his legal interests were too narrow, and that he did not have a "big heart."

As a fallback in case the Breyer nomination did not materialize, Bernard Nussbaum had placed Ruth Bader Ginsburg, a 13-year veteran of the prestigious U.S. Court of Appeals for the District of Columbia, on the list. She obviously was not a white male nonjurist, but Ginsburg catapulted to the top of Clinton's list after an hour-and-a-half meeting with him, during which Clinton reportedly "fell in love" with her story. The president found her life's narrative of family tragedy (her mother died of cancer when Ginsburg was 17, and her husband successfully battled the disease early in their marriage) and personal and professional struggles against gender discrimination to be compelling.

In announcing her nomination, Clinton propounded three reasons for her selection: First, her distinguished judicial career. Second, her towering efforts on behalf of women's issues made her, as he put it, "to the women's movement what Thurgood Marshall was to the movement for the rights of African-Americans." She was the victorious counsel of record and successful advocate before the Supreme Court in the first handful of gender discrimination cases to be decided by the Burger Court in the 1970s. Third was her proven ability as a consensus builder, as a healer, as a "moderate. "

Despite Ginsburg's seemingly impeccable feminist credentials, some women's groups did not immediately embrace her nomination. While feminism had evolved into a more radical variety, Ginsburg had grown increasingly centrist during her tenure on the circuit court bench. Although supporting the outcome of *Roe v. Wade*, she had questioned the rationale behind and the breadth of justice Harry Blackmun's majority opinion in a speech at New York University School of Law two months before her nomination. She remained clearly pro-choice, but abortion rights advocates, such as the president of the National Abortion Rights Action League, commented after Ginsburg's nomination that her interest group would monitor the confirmation hearings carefully to determine whether she "will protect a woman's fundamental right to privacy." Despite such doubts, the copresident of the National Women's Law Center asserted that "Ruth Ginsburg was as responsible as any one person for legal advances that women made under the Equal Protection Clause of the Constitution. As a result, doors of opportunity have been opened that have benefitted not only the women themselves but their families."

The Senate Judiciary Committee approved Ginsburg's nomination by a vote of 18–0, and the full Senate followed suit in August of 1993 by a 96–3 margin, with only conservative Republican Senators Jesse Helms of North Carolina, Bob Smith of New Hampshire, and Don Nickles of Oklahoma dissenting. Thus, Clinton's concentration on Ginsburg's meritorious record and her general moderation earned a smooth confirmation process.

It is difficult to determine the role that gender played in the Ginsburg nomination. Although Clinton's record of diversifying the federal judiciary along racial and gender lines is unsurpassed, that fact actually worked in favor of a white male, with whom Clinton intended to balance his appointment record. When his white male candidates did not prove acceptable, Clinton turned to Ginsburg. Therefore, although being a female did not work in Ginsburg's favor per se, her compelling story of overcoming gender discrimination motivated Clinton and certainly did not harm her in the Senate.

As the second female justice on the high bench, Ginsburg has often demonstrated her commitment to serving as a symbol for women of all ages. She often takes time from her busy schedule to meet with young women students. If she is unable to see them, she sends one of her female law clerks to serve as a role model. In December 1994, ABC's "Prime Time Live" presented a feature on Ginsburg, which opened with her attendance at her 35th law school class reunion at Columbia University. The broadcast not only focused on the discrimination that Ginsburg and her female colleagues had faced both in law school and beyond, it also emphasized her success in battling for women's equality. Interestingly, Ginsburg revealed that she rejects "politically correct" speech, which she believes puts women on a pedestal and removes them from the real world because they are treated, in the words of the old nursery rhyme, as "sugar and spice and everything nice." Yet symbolizing her own femininity, Ginsburg proudly toured her chambers with correspondent Diane Sawyer, who duly noted the light, airy decor of the justice's upstairs office, in contrast to the typical dark, masculine furnishings of her colleagues' downstairs chambers.

Joan Biskupic, Supreme Court reporter for the *Washington Post,* has also raised the issue of Ginsburg's gender, but more substantively in an April 1995 feature article, which claimed that she was using her position on the Court to advocate her "feminist message" in a way that no previous justice had done. Regardless of the relevancy of Biskupic's thesis regarding Ginsburg's supposed use of the Court to disseminate her feminist message, the very fact that journalists are drawn to such accounts illustrates the continued novelty of only the second women to serve on the Supreme Court.

While most commentators noted that Ginsburg would be the first Jew on the Court since Fortas's resignation almost 25 years earlier, her religion did not appear to play a role in her selection. Nevertheless, demonstrating pride in Ginsburg's position on the highest court in the land, the American Jewish Committee (AJC) invited her to speak at its annual meeting in May 1995. Broadcast on C-SPAN, Ginsburg's talk recalled the Jewish justices who had preceded her to the Court and the age-old Jewish commitment to law and scholarship. She quoted the late Justice Arthur Goldberg (former president of the AJC), who once commented, "My concern for justice, for peace, for enlightenment, all stem from my heritage," and she added, "I am fortunate to be linked to that heritage."

Justice Ginsburg's first four terms on the Supreme Court (October 1993-July 1997) demonstrated her to be the normally left-of-center pragmatist that Clinton had described in Ginsburg has often demonstrated her commitment to serving as a symbol for women of all ages. his nomination. In her first term, she voted most frequently with moderate to liberal justices David Souter and John Paul Stevens and most infrequently with justices Thomas and Scalia and Chief Justice William Rehnquist on the conservative side. In her second and third terms, she continued her agreement with Souter and Stevens, but she was most often aligned with newly appointed Justice Breyer, while continuing her basic disagreement with the Thomas Scalia-Rehnquist wing of the Court.

In cases related to gender or religion issues, Ginsburg has manifested a jurisprudence that usually aligns her with the Court's moderate to liberal wing. To date her most visible opinion came in the 1996 VMI decision in which she determined for a 7–1 majority (Thomas having recused himself because his son was a student there) that the state-funded Virginia Military Institute's exclusion of women from its corps of cadets was unconstitutional. Although Ginsburg's opinion for the Court did not boost gender into the "suspect classification" category urged by the Justice Department—under which the state must prove a compelling interest in order to treat genders differently—she did argue that the government needs an "exceedingly persuasive justification" for any classification based on sex.

Arguably, Ginsburg has also fulfilled the agenda of mainstream Jewish interest groups in religious establishment cases, in which the American Jewish Committee, for one, argues for a strict "wall of separation" between church and state as, indeed, have all Jewish Supreme Court justices. Ginsburg's separationist stance placed her among the majority of the Court in 1994 when it held that New York state may not carve out a separate school district to accommodate the special needs of a particular community of "highly religious Satmar Hasidic Jews. " In two 1995 cases, Ginsburg dissented from majority rulings requiring the University of Virginia to subsidize a student-run Christian religious magazine and upholding the Ku Klux Klan's erection of a cross on the state capitol grounds in Columbus, Ohio. In addition, she was among the dissenters in the 1997 case that held that public school teachers may now provide remedial instruction for children inside parochial schools under Title I of the Federal Aid to Elementary and Secondary Schools Act of 1965. In the free exercise realm, however, Ginsburg departed from the position of most religious interest groups by joining the six-justice majority that struck down the Religious Freedom Restoration Act in 1997. Nevertheless, regardless of Clinton's motivations in appointing the Court's second woman and sixth Jew, both liberal women's and Jewish interest groups have gained a generally reliable advocate for their causes.

STEPHEN BREYER

Like Ginsburg, Stephen Breyer, too, was an also ran choice. Not only had he been sandbagged at the 11th hour for the seat that eventually went to Ginsburg, he found himself again on a long list of candidates to replace Justice Harry Blackmun, who announced his retirement in the spring of 1994. Once more President Clinton placed a politician, retiring Senate majority leader and erstwhile federal judge George Mitchell, at the top of the list. After Mitchell declined, Clinton returned to his list of previous candidates, including Secretary Babbitt and federal judges Richard Arnold, Jose Cabranes, Amalia Kearse, and Breyer, whose names were sent up as trial balloons for media and political reaction.

Two factors proved to be decisive in Breyer's favor: First, he had an exemplary academic and professional record, having served in all three branches of government. Second, his tenure on the First Circuit Court of Appeals, including service as its chief judge, and as counsel to the Senate Judiciary Committee, revealed an uncanny ability to find common ground as a consensus builder. The Senate Judiciary Committee approved him 18–0, and the Senate confirmed him as the 108th justice by a vote of 87–9.

The press made little mention of the fact that Breyer would now be the second sitting Jewish member of the high bench. Although Breyer's personal life is more ecumenical than Ginsburg's (his British-born wife, the daughter of a leader of the Conservative Party, was a member of the Church of England, and they were married in an Anglican ceremony), he does not shrink from public references to his Jewish roots. In June 1995, for example, he presided over the swearing-in ceremony of the directors of the Holocaust Museum in Washington, D.C. He spoke movingly of his first trip through the exhibit and how emotional it was for him "as a Jew." Like Justice Ginsburg, he then emphasized the responsibility of lawyers and judges to uphold justice, in contrast to the dismal record of German judges during the Nazi era.

Justice Breyer quickly—indeed from the very first day of his tenure demonstrated alive, alert, and forceful participation in oral argument, a profound knowledge of history, a professorial approach to questioning, and remarkable analytical powers. Like his co-religionist on the Court, Breyer embraces civil rights and liberties generally, thus rather predictably almost always joining the Stevens-Souter-Ginsburg group in such issues. In his first two terms, Breyer was most frequently aligned with Justice Ginsburg—and least frequently with Justices Scalia and Thomas.

In religion cases, Breyer voted with Ginsburg on the separationist side (each time in dissent) in the University of Virginia Christian magazine case and in the New York decision allowing public school remedial instructors to teach in parochial schools. He parted company with her, however, in the Columbus, Ohio, KKK case, sanctioning that city's public forum, which is open to a variety of private expression, both religious and nonreligious. He also differed with Ginsburg in his dissenting vote to uphold the Religious Freedom Restoration Act.

After three terms, Breyer, like Ginsburg, has reflected the views of mainstream Jewish interest groups in several religion cases, but his "representativeness" has fallen primarily into the symbolic category.

ARTICLE 5

GEORGE W. BUSH, ET AL., PETITIONERS V. ALBERT GORE, JR., ET AL. (EXCERPTS), [DECEMBER 12, 2000]

PER CURIAM

I

On December 8, 2000, the Supreme Court of Florida ordered that the Circuit Court of Leon County tabulate by hand 9,000 ballots in Miami-Dade County. It also ordered the inclusion in the certified vote totals of 215 votes identified in Palm Beach County and 168 votes identified in Miami-Dade County for Vice President Albert Gore, Jr., and Senator Joseph Lieberman, Democratic Candidates for President and Vice President. The Supreme Court noted that petitioner, Governor George W. Bush asserted that the net gain for Vice President Gore in Palm Beach County was 176 votes, and directed the Circuit Court to resolve that dispute on remand. The court further held that relief would require manual recounts in all Florida counties where so-called "undervotes" had not been subject to manual tabulation. The court ordered all manual recounts to begin at once. Governor Bush and Richard Cheney, Republican Candidates for the Presidency and Vice Presidency, filed an emergency application for a stay of this mandate. On December 9, we granted the application, treated the application as a petition for a writ of certiorari, and granted certiorari.

The proceedings leading to the present controversy are discussed in some detail in our opinion in *Bush* v. *Palm Beach County Canvassing Bd., ante, (Bush I)*. On November 8, 2000, the day following the Presidential election, the Florida Division of Elections reported that petitioner, Governor Bush, had received 2,909,135 votes, and respondent, Vice President Gore, had received 2,907,351 votes, a margin of 1,784 for Governor Bush. Because Governor Bush's margin of victory was less than "one-half of a percent . . . of the votes cast," an automatic machine recount was conducted under §102.141(4) of the election code, the results of which showed Governor Bush still winning the race but by a diminished margin. Vice President Gore then sought manual recounts in Volusia, Palm Beach, Broward, and Miami-Dade Counties, pursuant to Florida's election protest provisions. Fla. Stat. §102.166 (2000). A dispute arose concerning the deadline for local county canvassing boards to submit their returns to the Secretary of State (Secretary). The Secretary declined to waive the November 14 deadline imposed by statute. §§102.111, 102.112. The Florida Supreme Court, however, set the deadline at November 26. We granted certiorari and vacated the Florida Supreme Court's decision, finding considerable uncertainty as to the grounds on which it was based *(Bush I)*. On December 11, the Florida Supreme Court issued a decision on remand reinstating that date.

On November 26, the Florida Elections Canvassing Commission certified the results of the election and declared Governor Bush the winner of Florida's 25 electoral votes. On November 27, Vice President Gore, pursuant to Florida's contest provisions, filed a complaint in Leon County Circuit Court contesting the certification. Fla. Stat. §102.168 (2000). He sought relief pursuant to §102.168(3)(c), which provides that "[r]eceipt of a number of illegal votes or rejection of a number of legal votes sufficient to change or place in doubt the result of the election" shall be grounds for a contest. The Circuit Court denied relief, stating that Vice President Gore failed to meet his burden of proof. He appealed to the First District Court of Appeal, which certified the matter to the Florida Supreme Court.

Accepting jurisdiction, the Florida Supreme Court affirmed in part and reversed in part. *Gore v. Harris,* (2000). The court held that the Circuit Court had been correct to reject Vice President Gore's challenge to the results certified in Nassau County and his challenge to the Palm Beach County Canvassing Board's determination that 3,300 ballots cast in that county were not, in the statutory phrase, "legal votes."

The Supreme Court held that Vice President Gore had satisfied his burden of proof under §102.168(3)(c) with respect to his challenge to Miami-Dade County's failure to tabulate, by manual count, 9,000 ballots on which the machines had failed to detect a vote for President ("undervotes"). Noting the closeness of the election, the Court explained that "[o]n this record, there can be no question that there are legal votes within the 9,000 uncounted votes sufficient to place the results of this election in doubt." *Id.* A "legal vote," as determined by the Supreme Court, is "one in which there is a 'clear indication of the intent of the voter'." *Id.* The court therefore ordered a hand recount of the 9,000 ballots in Miami-Dade County. Observing that the contest provisions vest broad discretion in the circuit judge to "provide any relief appropriate under such circumstances," Fla. Stat. §102.168(8) (2000), the Supreme Court further held that the Circuit Court could order "the Supervisor of Elections and the Canvassing Boards, as well as the necessary public officials, in all counties that have not conducted a manual recount or tabulation of the undervotes . . . to do so forthwith, said tabulation to take place in the individual counties where the ballots are located."

The Supreme Court also determined that both Palm Beach County and Miami-Dade County, in their earlier manual recounts, had identified a net gain of 215 and 168 legal votes for Vice President Gore. *Id.* Rejecting the Circuit Court's conclusion that Palm Beach County lacked the authority to include the 215 net votes submitted past the November 26 deadline, the Supreme Court explained that the deadline was not intended to exclude votes identified after that date through ongoing manual recounts. As to Miami-Dade County, the Court concluded that although the 168 votes identified were the result of a partial recount, they were "legal votes [that] could change the outcome of the election." *Id.* The Supreme Court therefore directed the Circuit Court to include those totals in the certified results, subject to resolution of the actual vote total from the Miami-Dade partial recount.

The petition presents the following questions: whether the Florida Supreme Court established new standards for resolving Presidential election contests, thereby violating Art. II, §1, cl. 2, of the United States Constitution and failing to comply with 3 U.S.C. § 5 and whether the use of standardless manual recounts violates the Equal Protection and Due Process Clauses. With respect to the equal protection question, we find a violation of the Equal Protection Clause.

II

A

The closeness of this election, and the multitude of legal challenges which have followed in its wake, have brought into sharp focus a common, if heretofore unnoticed, phenomenon. Nationwide statistics reveal that an estimated 2% of ballots cast do not register a vote for President for whatever reason, including deliberately choosing no candidate at all or some voter error, such as voting for two candidates or insufficiently marking a ballot. See Ho, More Than 2M

Ballots Uncounted, AP Online (Nov. 28, 2000); Kelley, Balloting Problems Not Rare But Only In A Very Close Election Do Mistakes And Mismarking Make A Difference, Omaha World-Herald (Nov. 15, 2000). In certifying election results, the votes eligible for inclusion in the certification are the votes meeting the properly established legal requirements.

This case has shown that punch card balloting machines can produce an unfortunate number of ballots which are not punched in a clean, complete way by the voter. After the current counting, it is likely legislative bodies nationwide will examine ways to improve the mechanisms and machinery for voting.

B

The individual citizen has no federal constitutional right to vote for electors for the President of the United States unless and until the state legislature chooses a statewide election as the means to implement its power to appoint members of the Electoral College. U.S. Const., Art. II, §1. This is the source for the statement in *McPherson* v. *Blacker,* 146 U.S. 1, 35 (1892), that the State legislature's power to select the manner for appointing electors is plenary; it may, if it so chooses, select the electors itself, which indeed was the manner used by State legislatures in several States for many years after the Framing of our Constitution. *Id.,* at 28–33. History has now favored the voter, and in each of the several States the citizens themselves vote for Presidential electors. When the state legislature vests the right to vote for President in its people, the right to vote as the legislature has prescribed is fundamental; and one source of its fundamental nature lies in the equal weight accorded to each vote and the equal dignity owed to each voter. The State, of course, after granting the franchise in the special context of Article II, can take back the power to appoint electors. See *id.,* at 35 ("[T]here is no doubt of the right of the legislature to resume the power at any time, for it can neither be taken away nor abdicated") (quoting S. Rep. No. 395, 43d Cong., 1st Sess.).

The right to vote is protected in more than the initial allocation of the franchise. Equal protection applies as well to the manner of its exercise. Having once granted the right to vote on equal terms, the State may not, by later arbitrary and disparate treatment, value one person's vote over that of another. See, e.g., *Harper* v. *Virginia Bd. of Elections,* 383 U.S. 663, 665 (1966) ("[O]nce the franchise is granted to the electorate, lines may not be drawn which are inconsistent with the Equal Protection Clause of the Fourteenth Amendment"). It must be remembered that "the right of suffrage can be denied by a debasement or dilution of the weight of a citizen's vote just as effectively as by wholly prohibiting the free exercise of the franchise." *Reynolds* v. *Sims,* 377 U.S. 533, 555 (1964).

There is no difference between the two sides of the present controversy on these basic propositions. Respondents say that the very purpose of vindicating the right to vote justifies the recount procedures now at issue. The question before us, however, is whether the recount procedures the Florida Supreme Court has adopted are consistent with its obligation to avoid arbitrary and disparate treatment of the members of its electorate.

Much of the controversy seems to revolve around ballot cards designed to be perforated by a stylus but which, either through error or deliberate omission, have not been perforated with sufficient precision for a machine to count them. In some cases a piece of the card—a chad—is hanging, say by two corners. In other cases there is no separation at all, just an indentation.

The Florida Supreme Court has ordered that the intent of the voter be discerned from such ballots. For purposes of resolving the equal protection challenge, it is not necessary to decide whether the Florida Supreme Court had the authority under the legislative scheme for resolving election disputes to define what a legal vote is and to mandate a manual recount implementing that definition. The recount mechanisms implemented in response to the decisions of the Florida Supreme Court do not satisfy the minimum requirement for non-arbitrary treatment of voters necessary to secure the fundamental right. Florida's basic command for the count of legally cast votes is to consider the "intent of the voter" *(Gore* v. *Harris).* This is unobjectionable as an abstract proposition and a starting principle. The problem inheres in the absence of specific standards to ensure its equal application. The formulation of uniform rules to determine intent based on these recurring circumstances is practicable and, we conclude, necessary.

The law does not refrain from searching for the intent of the actor in a multitude of circumstances; and in some cases the general command to ascertain intent is not susceptible to much further refinement. In this instance, however, the question is not whether to believe a witness but how to interpret the marks or holes or scratches on an inanimate object, a piece of cardboard or paper which, it is said, might not have registered as a vote during the machine count. The factfinder confronts a thing, not a person. The search for intent can be confined by specific rules designed to ensure uniform treatment.

The want of those rules here has led to unequal evaluation of ballots in various respects. See *Gore* v. *Harris.* (Wells, J., dissenting) ("Should a county canvassing board count or not count a 'dimpled chad' where the voter is able to successfully dislodge the chad in every other contest on that ballot? Here, the county canvassing boards disagree"). As seems to have been acknowledged at oral argument, the standards for accepting or rejecting contested ballots might vary not only from county to county but indeed within a single county from one recount team to another.

The record provides some examples. A monitor in Miami-Dade County testified at trial that he observed that three members of the county canvassing board applied different standards in defining a legal vote. 3 Tr. 497, 499 (Dec. 3, 2000). And testimony at trial also revealed that at least one county changed its evaluative standards during the counting process. Palm Beach County, for example, began the process with a 1990 guideline which precluded counting completely attached chads, switched to a rule that considered a vote to be legal if any light could be seen through a chad, changed back to the 1990 rule, and then abandoned any pretense of a *per se* rule, only to have a court order that the county consider dimpled chads legal. This is not a process with sufficient guarantees of equal treatment.

An early case in our one person, one vote jurisprudence arose when a State accorded arbitrary and disparate treatment to voters in its different counties. *Gray* v. *Sanders,* 372 U.S. 368 (1963). The Court found a constitutional violation. We relied on these principles in the context of the Presidential selection process in *Moore* v. *Ogilvie,* 394 U.S. 814 (1969), where we invalidated a county-based procedure that diluted the influence of citizens in larger counties in the nominating process. There we observed that "[t]he idea that one group can be granted greater voting strength than another is hostile to the one man, one vote basis of our representative government." *Id.,* at 819.

The State Supreme Court ratified this uneven treatment. It mandated that the recount totals from two counties, Miami-Dade and Palm Beach, be included in the certified total. The court also appeared to hold *sub silentio* that the recount totals from Broward County, which were not completed until after the original November 14 certification by the Secretary of State, were to be considered part of the new certified vote totals even though the county certification was not contested by Vice President Gore. Yet each of the counties used varying standards to determine what was a legal vote. Broward County used a more forgiving standard than Palm Beach County, and uncovered almost three times as many new votes, a result markedly disproportionate to the difference in population between the counties.

In addition, the recounts in these three counties were not limited to so-called undervotes but extended to all of the ballots. The distinction has real consequences. A manual recount of all ballots identifies not only those ballots which show no vote but also those which contain more than one, the so-called overvotes. Neither category will be counted by the machine. This is not a trivial concern. At oral argument, respondents estimated there are as many as 110,000 overvotes statewide. As a result, the citizen whose ballot was not read by a machine because he failed to vote for a candidate in a way readable by a machine may still have his vote counted in a manual recount; on the other hand, the citizen who marks two candidates in a way discernable by the machine will not have the same opportunity to have his vote count, even if a manual examination of the ballot would reveal the requisite indicia of intent. Furthermore, the citizen who marks two candidates, only one of which is discernable by the machine, will have his vote counted even though it should have been read as an invalid ballot. The State Supreme Court's inclusion of vote counts based on these variant standards exemplifies concerns with the remedial processes that were under way.

That brings the analysis to yet a further equal protection problem. The votes certified by the court included a partial total from one county, Miami-Dade. The Florida Supreme Court's decision thus gives no assurance that the recounts included in a final certification must be complete. Indeed, it is respondent's submission that it would be consistent with the rules of the recount procedures to include whatever partial counts are done by the time of final certification, and we interpret the Florida Supreme Court's decision to permit this. This accommodation no doubt results from the truncated contest period established by the Florida Supreme Court in *Bush I*, at respondents' own urging. The press of time does not diminish the constitutional concern. A desire for speed is not a general excuse for ignoring equal protection guarantees.

In addition to these difficulties the actual process by which the votes were to be counted under the Florida Supreme Court's decision raises further concerns. That order did not specify who would recount the ballots. The county canvassing boards were forced to pull together ad hoc teams comprised of judges from various Circuits who had no previous training in handling and interpreting ballots. Furthermore, while others were permitted to observe, they were prohibited from objecting during the recount.

The recount process, in its features here described, is inconsistent with the minimum procedures necessary to protect the fundamental right of each voter in the special instance of a statewide recount under the authority of a single state judicial officer. Our consideration is limited to the present circumstances, for the problem of equal protection in election processes generally presents many complexities.

The question before the Court is not whether local entities, in the exercise of their expertise, may develop different systems for implementing elections. Instead, we are presented with a situation where a state court with the power to assure uniformity has ordered a statewide recount with minimal procedural safeguards. When a court orders a statewide remedy, there must be at least some assurance that the rudimentary requirements of equal treatment and fundamental fairness are satisfied.

Given the Court's assessment that the recount process underway was probably being conducted in an unconstitutional manner, the Court stayed the order directing the recount so it could hear this case and render an expedited decision. The contest provision, as it was mandated by the State Supreme Court, is not well calculated to sustain the confidence that all citizens must have in the outcome of elections. The State has not shown that its procedures include the necessary safeguards. The problem, for instance, of the estimated 110,000 overvotes has not been addressed, although Chief Justice Wells called attention to the concern in his dissenting opinion.

Upon due consideration of the difficulties identified to this point, it is obvious that the recount cannot be conducted in compliance with the requirements of equal protection and due process without substantial additional work. It would require not only the adoption (after opportunity for argument) of adequate statewide standards for determining what is a legal vote, and practicable procedures to implement them, but also orderly judicial review of any disputed matters that might arise. In addition, the Secretary of State has advised that the recount of only a portion of the ballots requires that the vote tabulation equipment be used to screen out undervotes, a function for which the machines were not designed. If a recount of overvotes were also required, perhaps even a second screening would be necessary. Use of the equipment for this purpose, and any new software developed for it, would have to be evaluated for accuracy by the Secretary of State, as required by Fla. Stat. §101.015 (2000).

The Supreme Court of Florida has said that the legislature intended the State's electors to "participat[e] fully in the federal electoral process," as provided in 3 U.S.C. § 5; see also *Palm Beach Canvassing Bd.* v. *Harris,* 2000 WL 1725434, *13 (Fla. 2000). That statute, in turn, requires that any controversy or contest that is designed to lead to a conclusive selection of electors be completed by December 12. That date is upon us, and there is no recount procedure in place under the State Supreme Court's order that comports with minimal constitutional standards. Because it is evident that any recount seeking to meet the December 12 date will be unconstitutional for the reasons we have discussed, we reverse the judgment of the Supreme Court of Florida ordering a recount to proceed.

Seven Justices of the Court agree that there are constitutional problems with the recount ordered by the Florida Supreme Court that demand a remedy. See *post,* at 6 (Souter, J., dissenting); *post,* at 2, 15 (Breyer, J., dissenting). The only disagreement is as to the remedy. Because the Florida Supreme Court has said that the Florida Legislature intended to obtain the safe-harbor benefits of 3 U.S.C. § 5 Justice Breyer's proposed remedy—remanding to the Florida Supreme Court for its ordering of a constitutionally proper contest until December 18—contemplates action in violation of the Florida election code, and hence could not be part of an "appropriate" order authorized by Fla. Stat. §102.168(8) (2000).

* * *

None are more conscious of the vital limits on judicial authority than are the members of this Court, and none stand more in admiration of the Constitution's design to leave the selection of the President to the people, through their legislatures, and to the political sphere. When contending parties invoke the process of the courts, however, it becomes our unsought responsibility to resolve the federal and constitutional issues the judicial system has been forced to confront.

The judgment of the Supreme Court of Florida is reversed, and the case is remanded for further proceedings not inconsistent with this opinion.

Pursuant to this Court's Rule 45.2, the Clerk is directed to issue the mandate in this case forthwith.

It is so ordered.

CHIEF JUSTICE REHNQUIST, WITH WHOM JUSTICE SCALIA AND JUSTICE THOMAS JOIN, CONCURRING

We join the *per curiam* opinion. We write separately because we believe there are additional grounds that require us to reverse the Florida Supreme Court's decision.

I

We deal here not with an ordinary election, but with an election for the President of the United States. In *Burroughs* v. *United States,* 290 U.S. 534, 545 (1934), we said:

> "While presidential electors are not officers or agents of the federal government (*In re Green,* 134 U.S. 377, 379), they exercise federal functions

under, and discharge duties in virtue of authority conferred by, the Constitution of the United States. The President is vested with the executive power of the nation. The importance of his election and the vital character of its relationship to and effect upon the welfare and safety of the whole people cannot be too strongly stated."

Likewise, in *Anderson* v. *Celebrezze,* 460 U.S. 780, 794–795 (1983) (footnote omitted), we said:

"[I]n the context of a Presidential election, state-imposed restrictions implicate a uniquely important national interest. For the President and the Vice President of the United States are the only elected officials who represent all the voters in the Nation."

In most cases, comity and respect for federalism compel us to defer to the decisions of state courts on issues of state law. That practice reflects our understanding that the decisions of state courts are definitive pronouncements of the will of the States as sovereigns. Cf. *Erie R. Co.* v. *Tompkins,* 304 U.S. 64 (1938). Of course, in ordinary cases, the distribution of powers among the branches of a State's government raises no questions of federal constitutional law, subject to the requirement that the government be republican in character. See U.S. Const., Art. IV, §4. But there are a few exceptional cases in which the Constitution imposes a duty or confers a power on a particular branch of a State's government. This is one of them. Article II, §1, cl. 2, provides that "[e]ach State shall appoint, in such Manner as the *Legislature* thereof may direct," electors for President and Vice President. (Emphasis added.) Thus, the text of the election law itself, and not just its interpretation by the courts of the States, takes on independent significance.

In *McPherson* v. *Blacker,* 146 U.S. 1 (1892), we explained that Art. II, §1, cl. 2, "convey[s] the broadest power of determination" and "leaves it to the legislature exclusively to define the method" of appointment. *Id.,* at 27. A significant departure from the legislative scheme for appointing Presidential electors presents a federal constitutional question.

3 U.S.C. § 5 informs our application of Art. II, §1, cl. 2, to the Florida statutory scheme, which, as the Florida Supreme Court acknowledged, took that statute into account. Section 5 provides that the State's selection of electors "shall be conclusive, and shall govern in the counting of the electoral votes" if the electors are chosen under laws enacted prior to election day, and if the selection process is completed six days prior to the meeting of the electoral college. As we noted in *Bush* v. *Palm Beach County Canvassing Bd., ante,* at 6.

"Since §5 contains a principle of federal law that would assure finality of the State's determination if made pursuant to a state law in effect before the election, a legislative wish to take advantage of the 'safe harbor' would counsel against any construction of the Election Code that Congress might deem to be a change in the law."

If we are to respect the legislature's Article II powers, therefore, we must ensure that postelection state-court actions do not frustrate the legislative desire to attain the "safe harbor" provided by §5.

In Florida, the legislature has chosen to hold statewide elections to appoint the State's 25 electors. Importantly, the legislature has delegated the authority to run the elections and to oversee election disputes to the Secretary of State (Secretary), Fla. Stat. §97.012(1) (2000), and to state circuit courts, §§102.168(1), 102.168(8). Isolated sections of the code may well admit of more than one interpretation, but the general coherence of the legislative scheme may not be altered by judicial interpretation so as to wholly change the statutorily provided apportionment of responsibility among these various bodies. In any election but a Presidential election, the Florida Supreme Court can give as little or as much deference to Florida's executives as it chooses, so far as Article II is concerned, and this Court will have no cause to question the court's actions. But, with respect to a Presidential election, the court must be both mindful of the legislature's role under Article II in choosing the manner of appointing electors and deferential to those bodies expressly empowered by the legislature to carry out its constitutional mandate.

In order to determine whether a state court has infringed upon the legislature's authority, we necessarily must examine the law of the State as it existed prior to the action of the court. Though we generally defer to state courts on the interpretation of state law—see, e.g., *Mullaney* v. *Wilbur,* 421 U.S. 684 (1975)—there are of course areas in which the Constitution requires this Court to undertake an independent, if still deferential, analysis of state law.

For example, in *NAACP* v. *Alabama ex rel. Patterson,* 357 U.S. 449 (1958), it was argued that we were without jurisdiction because the petitioner had not pursued the correct appellate remedy in Alabama's state courts. Petitioners had sought a state-law writ of certiorari in the Alabama Supreme Court when a writ of mandamus, according to that court, was proper. We found this state-law ground inadequate to defeat our jurisdiction because we were "unable to reconcile the procedural holding of the Alabama Supreme Court" with prior Alabama precedent. *Id.,* at 456. The purported state-law ground was so novel, in our independent estimation, that "petitioner could not fairly be deemed to have been apprised of its existence." *Id.,* at 457.

Six years later we decided *Bouie* v. *City of Columbia,* 378 U.S. 347 (1964), in which the state court had held, contrary to precedent, that the state trespass law applied to black sit-in demonstrators who had consent to enter private property but were then asked to leave. Relying upon *NAACP,* we concluded that the South Carolina Supreme Court's interpretation of a state penal statute had impermissibly broadened the scope of that statute beyond what a fair reading provided, in violation of due process. See 378 U.S., at 361–362. What we would do in the present case is precisely parallel: Hold that the Florida Supreme Court's interpretation of the Florida election laws impermissibly distorted them beyond what a fair reading required, in violation of Article II.[1]

This inquiry does not imply a disrespect for state *courts* but rather a respect for the constitutionally prescribed role of state *legislatures.* To attach definitive weight to the pronouncement of a state court, when the very question at issue is whether the court has actually departed from the statutory meaning, would be to abdicate our responsibility to enforce the explicit requirements of Article II.

II

Acting pursuant to its constitutional grant of authority, the Florida Legislature has created a detailed, if not perfectly crafted, statutory scheme that provides for appointment of Presidential electors by direct election. Fla. Stat. §103.011 (2000). Under the statute, "[v]otes cast for the actual candidates for President and Vice President shall be counted as votes cast for the presidential electors supporting such candidates." *Ibid.* The legislature has designated the Secretary of State as the "chief election officer," with the responsibility to "[o]btain and maintain uniformity in the application, operation, and interpretation of the election laws." §97.012. The state legislature has delegated to county canvassing boards the duties of administering elections. §102.141. Those boards are responsible for providing results to the state Elections Canvassing Commission, comprising the Governor, the Secretary of State, and the Director of the Division of Elections. §102.111. Cf. *Boardman* v. *Esteva,* 323 So. 2d 259, 268, n. 5 (1975) ("The election process . . . is committed to the executive branch of government through duly designated officials all charged with specific duties. . . . [The] judgments [of these officials] are entitled to be regarded by the courts as presumptively correct . . .").

After the election has taken place, the canvassing boards receive returns from precincts, count the votes, and in the event that a candidate was defeated by .5% or less, conduct a mandatory recount. Fla. Stat. §102.141(4) (2000). The county canvassing boards must file certified election returns with the Department of State by 5 p.m.

on the seventh day following the election. §102.112(1). The Elections Canvassing Commission must then certify the results of the election. §102.111(1).

The state legislature has also provided mechanisms both for protesting election returns and for contesting certified election results. Section 102.166 governs protests. Any protest must be filed prior to the certification of election results by the county canvassing board. §102.166(4)(b). Once a protest has been filed, "the county canvassing board may authorize a manual recount." §102.166(4)(c). If a sample recount conducted pursuant to §102.166(5) "indicates an error in the vote tabulation which could affect the outcome of the election," the county canvassing board is instructed to: "(a) Correct the error and recount the remaining precincts with the vote tabulation system; (b) Request the Department of State to verify the tabulation software; or (c) Manually recount all ballots," §102.166(5). In the event a canvassing board chooses to conduct a manual recount of all ballots, §102.166(7) prescribes procedures for such a recount.

Contests to the certification of an election, on the other hand, are controlled by §102.168. The grounds for contesting an election include "[r]eceipt of a number of illegal votes or rejection of a number of legal votes sufficient to change or place in doubt the result of the election." §102.168(3)(c). Any contest must be filed in the appropriate Florida circuit court, Fla. Stat. §102.168(1), and the canvassing board or election board is the proper party defendant, §102.168(4). Section 102.168(8) provides that "[t]he circuit judge to whom the contest is presented may fashion such orders as he or she deems necessary to ensure that each allegation in the complaint is investigated, examined, or checked, to prevent or correct any alleged wrong, and to provide any relief appropriate under such circumstances." In Presidential elections, the contest period necessarily terminates on the date set by 3 U.S.C. § 5 for concluding the State's "final determination" of election controversies."

In its first decision, *Palm Beach Canvassing Bd. v. Harris* (Nov. 21, 2000) (*Harris I*), the Florida Supreme Court extended the 7-day statutory certification deadline established by the legislature.[2] This modification of the code, by lengthening the protest period, necessarily shortened the contest period for Presidential elections. Underlying the extension of the certification deadline and the shortchanging of the contest period was, presumably, the clear implication that certification was a matter of significance: The certified winner would enjoy presumptive validity, making a contest proceeding by the losing candidate an uphill battle. In its latest opinion, however, the court empties certification of virtually all legal consequence during the contest, and in doing so departs from the provisions enacted by the Florida Legislature.

The court determined that canvassing boards' decisions regarding whether to recount ballots past the certification deadline (even the certification deadline established by *Harris I*) are to be reviewed *de novo*, although the election code clearly vests discretion whether to recount in the boards, and sets strict deadlines subject to the Secretary's rejection of late tallies and monetary fines for tardiness. See Fla. Stat. §102.112 (2000). Moreover, the Florida court held that all late vote tallies arriving during the contest period should be automatically included in the certification regardless of the certification's deadline (even the certification deadline established by *Harris I*), thus virtually eliminating both the deadline and the Secretary's discretion to disregard recounts that violate it.[3]

Moreover, the court's interpretation of "legal vote," and hence its decision to order a contest-period recount, plainly departed from the legislative scheme. Florida statutory law cannot reasonably be thought to *require* the counting of improperly marked ballots. Each Florida precinct before election day provides instructions on how properly to cast a vote, §101.46; each polling place on election day contains a working model of the voting machine it uses, §101.5611; and each voting booth contains a sample ballot, §101.46. In precincts using punch-card ballots, voters are instructed to punch out the ballot cleanly:

> AFTER VOTING, CHECK YOUR BALLOT CARD TO BE SURE YOUR VOTING SELECTIONS ARE CLEARLY AND CLEANLY PUNCHED AND THERE ARE NO CHIPS LEFT HANGING ON THE BACK OF THE CARD.

Instructions to Voters, quoted in *Touchston* v. *McDermott*, 2000 WL 1781942, *6 & n. 19 (CA11) (Tjoflat, J., dissenting). No reasonable person would call it "an error in the vote tabulation," Fla. Stat. §102.166(5), or a "rejection of legal votes," Fla. Stat. §102.168(3)(c),[4] when electronic or electromechanical equipment performs precisely in the manner designed, and fails to count those ballots that are not marked in the manner that these voting instructions explicitly and prominently specify. The scheme that the Florida Supreme Court's opinion attributes to the legislature is one in which machines are *required* to be "capable of correctly counting votes," §101.5606(4), but which nonetheless regularly produces elections in which legal votes are predictably not tabulated, so that in close elections manual recounts are regularly required. This is of course absurd. The Secretary of State, who is authorized by law to issue binding interpretations of the election code, §§97.012, 106.23, rejected this peculiar reading of the statutes. See DE 00–13 (opinion of the Division of Elections). The Florida Supreme Court, although it must defer to the Secretary's interpretations, see *Krivanek* v. *Take Back Tampa Political Committee*, 625 So. 2d 840, 844 (Fla. 1993), rejected her reasonable interpretation and embraced the peculiar one. See *Palm Beach County Canvassing Board* v. *Harris*, No. SC00–2346 (Dec. 11, 2000) (*Harris III*).

But as we indicated in our remand of the earlier case, in a Presidential election the clearly expressed intent of the legislature must prevail. And there is no basis for reading the Florida statutes as requiring the counting of improperly marked ballots, as an examination of the Florida Supreme Court's textual analysis shows. We will not parse that analysis here, except to note that the principal provision of the election code on which it relied, §101.5614(5), was, as the Chief Justice pointed out in his dissent from *Harris II*, entirely irrelevant. See *Gore* v. *Harris*, No. SC00-2431, slip op., at 50 (Dec. 8, 2000). The State's Attorney General (who was supporting the Gore challenge) confirmed in oral argument here that never before the present election had a manual recount been conducted on the basis of the contention that "undervotes" should have been examined to determine voter intent. Tr. of Oral Arg. in *Bush* v. *Palm Beach County Canvassing Bd.*, 39–40 (Dec. 1, 2000); cf. *Broward County Canvassing Board* v. *Hogan*, 607 So. 2d 508, 509 (Fla. Ct. App. 1992) (denial of recount for failure to count ballots with "hanging paper chads"). For the court to step away from this established practice, prescribed by the Secretary of State, the state official charged by the legislature with "responsibility to . . . [o]btain and maintain uniformity in the application, operation, and interpretation of the election laws," §97.012(1), was to depart from the legislative scheme.

III

The scope and nature of the remedy ordered by the Florida Supreme Court jeopardizes the "legislative wish" to take advantage of the safe harbor provided by 3 U.S.C. § 5. *Bush* v. *Palm Beach County Canvassing Bd.*, *ante*, at 6. December 12, 2000, is the last date for a final determination of the Florida electors that will satisfy §5. Yet in the late afternoon of December 8th—four days before this deadline—the Supreme Court of Florida ordered recounts of tens of thousands of so-called "undervotes" spread through 64 of the State's 67 counties. This was done in a search for elusive—perhaps delusive—certainty as to the exact count of 6 million votes. But no one claims that these ballots have not previously been tabulated; they were initially read by voting machines at the time of the election, and thereafter reread by virtue of Florida's automatic recount provision. No one claims there was any fraud in the election. The Supreme Court of Florida ordered this additional recount under the provision of the election code giving the circuit judge the authority to provide relief that is "appropriate under such circumstances." Fla. Stat. §102.168(8) (2000).

Surely when the Florida Legislature empowered the courts of the State to grant "appropriate" relief, it must have meant relief that would have become final by the cut-off date of 3 U.S.C. § 5. In light of the inevitable legal challenges and ensuing appeals to the Supreme Court of Florida and petitions for certiorari to this Court, the entire recounting process could not possibly be completed by that date. Whereas the majority in the Supreme Court of Florida stated its confidence that "the remaining undervotes in these counties can be [counted] within the required time frame," it made no assertion that the seemingly inevitable appeals could be disposed of in that time. Although the Florida Supreme Court has on occasion taken over a year to resolve disputes over local elections, see, *e.g., Beckstrom* v. *Volusia County Canvassing Bd.,* 707 So. 2d 720 (1998) (resolving contest of sheriff's race 16 months after the election), it has heard and decided the appeals in the present case with great promptness. But the federal deadlines for the Presidential election simply do not permit even such a shortened process.

As the dissent noted:

> "In [the four days remaining], all questionable ballots must be reviewed by the judicial officer appointed to discern the intent of the voter in a process open to the public. Fairness dictates that a provision be made for either party to object to how a particular ballot is counted. Additionally, this short time period must allow for judicial review. I respectfully submit this cannot be completed without taking Florida's presidential electors outside the safe harbor provision, creating the very real possibility of disenfranchising those nearly 6 million voters who are able to correctly cast their ballots on election day."

The other dissenters echoed this concern: "[T]he majority is departing from the essential requirements of the law by providing a remedy which is impossible to achieve and which will ultimately lead to chaos." *Id.* (Harding, J., dissenting, Shaw, J. concurring).

Given all these factors, and in light of the legislative intent identified by the Florida Supreme Court to bring Florida within the "safe harbor" provision of 3 U.S.C. § 5 the remedy prescribed by the Supreme Court of Florida cannot be deemed an "appropriate" one as of December 8. It significantly departed from the statutory framework in place on November 7, and authorized open-ended further proceedings which could not be completed by December 12, thereby preventing a final determination by that date.

For these reasons, in addition to those given in the *per curiam,* we would reverse.

NOTES

1 Similarly, our jurisprudence requires us to analyze the "background principles" of state property law to determine whether there has been a taking of property in violation of the Takings Clause. That constitutional guarantee would, of course, afford no protection against state power if our inquiry could be concluded by a state supreme court holding that state property law accorded the plaintiff no rights. See *Lucas* v. *South Carolina Coastal Council,* 505 U.S. 1003 (1992). In one of our oldest cases, we similarly made an independent evaluation of state law in order to protect federal treaty guarantees. In *Fairfax's Devisee* v. *Hunter's Lessee,* 7 Cranch 603 (1813), we disagreed with the Supreme Court of Appeals of Virginia that a 1782 state law had extinguished the property interests of one Denny Fairfax, so that a 1789 ejectment order against Fairfax supported by a 1785 state law did not constitute a future confiscation under the 1783 peace treaty with Great Britain. See *id.,* at 623; *Hunter* v. *Fairfax's Devisee,* 1 Munf. 218 (Va. 1809).

2 We vacated that decision and remanded that case; the Florida Supreme Court reissued the same judgment with a new opinion on December 11, 2000.

3 Specifically, the Florida Supreme Court ordered the Circuit Court to include in the certified vote totals those votes identified for Vice President Gore in Palm Beach County and Miami-Dade County.

4 It is inconceivable that what constitutes a vote that must be counted under the "error in the vote tabulation" language of the protest phase is different from what constitutes a vote that must be counted under the "legal votes" language of the contest phase.

JUSTICE BREYER, WITH WHOM JUSTICE STEVENS AND JUSTICE GINSBURG JOIN EXCEPT AS TO PART I-A-1, AND WITH WHOM JUSTICE SOUTER JOINS AS TO PART I, DISSENTING

The Court was wrong to take this case. It was wrong to grant a stay. It should now vacate that stay and permit the Florida Supreme Court to decide whether the recount should resume.

I

The political implications of this case for the country are momentous. But the federal legal questions presented, with one exception, are insubstantial.

A

1

The majority raises three Equal Protection problems with the Florida Supreme Court's recount order: first, the failure to include overvotes in the manual recount; second, the fact that *all* ballots, rather than simply the undervotes, were recounted in some, but not all, counties; and third, the absence of a uniform, specific standard to guide the recounts. As far as the first issue is concerned, petitioners presented no evidence, to this Court or to any Florida court, that a manual recount of overvotes would identify additional legal votes. The same is true of the second, and, in addition, the majority's reasoning would seem to invalidate any state provision for a manual recount of individual counties in a statewide election.

The majority's third concern does implicate principles of fundamental fairness. The majority concludes that the Equal Protection Clause requires that a manual recount be governed not only by the uniform general standard of the "clear intent of the voter," but also by uniform subsidiary standards (for example, a uniform determination whether indented, but not perforated, "undervotes" should count). The opinion points out that the Florida Supreme Court ordered the inclusion of Broward County's undercounted "legal votes" even though those votes included ballots that were not perforated but simply "dimpled," while newly recounted ballots from other counties will likely include only votes determined to be "legal" on the basis of a stricter standard. In light of our previous remand, the Florida Supreme Court may have been reluctant to adopt a more specific standard than that provided for by the legislature for fear of exceeding its authority under Article II. However, since the use of different standards could favor one or the other of the candidates, since time was, and is, too short to permit the lower courts to iron out significant differences through ordinary judicial review, and since the relevant distinction was embodied in the order of the State's highest court, I agree that, in these very special circumstances, basic principles of fairness may well have counseled the adoption of a uniform standard to address the problem. In light of the majority's disposition, I need not decide whether, or the extent to which, as a remedial matter, the Constitution would place limits upon the content of the uniform standard.

2

Nonetheless, there is no justification for the majority's remedy, which is simply to reverse the lower court and halt the recount entirely. An appropriate remedy would be, instead, to remand this case with instructions that, even at this late date, would permit the Florida Supreme Court to require recounting *all* undercounted votes in Florida, including those from Broward, Volusia, Palm Beach, and Miami-Dade Counties, whether or not previously recounted prior to the end of the protest period, and to do so in accordance with a single-uniform substandard.

The majority justifies stopping the recount entirely on the ground that there is no more time. In particular, the majority relies on the lack of time for the Secretary to review and approve equipment needed to separate undervotes. But the majority reaches this conclusion in the absence of *any* record evidence that the recount could not have been completed in the time allowed by the Florida Supreme Court. The majority finds facts outside of the record on matters that state courts are in a far better position to address. Of course, it is too late for any such recount to take place by December 12, the date by which election disputes must be decided if a State is to take advantage of the safe harbor provisions of 3 U.S.C. § 5. Whether there is time to conduct a recount prior to December 18, when the electors are scheduled to meet, is a matter for the state courts to determine. And whether, under Florida law, Florida could or could not take further action is obviously a matter for Florida courts, not this Court, to decide. See *ante,* at 13 (*per curiam*).

By halting the manual recount, and thus ensuring that the uncounted legal votes will not be counted under any standard, this Court crafts a remedy out of proportion to the asserted harm. And that remedy harms the very fairness interests the Court is attempting to protect. The manual recount would itself redress a problem of unequal treatment of ballots. As Justice Stevens points out, see *ante,* at 4 and n. 4 (Stevens, J., dissenting opinion), the ballots of voters in counties that use punch-card systems are more likely to be disqualified than those in counties using optical-scanning systems. According to recent news reports, variations in the undervote rate are even more pronounced. See Fessenden, No-Vote Rates Higher in Punch Card Count, N. Y. Times, Dec. 1, 2000, p. A29 (reporting that 0.3% of ballots cast in 30 Florida counties using optical-scanning systems registered no Presidential vote, in comparison to 1.53% in the 15 counties using Votomatic punch card ballots). Thus, in a system that allows counties to use different types of voting systems, voters already arrive at the polls with an unequal chance that their votes will be counted. I do not see how the fact that this results from counties' selection of different voting machines rather than a court order makes the outcome any more fair. Nor do I understand why the Florida Supreme Court's recount order, which helps to redress this inequity, must be entirely prohibited based on a deficiency that could easily be remedied.

B

The remainder of petitioners' claims, which are the focus of the Chief Justice's concurrence, raise no significant federal questions. I cannot agree that the Chief Justice's unusual review of state law in this case, see *ante*, at 5–8 (Ginsburg, J., dissenting opinion), is justified by reference either to Art. II, §1, or to 3 U.S.C. § 5. Moreover, even were such review proper, the conclusion that the Florida Supreme Court's decision contravenes federal law is untenable.

While conceding that, in most cases, "comity and respect for federalism compel us to defer to the decisions of state courts on issues of state law," the concurrence relies on some combination of Art. II, §1, and 3 U.S.C. § 5 to justify the majority's conclusion that this case is one of the few in which we may lay that fundamental principle aside. *Ante*, at 2 (Opinion of Rehnquist, C. J. The concurrence's primary foundation for this conclusion rests on an appeal to plain text: Art. II, §1's grant of the power to appoint Presidential electors to the State "Legislature." *Ibid.* But neither the text of Article II itself nor the only case the concurrence cites that interprets Article II, *McPherson* v. *Blacker*, 146 U.S. 1 (1892), leads to the conclusion that Article II grants unlimited power to the legislature, devoid of any state constitutional limitations, to select the manner of appointing electors. See *id.*, at 41 (specifically referring to state constitutional provision in upholding state law regarding selection of electors). Nor, as Justice Stevens points out, have we interpreted the Federal constitutional provision most analogous to Art. II, §1–Art. I, §4–in the strained manner put forth in the concurrence. *Ante*, at 1–2 and n. 1 (dissenting opinion).

The concurrence's treatment of §5 as "inform[ing]" its interpretation of Article II, §1, cl. 2, *ante*, at 3 (Rehnquist, C. J., concurring), is no more convincing. The Chief Justice contends that our opinion in *Bush* v. *Palm Beach County Canvassing Bd., ante*, (per curiam) (*Bush I*), in which we stated that "a legislative wish to take advantage of [§5] would counsel against" a construction of Florida law that Congress might deem to be a change in law, *id.*, (slip op. at 6), now means that *this Court* "must ensure that post-election state court actions do not frustrate the legislative desire to attain the 'safe harbor' provided by §5." *Ante*, at 3. However, §5 is part of the rules that govern Congress' recognition of slates of electors. Nowhere in *Bush I* did we establish that *this Court* had the authority to enforce §5. Nor did we suggest that the permissive "counsel against" could be transformed into the mandatory "must ensure." And nowhere did we intimate, as the concurrence does here, that a state court decision that threatens the safe harbor provision of §5 does so in violation of Article II. The concurrence's logic turns the presumption that legislatures would wish to take advantage of § 5's "safe harbor" provision into a mandate that trumps other statutory provisions and overrides the intent that the legislature *did* express.

But, in any event, the concurrence, having conducted its review, now reaches the wrong conclusion. It says that "the Florida Supreme Court's interpretation of the Florida election laws impermissibly distorted them beyond what a fair reading required, in violation of Article II." *Ante,* at 4–5 (Rehnquist, C. J, concurring). But what precisely is the distortion? Apparently, it has three elements. First, the Florida court, in its earlier opinion, changed the election certification date from November 14 to November 26. Second, the Florida court ordered a manual recount of "undercounted" ballots that could not have been fully completed by the December 12 "safe harbor" deadline. Third, the Florida court, in the opinion now under review, failed to give adequate deference to the determinations of canvassing boards and the Secretary.

To characterize the first element as a "distortion," however, requires the concurrence to second-guess the way in which the state court resolved a plain conflict in the language of different statutes. Compare Fla. Stat. §102.166 (2001) (foreseeing manual recounts during the protest period) with §102.111 (setting what is arguably too short a deadline for manual recounts to be conducted); compare §102.112(1) (stating that the Secretary "may" ignore late returns) with §102.111(1) (stating that the Secretary "shall" ignore late returns). In any event, that issue no longer has any practical importance and cannot justify the reversal of the different Florida court decision before us now.

To characterize the second element as a "distortion" requires the concurrence to overlook the fact that the inability of the Florida courts to conduct the recount on time is, in significant part, a problem of the Court's own making. The Florida Supreme Court thought that the recount could be completed on time, and, within hours, the Florida Circuit Court was moving in an orderly fashion to meet the deadline. This Court improvidently entered a stay. As a result, we will never know whether the recount could have been completed.

Nor can one characterize the third element as "impermissibl[e] distort[ing]" once one understands that there are two sides to the opinion's argument that the Florida Supreme Court "virtually eliminated the Secretary's discretion." *Ante,* at 9 (Rehnquist, C. J, concurring). The Florida statute in question was amended in 1999 to provide that the "grounds for contesting an election" include the "rejection of a number of legal votes sufficient to . . . place in doubt the result of the election." Fla. Stat. §§102.168(3), (3)(c) (2000). And the parties have argued about the proper meaning of the statute's term "legal vote." The Secretary has claimed that a "legal vote" is a vote "properly executed in accordance with the instructions provided to all registered voters." Brief for Respondent Harris et al. 10. On that interpretation, punchcard ballots for which the machines cannot register a vote are not "legal" votes. *Id.,* at 14. The Florida Supreme Court did not accept her definition. But it had a reason. Its reason was that a different provision of Florida election laws (a provision that addresses damaged or defective ballots) says that no vote shall be disregarded "if there is a clear indication of the intent of the voter as determined by the canvassing board" (adding that ballots should not be counted "if it is impossible to determine the elector's choice"). Fla. Stat. §101.5614(5) (2000). Given this statutory language, certain roughly analogous judicial precedent, *e.g., Darby* v. *State ex rel. McCollough,* 75 So. 411 (Fla. 1917) (*per curiam*), and somewhat similar determinations by courts throughout the Nation, see cases cited *infra,* at 9, the Florida Supreme Court concluded that the term "legal vote" means a vote recorded on a ballot that clearly reflects what the voter intended. *Gore* v. *Harris,* (2000) (slip op., at 19). That conclusion differs from the conclusion of the Secretary. But nothing in Florida law requires the Florida Supreme Court to accept as determinative the Secretary's view on such a matter. Nor can one say that the Court's ultimate determination is so unreasonable as to amount to a constitutionally "impermissible distort[ion]" of Florida law.

The Florida Supreme Court, applying this definition, decided, on the basis of the record, that respondents had shown that the ballots undercounted by the voting machines contained enough "legal votes" to place "the results" of the election "in doubt." Since only a few hundred votes separated the candidates, and since the "undercounted" ballots numbered tens of thousands, it is difficult to see how anyone could find this conclusion unreasonable—however strict the standard used to measure the voter's "clear intent." Nor did this conclusion "strip" canvassing boards of their discretion. The boards retain their traditional discretionary authority during the protest period. And during the contest period, as the court stated, "the Canvassing Board's actions [during the protest period] may constitute evidence that a ballot does or does not qualify as a legal vote." *Id.,* at *13. Whether a local county canvassing board's discretionary judgment during the protest period not to conduct a manual recount will be set aside during a contest period depends upon whether a candidate provides additional evidence that the rejected votes contain enough "legal votes" to place the outcome of the race in doubt. To limit the local canvassing board's discretion in this way is not to eliminate that discretion. At the least, one could reasonably so believe.

The statute goes on to provide the Florida circuit judge with authority to "fashion such orders as he or she deems necessary to ensure that each allegation . . . is *investigated, examined, or checked*, . . . and to provide any relief appropriate." Fla. Stat. §102.168(8) (2000) (emphasis added). The Florida Supreme Court did just that. One might reasonably disagree with the Florida Supreme Court's interpretation of these, or other, words in the statute. But I do not see how one could call its plain language interpretation of a 1999 statutory change so misguided as no longer to qualify as judicial interpretation or as a usurpation of the authority of the State legislature. Indeed, other state courts have interpreted roughly similar state statutes in similar ways. See, *e.g., In re Election of U.S. Representative for Second Congressional Dist.*, 231 Conn. 602, 621, 653 A. 2d 79, 90–91 (1994) ("Whatever the process used to vote and to count votes, differences in technology should not furnish a basis for disregarding the bedrock principle that the purpose of the voting process is to ascertain the intent of the voters"); *Brown* v. *Carr*, 130 W. Va. 401, 460, 43 S. E.2d 401, 404–405 (1947) ("[W]hether a ballot shall be counted . . . depends on the intent of the voter . . . . Courts decry any resort to technical rules in reaching a conclusion as to the intent of the voter").

I repeat, where is the "impermissible" distortion?

II

Despite the reminder that this case involves "an election for the President of the United States," *ante*, at 1 (Rehnquist, C. J., concurring), no preeminent legal concern, or practical concern related to legal questions, required this Court to hear this case, let alone to issue a stay that stopped Florida's recount process in its tracks. With one exception, petitioners' claims do not ask us to vindicate a constitutional provision designed to protect a basic human right. See, e.g., *Brown* v. *Board of Education*, 347 U.S. 483 (1954). Petitioners invoke fundamental fairness, namely, the need for procedural fairness, including finality. But with the one "equal protection" exception, they rely upon law that focuses, not upon that basic need, but upon the constitutional allocation of power. Respondents invoke a competing fundamental consideration—the need to determine the voter's true intent. But they look to state law, not to federal constitutional law, to protect that interest. Neither side claims electoral fraud, dishonesty, or the like. And the more fundamental equal protection claim might have been left to the state court to resolve if and when it was discovered to have mattered. It could still be resolved through a remand conditioned upon issuance of a uniform standard; it does not require reversing the Florida Supreme Court.

Of course, the selection of the President is of fundamental national importance. But that importance is political, not legal. And this Court should resist the temptation unnecessarily to resolve tangential legal disputes, where doing so threatens to determine the outcome of the election.

The Constitution and federal statutes themselves make clear that restraint is appropriate. They set forth a road map of how to resolve disputes about electors, even after an election as close as this one. That road map foresees resolution of electoral disputes by *state* courts. See 3 U.S.C. § 5 (providing that, where a "State shall have provided, by laws enacted prior to [election day], for its final determination of any controversy or contest concerning the appointment of . . . electors . . . by *judicial* or other methods," the subsequently chosen electors enter a safe harbor free from congressional challenge). But it nowhere provides for involvement by the United States Supreme Court.

To the contrary, the Twelfth Amendment commits to Congress the authority and responsibility to count electoral votes. A federal statute, the Electoral Count Act, enacted after the close 1876 Hayes-Tilden Presidential election, specifies that, after States have tried to resolve disputes (through "judicial" or other means), Congress is the body primarily authorized to resolve remaining disputes. See Electoral Count Act of 1887, 24 Stat. 373, 3 U.S.C. § 5 6, and 15.

The legislative history of the Act makes clear its intent to commit the power to resolve such disputes to Congress, rather than the courts:

"The two Houses are, by the Constitution, authorized to make the count of electoral votes. They can only count legal votes, and in doing so must determine, from the best evidence to be had, what are legal votes. . . . The power to determine rests with the two Houses, and there is no other constitutional tribunal." H. Rep. No. 1638, 49th Cong., 1st Sess., 2 (1886) (report submitted by Rep. Caldwell, Select Committee on the Election of President and Vice-President).

The Member of Congress who introduced the Act added:

"The power to judge of the legality of the votes is a necessary consequent of the power to count. The existence of this power is of absolute necessity to the preservation of the Government. The interests of all the States in their relations to each other in the Federal Union demand that the ultimate tribunal to decide upon the election of President should be a constituent body, in which the States in their federal relationships and the people in their sovereign capacity should be represented." 18 Cong. Rec. 30 (1886).

"Under the Constitution who else could decide? Who is nearer to the State in determining a question of vital importance to the whole union of States than the constituent body upon whom the Constitution has devolved the duty to count the vote?" *Id.,* at 31.

The Act goes on to set out rules for the congressional determination of disputes about those votes. If, for example, a state submits a single slate of electors, Congress must count those votes unless both Houses agree that the votes "have not been . . . regularly given." 3 U.S.C. § 15. If, as occurred in 1876, one or more states submits two sets of electors, then Congress must determine whether a slate has entered the safe harbor of §5, in which case its votes will have "conclusive" effect. *Ibid.* If, as also occurred in 1876, there is controversy about "which of two or more of such State authorities . . . is the lawful tribunal" authorized to appoint electors, then each House shall determine separately which votes are "supported by the decision of such State so authorized by its law." *Ibid.* If the two Houses of Congress agree, the votes they have approved will be counted. If they disagree, then "the votes of the electors whose appointment shall have been certified by the executive of the State, under the seal thereof, shall be counted." *Ibid.*

Given this detailed, comprehensive scheme for counting electoral votes, there is no reason to believe that federal law either foresees or requires resolution of such a political issue by this Court. Nor, for that matter, is there any reason to that think the Constitution's Framers would have reached a different conclusion. Madison, at least, believed that allowing the judiciary to choose the presidential electors "was out of the question." Madison, July 25, 1787 (reprinted in 5 Elliot's Debates on the Federal Constitution 363 (2d ed. 1876)).

The decision by both the Constitution's Framers and the 1886 Congress to minimize this Court's role in resolving close federal presidential elections is as wise as it is clear. However awkward or difficult it may be for Congress to resolve difficult electoral disputes, Congress, being a political body, expresses the people's will far more accurately than does an unelected Court. And the people's will is what elections are about.

Moreover, Congress was fully aware of the danger that would arise should it ask judges, unarmed with appropriate legal standards, to resolve a hotly contested Presidential election contest. Just after the 1876 Presidential election, Florida, South Carolina, and Louisiana each sent two slates of electors to Washington. Without these States, Tilden, the Democrat, had 184 electoral votes, one short of the number required to win the Presidency. With those States, Hayes, his Republican opponent, would have had 185. In order to choose between the two slates of electors, Congress decided to appoint an electoral commission composed of five Senators, five Representatives, and five Supreme Court Justices. Initially the Commission was to be evenly divided between Republicans and Democrats, with Justice David Davis, an Independent, to possess the decisive vote. However, when at the last minute the Illinois Legislature elected Justice Davis to the United States Senate, the final position on the Commission was filled by Supreme Court Justice Joseph P. Bradley.

The Commission divided along partisan lines, and the responsibility to cast the deciding vote fell to Justice Bradley. He decided to accept the votes by the Republican electors, and thereby awarded the Presidency to Hayes.

Justice Bradley immediately became the subject of vociferous attacks. Bradley was accused of accepting bribes, of being captured by railroad interests, and of an eleventh-hour change in position after a night in which his house "was surrounded by the carriages" of Republican partisans and railroad officials. C. Woodward, Reunion and Reaction 159–160 (1966). Many years later, Professor Bickel concluded that Bradley was honest and impartial. He thought that "'the great question' for Bradley was, in fact, whether Congress was entitled to go behind election returns or had to accept them as certified by state authorities," an "issue of principle." The Least Dangerous Branch 185 (1962). Nonetheless, Bickel points out, the legal question upon which Justice Bradley's decision turned was not very important in the contemporaneous political context. He says that "in the circumstances the issue of principle was trivial, it was overwhelmed by all that hung in the balance, and it should not have been decisive." *Ibid.*

For present purposes, the relevance of this history lies in the fact that the participation in the work of the electoral commission by five Justices, including Justice Bradley, did not lend that process legitimacy. Nor did it assure the public that the process had worked fairly, guided by the law. Rather, it simply embroiled Members of the Court in partisan conflict, thereby undermining respect for the judicial process. And the Congress that later enacted the Electoral Count Act knew it.

This history may help to explain why I think it not only legally wrong, but also most unfortunate, for the Court simply to have terminated the Florida recount. Those who caution judicial restraint in resolving political disputes have described the quintessential case for that restraint as a case marked, among other things, by the "strangeness of the issue," its "intractability to principled resolution," its "sheer momentousness, . . . which tends to unbalance judicial judgment," and "the inner vulnerability, the self-doubt of an institution which is electorally irresponsible and has no earth to draw strength from." Bickel, *supra,* at 184. Those characteristics mark this case.

At the same time, as I have said, the Court is not acting to vindicate a fundamental constitutional principle, such as the need to protect a basic human liberty. No other strong reason to act is present. Congressional statutes tend to obviate the need. And, above all, in this highly politicized matter, the appearance of a split decision runs the risk of undermining the public's confidence in the Court itself. That confidence is a public treasure. It has been built slowly over many years, some of which were marked by a Civil War and the tragedy of segregation. It is a vitally necessary ingredient of any successful effort to protect basic liberty and, indeed, the rule of law itself. We run no risk of returning to the days when a President (responding to this Court's efforts to protect the Cherokee Indians) might have said, "John Marshall has made his decision; now let him enforce it!" Loth, Chief Justice John Marshall and The Growth of the American Republic 365 (1948). But we do risk a self-inflicted wound—a wound that may harm not just the Court, but the Nation.

I fear that in order to bring this agonizingly long election process to a definitive conclusion, we have not adequately attended to that necessary "check upon our own exercise of power," "our own sense of self-restraint." *United States* v. *Butler,* 297 U.S. 1, 79 (1936) (Stone, J., dissenting). Justice Brandeis once said of the Court, "The most important thing we do is not doing." Bickel, *supra,* at 71. What it does today, the Court should have left undone. I would repair the damage done as best we now can, by permitting the Florida recount to continue under uniform standards.

I respectfully dissent.

JUSTICE GINSBURG, WITH WHOM JUSTICE STEVENS JOINS, AND WITH WHOM JUSTICE SOUTER AND JUSTICE BREYER JOIN AS TO PART I, DISSENTING.

I

The Chief Justice acknowledges that provisions of Florida's Election Code "may well admit of more than one interpretation." *Ante,* at 3. But instead of respecting the state high court's province to say what the State's Election Code means, The Chief Justice maintains that Florida's Supreme Court has veered so far from the ordinary practice of judicial review that what it did cannot properly be called judging. My colleagues have offered a reasonable construction of Florida's law. Their construction coincides with the view of one of Florida's seven Supreme Court justices. *Gore* v. *Harris,* (Fla. 2000) (slip op., at 45–55) (Wells, C. J., dissenting); *Palm Beach County Canvassing Bd.* v. *Harris,* (Fla. 2000) (slip op., at 34) (on remand) (confirming, 6–1, the construction of Florida law advanced in *Gore*). I might join The Chief Justice were it my commission to interpret Florida law. But disagreement with the Florida court's interpretation of its own State's law does not warrant the conclusion that the justices of that court have legislated. There is no cause here to believe that the members of Florida's high court have done less than "their mortal best to discharge their oath of office," *Sumner* v. *Mata,* 449 U.S. 539, 549 (1981), and no cause to upset their reasoned interpretation of Florida law.

This Court more than occasionally affirms statutory, and even constitutional, interpretations with which it disagrees. For example, when reviewing challenges to administrative agencies' interpretations of laws they implement, we defer to the agencies unless their interpretation violates "the unambiguously expressed intent of Congress." *Chevron U.S. A. Inc.* v. *Natural Resources Defense Council, Inc.,* 467 U.S. 837, 843 (1984). We do so in the face of the declaration in Article I of the United States Constitution that "All legislative Powers herein granted shall be vested in a Congress of the United States." Surely the Constitution does not call upon us to pay more respect to a federal administrative agency's construction of federal law than to a state high court's interpretation of its own state's law. And not uncommonly, we let stand state-court interpretations of *federal* law with which we might disagree. Notably, in the habeas context, the Court adheres to the view that "there is 'no intrinsic reason why the fact that a man is a federal judge should make him more competent, or conscientious, or learned with respect to [federal law] than his neighbor in the state courthouse'." *Stone* v. *Powell,* 428 U.S. 465, 494, n. 35 (1976) (quoting Bator, Finality in Criminal Law and Federal Habeas Corpus For State Prisoners, 76 Harv. L. Rev. 441, 509 (1963)); see *O'Dell* v. *Netherland,* 521 U.S. 151, 156 (1997) ("[T]he *Teague* doctrine validates reasonable, good-faith interpretations of existing precedents made by state courts even though they are shown to be contrary to later decisions.") (citing *Butler* v. *McKellar,* 494 U.S. 407, 414 (1990)); O'Connor, Trends in the Relationship Between the Federal and State Courts from the Perspective of a State Court Judge, 22 Wm. & Mary L. Rev. 801, 813 (1981) ("There is no reason to assume that state court judges cannot and will not provide a 'hospitable forum' in litigating federal constitutional questions.").

No doubt there are cases in which the proper application of federal law may hinge on interpretations of state law. Unavoidably, this Court must sometimes examine state law in order to protect federal rights. But we have dealt with such cases ever mindful of the full measure of respect we owe to interpretations of state law by a State's highest court. In the Contract Clause case, *General Motors Corp.* v. *Romein,* 503 U.S. 181 (1992), for example, we said that although "ultimately we are bound to decide for ourselves whether a contract was made," the Court "accord[s] respectful consideration and great weight to the views of the State's highest court." *Id.,* at 187 (citation omitted). And in *Central Union Telephone Co.* v. *Edwardsville,* 269 U.S. 190 (1925), we upheld the Illinois Supreme Court's interpretation of a state waiver rule, even though that interpretation resulted in the forfeiture of federal constitutional rights. Refusing to supplant Illinois law with a federal definition of waiver, we explained that the state court's declaration "should bind us unless so unfair or unreasonable in its application to those asserting a federal right as to obstruct it." *Id.,* at 195.[1]

In deferring to state courts on matters of state law, we appropriately recognize that this Court acts as an "'outside[r]' lacking the common exposure to local law which comes from sitting in the jurisdiction." *Lehman Brothers* v. *Schein,* 416 U.S. 386, 391 (1974). That recognition has sometimes prompted us to resolve doubts about the meaning of state law by certifying issues to a State's highest court, even when federal rights are at stake. Cf. *Arizonans for Official English* v. *Arizona,* 520 U.S. 43, 79 (1997) ("Warnings against premature adjudication of constitutional questions bear heightened attention when a federal court is asked to invalidate a State's law, for the federal tribunal risks friction-generating error when it endeavors to construe a novel state Act not yet reviewed by the State's highest court."). Notwithstanding our authority to decide issues of state law underlying federal claims, we have used the certification devise to afford state high courts an opportunity to inform us on matters of their own State's law because such restraint "helps build a cooperative judicial federalism." *Lehman Brothers,* 416 U.S., at 391.

Just last Term, in *Fiore* v. *White,* 528 U.S. 23 (1999), we took advantage of Pennsylvania's certification procedure. In that case, a state prisoner brought a federal habeas action claiming that the State had failed to prove an essential element of his charged offense in violation of the Due Process Clause. *Id.,* at 25–26. Instead of resolving the state-law question on which the federal claim depended, we certified the question to the Pennsylvania Supreme Court for that court to "help determine the proper state-law predicate for our determination of the federal constitutional questions raised." *Id.,* at 29; *id.,* at 28 (asking the Pennsylvania Supreme Court whether its recent interpretation of the statute under which Fiore was convicted "was always the statute's meaning, even at the time of Fiore's trial"). The Chief Justice's willingness to *reverse* the Florida Supreme Court's interpretation of Florida law in this case is at least in tension with our reluctance in *Fiore* even to interpret Pennsylvania law before seeking instruction from the Pennsylvania Supreme Court. I would have thought the "cautious approach" we counsel when federal courts address matters of state law, *Arizonans,* 520 U.S., at 77, and our commitment to "build[ing] cooperative judicial federalism," *Lehman Brothers,* 416 U.S., at 391, demanded greater restraint.

Rarely has this Court rejected outright an interpretation of state law by a state high court. *Fairfax's Devisee* v. *Hunter's Lessee*, 7 Cranch 603 (1813), *NAACP* v. *Alabama ex rel. Patterson*, 357 U.S. 449 (1958), and *Bouie* v. *City of Columbia*, 378 U.S. 347 (1964), cited by The Chief Justice, are three such rare instances. See *ante*, at 4, 5, and n. 2. But those cases are embedded in historical contexts hardly comparable to the situation here. *Fairfax's Devisee*, which held that the Virginia Court of Appeals had misconstrued its own forfeiture laws to deprive a British subject of lands secured to him by federal treaties, occurred amidst vociferous States' rights attacks on the Marshall Court. G. Gunther & K. Sullivan, Constitutional Law 61–62 (13th ed. 1997). The Virginia court refused to obey this Court's *Fairfax's Devisee* mandate to enter judgment for the British subject's successor in interest. That refusal led to the Court's pathmarking decision in *Martin* v. *Hunter's Lessee*, 1 Wheat. 304 (1816). *Patterson*, a case decided three months after *Cooper* v. *Aaron*, 358 U.S. 1 (1958), in the face of Southern resistance to the civil rights movement, held that the Alabama Supreme Court had irregularly applied its own procedural rules to deny review of a contempt order against the NAACP arising from its refusal to disclose membership lists. We said that "our jurisdiction is not defeated if the nonfederal ground relied on by the state court is without any fair or substantial support." 357 U.S., at 455. *Bouie*, stemming from a lunch counter "sit-in" at the height of the civil rights movement, held that the South Carolina Supreme Court's construction of its trespass laws—criminalizing conduct not covered by the text of an otherwise clear statute—was "unforeseeable" and thus violated due process when applied retroactively to the petitioners. 378 U.S., at 350, 354.

The Chief Justice's casual citation of these cases might lead one to believe they are part of a larger collection of cases in which we said that the Constitution impelled us to train a skeptical eye on a state court's portrayal of state law. But one would be hard pressed, I think, to find additional cases that fit the mold. As Justice Breyer convincingly explains, see *post*, at 5–9 (dissenting opinion), this case involves nothing close to the kind of recalcitrance by a state high court that warrants extraordinary action by this Court. The Florida Supreme Court concluded that counting every legal vote was the overriding concern of the Florida Legislature when it enacted the State's Election Code. The court surely should not be bracketed with state high courts of the Jim Crow South.

The Chief Justice says that Article II, by providing that state legislatures shall direct the manner of appointing electors, authorizes federal superintendence over the relationship between state courts and state legislatures, and licenses a departure from the usual deference we give to state court interpretations of state law. *Ante*, at 5 ("To attach definitive weight to the pronouncement of a state court, when the very question at issue is whether the court has actually departed from the statutory meaning, would be to abdicate our responsibility to enforce the explicit requirements of Article II."). The Framers of our Constitution, however, understood that in a republican government, the judiciary would construe the legislature's enactments. See U.S. Const., Art. III; The Federalist No. 78 (A. Hamilton). In light of the constitutional guarantee to States of a "Republican Form of Government," U.S. Const., Art. IV, §4, Article II can hardly be read to invite this Court to disrupt a State's republican regime. Yet, the Chief Justice today would reach out to do just that. By holding that Article II requires our revision of a state court's construction of state laws in order to protect one organ of the State from another, The Chief Justice contradicts the basic principle that a State may organize itself as it sees fit. See, e.g., *Gregory* v. *Ashcroft,* 501 U.S. 452, 460 (1991) ("Through the structure of its government, and the character of those who exercise government authority, a State defines itself as a sovereign."); *Highland Farms Dairy, Inc.* v. *Agnew,* 300 U.S. 608, 612 (1937) ("How power shall be distributed by a state among its governmental organs is commonly, if not always, a question for the state itself.").[2] Article II does not call for the scrutiny undertaken by this Court.

The extraordinary setting of this case has obscured the ordinary principle that dictates its proper resolution: Federal courts defer to state high courts' interpretations of their state's own law. This principle reflects the core of federalism, on which all agree. "The Framers split the atom of sovereignty. It was the genius of their idea that our citizens would have two political capacities, one state and one federal, each protected from incursion by the other." *Saenz* v. *Roe,* 526 U.S. 489, 504, n. 17 (1999) (citing *U.S. Term Limits, Inc.* v. *Thornton,* 514 U.S. 779, 838 (1995) (Kennedy, J., concurring)). The Chief Justice's solicitude for the Florida Legislature comes at the expense of the more fundamental solicitude we owe to the legislature's sovereign. U.S. Const., Art. II, §1, cl. 2 ("Each *State* shall appoint, in such Manner as the Legislature *thereof* may direct," the electors for President and Vice President) (emphasis added); *ante,* at 1–2 (Stevens, J., dissenting).[3] Were the other members of this Court as mindful as they generally are of our system of dual sovereignty, they would affirm the judgment of the Florida Supreme Court.

II

I agree with Justice Stevens that petitioners have not presented a substantial equal protection claim. Ideally, perfection would be the appropriate standard for judging the recount. But we live in an imperfect world, one in which thousands of votes have not been counted. I cannot agree that the recount adopted by the Florida court, flawed as it may be, would yield a result any less fair or precise than the certification that preceded that recount. See, *e.g., McDonald* v. *Board of Election Commissioners of Chicago,* 394 U.S. 802, 807 (1969) (even in the context of the right to vote, the state is permitted to reform "'one step at a time'") (quoting *Williamson* v. *Lee Optical of Oklahoma, Inc.,* 348 U.S. 483, 489 (1955)).

Even if there were an equal protection violation, I would agree with Justice Stevens, Justice Souter, and Justice Breyer that the Court's concern about "the December 12 deadline," *ante,* at 12, is misplaced. Time is short in part because of the Court's entry of a stay on December 9, several hours after an able circuit judge in Leon County had begun to superintend the recount process. More fundamentally, the Court's reluctance to let the recount go forward—despite its suggestion that "[t]he search for intent can be confined by specific rules designed to ensure uniform treatment," *ante,* at 8—ultimately turns on its own judgment about the practical realities of implementing a recount, not the judgment of those much closer to the process.

Equally important, as Justice Breyer explains, *post,* at 12 (dissenting opinion), the December 12 "deadline" for bringing Florida's electoral votes into 3 U.S.C. § 5's safe harbor lacks the significance the Court assigns it. Were that date to pass, Florida would still be entitled to deliver electoral votes Congress *must* count unless both Houses find that the votes "ha[d] not been . . . regularly given." 3 U.S.C. § 15. The statute identifies other significant dates. See, *e.g.,* §7 (specifying December 18 as the date electors "shall meet and give their votes"); §12 (specifying "the fourth Wednesday in December"—this year, December 27—as the date on which Congress, if it has not received a State's electoral votes, shall request the state secretary of state to send a certified return immediately). But none of these dates has ultimate significance in light of Congress' detailed provisions for determining, on "the sixth day of January," the validity of electoral votes. §15.

The Court assumes that time will not permit "orderly judicial review of any disputed matters that might arise." *Ante,* at 12. But no one has doubted the good faith and diligence with which Florida election officials, attorneys for all sides of this controversy, and the courts of law have performed their duties. Notably, the Florida Supreme Court has produced two substantial opinions within 29 hours of oral argument. In sum, the Court's conclusion that a constitutionally adequate recount is impractical is a prophecy the Court's own judgment will not allow to be tested. Such an untested prophecy should not decide the Presidency of the United States.

I dissent.

NOTES

1 See also *Lucas* v. *South Carolina Coastal Council,* 505 U.S. 1003, 1032, n. 18 (1992) (South Carolina could defend a regulatory taking "if an *objectively reasonable application* of relevant precedents [by its courts] would exclude . . . beneficial uses in the circumstances in which the land is presently found"); *Bishop* v. *Wood,* 426 U.S. 341, 344–345 (1976) (deciding whether North Carolina had created a property interest cognizable under the Due Process Clause by reference to state law as interpreted by the North Carolina Supreme Court). Similarly, in *Gurley* v. *Rhoden,* 421 U.S. 200 (1975), a gasoline retailer claimed that due process entitled him to deduct a state gasoline excise tax in computing the amount of his sales subject to a state sales tax, on the grounds that the legal incidence of the excise tax fell on his customers and that he acted merely as a collector of the tax. The Mississippi Supreme Court held that the legal incidence of the excise tax fell on petitioner. Observing that "a State's highest court is the final judicial arbiter of the meaning of state statutes," we said that "[w]hen a state court has made its own definitive determination as to the operating incidence, . . . [w]e give this finding great weight in determining the natural effect of a statute, and if it is consistent with the statute's reasonable interpretation it will be deemed conclusive." *Id.,* at 208.

2 Even in the rare case in which a State's "manner" of making and construing laws might implicate a structural constraint, Congress, not this Court, is likely the proper governmental entity to enforce that constraint. See U.S. Const., amend. XII; 3 U.S.C. § 1–15; cf. *Ohio ex rel. Davis* v. *Hildebrant,* 241 U.S. 565, 569 (1916) (treating as a nonjusticiable political question whether use of a referendum to override a congressional districting plan enacted by the state legislature violates Art. I, §4); *Luther* v. *Borden,* 7 How. 1, 42 (1849).

3 "[B]ecause the Framers recognized that state power and identity were essential parts of the federal balance, see The Federalist No. 39, the Constitution is solicitous of the prerogatives of the States, even in an otherwise sovereign federal province. The Constitution . . . grants States certain powers over the times, places, and manner of federal elections (subject to congressional revision), Art. I, §4, cl. 1 . . . , and allows States to appoint electors for the President, Art. II, §1, cl. 2." *U.S. Term Limits, Inc.* v. *Thornton,* 514 U.S. 779, 841–842 (1995) (Kennedy, J., concurring).

JUSTICE SOUTER, WITH WHOM JUSTICE BREYER JOINS AND WITH WHOM JUSTICE STEVENS AND JUSTICE GINSBURG JOIN WITH REGARD TO ALL BUT PART C, DISSENTING.

The Court should not have reviewed either *Bush* v. *Palm Beach County Canvassing Bd., ante,* (*per curiam*), or this case, and should not have stopped Florida's attempt to recount all undervote ballots, by issuing a stay of the Florida Supreme Court's orders during the period of this review, see *Bush* v. *Gore.* If this Court had allowed the State to follow the course indicated by the opinions of its own Supreme Court, it is entirely possible that there would ultimately have been no issue requiring our review, and political tension could have worked itself out in the Congress following the procedure provided in 3 U.S.C. § 15. The case being before us, however, its resolution by the majority is another erroneous decision.

As will be clear, I am in substantial agreement with the dissenting opinions of Justice Stevens, Justice Ginsburg and Justice Breyer. I write separately only to say how straightforward the issues before us really are.

There are three issues: whether the State Supreme Court's interpretation of the statute providing for a contest of the state election results somehow violates 3 U.S.C. § 5; whether that court's construction of the state statutory provisions governing contests impermissibly changes a state law from what the State's legislature has provided, in violation of Article II, §1, cl. 2, of the national Constitution; and whether the manner of interpreting markings on disputed ballots failing to cause machines to register votes for President (the undervote ballots) violates the equal protection or due process guaranteed by the Fourteenth Amendment. None of these issues is difficult to describe or to resolve.

A

The 3 U.S.C. § 5 issue is not serious. That provision sets certain conditions for treating a State's certification of Presidential electors as conclusive in the event that a dispute over recognizing those electors must be resolved in the Congress under 3 U.S.C. § 15. Conclusiveness requires selection under a legal scheme in place before the election, with results determined at least six days before the date set for casting electoral votes. But no State is required to conform to §5 if it cannot do that (for whatever reason); the sanction for failing to satisfy the conditions of §5 is simply loss of what has been called its "safe harbor." And even that determination is to be made, if made anywhere, in the Congress.

B

The second matter here goes to the State Supreme Court's interpretation of certain terms in the state statute governing election "contests," Fla. Stat. §102.168 (2000); there is no question here about the state court's interpretation of the related provisions dealing with the antecedent process of "protesting" particular vote counts, §102.166, which was involved in the previous case, *Bush* v. *Palm Beach County Canvassing Board*. The issue is whether the judgment of the state supreme court has displaced the state legislature's provisions for election contests: is the law as declared by the court different from the provisions made by the legislature, to which the national Constitution commits responsibility for determining how each State's Presidential electors are chosen? See U.S. Const., Art. II, §1, cl. 2. Bush does not, of course, claim that any judicial act interpreting a statute of uncertain meaning is enough to displace the legislative provision and violate Article II; statutes require interpretation, which does not without more affect the legislative character of a statute within the meaning of the Constitution. Brief for Petitioners 48, n. 22, in *Bush* v. *Palm Beach County Canvassing Bd., et al.,* 531 U.S. ___ (2000). What Bush does argue, as I understand the contention, is that the interpretation of §102.168 was so unreasonable as to transcend the accepted bounds of statutory interpretation, to the point of being a nonjudicial act and producing new law untethered to the legislative act in question.

The starting point for evaluating the claim that the Florida Supreme Court's interpretation effectively re-wrote §102.168 must be the language of the provision on which Gore relies to show his right to raise this contest: that the previously certified result in Bush's favor was produced by "rejection of a number of legal votes sufficient to change or place in doubt the result of the election." Fla. Stat. §102.168(3)(c) (2000). None of the state court's interpretations is unreasonable to the point of displacing the legislative enactment quoted. As I will note below, other interpretations were of course possible, and some might have been better than those adopted by the Florida court's majority; the two dissents from the majority opinion of that court and various briefs submitted to us set out alternatives. But the majority view is in each instance within the bounds of reasonable interpretation, and the law as declared is consistent with Article II.

1) The statute does not define a "legal vote," the rejection of which may affect the election. The State Supreme Court was therefore required to define it, and in doing that the court looked to another election statute, §101.5614(5), dealing with damaged or defective ballots, which contains a provision that no vote shall be disregarded "if there is a clear indication of the intent of the voter as determined by a canvassing board." The court read that objective of looking to the voter's intent as indicating that the legislature probably meant "legal vote" to mean a vote recorded on a ballot indicating what the voter intended. *Gore* v. *Harris* (Dec. 8, 2000). It is perfectly true that the majority might have chosen a different reading. See, *e.g.,* Brief for Respondent Harris et al. 10 (defining "legal votes" as "votes properly executed in accordance with the instructions provided to all

registered voters in advance of the election and in the polling places"). But even so, there is no constitutional violation in following the majority view; Article II is unconcerned with mere disagreements about interpretive merits.

2) The Florida court next interpreted "rejection" to determine what act in the counting process may be attacked in a contest. Again, the statute does not define the term. The court majority read the word to mean simply a failure to count. That reading is certainly within the bounds of common sense, given the objective to give effect to a voter's intent if that can be determined. A different reading, of course, is possible. The majority might have concluded that "rejection" should refer to machine malfunction, or that a ballot should not be treated as "reject[ed]" in the absence of wrongdoing by election officials, lest contests be so easy to claim that every election will end up in one. Cf. *id.* (Wells, C. J., dissenting). There is, however, nothing nonjudicial in the Florida majority's more hospitable reading.

3) The same is true about the court majority's understanding of the phrase "votes sufficient to change or place in doubt" the result of the election in Florida. The court held that if the uncounted ballots were so numerous that it was reasonably possible that they contained enough "legal" votes to swing the election, this contest would be authorized by the statute.[1] While the majority might have thought (as the trial judge did) that a probability, not a possibility, should be necessary to justify a contest, that reading is not required by the statute's text, which says nothing about probability. Whatever people of good will and good sense may argue about the merits of the Florida court's reading, there is no warrant for saying that it transcends the limits of reasonable statutory interpretation to the point of supplanting the statute enacted by the "legislature" within the meaning of Article II.

In sum, the interpretations by the Florida court raise no substantial question under Article II. That court engaged in permissible construction in determining that Gore had instituted a contest authorized by the state statute, and it proceeded to direct the trial judge to deal with that contest in the exercise of the discretionary powers generously conferred by Fla. Stat. §102.168(8) (2000), to "fashion such orders as he or she deems necessary to ensure that each allegation in the complaint is investigated, examined, or checked, to prevent or correct any alleged wrong, and to provide any relief appropriate under such circumstances." As Justice Ginsburg has persuasively explained in her own dissenting opinion, our customary respect for state interpretations of state law counsels against rejection of the Florida court's determinations in this case.

C

It is only on the third issue before us that there is a meritorious argument for relief, as this Court's *Per Curiam* opinion recognizes. It is an issue that might well have been dealt with adequately by the Florida courts if the state proceedings had not been interrupted, and if not disposed of at the state level it could have been considered by the Congress in any electoral vote dispute. But because the course of state proceedings has been interrupted, time is short, and the issue is before us, I think it sensible for the Court to address it.

Petitioners have raised an equal protection claim (or, alternatively, a due process claim, see generally *Logan* v. *Zimmerman Brush Co.*, 455 U.S. 422 (1982)), in the charge that unjustifiably disparate standards are applied in different electoral jurisdictions to otherwise identical facts. It is true that the Equal Protection Clause does not forbid the use of a variety of voting mechanisms within a jurisdiction, even though different mechanisms will have different levels of effectiveness in recording voters' intentions; local variety can be justified by concerns about cost, the potential value of innovation, and so on. But evidence in the record here suggests that a different order of disparity obtains under rules for determining a voter's intent that have been applied (and could continue to be applied) to identical types of ballots used in identical brands of machines and exhibiting identical physical characteristics (such as "hanging" or "dimpled" chads). See, *e.g.*, Tr., at 238–242 (Dec. 2–3, 2000) (testimony of Palm Beach County Canvassing Board Chairman Judge Charles Burton describing varying standards applied to imperfectly punched ballots in Palm Beach County during precertification manual recount); *id.*, at 497–500 (similarly describing varying standards applied in Miami-Dade County); Tr. of Hearing 8–10 (Dec. 8, 2000) (soliciting from county canvassing boards proposed protocols for determining voters' intent but declining to provide a precise, uniform standard). I can conceive of no legitimate state interest served by these differing treatments of the expressions of voters' fundamental rights. The differences appear wholly arbitrary.

In deciding what to do about this, we should take account of the fact that electoral votes are due to be cast in six days. I would therefore remand the case to the courts of Florida with instructions to establish uniform standards for evaluating the several types of ballots that have prompted differing treatments, to be applied within and among counties when passing on such identical ballots in any further recounting (or successive recounting) that the courts might order.

Unlike the majority, I see no warrant for this Court to assume that Florida could not possibly comply with this requirement before the date set for the meeting of electors, December 18. Although one of the dissenting justices of the State Supreme Court estimated that disparate standards potentially affected 170,000 votes, *Gore* v. *Harris, supra,* the number at issue is significantly smaller. The 170,000 figure apparently represents all uncounted votes, both undervotes (those for which no Presidential choice was recorded by a machine) and overvotes (those rejected because of votes for more than one candidate). Tr. of Oral Arg. 61–62. But as Justice Breyer has pointed out, no showing has been made of legal overvotes uncounted, and counsel for Gore made an uncontradicted representation to the Court that the statewide total of undervotes is about 60,000. *Id.,* at 62. To recount these manually would be a tall order, but before this Court stayed the effort to do that the courts of Florida were ready to do their best to get that job done. There is no justification for denying the State the opportunity to try to count all disputed ballots now.

I respectfully dissent.

NOTES

<u>1</u> When the Florida court ruled, the totals for Bush and Gore were then less than 1,000 votes apart. One dissent pegged the number of uncounted votes in question at 170,000. *Gore* v. *Harris, supra* (opinion of Harding, J.). Gore's counsel represented to us that the relevant figure is approximately 60,000, Tr. of Oral Arg. 62, the number of ballots in which no vote for President was recorded by the machines.

JUSTICE STEVENS, WITH WHOM JUSTICE GINSBURG AND JUSTICE BREYER JOIN, DISSENTING

The Constitution assigns to the States the primary responsibility for determining the manner of selecting the Presidential electors. See Art. II, §1, cl. 2. When questions arise about the meaning of state laws, including election laws, it is our settled practice to accept the opinions of the highest courts of the States as providing the final answers. On rare occasions, however, either federal statutes or the Federal Constitution may require federal judicial intervention in state elections. This is not such an occasion.

The federal questions that ultimately emerged in this case are not substantial. Article II provides that "[e]ach *State* shall appoint, in such Manner as the Legislature *thereof* may direct, a Number of Electors." *Ibid.* (emphasis added). It does not create state legislatures out of whole cloth, but rather takes them as they comeñas creatures born of, and constrained by, their state constitutions. Lest there be any doubt, we stated over 100 years ago in *McPherson* v. *Blacker,* 146 U.S. 1, 25 (1892), that "[w]hat is forbidden or required to be done by a State" in the Article II context "is forbidden or required of the legislative power under state constitutions as they exist." In the same vein, we also observed that "[t]he [State's] legislative power is the supreme authority except as limited by the constitution of the State." *Ibid.*; cf. *Smiley* v. *Holm,* 285 U.S. 355, 367 (1932).[1] The legislative power in Florida is subject to judicial review pursuant to Article V of the Florida Constitution, and nothing in Article II of the Federal Constitution frees the state legislature from the constraints in the state constitution that created it. Moreover, the Florida Legislature's own decision to employ a unitary code for all elections indicates that it intended the Florida Supreme Court to play the same role in Presidential elections that it has historically played in resolving electoral disputes. The Florida Supreme Court's exercise of appellate jurisdiction therefore was wholly consistent with, and indeed contemplated by, the grant of authority in Article II.

It hardly needs stating that Congress, pursuant to 3 U.S.C. § 5 did not impose any affirmative duties upon the States that their governmental branches could "violate." Rather, §5 provides a safe harbor for States to select electors in contested elections "by judicial or other methods" established by laws prior to the election day. Section 5, like Article II, assumes the involvement of the state judiciary in interpreting state election laws and resolving election disputes under those laws. Neither §5 nor Article II grants federal judges any special authority to substitute their views for those of the state judiciary on matters of state law.

Nor are petitioners correct in asserting that the failure of the Florida Supreme Court to specify in detail the precise manner in which the "intent of the voter," Fla. Stat. §101.5614(5) (Supp. 2001), is to be determined rises to the level of a constitutional violation.[2] We found such a violation when individual votes within the same State were weighted unequally, see, *e.g., Reynolds* v. *Sims,* 377 U.S. 533, 568 (1964), but we have never before called into question the substantive standard by which a State determines that a vote has been legally cast. And there is no reason to think that the guidance provided to the factfinders, specifically the various canvassing boards, by the "intent of the voter" standard is any less sufficient— or will lead to results any less uniform—than, for example, the "beyond a reasonable doubt" standard employed everyday by ordinary citizens in courtrooms across this country.[3]

Admittedly, the use of differing substandards for determining voter intent in different counties employing similar voting systems may raise serious concerns. Those concerns are alleviated—if not eliminated—by the fact that a single impartial magistrate will ultimately adjudicate all objections arising from the recount process. Of course, as a general matter, "[t]he interpretation of constitutional principles must not be too literal. We must remember that the machinery of government would not work if it were not allowed a little play in its joints." *Bain Peanut Co. of Tex. v. Pinson,* 282 U.S. 499, 501 (1931) (Holmes, J.). If it were otherwise, Florida's decision to leave to each county the determination of what balloting system to employ—despite enormous differences in accuracy[4]— might run afoul of equal protection. So, too, might the similar decisions of the vast majority of state legislatures to delegate to local authorities certain decisions with respect to voting systems and ballot design.

Even assuming that aspects of the remedial scheme might ultimately be found to violate the Equal Protection Clause, I could not subscribe to the majority's disposition of the case. As the majority explicitly holds, once a state legislature determines to select electors through a popular vote, the right to have one's vote counted is of constitutional stature. As the majority further acknowledges, Florida law holds that all ballots that reveal the intent of the voter constitute valid votes. Recognizing these principles, the majority nonetheless orders the termination of the contest proceeding before all such votes have been tabulated. Under their own reasoning, the appropriate course of action would be to remand to allow more specific procedures for implementing the legislature's uniform general standard to be established.

In the interest of finality, however, the majority effectively orders the disenfranchisement of an unknown number of voters whose ballots reveal their intent—and are therefore legal votes under state law—but were for some reason rejected by ballot-counting machines. It does so on the basis of the deadlines set forth in Title 3 of the United States Code. *Ante,* at 11. But, as I have already noted, those provisions merely provide rules of decision for Congress to follow when selecting among conflicting slates of electors. *Supra,* at 2. They do not prohibit a State from counting what the majority concedes to be legal votes until a bona fide winner is determined. Indeed, in 1960, Hawaii appointed two slates of electors and Congress chose to count the one appointed on January 4, 1961, well after the Title 3 deadlines. See Josephson & Ross, Repairing the Electoral College, 22 J. Legis. 145, 166, n. 154 (1996).[5] Thus, nothing prevents the majority, even if it properly found an equal protection violation, from ordering relief appropriate to remedy that violation without depriving Florida voters of their right to have their votes counted. As the majority notes, "[a] desire for speed is not a general excuse for ignoring equal protection guarantees." *Ante,* at 10.

Finally, neither in this case, nor in its earlier opinion in *Palm Beach County Canvassing Bd. v. Harris,* 2000 WL 1725434 (Fla., Nov. 21, 2000), did the Florida Supreme Court make any substantive change in Florida electoral law.[6] Its decisions were rooted in long-established precedent and were consistent with the relevant statutory provisions, taken as a whole. It did what courts do[7]—it decided the case before it in light of the legislature's intent to leave no legally cast vote uncounted. In so doing, it relied on the sufficiency of the general "intent of the voter" standard articulated by the state legislature, coupled with a procedure for ultimate review by an impartial judge, to resolve the concern about disparate evaluations of contested ballots. If we assume—as I do—that the members of that court and the judges who would have carried out its mandate are impartial, its decision does not even raise a colorable federal question.

What must underlie petitioners' entire federal assault on the Florida election procedures is an unstated lack of confidence in the impartiality and capacity of the state judges who would make the critical decisions if the vote count were to proceed. Otherwise, their position is wholly without merit. The endorsement of that position by the majority of this Court can only lend credence to the most cynical appraisal of the work of judges throughout the land. It is confidence in the men and women who administer the judicial system that is the true backbone of the rule of law. Time will one day heal the wound to that confidence that will be inflicted by today's decision. One thing, however, is certain. Although we may never know with complete certainty the identity of the winner of this year's Presidential election, the identity of the loser is perfectly clear. It is the Nation's confidence in the judge as an impartial guardian of the rule of law.

I respectfully dissent.

NOTES

1 "Wherever the term 'legislature' is used in the Constitution it is necessary to consider the nature of the particular action in view." 285 U.S., at 367. It is perfectly clear that the meaning of the words "Manner" and "Legislature" as used in Article II, §1, parallels the usage in Article I, §4, rather than the language in Article V. *U.S. Term Limits, Inc. v. Thornton,* 514 U.S. 779, 805 (1995). Article I, §4, and Article II, §1, both call upon legislatures to act in a lawmaking capacity whereas Article V simply calls on the legislative body to deliberate upon a binary decision. As a result, petitioners' reliance on *Leser v. Garnett,* 258 U.S. 130 (1922), and *Hawke v. Smith* (No. 1), 253 U.S. 221 (1920), is misplaced.

2 The Florida statutory standard is consistent with the practice of the majority of States, which apply either an "intent of the voter" standard or an "impossible to determine the elector's choice" standard in ballot recounts. The following States use an "intent of the voter" standard: Ariz. Rev. Stat. Ann. §16–645(A) (Supp. 2000) (standard for canvassing write-in votes); Conn. Gen. Stat. §9–150a(j) (1999) (standard for absentee ballots, including three conclusive presumptions); Ind. Code §3–12–1–1 (1992); Me. Rev. Stat. Ann., Tit. 21–A, §1(13) (1993); Md. Ann. Code, Art. 33, §11–302(d) (2000 Supp.) (standard for absentee ballots); Mass. Gen. Laws §70E (1991) (applying standard to Presidential primaries); Mich. Comp. Laws §168.799a(3) (Supp. 2000); Mo. Rev. Stat. §115.453(3) (Cum. Supp. 1998) (looking to voter's intent where there is substantial compliance with statutory requirements); Tex. Elec. Code Ann. §65.009(c) (1986); Utah Code Ann. §20A–4–104(5)(b) (Supp. 2000) (standard for write-in votes), §20A–4–105(6)(a) (standard for mechanical ballots); Vt. Stat. Ann., Tit. 17, §2587(a) (1982); Va. Code Ann. §24.2–644(A) (2000); Wash. Rev. Code §29.62.180(1) (Supp. 2001) (standard for write-in votes); Wyo. Stat. Ann. §22–14–104 (1999). The following States employ a standard in which a vote is counted unless it is "impossible to determine the elector's [or voter's] choice": Ala. Code §11–46–44(c) (1992), Ala. Code §17–13–2 (1995); Ariz. Rev. Stat. Ann. §16–610 (1996) (standard for rejecting ballot); Cal. Elec. Code Ann. §15154(c) (West Supp. 2000); Colo. Rev. Stat. §1–7–309(1) (1999) (standard for paper ballots), §1–7–508(2) (standard for electronic ballots); Del. Code Ann., Tit. 15, §4972(4) (1999); Idaho Code §34–1203 (1981); Ill. Comp. Stat., ch. 10, §5/7–51 (1993) (standard for primaries), *id.*, ch. 10, §5/17–16 (1993) (standard for general elections); Iowa Code §49.98 (1999); Me. Rev. Stat. Ann., Tit. 21–A §§696(2)(B), (4) (Supp. 2000); Minn. Stat. §204C.22(1) (1992); Mont. Code Ann. §13–15–202 (1997) (not counting votes if "elector's choice cannot be determined"); Nev. Rev. Stat. §293.367(d) (1995); N. Y. Elec. Law §9–112(6) (McKinney 1998); N. C. Gen. Stat. §§163–169(b), 163–170 (1999); N. D. Cent. Code §16.1–15–01(1) (Supp. 1999); Ohio Rev. Code Ann. §3505.28 (1994); 26 Okla. Stat., Tit. 26, §7–127(6) (1997); Ore. Rev. Stat. §254.505(1) (1991); S. C. Code Ann. §7–13–1120 (1977); S. D. Codified Laws §12–20–7 (1995); Tenn. Code Ann. §2–7–133(b) (1994); W. Va. Code §3–6–5(g) (1999).

3 Cf. *Victor* v. *Nebraska,* 511 U.S. 1, 5 (1994) ("The beyond a reasonable doubt standard is a requirement of due process, but the Constitution neither prohibits trial courts from defining reasonable doubt nor requires them to do so").

4 The percentage of nonvotes in this election in counties using a punch-card system was 3.92%; in contrast, the rate of error under the more modern optical-scan systems was only 1.43%. *Siegel* v. *LePore,* No. 00–15981, 2000 WL 1781946, *31, *32, *43 (charts C and F) (CA11, Dec. 6, 2000). Put in other terms, for every 10,000 votes cast, punch-card systems result in 250 more nonvotes than optical-scan systems. A total of 3,718,305 votes were cast under punch-card systems, and 2,353,811 votes were cast under optical-scan systems. *Ibid.*

5 Republican electors were certified by the Acting Governor on November 28, 1960. A recount was ordered to begin on December 13, 1960. Both Democratic and Republican electors met on the appointed day to cast their votes. On January 4, 1961, the newly elected Governor certified the Democratic electors. The certification was received by Congress on January 6, the day the electoral votes were counted. Josephson & Ross, 22 J. Legis., at 166, n. 154.

6 When, for example, it resolved the previously unanswered question whether the word "shall" in Fla. Stat. §102.111 or the word "may" in §102.112 governs the scope of the Secretary of State's authority to ignore untimely election returns, it did not "change the law." Like any other judicial interpretation of a statute, its opinion was an authoritative interpretation of what the statute's relevant provisions have meant since they were enacted. *Rivers* v. *Roadway Express, Inc.,* 511 U.S. 298, 312–313 (1994).

7 "It is emphatically the province and duty of the judicial department to say what the law is." *Marbury* v. *Madison.,* 1 Cranch 137, 177 (1803).

PART 2

POLITICAL PARTIES AND INTEREST GROUPS

D uring the founding period of our democracy, leading figures warned against the divisive politics generated by political parties and factions. Most famously James Madison wrote of the dangerous potential for a majority faction to take control of political power and to use government to press its own advantages at the expense of smaller groups. Madison believed that the only solution to the "mischief of faction" was to enable a large number of diverse factions to thrive in the polity so that no one of them can become too powerful. In his farewell address upon leaving the presidency, George Washington warned against the dangers of establishing permanent party competition in the United States. The leaders of political parties, Washington reasoned, would not see themselves as leaders of all the people and would work to enhance the interests of party over those of the nation.

Madison's theory of factions appears to thrive in today's competitive interest group environment. Yet not all agree that this competition has always been good for democracy. Some critics argue that the interest group system favors those with the most resources in society whereas those in most need of government assistance have the least say. Others perceive such groups as labor and the education community pressing issues to their own professional advantage that hurt the economy, education, and so forth. Political scientist Jeffrey Berry studied the impact of citizen lobbying groups during the era of GOP leadership of Congress. He found that despite predictions of their demise, the citizen organizations not only survived the Republican revolution, but were actually thriving. Berry explains how these groups continue to exert real influence in policy even while some traditional Democratic party groups such as labor appear to wane.

Despite Washington's pleas, political parties are now a long-established feature of the U.S. political system. It is hard to imagine elections or governing in the U.S. without the presence of the major parties. Scholar Paul Herrnson explores the reasons for the persistence of the two-party system in the U.S. He examines the efforts of third parties to become competitive and makes it clear why our system appears wedded to primarily two-party competition over the long term. Nonetheless, he sees a valid role for third parties in our system and explores their impact on elections and governing.

One of the hallmarks of the two-party system has been its moderating influence on political debates in the U.S. That is, political parties seek first and foremost to win elections and hold power. In so doing, they stake out generally centrist positions on issues to appeal to as wide a segment of the electorate as possible. Yet sometimes parties stray from that principle and behave in a more contentious and ideological fashion. The essay "Federalism, the Republican Party, and the New Politics of Absolutism" shows the difficulties posed to major parties when they behave more ideologically than pragmatically. Perhaps the greatest challenge is for President Bush, who promises a politics of "compassionate conservatism" when many leaders in the GOP favor a full-fledged conservative revolution.

Americans may favor the continuation of two-party competition, but they strongly dislike the ways in which parties and candidates fund political campaigns. As political scientist Clyde Wilcox shows, overwhelming majorities of Americans express a strong opposition to the current campaign finance system. Nonetheless, popular proposals for campaign finance reform hit roadblock after roadblock in Congress, stalled by incumbent members who benefit from the current system. Wilcox's essay demonstrates why campaign finance is both a contentious issue today and so difficult to resolve to the satisfaction of our elected officials.

ARTICLE 6

TWO-PARTY DOMINANCE AND MINOR PARTY FORAYS IN AMERICAN POLITICS

Paul S. Herrnson

T he United States has experienced numerous minor party and independent candidacies over the course of its history. Minor party (or third-party) candidates have run for offices ranging from city council to president. A small number, including the former governor of Connecticut, Lowell Weicker, and the U.S. representative from Vermont, Bernard Sanders, have been successful. Others, like Theodore Roosevelt, who was the Progressive (or Bull Moose) party's presidential nominee in 1912, won significant numbers of votes and influenced the outcome of an election, but failed to get elected. More common, however, was the experience of Margaret Byrnes, who in 1994 ran for New York's eighth congressional district seat under the Conservative party label and received only 2 percent of the vote.

The success rates and political influence of minor parties are no better or worse than those of their candidates. The parties' limited success, and the ability of the two major parties to monopolize power, places the United States in a relatively small group of modern democracies that are classified as having two-party rather than multiparty systems. The first section of this chapter describes the historical continuity of two-party dominance and analyzes the institutional structures and behavioral norms that provide its foundations. The second section analyzes the types of minor parties that have participated in American politics, the conditions that help them garner support, and their roles in American politics. The

Paul S. Herrnson, "Two-Party Dominance and Minor Party Forays in American Politics" (as appeared in *Multiparty Politics in America,* 1997, pp. xx–xx). Copyright ownership by Rowan & Littlefield, 1997. Reprinted by permission.

chapter concludes with comments on the limitations and contributions of minor parties in the two-party system.

THE TWO-PARTY SYSTEM

American politics have almost always been dominated by two parties. Major parties differ from their minor party counterparts in a variety of ways, including the sizes and compositions of their followings, their pragmatism in selecting issues and candidates, their location on the ideological spectrum, the types and amounts of politically relevant resources under their control, and the number of offices their candidates contest. Perhaps the most important difference between major and minor parties concerns power. As a result of recent successes at the polls, the major parties have sufficient numbers of public officeholders to exercise substantial power over the nation's political agenda and the policy-making processes. Although a few minor parties elect some of their members to public office, they do not qualify as major parties because they do not control enough elective offices, or have not done so in the recent past, to be contenders for power.

Historical Development

The seeds for the two-party system were sown during the Colonial era and firmly rooted by the time the Federalists and Anti-Federalists battled over ratification of the U.S. Constitution. Since then, the nation's political history has been largely defined by five separate party eras or party systems (e.g., Burnham 1970; Bibby 1987, 21–34).

Under the first party era, the Federalists and the Democratic Republicans battled over whether the nation should develop into a commercial republic or remain a largely agrarian society. The Federalists, who were primarily supported by landowners, merchants, and other established families of the Northeast and Atlantic regions, favored a strong national government. The Democratic Republican party, which was founded by Thomas Jefferson, attracted small farmers, workers, and others of modest means. It championed the extension of suffrage, decentralized power, and other ideals of popular self-government. Although the Federalists won the nation's first contested presidential election, the party's narrow base prevented it from again capturing the White House and resulted in its disintegration.

The second period of two-party competition began following a short period of one-party dominance that was characterized by bifactional politics within the Democratic Republican party. This era, which lasted from 1836 into the 1850s, pitted the Democratic party of Andrew Jackson against the Whigs, who were led by Henry Clay and Daniel Webster. Both parties were broad-based popular parties. The Democrats were primarily aligned with the interests of frontiersmen, immigrants, and other less privileged voters. The Whigs attracted more support from manufacturers, trading interests, and citizens of Protestant stock. Conflicts over slavery led to the second party system's demise.

The slavery issue cut across existing party cleavages and led to the formation of several short-lived minor parties, the birth of the modern Republican party, and ultimately the start of the third party era. Lincoln's successful prosecution of the Civil War led the Republican party to be identified with victory, patriotism, reconstruction, and the abolition of slavery. The party was also identified with a concern for mercantile and propertied interests. The Republicans drew their support from the North and West, while their Democratic opponents enjoyed strong support in the South. The Democratic party also attracted significant votes from Roman Catholics who lived in northern cities.

The 1896 election marked the dawning of the fourth party era and a new period of Republican dominance in national politics. William McKinley, the Republican standard-bearer, increased support for his party in northeastern cities and among the population in general. Democratic (and Populist) nominee William Jennings Bryan's campaign to expand the money supply attracted support from farmers in the South and the Plains states and silver miners in the West. It failed, however, to win many votes from the industrial centers of the East and Midwest. McKinley defeated Bryan twice and the GOP won every presidential contest from 1896 through 1932, except for Wilson's two victories, the first of which was largely the result of Theodore Roosevelt's minor party candidacy.

The Great Depression and the election in 1932 launched the fifth party era. President Herbert Hoover and his fellow Republicans received the brunt of the blame for the nation's economic woes. In 1932 and over the course of the next decade, Franklin Roosevelt and the Democrats pieced together a majority coalition comprised of blue-collar workers, urban dwellers, Southerners, ethnic minorities, and blacks. The Democratic and Republican parties battled over the federal government's role in the economy and the welfare state. During the 1960s, civil rights and a variety of social issues began to erode the original economic foundation of the New Deal coalition and contributed to the election of several Republican presidents. Whether the election of a Republican-controlled Congress in 1994 marks the beginning of a sixth party system remains a matter of debate (Beck 1997, 13–136; Aldrich and Niemi 1996).

Institutional Foundations

Institutional arrangements have played a major role in perpetuating the U.S. two-party system. The Constitution is challenging to political parties in general, but particularly inhospitable to minor parties. Federalism, the separation of powers, and bicameralism provide a strong foundation for candidate-centered politics and impede party-focused election efforts, especially the efforts of parties that do not enjoy a broad constituent base.

Single-member, simple-plurality elections, which are not delineated in the Constitution, also make it very difficult for minor parties to have a major impact on elections or policy making (Duverger 1954, 217). This winner-take-all system denies any elected offices to candidates or parties that do not place first in an election, even when the party garners a significant share of the national vote or runs a close second in several contests. This is especially harmful to minor parties, which are usually considered successful when their candidates place second at the polls. By depriving minor parties of seats in Congress or state legislatures, ensuring that few of their members become presidents or governors, and depriving their supporters of judgeships, cabinet posts, and other forms of patronage, the electoral system discourages their institutional development and growth. Most minor parties survived for only a relatively short time because of their inability to play a significant role in governing.

The Electoral College poses particular difficulties for minor parties. The contest for the nation's highest office actually consists of fifty-one separate elections—one held in each of the states and the District of Columbia. In order to win any Electoral College votes, a presidential candidate needs to capture a majority of votes in at least one state or the District. Winning the election requires a candidate to win a majority of Electoral College votes.[1] Nationally based minor parties, such as the Libertarian party, may win a significant share of the popular vote, but they rarely receive enough support to capture a state's electoral votes. Regional minor parties, such as the Dixiecrat (or States' Rights) party, which nominated then Democratic Senator Strom Thurmond of South Carolina in 1948, may win the popular vote in a number of states. However, because their vote is concentrated in those states, these parties often win more popular votes than they need to win Electoral College votes from states in their region and too few popular votes to capture Electoral College votes elsewhere. Their failure to capture political offices does little to help minor parties expand their bases of support or survive for long periods.

Institutional recognition also gives the two major parties ballot access advantages over minor parties. Because they receive automatic placement on the ballot, the two major parties are able to focus most of their energies on winning the support of voters. In many states, minor party and independent candidates can only remain on the ballot by winning a threshold of votes. Those that receive fewer are treated like new parties: to qualify for a place on the ballot they may need to pay a filing fee or submit a minimum number of signatures to local or state election officials prior to the general election or, in some cases, the primary contest (Winger 1995).

The number of signatures required to gain access to the ballot varies widely across the states. In New Jersey, a minor party candidate needs to collect a mere 800 signatures to qualify as a candidate for the Senate, whereas in Florida one needs 196,788. Moreover, minor parties that wish to compete in all fifty states are often penalized at lower ends of the ballot. In 1996, a minor party needed to collect roughly 750,000 signatures to secure a place on the ballot for its presidential candidate in all fifty states, but had to gather more than 1.6 million signatures to place its House candidates on the ballot in all 435 congressional districts (Jost 1995, 1143).

Participatory nominations enable the major parties to absorb protest and discourage the formation of minor parties (Epstein 1986, 129–132). State-regulated caucuses and state-administered primaries give dissident groups from outside or inside the party the opportunity to run candidates for a major party nomination, thereby discouraging them from forming new minor parties.

The campaign finance system also penalizes minor parties. The Federal Election Campaign Act of 1974 and its amendments (collectively referred to as the FECA) provide subsidies for major party candidates for the presidency. During the 1996 presidential election, candidates for major party nominations who raised $5,000 in individual contributions of $250 or less in at least twenty states qualified for up to $15.45 million in federal matching funds, enabling them to spend $37.92 million to contest the nomination. Minor party candidates can also qualify for matching funds, if they meet the same requirements as their major party counterparts. As a practical matter however, these requirements are easily met by serious major party nomination candidates, but pose substantial barriers to minor party contestants because of the lack of support their parties enjoy among individuals who make campaign contributions.

Major parties also automatically receive funds to help them pay for their national conventions. In 1996, the Democratic and Republican national committees each received just over $12.36 million for that purpose. Minor parties can also qualify for convention subsidies, but only if their presidential nominee garners 5 percent or more of the popular vote in the previous presidential election.[2] A minor party has yet to qualify for convention funding under the FECA.

The FECA also provides substantial federal grants to major party presidential nominees. In 1996, President Bill Clinton and former Senator Bob Dole each received $61.8 million to wage their general election campaigns. Minor party and independent candidates can also qualify for federal funding in the general election, but they typically receive much smaller amounts. Newly emergent minor parties and first-time presidential candidates can only qualify for federal subsidies retroactively. Candidates who receive more than 5 percent of the popular vote are rewarded with campaign subsidies, but only after the election when it is too late to have any impact on the outcome. Minor parties that have made a good showing in a previous election automatically qualify for campaign subsidies during the current contest, but they get only a fraction of the money given to the major parties. Ross Perot's 19 percent of the popular vote in 1992 qualified him for $29.2 million in federal funds in 1996. His acceptance of those funds severely limited his ability to compete because he began with fewer funds than his major party opponents, could contribute a maximum of $50,000 to his own campaign, and had to stay within the legal contribution limits when trying to make up his campaign's $32.6 million deficit.

Minor party candidates who cannot or choose not to finance their own campaigns are severely handicapped because of the legal limits on contributions they can collect from others. Ceilings of $1,000 for individuals and $5,000 for political action committees (PACs) prohibit minor party candidates from underwriting their campaigns with large contributions from a small group of backers. Ceilings on party contributions and expenditures also limit the extent to which candidates can depend on a minor party for support. The modest levels of public support that most minor party candidates enjoy make it virtually impossible for them to raise large sums in the form of small donations. Only a few extremely wealthy minor party candidates have been able to amass the resources needed to wage campaigns that rival the efforts mounted by major party contenders.

Candidates for Congress do not receive public subsidies, but the FECA's contribution limits disadvantage minor party candidates for the House and Senate. These candidates can make unlimited contributions to their own campaigns, but are limited in the amounts they can accept from others. Individuals can contribute up to $1,000 and PACs can contribute up to $5,000 in each phase of the election— primary, runoff, and general. National, congressional, and state party campaign committees can each contribute up to $5,000 to individual House candidates in each stage of the election. State parties can give $5,000 to Senate candidates and a party's national organizations can contribute a combined total of $17,500.

Parties can also spend larger sums on behalf of candidates as "coordinated expenditures" that typically are given as polls, radio advertisements, television commercials, fund-raising events, direct-mail solicitations, or issue and opposition research (Herrnson 1988, ch. 3; 1995, ch. 4). Originally set at $10,000 each for a state and national committee, the limits for coordinated expenditures on behalf of House candidates are adjusted for inflation and reached $30,910 per committee in 1996.[3] The coordinated expenditure limits for Senate elections vary by state population and are also indexed to inflation. In 1996, they ranged from $61,820 per committee in the smallest states to $1.41 million per committee in California. The coordinated expenditure limits for presidential elections are also based on population; they reached $11.9 million in 1996.

Parties can also make other kinds of expenditures on behalf of their federal candidates. Since the FECA was amended in 1979, parties have been allowed to use soft money (which is raised and spent outside of the federal election system) on party-building activities, voter mobilization drives, and generic party-focused campaign advertisements that are intended to benefit their entire ticket.[4]

In addition, several Supreme Court rulings that were handed down in the midst of the 1996 election cycle made it permissible for parties to make unlimited expenditures on behalf of their candidates as long as they did not expressly advocate a candidate's election or defeat, or they were made independently of the candidate's campaign and without its knowledge or consent.[5]

One of the major effects of the FECA's matching funds, contribution, and expenditure provisions is that they leave minor party congressional and presidential candidates starved for resources. Few individuals or PACs are willing to invest in minor party candidacies, and those willing to make such investments give only limited amounts. Moreover, most minor parties, especially new ones, lack the funds to match the expenditures made by the two major parties. Campaign finance laws make it difficult for minor parties to compete in federal elections.

The mass media, while not considered a formal political institution, are an important part of the strategic environment in which candidates campaign. Positive media coverage can improve a candidate's name recognition and credibility, whereas negative coverage or an absence of press attention can undermine a candidate's prospects. Many major party candidates complain about the media, but virtually all of them are treated better than their minor party counterparts. Minor party candidates receive less coverage because the media are preoccupied with the horse-race aspects of elections, focusing most of their attention on the probable victors—usually

Democrats and Republicans—and ignoring others (Clarke and Evans 1983, 60–62; Graber 1993, 262–70).

Sometimes the media are openly hostile to minor parties. The press has historically been hostile to third-party candidates, and the coverage afforded to the New Alliance party, the Socialist Workers party, and other contemporary minor parties is often distorted and rarely favorable (e.g., Goodwyn 1978, 210; Schmidt 1960; Rosenstone et al. 1984, 90–91, 133–34, 229–33). A *Washington Post* article that appeared in the paper's style section in September 1996 illustrates the kind of ridicule to which minor party candidates are often subjected. The article, titled "There's the Ticket . . . A Selection of Running Mates for Ross Perot," listed Binti, the gorilla who rescued a toddler who had fallen into her cage, first. Also listed were Prince Charles of Great Britain and Jack Kevorkian, known as "Doctor Death" because of his involvement in physician-assisted suicides (*Washington Post* 1996).

The anti-minor party bias of the American election system stands in sharp contrast to the electoral institutions in other countries. Multimember, proportional representation systems, such as those used in most other democracies, virtually guarantee at least some legislative seats to any party—no matter how small, transient, or geographically confined—that wins a threshold of votes. Public funding provisions and government-subsidized broadcast time ensure that minor parties have a reasonable amount of campaign resources at their disposal (Nassmacher 1993, 239–44). All of these factors give the media incentives to provide significant and respectful coverage to many minor parties and their candidates. American political institutions buttress a two-party system, whereas political institutions in other democracies support multiparty systems.

Behavioral Underpinnings

Institutional impediments are not the only hurdles that must be cleared in order for minor parties to survive. Partisan identification and voting cues may have declined in importance during the past few decades, but most voters continue to identify with one of the two major parties (Keith et al. 1992, 17–23). Most voters' socialization to politics encourages them to consider minor parties outside the mainstream and unworthy of support. Some voters refuse to support minor party candidates for this reason or because of the outright hostility with which their campaigns are treated by the press. Others recognize that casting a ballot for a minor party candidate could contribute to the election of the major party candidate that they least prefer (Brams 1978, ch. 1; Riker 1982).

The relative ideological homogeneity of the electorate also deprives minor parties of bases of support that exist in more ideologically heterogeneous nations. Trying to outflank the major parties by occupying a place to the far left or the far right of the political spectrum rarely succeeds because Americans' moderate views do little to provide extremist parties with bases of support. The fact that the vast majority of Americans hold opinions that are close to the center of a fairly narrow ideological spectrum means that most elections, particularly those for the presidency, are primarily contests to capture the middle ground. At their very essence, Democratic strategies involve piecing together a coalition of moderates and voters on the left, and Republican strategies dictate holding their party's conservative base while reaching out for the support of voters at the center. Democracies whose voters have a broader array of ideological perspectives, or have higher levels of class or ethnic consciousness, generally provide more fertile ground for minor party efforts.

The career paths of the politically ambitious are extremely important in explaining the weakness and short-term existence of most minor party movements in the United States. Budding politicians learn early in their careers that the Democratic and Republican parties can provide them with useful contacts, expertise, financial assistance, and an orderly path of entry into electoral politics. Minor parties and independent candidacies simply do not offer most of these benefits. As a result, the two parties tend to attract the most talented among those interested in a career in public service. A large part of the parties' hegemony can be attributed to their advantages in candidate recruitment.

Voters are able to discern differences in the talents and levels of experience of minor party and major party candidates and, not surprisingly, they hesitate to cast votes for less qualified minor party contestants. As fluctuations in the support that minor party candidates register in public opinion polls demonstrate, even voters who declare their support for a minor party or independent contestant early in the campaign season often balk at casting their ballot for one of these candidates on election day. Major party candidates and their supporters prey upon Americans' desire to go with a winner—or at least affect the election outcome—when they discourage citizens from "throwing away their votes" on fringe candidates.

Mainstream politicians also respond to minor parties by trying to delegitimize their efforts. Major party officials have subjected minor parties to court challenges to keep them off the ballot. Major party nominees have often refused to debate minor party candidates. The 1992 presidential debates, which featured Perot, were the exception to the rule in that they included an independent. It is more common for minor party and independent contestants to be denied a place on the podium, as was Perot in 1996 and the nominees of the Libertarian party, the Natural Law party, and the nearly twenty other minor party and independent candidates who contested the 1992 or 1996 presidential elections. Major party nominees prefer to label minor party candidates as extremists and cast them as irrelevant in order to minimize their influence.

When a minor party or independent candidate introduces an issue that proves to be popular, Democratic and Republican leaders are quick to co-opt it. Perot proclaimed himself to be an agent of change and campaigned to cut the deficit and reform the political process. When these issues became popular many major party candidates, including then President George Bush and Democratic nominee Bill Clinton, staked out similar positions. By adopting positions espoused in popular movements, party leaders are able to better represent their followers, expand their constituencies, and attract votes (Eldersveld 1982, 40–43). Strategic adjustments that rob minor party and independent movements of their platforms are common in American history. They enable the two major parties to absorb, protest, and help maintain the existence of the two-party system.

MINOR PARTY FORAYS

Despite the hurdles they must jump, a variety of minor parties have participated in the electoral process. Some have occupied an extreme position on the ideological spectrum, while others have tried to carve out a niche in the center. Some have taken stances on a wide array of issues, but others have mobilized around only one or two causes. Most minor parties have sought to elect presidential candidates, but some have focused on the state and local levels, and others have been more concerned with raising issues than electing candidates. A few have endorsed and even formally nominated candidates that have already won major party nominations. Some minor parties have survived for decades, but many last only one election. Minor parties can be classified using a variety of schemes (e.g., Key 1964, ch. 10). The scheme that follows divides them into four groups: minor parties that resemble major parties in their endurance and activities, those that form primarily around a single candidate, those that revolve around one or a small number of related issues, and those that survive largely by playing a supporting role for major party candidates.

Enduring Comprehensive Parties

Many of the minor parties resembled the major parties of their time (Rosenstone et al. 1984, 78–80). These parties were united by issues or an ideology and put forward candidates for Congress, the presidency, and state and local offices. They held contested nominations and selected their presidential candidates at conventions. They also employed campaign strategies and tactics that were similar to those used by the two major parties: they framed issues and adopted slogans that would help them secure their base and attract new voters; they used their resources to mobilize specific voting blocs whose support was necessary for electoral success. Moreover, they lasted for several elections. A few contemporary minor parties, such as the Libertarian party, founded in 1971, are similar to their predecessors in that they bear a resemblance to the major parties of their time (Hazlett 1992; Flood and Mayer 1996, 313–16).

During the nineteenth century, several enduring comprehensive parties enjoyed significant electoral success. The American (or Know-Nothing) party won control of the Massachusetts governorship and both chambers of the state legislature in 1854. Like its major party counterparts, and other successful minor parties, it used its control of the government to reward supporters with patronage and government contracts (Rosenstone et al. 1984, 57). Those minor parties that were in a position to distribute patronage and influence public policy usually survived for more than one election. The Greenback, Populist, and several other nineteenth-century minor parties lasted for over a decade.

Their extended presence on the political scene and their organizational strength made these parties attractive vehicles for politicians who wished to bolt from a major party. Politicians who were denied a major party nomination or found themselves unable to influence the party platform could advance their causes by joining an existing minor party. Former Whig President Millard Fillmore pursued this route of influence when he accepted the American party's presidential nomination in 1856, as did Tennessee Senator John Bell, who left the Whig party to become the Constitutional Union party's standard-bearer in 1860.

Contemporary enduring comprehensive parties, most notably the Libertarian party, rarely recruit candidates from the two dominant parties. Their weak political organizations, ideological extremism, and lack of electoral success reduce the attractiveness of these parties to successful major party politicians. Their inability to distribute political favors and limited influence over public policy have prevented these parties from amassing large followings and caused their number to dwindle. These parties have been largely replaced by less enduring candidate-focused parties.

Candidate-Focused Parties

Many of the minor parties that left their mark on the twentieth-century political landscape were highly candidate-centered. The same legal, technological, and cultural changes that influenced the development of the two major parties helped to shape the nature of their minor party contemporaries. The rise of the participatory primary, the enactment of the FECA, the introduction of polling, the electronic media, and modern marketing techniques into the political arena, and the decline of partisanship in the electorate helped foster the emergence of candidate-centered elections (e.g., Sorauf 1980).

Under the candidate-centered system, campaigns revolve around individual candidates, not parties. Elections are characterized by self-recruited candidates who field professionally staffed, money-driven campaign organizations that are not dependent on party workers. The two major parties play important supporting roles in the candidate-centered system, as do most twentieth-century minor parties (Herrnson 1988, chs. 3–4; 1995, ch. 4). However, the major parties enjoy an existence that is independent of and extends beyond their individual candidates' campaigns, whereas most candidate-focused minor party movements are merely extensions of individual candidates. They live and die with their candidates' campaigns.

The Progressive party, which was an offshoot of the Republican party, exemplifies modern candidate-focused minor parties. The Progressive party was constructed by former Republican Theodore Roosevelt after the tumultuous 1912 Republican Convention for the purpose of challenging his successor, William Howard Taft (Sundquist 1973, 164; Pinchot 1958, 172, 226–27). Roosevelt opposed Taft for the Republican nomination because Taft failed to continue his predecessor's battle to curb the power of corporate barons and improve the lives of ordinary workers. After losing the nomination to Taft, Roosevelt and his followers bolted the GOP and formed the Progressive party to mount Roosevelt's general election campaign.

Because it was a splinter group that drew its votes mainly from the progressive faction of the GOP, the Progressive party contributed to Taft's defeat at the hands of Democratic candidate Woodrow Wilson. Following the election, the Progressives failed to maintain a permanent organization or expand their efforts. In 1916, after extensive negotiations with Republican leaders, Roosevelt decided to return to the Republican fold. Many Progressives followed him, leading to the party's demise (Pinchot 1958, 226–27).

The Progressive party differed from the minor parties that preceded it in that it was little more than a vehicle for an individual politician (Rosenstone et al. 1984, 82). Previous minor parties had been built around causes, nominated candidates, and then waged their campaigns. The Progressive party drastically changed this pattern: it was organized for the purpose of campaigning for a preordained candidate.

A number of other minor parties were organized to promote individual candidacies. They included a new Progressive party that was formed in 1924 to support the presidential candidacy of former

Republican Governor and Senator Robert M. La Follette of Wisconsin and the Union party that was organized in 1936 to promote the presidential candidacy of Republican House member William Lemke of North Dakota. These parties were all short-lived, disintegrating after their candidates lost the election (Rosenstone et al. 1984, 96, 101–02, 108–10).

The presidential candidacies of Democratic Senator Eugene McCarthy in 1976 and Republican Representative John Anderson in 1980 were conducted without the pretense of a minor party. These individuals were self-selected candidates, who assembled their own political organizations and mounted independent campaigns. They made little effort to ally their campaigns with those of candidates for lower office and their organizations were dismantled after the election was held.

Wealthy businessman Ross Perot's 1992 United We Stand America (UWSA) campaign bore many similarities to McCarthy's and Anderson's efforts. However, the Perot campaign differed in that the candidate was able to spend sufficient funds—$60 million—to mount a credible campaign. Perot's effort also differed in that after the election Perot transformed his independent candidacy into a new political party.

Recent events indicate that the new Reform party will probably fit the model of a short-lived candidate-focused party rather than become an enduring comprehensive party. First, Perot's money is the overwhelming source of the party's funds. Perot invested roughly $6.7 million to transform UWSA into the Reform party (Baker 1996a). Second, the party's nomination process appears to have been designed to provide a coronation for Perot rather than to select a nominee from among competing aspirants. In the first step of the process, each voter who signed a Reform party petition was supposed to be sent a nomination ballot that included the names of Perot, other self-declared candidates, and a place for a write-in candidate. In the second step, each candidate who received more than 10 percent of the nomination ballots—only Perot and former Colorado Governor Richard Lamm qualified—was given the opportunity to speak at the first Reform party convention. In the third step, a second set of ballots was sent to Reform party petition-signers, who were instructed to vote for Perot or Lamm by mail, telephone, or e-mail. In the final step, party officials announced the results of the second round of balloting and designated the party's nominee at a second Reform party convention (Greenblatt 1996).

News reports and the complaints of Perot's opponent indicate that the process may have been well planned for attracting media coverage, but it was poorly planned for the conduct of a competitive nominating contest. The balloting process was not well planned or executed. Many petition-signers received their ballots late. Others, including such prominent Reform party members as Lamm and Michael Farris, chairman of the California Reform party, never received a ballot. Still others received several ballots (Greenblatt 1996). Perot's influence over the process partially stems from his financing the party, including paying the firm hired to count the ballots. Moreover, flawed balloting procedures and a lack of interest among Reform party petition-signers resulted in only 43,057 returning first-round ballots and only 49,266 returning second-round ballots. Less than 5 percent of the petitioners participated in either round of balloting (Babbington 1996).

The nomination process also denied Lamm the opportunity to compete on a level playing field. Lamm's request for access to the list of petition-signers was refused by party officials, depriving him of one of the few means available to communicate with Reform party supporters.[6] Perot was the only Reform party candidate who had access to the party's supporter list, and he benefited from a direct-mail piece that featured his but not Lamm's picture (Fisher 1996). Another major avenue for communicating with petition-signers—a televised one-on-one debate—was never planned. Lamm's opportunities to communicate directly with party supporters were largely limited to speeches he gave at the party's state conventions in Florida and Maine.

The Reform party's decision to stack the deck so heavily in favor of Perot suggests that it will have difficulty making the transition from a movement dominated by a single charismatic leader to an enduring comprehensive party. This transition would require the party to develop a formal governing body that is independent of Perot, an independent source of financing, and a routinized system of candidate selection. It would also require the party to nominate candidates for state, local, and congressional office and to develop a permanent organization capable of assisting its candidates with their general election campaigns.[7]

It is more than likely that the Reform party will fold once Perot loses interest in politics and withdraws his financial backing. Perot's decision not to help other Reform party candidates on the ticket—he failed to appear with or endorse any of them (Baker 1996b)—did little to help their campaigns or to generate the kind of grassroots support that would be needed to enable the party to continue to build after it failed to achieve any significant success in the 1996 contest.

Single-Issue Parties

The source of strength for most single-issue parties (sometimes called ideological parties) is a salient, often highly charged cause or related set of causes. These parties differ from candidate-centered and enduring comprehensive minor parties, and from the two major parties, in that they are more concerned with advancing their issue positions than winning elections. Elections are typically viewed as an opportunity to raise public awareness for a party's cause, influence the political debate and the issue positions of major party contenders, raise funds, and recruit new members. Single-issue parties are often considered successful when they are able to get one or both of the major parties to adopt their core policy positions and enact those positions into law. Ironically, it is precisely that success that usually leads to a single-issue party's demise. Deprived of the core issue that unites it, the party frequently lapses into decline.

The Green party and the New York Right-to-Life party are examples of single-issue parties. The Green party grew out of the environmental movement that swept through the United States and Western Europe in the 1980s and 1990s. The party takes positions on a broad array of environmental concerns, including recycling, ecological economics, toxic wastes, energy, and organic farming. In addition to the environmental issues that form its doctrinal core, the party maintains positions on social justice, international, and political reform issues (Green Party of California 1996).

The Green party has enjoyed a degree of electoral success. Following the 1994 elections, twenty-nine Green party officials held elective office in ten states. During the 1996 election cycle, the Green party selected renowned consumer advocate and environmentalist Ralph Nader to be its presidential nominee. Although Nader won less than 1 percent of the popular vote, the fact that his name appeared on the ballot in twenty-two states helped to elevate the Greens' visibility and ensure that environmental issues would be discussed in the election. The campaigns that the party has waged on environmental initiatives and referendums have helped to raise its visibility and increase support for its goals, particularly in California—home of the strongest Green party state committee.

Unlike most contemporary parties the Green party has maintained a strong grassroots activist agenda. It continues to carry out local projects at cleaning up the environment and educating citizens about pollution control, recycling, and other environmental issues. Literature circulated by the California Green party emphasizes that community projects and grassroots activities form one of the party's "two legs."

The Right-to-Life party also grew out of a social movement, but it has maintained a narrower focus than the Green party. Although the antiabortion movement has national foundations, the Right-to-Life party has had little impact beyond New York's borders. The party ran token campaigns for the presidency in 1976 and 1980, but as the next section shows, most of its influence has been through the cross-endorsements it has given to major party candidates running for office in New York State.

Fusion Parties

A fourth type of minor party—the fusion or alliance party—conducts many of the same activities as the two major parties and some of its minor party brethren, but differs in that it actively supports other parties' candidates. Some fusion parties can be categorized as comprehensive enduring minor parties, while others fit into the single-issue category. What makes these parties unique is that they engage in a practice known as "cross-endorsement," which enables a candidate to appear on more than one party's line on the ballot (Gillespie 1993, 255). Presidential candidate William Jennings Bryan, for example, appeared on more than one party's ballot in 1896 when he received the nomination of both the Democratic and the Populist parties. Fusion candidacies, such as Bryan's, became rare with the introduction of the Australian ballot. When they began printing ballots, many states enacted prohibitions against a candidate's name appearing more than once in the same contest. During the 1990s, ten states allowed a candidate's name to appear on more than one ballot line. Most fusion candidacies take place in New York.

New York has historically been the home of several fusion parties, most notably the Liberal, Conservative, and Right-to-Life parties. These parties resemble major parties and some minor parties in that they are enduring, have formal organizations, hold conventions, and attract volunteers and activists (e.g., Gillespie 1993, 258, 260). The Liberal party was founded in 1944, the Conservative party in 1962, and the Right-to-Life party in 1970. New York's fusion parties also resemble major parties in that they run local, state, and congressional candidates under their own label. Where they differ is that they routinely give their nominations to candidates who have been nominated by the two major parties and occasionally endorse each other's nominees. Most of New York's state legislators are elected on fusion tickets. The same is true of the state's congressional delegation. Of the fifty-seven major party candidates who ran for Congress in 1994, thirty-six were cross-endorsed by one of New York's minor parties. Both of New York's senators were also recipients of minor party cross-endorsements: Daniel Patrick Moynihan ran on both the Democratic and Liberal party lines and Alfonse D'Amato received the Republican, Conservative, and Right-to-Life nominations.

Fusion parties play important supporting roles to the major parties. They provide major party candidates with endorsements and grassroots campaign assistance. More importantly, fusion parties provide candidates with an extra place on the ballot that can be used to capture independent-minded voters who object to casting a ballot for a major party. This extra ballot line can also function as a safeguard for candidates who are unpopular with party activists. Republican incumbent John Lindsay, for example, was able to win the

1969 New York City mayoral contest after being defeated in the GOP primary because his name also appeared on the Liberal line of the general election ballot.

New York's fusion parties receive both material and policy benefits from their efforts (e.g., Gillespie 1993, 256, 259). They extract patronage from major party candidates in exchange for granting the candidates the opportunity to occupy their party's line on the ballot. They also influence the issues stances that are adopted by the major party candidates who seek their endorsements. The Liberal party pushes the candidates it endorses to the left, the Conservative party pushes them to the right, and the Right-to-Life party requires them to campaign on the party's antiabortion position. Ironically, a fusion party that succeeds in influencing the positions adopted by major party candidates can undercut its own constituent base.

Fusion parties do not automatically support the parties that are closest to them on the ideological spectrum. This occasionally causes the parties' endorsement strategies to backfire. In 1980, the Liberal party nominated incumbent Republican Senator Jacob Javits. After Javits lost the GOP nomination to Town of Hempstead Supervisor Alfonse D'Amato, his, D'Amato's, and Democratic nominee Elizabeth Holtzman's names all appeared on the general election ballot. Holtzman and Javits split the liberal vote, enabling D'Amato, who was the most conservative of the three candidates, to win. Given that most states ban fusion candidacies, it is likely that fusion parties, and the complications they sometimes cause, will continue to remain isolated to a few states.

Conditions for Strong Minor Party Performances

Support for minor parties ebbs and flows in response to national conditions, the performance of the two major parties, and the efforts of minor parties themselves. Minor parties usually attract more support under conditions of economic adversity, particularly when the agricultural sector is suffering. Minor parties also do well when the two major parties fail to address salient issues or when they nominate unappealing candidates (Mazmanian 1974; Rosenstone et al. 1984, ch. 5; Abramson 1995). As dissatisfaction with the major parties increases, minor parties increase in strength and number (Ranney and Kendall 1956, 458).

Minor parties can directly help their own causes by nominating popular candidates, particularly those who have previously held public office. Theodore Roosevelt, who occupied the White House as a Republican from 1901 to 1907, was the most successful of all minor party presidential candidates when in 1912, as the Progressive party nominee, he garnered 27.4 percent of the popular vote and 88 Electoral College votes. Former Democratic President Martin

Van Buren, former Republican Senator Robert La Follette, and former Democratic Governor of Alabama George Wallace each picked up over 10 percent of the popular vote when they ran as minor party candidates for president. La Follette and Wallace also picked up significant Electoral College votes.

Of course, attractive minor party candidacies, national conditions, major party failures, and minor party successes are systematically related to one another. Celebrity candidates are strategic. They are most likely to run on a minor party ticket when their prospects for success are greatest—that is, when voters are dissatisfied with the performance of government, the incumbent president is unpopular, the two major parties have difficulty containing internal dissent or fail to adequately address the major issues, and one of the major parties did poorly in the previous election. The candidacies of these individuals, in turn, add to their party's ability to win votes (Rosenstone et al. 1984, ch. 6).

Systemic factors related to the emergence of the candidate-centered system have contributed to voter support for minor parties in the latter half of the twentieth century. The unraveling of the New Deal coalition and the rise of issue-oriented voting have weakened voter identification with the Democratic and Republican parties, which has benefited their minor party opponents. The transition from a grassroots, volunteer-based style of campaigning to a high-tech, money-driven style also may have worked to the advantage of minor parties. Parties and candidates that can afford to purchase polls, direct mail, television and radio advertisements, and the services of professional campaign consultants are no longer penalized by their lack of volunteers and party activists.

These conditions, the nature of their constituencies, and their prior political records made important contributions to Lowell Weicker's successful gubernatorial campaign in Connecticut and Bernard Sanders's ability to win election to Congress from Vermont.

The Historic Roles of Minor Parties

Minor parties have historically performed many of the same functions as the major parties. They provide symbols for citizen identification and loyalty, educate and mobilize voters, select and campaign for candidates for office, aggregate and articulate interests, raise issues, advocate and help to formulate public policies, organize the government, provide loyal opposition, institutionalize political conflict and foster political stability. As their relative status indicates, minor parties tend to be less adept at performing many of these roles than are their major party counterparts.

Minor parties also play four additional roles that are important to the functioning of the political system: they raise issues that have been ignored by the two major parties, serve as vehicles for voters to express their discontent with the two major parties, help propel the transition from one party era to another, and occasionally act as laboratories for political innovation. Minor parties have raised issues that have been ignored or inadequately addressed by the major parties during many key junctures in American history (Sundquist 1983). The Free Soil and Liberty parties took important stands on slavery prior to the Civil War. The National Women's, Equal Rights, Prohibition, Greenback, Populist, and Socialist parties and the Progressive party of 1912 advocated female suffrage (Gillespie 1993, 284). More recently, the Green party has raised environmental concerns to new heights. In the first example, minor parties propelled the formation of a new political party—the modern Republican party. In the second two, they forced the major parties to confront significant issues, and in one case this resulted in an amendment to the Constitution. In all three examples minor parties made it possible for a variety of groups and issues to be better represented in the political process.

In providing outlets for protest, minor parties function as safety valves that channel societal frustrations into mainstream forums. Minor parties institutionalize conflict by championing the causes of alienated voters and encouraging them to express their dissatisfaction at the polls rather than in the streets. The Populist, Progressive, and Socialist Workers parties, for example, have harnessed the anger of some of the poorer elements of society. This anger might have otherwise been directed toward overthrowing the political system. During the 1990s, a new minor party movement gave alienated and apathetic voters who were turned off by the major party nominees a way to register their displeasure without resorting to violence.

The regularity with which minor party forays precede political realignments indicates how they help to redefine the political cleavages that divide the major parties. By raising new issues and loosening the ties that bind voters to the major parties, minor parties promote political realignments (Freie 1982; Burnham 1970; Sundquist 1983). The efforts of the Free Soil, Liberty, and other pre-Civil War minor parties hastened the development of the modern GOP and the third party era. The Populist party's efforts to expand the money supply helped usher in the fourth party system. The campaign waged by the La Follette Progressives helped pave the way for Franklin D. Roosevelt and the Democrats to expand the role of the federal government. Perhaps Perot's UWSA campaign and Reform party efforts will some day be interpreted as precursors to a sixth party system that is structured around deficit-related issues.

Another role that has been historically performed by minor parties is concerned more with political processes than public policy.

Because minor parties are born and die with some frequency, they are important sources of political experimentation and innovation. In 1831, the National Republican party introduced a major innovation in the presidential selection process when it held the first national nominating convention (Ranney 1975, 16). During the 1990s, Perot's minor party movement capitalized on modern technology and voters' desires for direct political involvement when it aired the first televised infomercial and held the first national presidential primary. If voter response to these innovations is favorable, they may some day be adopted by one or both of the major parties.

CONCLUSION

For most of its history, the United States has maintained a two-party system, This system has been shored up by the nation's political institutions and the activities of voters, the media, politicians, and the two parties themselves. Nevertheless, minor parties have raised critical issues, provided outlets for frustrated voters, and helped realign the nation's politics at key points in history. They have also introduced innovations into the political process. Minor parties have played, and continue to play, important roles in the American two-party system.

NOTES

1 The Constitution provides that when no candidate wins a majority of the Electoral College votes, the election is to be decided in the House of Representatives.

2 Once they qualify for federal funding, major and minor party candidates lose their eligibility for additional public funds if they win less than 10 percent of the vote in two consecutive primaries in which they compete. Candidates that lose their eligibility can requalify for public funds by winning at least 20 percent of the vote in a subsequent primary.

3 Coordinated expenditure limits for states with only one House member were set at $61,820 per committee in 1996.

4 Soft money is considered largely outside of federal law and is subject to the limits imposed by state laws (e.g., Alexander and Corrado 1995, ch. 6; Biersack 1994).

5 The most important of these are *Massachusetts Citizens for Life v. Federal Election Commission,* 479 U.S. 238 (1986) and *Colorado Republican Federal Campaign Committee v. Federal Election Commission,* U.S., 64 U.S.L.2 4663 (1996).

<u>6</u> Party officials claimed that making the list available would violate federal election laws.

<u>7</u> The party nominated and elected a few candidates for local office in 1995 in a small number of states and it endorsed some congressional contestants in 1996. However, the numbers who were nominated are too small to classify it as an enduring, comprehensive minor party.

ARTICLE 7

FEDERALISM, THE REPUBLICAN PARTY, AND THE NEW POLITICS OF ABSOLUTISM

John Kenneth White

D uring the early nineteenth century, Alexis de Tocqueville saw formative characteristics in the American polity that made it distinctive from his native France. In 1832, Tocqueville observed that most Americans had "acquired or retained sufficient education and fortune to satisfy their own wants. They owe nothing to any man, they expect nothing from any man, they acquire the habit of always considering themselves as *standing alone,* and they are apt to imagine that their whole destiny is in their own hands."[1] From the agricultural era that informed Tocqueville's observations to today's Information Age, the American penchant for standing alone has remained constant. Sociologist Robert Putnam sees its present-day manifestations in the decline of bowling leagues.[2] A nation that "stands alone" now "bowls alone." During the 1990s, what was once the peculiar habit of standing alone mutated into a disturbing alienation within the public square. In 1995, *The Washington Post* and the Henry J. Kaiser Family foundation uncovered a profound sense of mutual distrust. When asked whether "most people can be trusted or that you can't be too careful in dealing with people," 63 percent responded "can't be too careful." Forty-eight percent said most people "would take advantage of you if they got a chance." An equal number thought that their fellow citizens were "mostly just looking out for themselves."[3]

Along with this super-charged hyper-individualism and intense cynicism has come a conviction that government cannot be depended upon to solve most problems. Fifty-two percent of those leaving the polls on Election Day 1996 wanted the federal government to "do less;" only 41 percent thought it should "do more."[4] Like his fellow Democrat Thomas Jefferson, who won in 1800 by promising to shrink the federal government (even as he expanded its authority), Bill Clinton triumphed in 1996, by proclaiming that "the era of big government is over."[5]

FROM LANDON TO DOLE: PREACHING THE GOSPEL OF SELF-RELIANCE

Individualism and self-reliance have characterized the American polity since its inception. The phrase "American Exceptionalism" is often used to highlight the fact that the United States is less rooted in its soil and grounded more in the realm of ideas.[6] In a land where "becoming American" means accepting the classical liberal notions of individualism, freedom, and equality of opportunity, the Republican party, if it did not exist, would have to be invented.

For the past six decades, Republicans have staunchly opposed most government innovations proposed by Democratic presidents. Two Kansans, Alf Landon and Bob Dole, serve as bookends in the Republican annals extolling the virtues of frugality and self-reliance. Campaigning for the presidency in 1936, Landon assailed the "folly" of Franklin D. Roosevelt's New Deal and denounced the "vast multitude of new offices" and the "centralized bureaucracy" from which "swarms of inspectors" had swooped over the country-side "to harass our people."[7] Landon proposed to save the country from well-intentioned "do-gooders," citing the newly-enacted Social Security Act as a typical example of Democratic "bungling and waste":

> Imagine the vast army of clerks which will be necessary to keep these records. Another army of field investigators will be necessary to check up on the people whose records are not clear, or regarding whom current information is not coming in. And so bureaucracy will grow and grow, and Federal snooping will flourish.[8]

Sixty years later Bob Dole preached the same gospel of self-reliance. Seeking to reverse the tendency toward big government, Dole cited his opposition to the 1993 Family and Medical Leave Act (once vetoed by George Bush) and the Clinton universal health care plan (which many Republicans likened to socialism). Dole pledged to restore the Tenth Amendment—that part of the Constitution that says that "the powers not delegated to the United States by the Constitution, nor prohibited by it to the states, are reserved to the states respectively, or to the people." In a televised debate, Dole told how he carries "a little card around in my pocket called the Tenth Amendment. Where possible, I want to give power back to the states and back to the people. That's my difference with the president."[9] In keeping with the spirit of the Tenth Amendment, Dole promised to eliminate the Cabinet departments of Housing and Urban Development, Commerce, Education, and Energy, and "defund" other agencies including the National Endowment for the Humanities, the Corporation for Public Broadcasting, and the Legal Services Corporation.

Landon and Dole's warning of an encroaching federal establishment has its roots with the Anti-Federalists, who feared that in a large republic the people "will have no confidence in their legislature, suspect them of ambitious views, be jealous of every measure they adopt, and will not support the laws they pass." Historian Ralph Ketcham has written: "Anti-Federalists saw mild, grassroots, small-scale governments in sharp contrast to the splendid edifice and overweening ambitions implicit in the new Constitution. . . . The first left citizens free to live their own lives and to cultivate the virtue (private and public) vital to republicanism, while the second soon entailed taxes and drafts and offices and wars damaging to human dignity and thus fatal to self-government."[10] Indeed, the 1936 Republican platform has more ties to the Anti-Federalists than it does to the Republican party of Abraham Lincoln. In making their pitch for a downsized federal government and more state and local autonomy, Republicans expressed their "inalterable conviction that, in the future as in the past, the fate of the nation will depend, not so much on the wisdom and power of government, as on the character and virtue, self-reliance, industry and thrift of the people and on their willingness to meet the responsibilities essential to the preservation of a free society."[11]

The defeat of the Anti-Federalists, and the subsequent losses of Landon and Dole, reveal contradictory trends in the public psyche. While individualism and self-reliance are distinct American impulses, so, too, is the desire for forceful government action in the face of pressing national problems. Hamiltonian Nationalists adhere to former New York Governor Mario Cuomo's proposition that Americans are inextricably joined to each other as one large family. Thus, in 1936 Democrats thought it "self-evident" that pressing national problems such as "drought, dust storms, floods, minimum wages, maximum hours, child labor and working conditions in industry, monopolistic and unfair business practices cannot be handled by forty-eight separate State Legislatures, forty-eight separate State administrations, and forty-eight separate State courts."[12] Given this "one-nation" viewpoint, Hamiltonian Nationalists recoil against any assertions of "special interests"—agreeing with Alexander Hamilton that such expressions are "mischievous."[13] Thus, the Roosevelt Democrats proposed amending the Constitution to allow the federal government to act in the best interests of "the family and the home."[14]

Jeffersonian Localists, like Landon and Dole, see the nation as a series of diverse communities each standing alone. In painting this small-town vision of America, Landon embraced Thomas Jefferson as heir to the Republican party's determination "to establish the rights and institutions of free men upon this continent."[15] Acting in this same spirit, the Reagan Republicans promised to "reemphasize those vital communities like the family, the neighborhood, the workplace, and others which are found at the center of our society between government and the individual."[16] Observing these contrasting strains of American thought, *New Republic* founder Herbert Croly wrote in 1909 that Hamilton "perverted the national idea as much as Jefferson perverted the American democratic idea, and the proper relation of these two fundamental conceptions one to another cannot be completely understood until this double perversion is corrected."[17]

Ever since the New Deal, Democrats have adhered to the idea of Hamiltonian Nationalism, while Republicans have remained loyal to Jeffersonian Localism. Texas Senator Phil Gramm proudly boasts: "We are Jeffersonians. The longer I live, the more convinced I am that there are only two ideas in the history of government: government and freedom. When government is the answer, the Democrats are in the ascendancy. When freedom is the answer, we are in the ascendancy."[18] During the fierce budget debates of the last two decades, Gramm and his Republican allies adhered to Alf Landon's 1936 dictum: "I want the Secretary of the Treasury to be obliged to say to committees of Congress every time a new appropriation is proposed, 'Gentlemen, you will have to provide some new taxes if you do this.'"[19] But Americans overwhelmingly rejected Landon's dour vision of government's usefulness. Garnering a mere 37 percent of the vote, Landon said he had been so badly beaten that it was like the Kansas cyclone that left the farmer and his wife standing on bare ground. The husband started laughing, and when his wife wondered why, the farmer replied, "The completeness of it all."[20]

Fifty years later, Ronald Reagan and his followers gloated that Jeffersonian Localism had finally triumphed. Today, numerous public opinion surveys show an increased skepticism of government by a public severely disappointed by foreign policy failures (Vietnam and Iranian hostages), scandal (Watergate, Whitewater, Filegate, and Monica Lewinsky), and the economic stagflation of the 1970s and industrial dislocations of the 1990s. One 1995 poll conducted by Democrat Peter D. Hart and Republican Robert M. Teeter found 56 percent believing that government does more to hinder the American dream than enhance it. Moreover, in such diverse areas as improving education, dealing with jobs and the economy, reducing crime, protecting the environment, enhancing minority opportunity, promoting culture, improving morals, and strengthening families, most wanted these tasks performed by businesses, individuals, or community leaders.[21]

These results are in sharp contrast to 1936 when George Gallup found a majority wanting an activist federal government. When asked, "Which theory of government do you favor: concentration of power in the federal government, or concentration of power in the state government?," 56 percent answered the federal government while 44 percent said state government. Yet, by 1987 the tables had turned: only 34 percent wanted power concentrated in the federal government, while a whopping 63 percent preferred their state governments have the lion's share of power.[22] Thus, when Ronald Reagan called for a "new federalism," saying it was time to "use the level of government closest to the community involved for all the public functions it can handle,"[23] his words were welcomed by a receptive electorate. Campaigning for the presidency in 1996, Bob Dole told the Republican National Committee that he would be another Reagan, "if that's what you want."[24] It was certainly what they expected. But there remained one lingering problem: each of Franklin Roosevelt's Republican successors has governed in Hamilton's America. Once having been beseeched by his conservative brother Edgar to be more faithful to the party of Landon and abandon the New Deal, Dwight Eisenhower replied: "Should any political party attempt to abolish social security and eliminate labor laws and farm programs, you would not hear of that party again in our political history."[25] Even Bob Dole found it advantageous to cooperate with Senate Democrats Hubert H. Humphrey, Edward M. Kennedy, and George S. McGovern in enlarging the scope of the federal government.

Ronald Reagan is the penultimate example of Hamilton's triumph: during two terms, government never shrank, only its rate of growth did. In 1983, then-Senator Daniel Patrick Moynihan captured the essence of Reaganism's charm:

> There is a tendency for any government to live beyond its income. The Reagan administration transformed this temptation from a vice into an opportunity. Put plainly, under Ronald Reagan, big government became a bargain. For seventy-five cents worth of taxes, you got a dollar's worth of return. Washington came to resemble a giant discount house. If no tax would balance the budget, and no outlay would make it any worse, why try?[26]

It was the freshman class of the Republican-controlled 104th Congress, which worshiped Reagan, that offered to make good on his promise to cut government's allowance by staging two shutdowns in 1995. Their reward was a strong rebuke by a middle-class that suddenly realized it was more dependent on government than it had previously thought. Baby-boomers saw value in having their elderly parents cared for by Social Security and Medicare, and worried that these Democratic programs might not be there for them. Education, which had long been a state and local issue, also emerged as a top federal concern. Public schools received poor grades from parents concerned about the failure of teachers to teach, and the random gun violence in Arkansas, Mississippi, and Colorado struck a deep chord in an electorate that believed something was seriously amiss. Just as the 1950s Republicans had to accommodate the New Deal by becoming "me-tooers" (the derisive phrase applied by apoplectic conservatives to any concession to Democratic orthodoxy), present-day Republicans were searching for new ways to present their ideas to voters no longer eager to view the government as an enemy. President George W. Bush has described his governing philosophy as "compassionate conservatism," citing his education reforms that gave poorer school districts more state aid, even as property taxes and welfare rolls were cut. Yet, some of Bush's opponents for the 2000 GOP presidential nomination saw "compassionate conservatism" as code words for "me-too" Clintonism. Lamar Alexander denounced "compassionate conservatism" as nothing more than "weasel words." Dan Quayle was even more caustic: "I have ordered my staff to never—ever—utter the words 'compassionate conservative.' This silly and insulting term was created by liberal Republicans and is nothing more than code for surrendering our values and principles."[27]

The Republican dilemma has been compounded by a series of stunning political victories. It is an axiom of American politics that failure is not the greatest danger a political party faces; rather, it is when that party enjoys an unexpected success. The New Deal, for example, was a rousing Democratic triumph, transforming millions of Americans from "have-nots" to "haves." Once that happened, middle-class Americans saw themselves as taxpayers rather than beneficiaries of federal largesse. Suddenly, the Landon-Dole mantra of "economy and efficiency" became their watchwords. Democrats learned to watch their language. Upon hearing that John Kennedy had planned to submit a $100 billion spending plan to Congress in 1964, Lyndon Johnson told his staff that he would not become the first Democratic president to bust the budget:

> I know that this room is full of mean, scheming little s.o.b.'s who've got special plans to put their special little pet projects into this budget so I'll be the first damn fool in history to send a $100-billion budget to the United States Congress.
>
> Let me tell you, you are not going to succeed because I'm gonna make you wish you were never born. I'm gonna make you so unhappy because I'm never gonna let you go easy. It's going to be long, and slow, and hard. It's gonna hurt.[28]

Today it is the Republicans who are suffering from a malaise generated by their successes. The demise of the Soviet Union in 1991 temporarily left the GOP bereft of a rationale for winning the presidency. For decades, Republican commanders-in chief promised to maintain a strong defense, hold the Soviet Union at bay, and uphold traditional values such as freedom and democracy as a beacon to the rest of the world. By 1992, with the Berlin Wall a mass of rubble and the Soviet Union wiped off the maps, George Bush was a Cold War president without the Cold War—thus making Bill Clinton's victory possible.[29] This Republican success was compounded by still another achievement—a balanced federal budget. For years, Republicans sought the promised land of a balanced budget— even devising such euphemisms as a "full-employment budget" (a Richard Nixon concoction) as a means of saying they had reached their nirvana. No one believed it, and by the Reagan era all pretense of claiming that the federal ledgers were balanced had given way to the ease of supply-side economics—a symbol of Hamilton's substantive victory, even as Republicans used Jeffersonian language to make their case. The $4 *trillion* deficit racked up by Reagan stymied the Democrats from any further New Deal or Great Society-like government experiments. As a political device, this worked quite nicely. Hillary Clinton has called this "Stockman's revenge," a reference to Ronald Reagan's ill-fated first budget director.[30] But by 1997, a balanced budget found the Reagan Republicans in disarray. Some wanted the surplus used for tax cuts; others wanted the money spent in their districts; still others wanted targeted tax cuts aimed at middle-class families; and another group wanted to use the surplus to draw down the federal debt. Senator Charles E. Grassley, a Landon-like balance-the-budget conservative from Iowa, recently declared: "I'm impressed with how difficult it is to manage the surplus. It's almost as difficult as managing the deficit."[31] Success is transforming the Republican party in ways as damaging to its prospects as the New Deal-Fair Deal-Great Society successes once proved fatal to the Democratic party.

THE RISE OF ABSOLUTIST POLITICS

The Republican philosophy of more individualism and less government, as advocated by Alf Landon and Bob Dole, has always contained its strain of puritanism. Landon's zealotry prompted the 1936 Republican platform writers to ominously warn that "America is in peril. The welfare of American men and women and the future of our youth are at stake. We dedicate ourselves to the preservation of their political liberty, their individual opportunity, and their character as full citizens which today are threatened by government itself."[32] Landon lauded the Republican delegates as "living proof that there are men and women able enough and brave enough to see the facts of our national problems and to meet them in the American way."[33] Sixty years later, Bob Dole saw American heretics in the baby-boomers who had risen to high positions in the Clinton administration. Dole contemptuously cited Hillary Rodham Clinton as a threat to traditional family values, taking exception to her claim that "it takes a village" to raise a child:

> After the virtual devastation of the American family, the rock upon which this country was founded, we are told that it takes a village, that is collective, and thus the state to raise a child. The state is more involved than it has ever been in the raising of children. And children are now more neglected and abused, and more mistreated than they ever have been in our time. This is not a coincidence. And with all due respect I am here to tell you it does not take a village to raise a child. It takes a family to raise a child.[34]

In 1964, political scientist Aaron Wildavsky wrote that Barry Goldwater's nomination had awakened puritanical strains that had long been suppressed. Interviewing the Goldwater delegates at the 1964 Republican National Convention, Wildavsky was overwhelmed by their passion and their willingness to sacrifice victory for adherence to conservative principles. One delegate, asked if the primary qualification of a candidate should be an ability to win votes, replied: "No; principles are more important. I would rather be one against 20,000 and believe I was right. That's what I admire about Goldwater. He's like that." In their zealous effort to purge the GOP of any remaining "me-too" Republicans, Wildavsky worried that the Goldwaterites represented a dangerous development in the American democratic experiment: "Could it be that the United States is producing large numbers of half-educated people with college degrees who have learned that participation (passion and commitment) is good but who do not understand (or cannot stand) the normal practices of democratic politics?"[35]

The successes Republicans enjoyed with victory in the Cold War and a balanced federal budget have produced a new form of absolutism that threatens to tear the party apart at the seams. This absolutism has its roots in the emphasis placed by the Anti-Federalists and their Republican successors, such as Landon and Dole, in the gospel of self-reliance. In extolling the individual, Republicans attached great importance to local civic virtue. Individuals, because they were of sound character, could do the work of government—or so the Republican argument went. Such appeals to a virtuous republic remain a staple of Republican rhetoric. But the GOP view of a relatively virtuous electorate has been turned on its head. In the minds of many Republicans, a culture war has replaced the Cold War. Bob Dole has likened contemporary liberals to the post-Cold War equivalent of political subversives: "It's as though our government, our institutions, and our culture have been hijacked by liberals and are careening dangerously off course."[36] Neoconservative intellectual Irving Kristol agrees: "There is no 'after the Cold War' for me. So far from having ended, my cold war has increased in intensity, as sector after sector of American life has been ruthlessly corrupted by the liberal ethos. It is an ethos that aims simultaneously at political and social collectivism on the one hand, and moral anarchy on the other."[37]

Fighting communism allowed the Republican party to unite its disparate elements. Dwight Eisenhower, Richard Nixon, Ronald Reagan, George Bush, Barry Goldwater, Pat Buchanan, and Dan Quayle could be counted on to rally the rank-and-file in their battle against the "evil empire." In making their pitch, Republicans cited a public willingness to make substantial sacrifices—both in their willingness to appropriate money to the Pentagon and commit American lives—as examples of virtue. Addressing the American Legion Convention in 1995, Bob Dole praised the Legionnaires, calling them "Freedom's heroes" who answered "America's call . . . [and know] what it means to wear the uniform of your country, to put your country first and to be willing to bear any sacrifice to keep her free."[38]

Today, Republicans long for virtue, but see it lacking. Gary Bauer, once a contender for the 2000 GOP presidential nomination, speaks of a "virtue deficit."[39] Such talk has led to a politics of absolutism. Its earliest manifestations were in the 1970s when voter concerns about violent crime prompted Republicans to back legislation that removed judicial discretion and required judges to impose mandatory jail sentences. This form of values politics was perfected during the 1990s, when state governors like Pete Wilson of California and Christine Todd Whitman of New Jersey signed versions of a "three-strikes-and-you're-out" law. These statutes mandated that judges institute life sentences for any violent criminal convicted for a third time. During the 1970s and 1980s, several Republican governors reinstituted capital punishment, and in the 1990s there is a rush to see how many death-row inmates can be executed. Democratic holdouts, like Mario Cuomo of New York, were defeated at the polls. Even Bill Clinton converted and imposed the death penalty on a mentally-impaired inmate in 1992. Dole tried to resurrect the crime issue in 1996, telling cheering Republican delegates: "As our many and voracious criminals go to bed tonight, at, say six in the morning, they had better pray that I lose the election. Because if I win, the lives of violent criminals are going to be hell."[40]

An especially striking example of absolutist politics was the congressional rush to judgment in supporting Megan's Law in 1996. The law was prompted by the slaying of Megan Kanka in the prosperous white middle-class town of Hamilton Township, New Jersey, back in July 1994. Kanka, who was only seven-years-old, was lured by her neighbor, thirty-two-year-old Jesse Timmendequas, into his home by offering to show her a puppy. Timmendequas strangled Kanka, and raped her as she lay dying. Twice before, Timmendequas had been convicted for committing child sex offenses, and was living with two other sex offenders in a house across the street from Megan. Megan's Law required child molesters to register with the state, and have their names and addresses released to the public.

Republicans (and Democrats) viewed this heinous crime as an example of the moral degeneration that had gripped the American psyche. On May 7, 1996, Megan's Law passed the House by a vote of 418 to zero. Two days later, the Senate unanimously passed Megan's Law by a voice vote. On May 17, 1996, President Clinton signed the measure into law. Despite the rare congressional unity, there were Democratic voices that expressed some disquiet. Rep. John Conyers, Jr., of Michigan questioned whether the registration requirement imposed an unconstitutional ex-post-facto punishment. He also raised the heretofore-Republican-like Landon and Dole federalist argument, noting that while the bill is not an unfunded mandate, it does impose a penalty on the states for non-compliance. Rep. Mel Watt (NC) agreed, questioning the prudence of not allowing states "to make their own decisions about whether they want a Megan's Law or do not want a Megan's Law." Watt criticized "Big Brother Government" for trying to force state compliance with something that is not necessarily a federal issue.[41] Despite their doubts, both men saw the political writing on the wall and voted for the measure.

Absolutist-minded Republicans felt they had another winner with the Flag Protection Act. Back in 1984 at the Republican National Convention held in Dallas, a protester burned an American flag in violation of a Texas statute that prohibited desecration of a venerated object. By a 5-to-4 decision, the U.S. Supreme Court invalidated laws in forty-eight states, and maintained that flag-burning was a form of expressive conduct protected by the First Amendment. Congress reacted by passing the Flag Protection Act of 1989. The new law criminalized the conduct of anyone who "knowingly mutilates, defaces, physically defiles, burns, maintains on the floor or ground, or tramples upon" a United States flag. Immediately after Congress passed the legislation and George H. W. Bush signed it, protestors burned American flags on the Capitol steps. Prosecutions began, and the matter became entangled in the courts. A federal district judge declared the new law unconstitutional, and the Supreme Court affirmed the decision with another 5-to-4 vote.

These court rulings have prompted an intense effort to pass a constitutional amendment that would restrict the First Amendment and place this form of political expression outside the realm of protected speech or assembly. In 1995, 1997, 1999, and 2001, the House mustered the necessary two-thirds needed to pass a flag protection amendment. Support for the amendment was especially strong among World War Two veterans who remembered the raising of the American flag at Iwo Jima. Opponents argued that the amendment was unworkable, since it might prohibit displaying the flag on clothes or commercial products highly sought after by the younger generation. Republicans paid the opposition no mind, and supported the amendment by overwhelming majorities. In 1997, for instance 219 Republican House members supported the amendment; only 12 voted against it. Democrats were more evenly split with 93 in favor and 107 against. The measure was stymied in the Senate, but only barely as the GOP fell four votes short of the two-thirds required. Forty-nine Republican senators supported the amendment, only 4 were against it. By a better than two-to-one margin, Democratic senators opposed the measure, with 14 in favor and 32 opposed. Nonetheless, the Republicans remained undeterred. In 1999, the House Judiciary Constitution subcommittee on a straight 7-to-4 party-line vote passed a new amendment that would permit Congress to pass legislation to restrain conduct, but not expression, concerning the flag. Rep. Charles Canady (FL), chairman of the Judiciary subcommittee, captured the prevailing GOP sentiments: "The flag of the United States represents values that bind America together. It warrants our respect and protection."[42]

An absolutist politics targeted against assorted rapists, criminals, and those who burn American flags proved popular at the polls. Republicans became entrusted to safeguard the traditional sanctuaries of hearth and home. Suddenly, Democrats were challenged to explain why they should be entrusted with the authority to govern, given their propensity to defend the rights of the accused. This form of "wedge politics" practiced by the Republicans reached its zenith in 1988 when George H. W. Bush accused Michael Dukakis of being a "card-carrying" member of the American Civil Liberties Union. Dukakis's opposition to a state law requiring students to recite the Pledge of Allegiance along with the revelation that convicted murderer Willie Horton raped a woman while on a weekend furlough from a Massachusetts prison while Dukakis was governor, made him a tempting target of Republican attacks.

But during the 1990s, this Republican form of absolutist politics began to backfire. First came the attacks on illegal immigrants. For some time, resentment had been building among whites in vote-rich states—including California, Florida, New Jersey, Texas, Illinois, and New York—against an onslaught of illegal immigrants who voters saw as threats to their livelihoods. Republicans thought they had a wedge issue they could exploit. In 1994, California Governor Pete Wilson backed Proposition 187 which banned all state spending on illegal immigrants and required the police to report any suspected illegals to the California Department of Justice and the U.S. Immigration Service. Wilson's television campaign featured spots showing dozens of illegal Mexicans swarming across the border as an announcer intoned, "They just keep coming." Despite the opposition of prominent Republicans Jack Kemp and William Bennett, who argued that Proposition 187 was "politically unwise and fundamentally at odds with the best tradition and spirit of our party,"[43] Wilson and Proposition 187 went on to easy victories.[44]

Proposition 187 marked the first time since 1988 that the values politics of "us versus them" went awry. Legal immigrants, whose numbers are especially large in vote-rich states, saw the Republican party as targeting them for expulsion. In fact, the Republican-controlled Congress passed legislation doubling the number of U.S. Border Patrol agents to 10,000 and hastening the deportation of immigrants who used false documents. Moreover, Republicans attached an amendment to the 1996 welfare reform bill denying benefits to the illegals. Suddenly, there was a rush of legal immigrants lining up to become naturalized citizens. Alfredo Alvarez was one. He told *The Washington Post*: "I love this country, but I feel unwanted. I feel like unless I am a true American, the government could one day knock on my door and tell me, 'Alfredo, go back to Honduras!'"[45]

These stances hurt Republicans with Hispanic voters. In 1996, Bill Clinton's nationwide support among this strategically placed group rose 11 percent from four years earlier. California Hispanics were especially hostile to Dole, awarding him a mere 18 percent of their votes. In 1998, Democrat Gray Davis became California's new governor—thanks in part to the 78 percent backing he received from Hispanics. Moreover, Cruz Bustamante won the Lieutenant Governorship (a separate race in California), becoming the first Latino elected to statewide office since 1871. Jesse Henriquez, an El Salvador immigrant, captured the sentiments of many Californian Hispanics: "The only way we can tell the people that we are working hard and that Latinos should not be blamed for all the country's problems is to register and vote. . . . Little by little, we are telling people, 'No more Proposition 187s.'"[46] California is rapidly becoming a safe bastion for Democrats—a reversal from the staunch Republicanism that characterized state politics during the Reagan years.

Undeterred in their belief that there is a virtue deficit in the American electorate, Republicans have sought other targets. One is homosexuals. In 1996, Bob Dole returned a $1,000 check from a gay Republican group, saying he did not want to create "the perception that we were buying into some special rights for any group, whether it is gays or anyone else."[47] For some time, Republicans argued that gays should not be given "special treatment" when it comes to protecting their job security, health care, or housing. But sensing an opportunity to score political points, Republicans abandoned their "we're all equal" stance in 1996 by passing the Defense of Marriage Act. Proposed by Georgia Congressman Bob Barr, the legislation forbade any state from recognizing a marriage ceremony involving couples of the same sex. At the time, Hawaii was on the verge of recognizing same-sex marriages—meaning that all states would have to acknowledge the validity of any marriage performed there, as required under the full faith and credit clause of the U.S. Constitution. For federal benefit purposes, Barr defined marriage as the legal union of one man and one woman.

The legislation stirred emotions on both sides. Barr saw himself as a hero in the culture wars, telling his colleagues: "The flames of hedonism, the flames of narcissism, the flames of self-centered morality are licking at the very foundations of our society, the family unit."[48] Even some Republicans who might have been counted on to oppose the law, supported it. Arizona Congressman Jim Kolbe voted for the act even though he is gay. Afterwards, he was outed by several gay organizations. The late Sonny Bono, Congressman and former singer and partner of Cher, whose daughter Chastity is gay, told Massachusetts Democrat Barney Frank (a self-professed homosexual): "I simply can't handle it yet, Barney. I wish I was ready, but I can't tell my son it's OK."[49]

Democrats saw the legislation as gay-baiting. Barney Frank declared, "I find it implausible that two men who decide to commit themselves to each other threaten the marriage of people who live two blocks away."[50] Senator Carol Moseley-Braun said the bill was "really about the politics of fear and division."[51] Ted Kennedy tried unsuccessfully to attach a provision prohibiting job discrimination against gays, losing by a single vote of 49 to 50. Democrats voted 41 to 5 for the Kennedy amendment; but Republicans solidly opposed it with only 8 in favor and 45 against. The Defense of Marriage Act won Senate approval by a vote of 85 to 14. The House had earlier passed the legislation by a 342 to 67 margin. Presidential spokesman Michael McCurry condemned the legislation as a "classic use of wedge politics designed to provoke anxieties and fears."[52] But McCurry's boss had other ideas. Fearing that he would be on the wrong side of the culture wars during his reelection campaign, Bill

Clinton signed the bill into law; but did so at the unusual hour of 12:50 A.M., on an otherwise quiet September night at the White House.

Abortion is another example of the dangers posed by the new politics of absolutism. During the Clinton years, Republicans twice sought to outlaw partial-birth abortions, only to be rebuffed with a presidential veto. The debate on both sides of this controversial procedure has been particularly vehement. Illinois Congressman Henry Hyde bemoaned the "abortion culture" which he believes Clinton has spawned saying, "Our beloved America is becoming 'The Killing Fields.' "[53] Believing that partial-birth abortions were symptomatic of the virtue deficit, House Republicans twice mustered the two-thirds needed to override Clinton's vetoes. In 1997, 219 House Republicans supported overriding Clinton; just 8 were opposed. The Senate has upheld Clinton's vetoes, but only by the barest of margins.

The Republican-led effort to ban partial-birth abortions was only one of many legislative initiatives designed to limit abortions. Republicans have lobbied to restore Reagan-era prohibitions against federal funding for family planning organizations promoting overseas abortions. They sought to impose an abortion ban in all U.S. military hospitals. Roger Wicker, a Mississippi House Republican who was elected president of the 1994 freshman class, sponsored legislation outlawing fetal tissue research. Each of these bills met with Clinton's strong disapproval. At a White House ceremony featuring women who had partial-birth abortions because their malformed babies would have made them barren, Clinton deplored the fact that these parents had become "political pawns."[54] Clinton supported a partial-birth abortion ban if the Republicans had included language protecting the life of the mother (which they did) and an "appropriate exception" for health (which they did not).[55]

Clinton's staunch pro-choice stance accentuated the pro-life decibels heard among Republican party activists. Texas delegates to the 1996 Republican National Convention signed a pledge promising to support an anti-abortion plank and oppose any vice presidential candidate who was not pro-life. Those opposed were sent home by the state party. One of the prospective delegates who packed his bags said of the pro-lifers, "These people don't understand and don't care about traditional politics."[56] But the power of the evangelical wing is such that no pro-choice Republican—including General Colin Powell and New Jersey Governor Christine Todd Whitman—can aspire to their party's presidential or vice-presidential nomination. In a vain attempt to dilute the pro-life influence, Bob Dole tried to insert tolerance language into the 1996 platform—only to receive a stinging rebuke from the convention delegates. Both Elizabeth

Dole and George W. Bush agree that passing a pro-life constitutional amendment is unlikely, and each hopes to mollify the anti-abortion language found in the 1996 platform. Their joint efforts are likely to be greeted by howls of protest from Republican absolutists.

The Republican party's dalliance with absolutist politics was in full public view during the impeachment inquiry and trial against President Clinton. Clinton's affair with White House intern Monica Lewinsky and his clumsy attempts to hide his extramarital relationship from Paula Jones's lawyers, provided Republicans with a vivid example of the virtue deficit in the White House. Representative Dan Burton (IN) described Clinton as a "scumbag," adding: "That's why I'm out to get him."[57] Charles Canady, a member of the House Judiciary Committee, used biblical language to castigate Clinton: "Unfortunately, the president's sins led him to commit crimes."[58] Canady and his fellow House impeachment managers attempted to make this case to the U.S. Senate. Although they never came close to mustering the two-thirds vote needed to remove Clinton from office, Senate Republicans were persuaded: 46 voted guilty on the perjury charge and 50 said Clinton had obstructed justice. In each instance, the Senate GOP defectors were 1960s-style "me-too" Northeast moderates accustomed to the art of political compromise.[59] Party voting also dominated in the House. The Judiciary Committee approved three of four articles of impeachment on a straight-line party vote of 21 to 16. In the full House, 98 percent of House Republicans supported Article One (accusing Clinton of lying before a federal grand jury); 88 percent passed Article Two (which claimed that Clinton gave false testimony in his Paula Jones deposition); 95 percent approved Article Three (which charged Clinton with obstruction of justice); and 64 percent backed Article Four (which stated that Clinton had abused his office).

What is especially striking about Clinton's impeachment is the Republican uniformity exhibited on the legislative examples of absolutist politics cited in this article. This unanimity, and Clinton's desire to undercut the GOP by stealing their most popular issues, served to increase the vehemence of the absolutists. Presidential Press Secretary Mike McCurry warned in 1996 that if Clinton adopted Republican-centrist style policies, then the GOP "can only win by doing the single most dangerous thing [to] Clinton . . . which is to totally destroy him as a human being."[60] By endorsing such measures as the Defense of Marriage Act, Clinton aroused the ire of the absolutists who hated him even more than the Republican recalcitrants of the 1930s loathed FDR. Many of the House impeachment managers had been leaders in the new politics of absolutism. Congressman Bob Barr of Georgia wrote the Defense of Marriage

TABLE ONE

The Absolutist Politics of the House Impeachment Managers

Impeachment Managers	Megan's Law	Flag Amendment (1997 vote)	Curbing Illegal Immigration	Defense of Marriage Act	Partial-Birth Abortion Override Vote
Henry Hyde	Yea	Yea	Yea	Yea	Yea
James Sensenbrenner	Yea	Yea	Yea	Yea	Yea
Bill McCollum	Yea	Yea	Yea	Yea	Yea
George Gekas	Yea	Yea	Yea	Yea	Yea
Charles Canady	Yea	Yea	Yea	Yea	Yea
Steve Buyer	Yea	Yea	Yea	Yea	Yea
Ed Bryant	Yea	Yea	Yea	Yea	Yea
Steve Chabot	Yea	Yea	Yea	Yea	Yea
Bob Barr	Yea	Yea	Yea	Yea	Yea
Asa Hutchinson	Yea	Yea	Yea	Yea	Yea
Christopher Cannon	Not in Congress	Yea	Not in Congress	Not in Congress	Yea
James Rogan	Not in Congress	Yea	Not in Congress	Not in Congress	Yea
Lindsay Graham	Yea	Yea	Yea	Yea	Yea

Act, and he was joined by James Sensenbrenner of Wisconsin and Charles Canady who served as a co-sponsors floor managers of the bill. As Table One makes clear, the House impeachment managers were reliable yeas when it came to voting for measures that would impose their virtues on the larger body politic.

The development of absolutist politics within GOP circles poses a serious electoral danger to a party operating in an increasingly secular society. Having talked about almost nothing else except impeachment for two years, Republican absolutism received a black eye from the voters. In 1998, Democrats added five House seats—a feat not seen by the president's party in a midterm election since Franklin Roosevelt's Democrats improved on their scores in 1934. The GOP scored poorly on what voters described as "very important" issues in the 2000 elections (see Table Two). Even on matters such as handling the economy and managing the federal budget—issues once copyrighted by the Republicans— Democrats surged ahead. Not surprisingly, 47 percent wanted the country to continue moving in Clinton's direction; just 29 percent preferred the path outlined by congressional Republicans.[61]

TABLE TWO

Issues and Party Images in the 2000 Elections (in percentages)

Issue	Percent who say issue will be "very important" in 2000 vote	Democrats	Republicans	Both	Neither	No Opinion
Handling the economy	80	47	42	2	4	5
Managing the federal budget	74	43	40	5	10	2
Protecting the Social Security System	74	52	29	3	8	8
Improving education and the schools	73	51	35	3	6	5
Protecting patients' rights in the health care system	71	53	27	4	9	7

Source: "Democrats Have Edge on Election Issues," *Washington Post,* March 17, 1999, p. A-5.

In his closing argument before the U.S. Senate advocating the impeachment of President Clinton, Henry Hyde declared: "Equal justice is what moves me and animates me and consumes me. And I'm willing to lose my seat any day in the week rather than sell out on those issues. Despite all the polls and the hostile editorials, America is hungry for people who believe in something. You may disagree with us, but we believe in something."[62] Hyde's contention is irrefutable. Operating against all conventional wisdom, and a plethora of public opinion polls showing an overwhelming majority opposed to impeachment, Republicans pushed ahead. The result was that Clinton survived not because of who he was, but thanks to his enemies. Collectively, the Newt Gingriches, Rush Limbaughs, Pat Robertsons, Kenneth Starrs, Henry Hydes, members of the Religious Right, and other assorted Clinton-haters constituted the most unappealing political opposition since the obdurate Landonites who railed against Franklin Roosevelt's New Deal. Unless Republicans can solve their absolutist dilemma and return to their Landon-Dole heritage of less government and more individualism, the dialogue in the public square is likely to remain very nasty indeed.

NOTES

1 Alexis de Tocqueville, *Democracy in America* (New York: New American Library, 1956), p. 194, emphasis added.

2 Robert D. Putnam, "Bowling Alone: America's Declining Social Capital," *Journal of Democracy,* January 1995.

3 Cited in Robert M. Eisinger, "Cynical America? Misunderstanding the Public's Message," *The Public Perspective,* April/May 1999, p. 47.

4 Voter Research and Surveys, exit poll, November 5, 1996.

5 Bill Clinton, State of the Union Address, Washington, D.C., January 23, 1996.

6 The best of these works is Seymour Martin Lipset, *American Exceptionalism: A Double-Edged Sword* (New York: W.W. Norton, 1996).

7 1936 Republican National Platform, as reprinted in the *New York Times,* June 12, 1936, p. 1.

8 Alfred M. Landon, "Text of Governor Landon's Milwaukee Address on Social Security," Milwaukee, Wisconsin, September 27, 1936; World Wide Web: Internet citation, http://199.173.224.3/history/alfspeech.html.

9 "Transcript of the First Presidential Debate," *Washington Post,* October 7, 1996.

10 Jean Bethke Elshtain, *Democracy on Trial* (New York: Basic Books, 1982), p. 9.

11 1936 Republican National Platform.

12 1936 Democratic National Platform, as reprinted in *The New York Times,* June 26, 1936, p. 1.

13 See Morton J. Frisch, ed., *Selected Writings and Speeches of Alexander Hamilton* (Washington, D.C.: American Enterprise Institute, 1985), p. 316.

14 1936 Democratic Platform.

15 "Landon's Message to Convention," *New York Times,* June 13, 1936, p. 7.

16 1980 Republican National Platform (Washington, D.C.: Republican National Committee, 1980).

17 Herbert Croly, *The Promise of American Life* (New York: Archon Books reprint, 1963), p. 29.

18 Robert D. Novak, "Big Government Conservatism," *Washington Post,* September 25, 1997, p. A-25.

19 Landon, "Text of Governor Landon's Milwaukee Address on Social Security."

20 Ted Morgan, *FDR: A Biography* (New York: Simon and Schuster, 1985), p. 441.

21 Hart-Teeter survey, March 16-18, 1995.

_22_ George Gallup, survey, 1936 and Decision/Making/Information, survey, for the Republican National Committee, April 21-23, 1987. Cited in John Kenneth White, *The New Politics of Old Values* (Hanover, New Hampshire: University Press of New England, 1990), p. 131.

_23_ Ronald Reagan, "Economic Report of the President's Annual Message to Congress," Washington, D.C., February 10, 1982.

_24_ Samuel G. Freedman, "Why Bob Dole Can't Be Reagan," *New York Times,* October 27, 1996, p. E-4.

_25_ Fred I. Greenstein, *The Hidden-Hand Presidency: Eisenhower as Leader* (New York: Basic Books, 1982), p. 50.

_26_ Daniel Patrick Moynihan, *Came the Revolution: Argument in the Reagan Era* (New York: Harcourt Brace Jovanovich, 1988), pp. 156-157.

_27_ E.J. Dionne, Jr., "Construction Boon: It's No Accident That the GOP Is Being Rebuilt by Its Governors," *Washington Post,* March 14, 1999, p. B-4.

_28_ Moynihan, *Came the Revolution,* p. 76.

_29_ See John Kenneth White, *Still Seeing Red: How the Cold War Shapes the New American Politics* (Boulder: Westview Press, 1998), especially pp. 107-253.

_30_ George Stephanopoulos, *All Too Human: A Political Education* (Boston: Little Brown and Company, 1999), p. 387.

_31_ George Hager, "GOP Tax-Cutting Budget Plans Open Double-Barrel Hill Debate," *Washington Post,* March 18, 1999, p. A-4.

_32_ 1936 Republican platform.

_33_ "Landon's Message to Convention," *New York Times,* June 13, 1936, p. 7.

_34_ Dole, Acceptance Speech, August 15, 1996.

_35_ Aaron Wildavsky, "The Goldwater Phenomenon: Purists, Politicians, and the Two-Party System," in Norman L. Zucker, ed., *The American Party Process: Readings and Comments* (New York: Dodd, Mead, 1968), pp. 445-446, 460.

_36_ Robert J. Dole, "State of the Union: The Republican Response," Washington, D.C., January 23, 1996.

_37_ Irving Kristol, *Neoconservatism: The Autobiography of an Idea* (New York: Free Press, 1995), p. 486.

_38_ Bob Dole, "Remarks Prepared for Delivery," American Legion Convention, Indianapolis, Indiana, September 4, 1995.

_39_ Gary Bauer, "A Conservative View of American Foreign Policy," John F. Kennedy School of Government, Harvard University, Cambridge, Massachusetts. Internet citation http://www.ksg.harvard.edu/ksgpress/ ksg_news/transcripts/bauer.htm.

_40_ Robert J. Dole, Acceptance Speech, Republican national Convention, San Diego, August 15, 1996.

_41_ Paul Koenig, "Does Congress Abuse Its Spending Clause Power by Attaching Conditions on the Receipt of Federal Law Enforcement Funds to a State's Compliance with 'Megan's Law'," *Journal of Criminal Law and Criminology,* Winter 1998, volume 88, number 2, pp. 721-765.

42 Jim Abrams, "Congress Moves on Flag Desecration Constitutional Amendment," CNN/AllPolitics, Website, April 14, 1999. Internet citation http://www.allpolitics.com.

43 Dick Kirschten, "Second Thoughts," *National Journal,* January 21, 1995, p. 150.

44 Wilson also supported Proposition 227 which would have ended bilingual education in public schools and Proposition 209 which would have curtailed affirmative action.

45 William Booth, "In a Rush, New Citizens Register Their Political Interest," *Washington Post,* September 26, 1996, p. A-1.

46 William Claiborne, "Democrats Don't Have Lock on Hispanic Vote, Latino Leaders Say," *Washington Post,* November 24, 1996, p. A-12. Texas Governor George W. Bush admonishes his fellow Republicans to be an "inclusive" party. Toward that end, Bush speaks fluent Spanish and won impressive support from Hispanics in his 1998 reelection bid.

47 Robert J. Dole, transcript, "This Week with David Brinkley," ABC News broadcast, September 17, 1995.

48 CNN/AllPolitics, "House Votes to Bar Gay Marriages Under Federal Law," July 12, 1996. Internet citation http://allpolitics.com.

49 Michael Barone and Grant Ujifusa, *The Almanac of American Politics, 1998* (Washington, D.C.: National Journal, 1997), p. 254.

50 "House Votes to Bar Gay Marriages Under Federal Law."

51 "Senate Says No to Gay Marriage," CNN/AllPolitics Website, September 10, 1996. Internet citation http://allpolitics.com.

52 CNN/AllPolitics, "House Says No to Same-Sex Marriages," July 12, 1996. Internet citation http://allpolitics.com.

53 Henry Hyde, "Consideration of the Veto Message on HR 1122, Partial-Birth Abortion Ban Act," *The Human Life Review,* Fall 1998, p. 95.

54 Bill Clinton, "Remarks on Returning Without Approval to the House of Representatives Partial-Birth Abortion Legislation," *Weekly Compilation of Presidential Documents,* April 15, 1996, p. 643.

55 Bill Clinton, "Message to the House of Representatives Returning Without Approval Partial-Birth Abortion Legislation," *Weekly Compilation of Presidential Documents,* October 13, 1997, p. 1545.

56 Jerelyn Eddings, "A Republican Civil War: Can Dole Unite a Party Divided Over Abortion?," *U.S. News and World Report,* July 8, 1996, p. 38.

57 White, *Still Seeing Red,* p. 301.

58 "We Stand Poised on the Edge of a Constitutional Cliff," *Washington Post,* December 11, 1998, p. A-28.

59 They were Arlen Specter, Pennsylvania; John Chafee, Rhode Island; James Jeffords, Vermont; Olympia Snowe and Susan Collins, Maine. Clinton had twice carried their states.

60 Lars-Erik Nelson, "The Republicans' War," *New York Review of Books*, February 4, 1999, p. 6.

61 "Democrats Have Edge on Election Issues," *Washington Post*, March 17, 1999, p. A-5.

62 Peter Baker, "Judge Orders Lewinsky to Cooperate," *Washington Post*, January 24, 1999, p. A-18.

ARTICLE 8

CAMPAIGN FINANCE AFTER THE 2000 ELECTIONS: A NEW REGIME?

Clyde Wilcox
Georgetown University

"There's no doubt that special interests and their representatives have taken over the legislative process, and more and more money is pouring into political campaigns from these interests . . . We will have blood all over the floor of the Senate until we exceed to the demands . . . of the American people to be represented in Washington again." John McCain, interviewed by Jim Leher, August 1, 2000."

"If we choose to be angry, let it be in defense of our standing as a self-governing people. Let its poison harden us in battle against those who, in exchange for campaign contributions, sell policy and sell access to power—which belongs rightfully to all of us. For how can we serve each other's needs and preserve our very earth if we allow greedy interests to steal from us the reins of our own democracy? There's the issue, friends: not the theft of an election, but the theft of a democracy." Doris Haddock—"Granny D", speech at DuPont Circle Park, Washington, D.C. Jan 20, 2001.

On Feb. 29, 2000, Doris Haddock, popularly known as "Granny D," completed a walk from Los Angeles, California to Washington, D.C. to focus public attention on campaign finance reform. Haddock, who was 90 years old, averaged 10 miles a day on foot and on cross-country skis, walking in the hot sun, the cool rain, and blinding snowstorms. She arrived accompanied by more than 2000 supporters, who listened while she began reading the Bill of Rights in the Capitol Rotunda, where she was promptly arrested.

At about the same time, Senator John McCain was seeking the Republican presidential nomination. McCain's most important legislative agenda had been to seek the elimination of large "soft money" contributions by interest groups and rich individuals to political parties, which he charged corrupted the political process and led legislators to support policies or amendments that they would otherwise oppose. McCain eventually lost the nomination to George W. Bush, who raised more money than any presidential candidate in history.

Granny D and John McCain did not succeed in elevating campaign finance reform to the top of the public's agenda. Surveys showed that although the public greatly dislikes the current system of funding elections, they care more about schools, the environment, taxes, and other issues that affect them on a daily basis. An April, 2000 poll by ABC-News and the Washington Post found that 2/3 of Americans support campaign finance reform, but that Americans rated the issue last in importance in a list of 15 policy issues.[1]

Yet there is also evidence that public attitudes about campaign finance are a major source of alienation from government. John Hibbing, a political scientist who studies attitudes toward government, argues that many Americans believe they are being "played for a sucker" by a government that listens to wealthy interest groups instead of average citizens. They believe this in part because of what they read about large contributions to campaigns and parties by interest groups. A Washington Post survey in 1997 showed that 82% of the public thought that the campaign finance system was either broken or had serious problems. A New York Times poll in 1997 showed that contrary to popular opinion, the public is not apathetic about campaign finance reform, but instead believes that politicians are unwilling to act on the issue (Clines, 1997).

Although scholars, journalists, and campaign finance professionals disagree about the role of money in elections, the importance of contributions in influencing legislation, and about the best course for reform, there is a growing agreement that the current campaign finance system is not working. Americans spent approximately $4 billion dollars in national, state, and local levels in 2000, making the elections the most expensive in history. Those who give this money are becoming increasingly irritated by the constant pleas to give more, and those who watch the seemingly endless barrage of campaign commercials purchased by this money are generally unhappy with the tone of the messages and their saturation of prime-time television.

In the aftermath of the election, attention was focused on the mechanisms of casting and counting votes, but perhaps an even more important story was that the 2000 election marked the end of the system of campaign finance regulation that had been enacted more than 25 years before. This regulatory framework has been

---

[1]"NEW POLLS REVEAL PUBLIC SUPPORT GROWING FOR CAMPAIGN REFORM" Political Finance & Lobby Reporter, April 12, 2000.

unraveling for some time, but by the end of the 2000 election cycle it was evident that we had entered a new regime of financing campaigns. There are widespread calls for reform of the system, but no consensus yet on precisely what reforms are needed.

To fully understand what transpired in 2000, and to think clearly about reforms, it is first necessary to understand how campaigns were financed before the Federal Election Campaign Act (FECA) amendments were enacted in 1974, to describe the nature of the reforms enacted in the FECA, and to show how those regulations have systematically lost their force over time.

PRE-FECA

Although campaign costs today dwarf those of earlier times, campaigning for office has always cost money. During the nation's first century, political parties printed newspapers to advance their ideas and candidates, and often solicited private contributions to pay for those publications. By the 1840s, campaigns were spending money on buttons, pamphlets, banners, and other items. Twenty years later Stephen Douglas barnstormed the U.S. in his unsuccessful campaign against Abraham Lincoln, although there are no estimates of the costs of his travels.

In 1896, Ohio mining magnate Mark Hanna gave $100,000 to GOP candidate William McKinley—the equivalent of more than $1,000,000 today—and raised between 3.5 and 10 million dollars by assessing banks and corporations a fee based on their assets. Standard Oil and J.P. Morgan each gave $250,000, and other corporations, banks, and industrialists gave large sums (Baida, 1992). While Democratic nominee William Jennings Bryan mobilized farmers, workers, and evangelical Christians, the GOP tapped the deep pockets of corporate America—outspending the Democrats by perhaps as much as 20-1.

Congress enacted the Tilman Act of 1907, which banned contributions by banks and corporations to candidates for national office. A series of scandals in the Harding Administration led to the passage of the Federal Corrupt Practices Act in 1925, which continued the ban on corporate and bank contributions, and required campaigns to report their receipts and expenditures. During World War II, the ban on corporate and bank contributions was extended to labor unions.

By the 1950s, laws banned corporate and labor contributions to campaigns, capped spending, and required disclosure of receipts and expenditures, but none of these laws had much force. The spending limits had loopholes, for they applied only to the candidates themselves and not to special committees organized on their behalf by the political parties. Corporations and banks avoided their contribution ban by awarding large bonuses to executives, who promptly contributed that money to candidates in their capacity as an individual citizen. Labor unions avoided the ban on their contributions by forming Political Action Committees—organizations which were run by the unions, but which were not unions. The documents that disclosed campaign receipts and expenditures were jammed into locked closets controlled by congressional staff. There was not a single prosecution for violation of these laws (Sorauf, 1992).

Overacker (1932) reported that in 1928 more than 2/3 of contributions to the Democratic and Republican national committees came in amounts of $1,000 or more, and more than half came in gifts of more than $5000. By the 1950s, industries were making coordinated contributions to party leaders, who redistributed the money to aid campaigns. Lyndon Johnson's political career was greatly enhanced by his ability to channel money from independent oil companies to Democratic candidates (Caro, 1982). Heard (1960) reported that campaigns in the 1950s were financed primarily by business, although labor unions played a major role for Democrats. Campaign money was channeled through party leaders during this period, who could use the money as part of their efforts to build majorities for legislation.

It was the two campaigns of Richard Nixon, however, which precipitated campaign finance reform. By the time of the 1968 campaign, parties had declined in importance, and individual candidates raised their own money. Campaigns were waged on television, leading to a sharp increase in spending. Total campaign spending increased by 50% from 1964 to 1968. In response, Congress in 1971 passed the Federal Election Campaign Act, which required disclosure of receipts and expenditures, and codified the existence of Political Action Committees.

As Congress examined the Nixon campaign's activities in 1972 as part of its Watergate investigation, they discovered illegal corporate contributions that had been solicited by Nixon fundraisers, and laundered through complex schemes. These contributions were already illegal, but they were difficult to trace because of the lack of effective disclosure. The investigations also revealed sizable contributions made by individuals who were appointed as ambassadors (Alexander, 1984; Drew, 1983). In 1974, Congress replaced the Federal Election Campaign Act with a set of comprehensive amendments.

The FECA Framework

The FECA amendments provided a comprehensive set of regulations on campaign fundraising, spending, and disclosure, and provided limited public funding. It had four main elements.

1) Contribution limits. Individuals were limited to contributions of $1000 to any one candidate during a primary or general election, and were not permitted to give to the presidential candidates during the general elections. For most Congressional candidates who run in the general election, this means that contributions were capped at $2000—$1000 for the primary election and an additional $1000 for the general election. In presidential elections, contributions were only allowed during the primary election, for the general election was funded by a public grant.

   Interest groups could form political action committees (PACs) which could raise money up to $5000 from each of their members, and give up to $5000 to candidates in each election. This was the only way that interest groups could give money in the FECA framework. Corporations, unions, and other interest groups were prohibited from making contributions from their treasuries.

   Parties could give money to candidates in the primary election campaigns, and spend on behalf of the candidates in the general elections. Candidates could give their own campaign $50,000 of their personal wealth. Contribution limits were not indexed to inflation, so that these limits today are far more constraining than they were in 1974.

2) Spending limits. Congressional candidates were limited in their spending in primary and general election campaigns. Limits were placed on the amounts of their own money that wealthy individuals could spend on their own or other's campaigns. Presidential primary candidates were limited both in their overall spending, and also in their spending in each state.

3) Disclosure. The FECA created a new federal agency, the Federal Election Commission (FEC), which would audit the campaigns, disburse the federal fund, and maintain records of the fundraising and spending of candidates, parties, and PACs. Candidates, parties and PACs were required to file regular reports detailing the names, occupations, and addresses of their contributors, and also the way they have spent their money. This information was made available to the public by the FEC in a variety of formats, enabling saavy reporters to determine when there is a coordinated effort by a particular industry to support a given candidate. The FEC maintains a web page that provides a great deal of summary information at *www.fec.gov,* and allows the public to download databases of contributions and expenditures free of charge.

4) Public Funding A public fund was created, financed by a checkoff on federal tax forms. This fund was used to partially finance Presidential primary elections by providing candidates with a subsidy that matched the first $250 of contributions from any citizen, up to a maximum amount. Thus a contribution of $1000 was worth $1250, while a gift of $25 was worth $50 because of federal matching funds. Candidates could borrow against the promise of matching funds, making that money available early in the campaign. Candidates could receive these matching funds even if they run unopposed in their party's primaries, as Reagan did in 1984 and Clinton did in 1996.

The public fund was also used to finance the Republican and Democratic party conventions. Finally, the public fund was used to finance the general election campaigns of the two major parties with equal-sized grants, and to provide more limited funding to the candidates of other parties which had done well in the previous election. Congress considered public financing for congressional elections, but the provision was dropped in conference committee.

Thus the FECA regulatory system limited contributions and spending, required that candidates and other actors disclose their activity, and provided for some partial public funding. This framework was never fully implemented, for the act was immediately challenged in court by an unusual coalition of liberal and conservative actors, who argued among other things that giving money and spending it in campaigns is a form of free speech, and therefore cannot be limited by Congress.

The Supreme Court was faced with a difficult dilemma. On the one hand, unlimited contributions by individuals and groups would increase the chance of corruption, and might erode public confidence in government. On the other hand, candidates and groups must spend money in order to make their speech heard by the larger public, and it is election campaigns that free speech is perhaps the most important. The Court tried to satisfy both principles, holding that spending was indeed speech and therefore could not be limited, but that contributions create the possibility of corruption and therefore could be limited. Spending by presidential candidates could be limited if they agreed to accept public funding, essentially voluntarily foregoing their unlimited right to speech in exchange for a subsidy from the government. Groups and individuals were also allowed to spend unlimited amounts to independently advocate the election or defeat of candidates, but groups could finance these expenditures only through the voluntary contributions of their members to their PACs as regulated by FECA limits.

The distinction between spending and contributing makes little practical sense. If spending is speech, then why not allow a citizen to give money to a candidate who speaks for her cause? And if a contribution can lead to corruption, surely spending money on behalf of the candidate can as well. Yet the distinction has continued in campaign law. This means that an individual can give only $2000 to a congressional candidate for her primary and general election races, but can spend millions urging citizens to cast their ballots for her.

In the aftermath of this decision, the FECA regime included contribution limits, spending limits for most presidential candidates, full disclosure of contributions and spending, and limited public funding. One of the most important developments in the early years of this regime was the rapid formation of Political Action Committees (PACs). Although corporations and labor unions were banned from giving money directly to candidates, they were allowed to form committees that would raise money from their members and give that money to candidates. PACs were regulated by the FECA—there were limits on the size of contributions they could receive from members, on who precisely was considered a member and therefore eligible to give, and on how much they could give to candidates. Within a few years there were thousands of PACs representing corporations, trade associations, labor unions, and citizen groups. Campaigns under the FECA regime were more candidate centered, for individual candidates raised their own money rather than receiving it filtered through party leaders.

Over the next 24 years, the FECA framework began to erode. By the end of the 2000 campaign, it was essentially defunct.

The Unraveling of the FECA Regulations

Each of the four main pillars of the FECA have been undermined by subsequent decisions by the courts, by the FEC, and by practices of candidates and campaigns.

1) Spending limits. The Supreme Court voided most spending limits in 1976 in *Buckley* v. *Valeo*. It left spending limits in place in presidential elections, however, for primary election candidates who accept matching funds, and for general election candidates who accept the public grant. The limits on spending in particular states were always violated by campaigns in relatively obvious ways, including buying advertising on Boston television that is beamed into New Hampshire in advance of that state's primary, but charging the expenditure against the Massachusetts limit. Overall spending limits were a factor in several races, including the 1996 campaign. In that election, GOP candidate Bob Dole

spent all of his allowable primary election money by late spring, and was thus unable to spend campaign funds until the convention which signaled the start of the general election campaign.

In 2000, George W. Bush became the first serious presidential candidate to forgo matching funds during the primary election in order to be able to spend an unlimited amount in the primaries. Bush subsequently raised more than $90 million dollars during the primary elections, mostly in contributions of $1000. Bush's fundraising success was probably due to his combined status as the governor of a wealthy state and son of a former president with ties to the moderate wing of the GOP, but it is clear that other mainstream candidates could also refuse matching funds and thereby avoid spending limits. Al Gore could easily have raised more money than the government provided in matching funds, but he feared the political cost of such an action. Bush's victory will clear the way for future mainstream candidates to follow his lead.

The spending limits remain in effect for the general election, but they have little force. The campaigns officially spend the public grant, but presidential candidates also effectively coordinate the spending of party soft money, described below. The Bush and Gore campaigns controlled much more money than was provided by the federal government, and there is no effective limit to the amount of soft money that parties can spend on behalf of issues or candidates.

2) Contribution limits. The contribution limits established in the FECA remain in force, and the amounts have not been adjusted for inflation. Money contributed directly to candidates, and much of the money controlled by parties and PACs is called "hard money," and is subject to those limits. But decisions by Congress and the FEC have created a special category of contributions that are not capped—"soft money." Soft money differs from hard money in two main characteristics. First, soft money can come directly from interest group treasuries, and need not be raised through PACs. Second, there are no limits to the amount of money that an individual, corporation, union, or other interest group can give.

Soft money contributions cannot be made to candidates, but instead go to the political parties. Parties are supposed to spend this money on party building activity, voter mobilization, and state and local elections. In practice, however, presidential candidates and party leaders raise soft money and control how it is allocated. After the 1996 election, the FEC ruled that both Clinton and Dole had controlled soft money spending by parties and thereby violated the law, but it fined both campaigns $0.

Soft money contributions to national party committees are disclosed to the Federal Election Commission, but in the 2000 campaign Republicans directed some donors to split their money between national and state party committees, thereby avoiding the disclosure of some of those contributions (Van Natta and Broder, 2000).

3) Disclosure. The requirement that candidates and parties disclose receipts and expenditures remains in effect, and covers soft money contributions as well. Yet the Court has created a new category of spending, called "issue advocacy," that is not covered under the FECA. Issue ads cannot explicitly call for the election or defeat of a candidate, but they can raise issues, and feature the picture and name of a candidate. To understand the distinction, consider two hypothetical ads, run by interest groups.

"Congressman X (picture) has voted to raise your taxes 10 times. He lives in a posh home in Washington (picture), so he doesn't understand how average citizens of our state live. Congressman X promised that he would support elderly citizens, but voted five times against bills that would have saved Medicare (picture of candidate). Send Candidate X a message" : vote for Candidate Y in November."

That was a campaign advertisement, fully governed by FECA limits. Now consider a similar ad:

"Congressman X (picture) has voted to raise your taxes 10 times. He lives in a posh home in Washington (picture), so he doesn't understand how average Americans live. Congressman X promised that he would support elderly citizens, but five times twice against bills that would have saved Medicare (picture of candidate). Tell Congressman X how you feel about his breaking his promises, and be sure to vote in November."

This latter advertisement does not explicitly use the words "defeat" or "vote for," and is therefore an issue advertisement. Issue advertisements are not considered campaign ads, and therefore lie outside of the FECA disclosure guidelines. Moreover, the money for these ads can come from the treasuries of unions or corporations, or from membership dues of interest groups. Congress in 2000 voted to require disclosure for issue advertising run by certain types of committees, but it is still quite difficult to trace the source of money spent in issue advertising, and it is very difficult to accurately estimate the aggregate amounts spent. Loopholes in disclosure requirements allow many groups to avoid disclosure altogether.

4) Public Financing. The FECA provision for public funds to match small contributions during presidential primaries, to help pay for the presidential conventions, and to finance the general election campaigns remains in place. These funds remain in effect, and are valuable for poorly financed candidates, or those from the ideological wings of the parties. It is likely that future mainstream primary election candidates will refuse matching funds in the primaries in order to avoid spending limits, as noted above.

The public funds for the convention and general election campaigns will continue to be used, but their original purpose no longer applies. The public grant was intended to pay for the presidential conventions, but today private corporations pay for much of the event, and provide lavish parties and for delegates and especially for policymakers. The public grant for the general election was intended to provide a level playing field for the major parties and to free candidates from fundraising, but now soft-money events are prominent in candidate schedules, and soft money is a significant portion of all presidential general election spending—far more than the total provided by the public grant. From June 1 to September 20, 2000, for example, the two parties spent some $52 million on commercials in the presidential race, compared with $21 million total for the two presidential campaigns (Marks, 2000).

Thus the post-FECA system resembles the pre-FECA system. Spending limits are in effect for only some elections, and are easily circumvented. Contribution limits do not apply to soft money, so parties continue to solicit large contributions from wealthy individuals, from corporations, and from other interest groups. Disclosure is far better than it was before the FECA was adopted, but an increasing portion of activity takes place outside the system. Finally, the limited public funding no longer frees up candidates from fundraising concerns so that they can concentrate on campaigning. Instead, it merely acts as a supplement to the private money raised by parties and campaigns. The new regime shifts the focus of campaign spending away from candidates, toward political parties and interest groups.

The extent to which the new post-FECA system resembles the pre-FECA system is striking. Before the FECA, industries often gave large sums in coordination to influence legislation: in 2001 the banking and financial sector gave large amounts to try to induce Congress to pass a bill making it harder for individuals to declare bankruptcy. Before FECA, presidents rewarded their financial backers with ambassadorships and subtly hinted of that possibility in soliciting the contributions. In 2001, the New York Times reported that Bush's financial backers were lining up for choice ambassadorships. ("A Mad Scramble by Donors for Plum Ambassadorships", by Marc Lacey and Raymond Bonner. New York Times, March 17, 2001, page A1.)

Rules are not neutral; some campaign finance actors benefit from the post-FECA system. Corporations find it easier to contribute large sums of soft money from their profits than to raise money through PACs. Labor unions, environmental groups, Christian conservative groups, and feminist groups all have an easier time spending large sums under the post-FECA rules. Candidates find that they control less of the spending in their races, however, and therefore have a harder time directing the message. Party committees now have more money to spend, but they most compete with interest groups to make their voice heard.

With the regulatory regime in tatters, there are many proposals for reform. Dozens of campaign finance reform proposals are introduced into every session of Congress, and academics generate many reports that include suggestions for reform every year. Three sets of proposals are most often mentioned: banning or limiting soft money, regulating or disclosing issue advocacy, and scrapping limits altogether and simply requiring disclosure.

The Reform Agenda

Banning Soft Money At the top of the reform agenda is a ban on soft money contributions to the political parties. Banning soft money is at the heart of the McCain-Feingold bill—the most seriously debated campaign finance reform measure in the most recent Congressional sessions. The principal argument for banning soft money is that contributions of unlimited size have a significant potential to corrupt policymakers, and are a source of public perceptions that Congress is bought by special interests.

Senator John McCain, cosponsor of the bill, argued on the Senate floor: "I believe, even if some of my colleagues do not, that these amounts [of soft money] have impaired our integrity. I believe that as strongly as I believe anything. Unlimited amounts of money given to political campaigns have impaired our integrity as political parties and as a legislative institution. Those interests enjoy greater influence here than the working men and women who cannot afford to buy our attention but who are affected, sometimes adversely, by the laws we pass. For me, Mr. President, that seems to be a good working definition of an impairment of our integrity, which is, as I noted, Webster's definition of corruption." (speech on Senate floor, October 14, 1999).

In recent years, party soft money fundraising has become increasingly frantic, and has occurred in many ethically dubious settings. It is not uncommon, for example, for the majority party to hold a soft money fundraising event the day before marking up a piece of legislation, inviting groups interested in the bill to contribute and then to share their views with legislators. In 2000, Republican state attorney generals solicited large contributions from corporations that were embroiled in, or seeking to avoid, lawsuits by the states (Lardner and Schmidt, 2000). Both parties are engaged in a seemingly desperate scramble to raise larger and larger sums of soft money. Some groups give millions of dollars to party committees year after year. (A list of top soft money donors is available and regularly updated at *www.opensecrets.org.*) Reformers argue that the potential for corruption is obvious with unlimited contributions, and that corruption has in fact already occurred, in both parties.

Soft money has come to constitute an increasingly important part of party spending. Figure 1 shows the hard money and soft money raised by national Republican and Democratic party committees in every election cycle since 1992, according to FEC figures. Party fundraising is consistently higher in presidential elections than in off-year elections, and Republicans consistently have a large advantage in "hard money." But one of the striking trends in the figure is the increase in soft money raised by the parties. For Democrats, the total increases from $36 million in 1992 to more than $240 million in 2000, for Republicans the increase is from just under $50 million to more than $240 million in 2000. Although both parties raised an almost identical amount of soft money, this is in marked contrast to a large GOP advantage in hard money—Democrats depend more on soft money to remain competitive in elections. The totals in Figure 1 do not include soft money raised by state and local party organizations, which grew significantly in 2000 as well.

There is little controversy that soft money gives its donors greater access to policymakers. Soft money is raised in intimate settings. In the New York Senate race, Republicans held cocktail parties at which the price of admission varied from $1000 to $100,000, providing opportunities to have personal conversations with state GOP policymakers. Mrs. Clinton held dinners in the homes of backers, where groups and individuals gave as much as $25,000 per person. Major soft money donors—labor unions, tobacco companies,

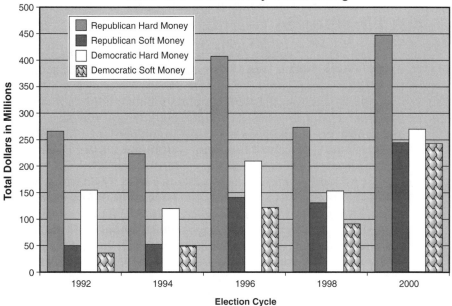

FIGURE 1. Hard and Soft Money Fundraising

Microsoft Corporation, the National Rifle Association—are often invited to meetings in attractive settings where they are given access to party leaders. For example, one new Democratic soft money donor was visited personally by Senator Robert Torricelli, chief fundraiser for the Senate Democrats, and then invited to a Washington dinner with President Clinton. (Schmidt, 2000). The Clinton administration invited large soft money donors to spend the night in the White House.

If soft money donors get special access, does this translate into policy payoffs? This is perhaps surprisingly a much more complex question than it initially appears. Many groups that give money to one political party get substantial support from the members of that party in legislative action. Yet political scientists note that many soft money contributions are made to reward a party or policymaker who has promoted a policy, not to influence future decisions. Thus, unions give to the Democratic party because most Democrats are more sympathetic to labor concerns than most Republicans. Pro-life groups spend money to help the Republican party because they believe it is the party that will promote its interests, not because they fear that pro-choice groups will outbid them for the support of Jesse Helms. Many of the most highly publicized soft money donors—Charles Keating and Roger Tamraz, for example, did not ultimately receive the policy payoffs they sought. Some corporations have concluded that party soft money is simply a poor investment, because they do not perceive that they receive sufficient policy for their money.

Yet potential rewards can influence behavior. It is often charged that otherwise liberal Torecilli backed a bankruptcy bill that favored the credit card industry in order to solicit their money for the Democratic party, and that the GOP supports tobacco interests in order to solicit large contributions (Schmidt, 2000). One of the most visible, and controversial, charge is that Bill Clinton pardoned Marc Rich in exchange for large contributions to the Clinton Library and the Democratic party by Rich's ex-wife.

As political scientist Thomas Mann notes, "And yet who can doubt that politicians sometimes pay back contributors in the only coin they possess in abundance. . . ? In the countless decisions elected officials make every day—whose phone call to return, whether to support an amendment in committee or even be present when a vote is taken, or which matters to devote one's legislative energies to—dollars may well amplify the voices of important financial benefactors over those of ordinary citizens." (Mann, 1999).

Donors themselves favor a ban on soft money, by a large margin. One survey of House and Senate contributors in 1996 showed that more than three quarters of donors favored an outright ban on soft money. Many soft money donors are tired of the incessant demands that they give more and give more often, others fear that if they do not give more they will lose access to those who do (Webster, Wilcox, Francia, Green, Herrnson, and Powell, 2001).

Opponents of a ban on soft money point out that soft money finances voter mobilization drives in a country with an embarrassingly low voter turnout, that it pays for issue advertising that helps inform an electorate of the positions of candidates and parties on complex policy matters. Without soft money, they argue, party mobilization and campaign spending would be significantly reduced. And although American elections are amazingly expensive compared to those in other countries, they cost less than the nation spends to market consumer goods like beer and toilet paper. Moreover, American elections must convey complex information—not just the position of party leaders, but the nuanced positions of candidates who may agree with party leaders on some matters and oppose them on others. There is evidence that campaign spending does help educate voters (Coleman and Manna, 2000). For this reason, many political scientists who favor limiting soft money either would allow some soft money for the parties, or would make it easier for parties to raise hard money by raising the individual contribution limit of hard money to parties.

In early 2001, Republicans in Congress were arguing that any ban on soft money must also include a prohibition on labor unions spending any of the money they raise from dues on politics. Efforts to enact this kind of restriction at the state level have failed in ballot measures. At first glance this seems uncontroversial, since many workers are bound by law to join a labor union if they work for a unionized company, and thus do not have the privilege of withholding their membership if they disapprove of union political action. In fact, this provision is a "poison pill," designed to prevent the soft money ban. If labor unions were prohibited from spending their dues but corporations were allowed to spend their profits without shareholder approval, the balance of power between these two groups would tilt even more toward companies, and by extension to the Republicans.

Regulating Issue Advocacy   Perhaps the most pressing reform for many observers is the need to disclose issue advocacy by interest groups and parties. Today interest groups and political parties can spend unlimited amounts of money on issue advertisements. If these ads do not mention the magic words such as "vote for" or "defeat," then the money need not be raised through FECA guidelines, which means that groups can pay for the activity from their treasury funds. Corporations can fund issue ads from their profits, and interest groups can fund them from their dues. Wealthy individuals can avoid contribution limits by giving not only to parties and PACs but to special committees designed to spend money on issue advocacy. Indeed, some committees are wholly funded by a few or even one donor.

If a group does this activity from a different account than their PAC, then they disclose this activity to the IRS, not the FEC. We have little experience with this system of disclosure, for it went into effect for the first time on July 1, 2000. The rapid passage of this disclosure requirement in the House and Senate was a surprise to all observers, and is a testimony to the possibilities of campaign finance reform even when the odds look daunting. Yet there remain significant holes in the disclosure of issue advocacy, and one major study of the funding of the 2000 congressional elections by David Magleby concluded that "Disclosure, another cornerstone of FECA and an idea that has widespread appeal, is now so incomplete that voters will be hardpressed to know who is paying for the communications designed to influence their vote." (Magleby, 2001).

Many issue advocacy groups reorganized soon after passage of the disclosure requirements, and claimed IRS status as 501 (c) 4 organizations, thereby avoiding disclosure. Citizens for Better Medicare, and the American Federation of State, County, and Municipal

Employees (AFSCME) are but two of the largest organizations to began to channel their issue advocacy through this route. To determine how much groups spend on issue advocacy, academics resort to tracing commercials and estimating their costs (Slass, 2001). Mailings, phone calls, and other communications are of course missed by this technique.

Thus it is possible to find the source for some but not all issue advocacy activity. Moreover, issue advocacy can be funded from group treasuries, or from contributions of very large sums from a few individuals, a change from independent expenditures channeled through PACs, which must be funded by contributions that meet FECA limits. In addition, groups or individuals can form new organizations with new names, and thus hide the purpose and source of their activity. Although it is often possible for journalists to eventually identify most of the groups that are involved in issue advocacy, it requires hard work and often comes after an election is completed. During the New York GOP primary, for example, a group calling itself "Republicans for Clean Air" spent significant amounts in advertisements that criticized Senator John McCain's record on the environment. The McCain campaign later charged that the ads were funded by a few individuals in Texas who had benefited from George W. Bush's lax enforcement of environmental laws, yet the name of the organization that paid for the advertisements was designed to lead voters to believe that it was an environmental organization.

Issue advocacy falls outside the scope of the FECA regulations because it is supposed to be used to promote issue, not candidates. But no serious observer of campaign finance believes that these advertisements are not made to influence elections, and one academic study of issue advertising revealed that voters do not distinguish between these ads and campaign ads. David Magleby (2000) conducted focus groups and surveys of citizens who watched campaign and issue advocacy advertisements. He concluded that "Our research documents well the ability of media consultants to craft electioneering messages that avoid the magic words but still convey a message to vote for or against a candidate . . . 90 percent of the respondents thought that mentioning a candidate's name indicates that an ad was trying to persuade their vote, and over 80% felt the same about ads that showed a candidate's likeness or image." (p13).

The most common reform proposal for issue advocacy is more comprehensive legislation requiring disclosure (Campaign Finance Institute, 2000). Such efforts often center on defining campaign spending by focusing on the date of the activity (e.g. how close it is to an election), whether a candidate is mentioned by name or is represented by an image, and by other means. Campaign spending would be required to be disclosed fully to the FEC. This would allow journalists, citizens, and scholars to trace the source of money and hold politicians responsible for legislative favors to their financial benefactors.

Other proposals would force any issue advertisement that met certain criteria to be financed through Political Action Committees that must raise money under FECA limits. This would prevent individuals and groups from avoiding contribution limits through issue advocacy committees, and remove once again labor union dues and corporate profits from directly financing elections.

Opponents of these reforms argue that issue advocacy is free speech, and that disclosure requirements pose a chilling effect on this speech. Some argue, often with a wink, that their advertisements are not really electoral activity. Others suggest that limiting spending by groups to money raised through FECA limits is a barrier to their effective and unlimited speech in elections.

Reform: Disclose with No Limits   Some politicians favor a very different approach—removing all limits on contributions and spending, and instead merely requiring disclosure of financial activity. Some campaign finance observers argue that all limits to giving and spending money are ineffective, because money will always find a way into campaigns. Moreover, they argue that limits tend to channel money in unexpected directions—so limits on contributions to candidates lead to more and larger soft money contributions to parties, and if limits are placed on soft money, financial support will flow into issue advocacy. As a result, any regime of limits will inevitably be ineffective.

Moreover, several Republican legislators argue that all limits violate freedom of speech. Spending and giving money are speech, they argue, and thus limits violate first amendment guarantees of free speech. Some argue that James Madison sought to control faction not by government regulation, but by providing a government with many power centers, and by letting multiple factions offset and balance one another. Thus corporate money is opposed by labor and environmentalist money, and abolishing all limits fits the original intent of the framers.

With no limits but strict disclosure, they argue, voters could decide if they care about the financial backers of a candidate, and can look at the incumbent's legislative activity with reference to the sources of her/his funds. Thus voters, not laws, can check the excesses of campaign finance. John Doolittle (R, CA) has offered a bill that would remove all limits and require full and prompt disclosure. Most of the support for this position comes from Republicans, and Democrats argue that the policy would give Republicans an enormous fundraising advantage in elections. The proposal does not even draw support of a majority of GOP donors (Webster, et al, 2001).

Critics of this proposal argue that the Doolittle bill does not in fact require full disclosure of issue advocacy, and thus would not fulfill its supposed goal. Moreover, it is unlikely that a citizenry that often fails to take the time to be fully informed about the few leading issues in a campaign would be able to sort through the charges and countercharges about campaign finance, and thereby serve as a check on corruption. Instead, it is likely that deregulation would lead to increased cynicism and distrust of government. Thomas Mann notes that if deregulation were to occur, "the unrestrained use of economic wealth and state power in the electoral process would almost certainly lead to insistent public demands to restore its regulation." (1999, p 10).

CONCLUSION

Although there is no clear consensus on precisely which reforms are needed, the FECA regulatory regime is clearly broken. Surveys show that the public believes that the system favors rich interests, to whom the government listens instead of average citizens. John Hibbing reports that many citizens admit that they might also be corrupted by large contributions if they were lawmakers. They want elected officials to pass laws to limit the influence of wealth interests. When elected officials jockey for advantage over campaign finance rules instead of passing reforms, their cynicism grows (Hibbing, 2001).

Yet reform is not easy or straightforward, it requires careful planning. Thomas Mann's argument, cited above, that a ban on soft money would merely lead to more money channeled into issue advocacy is almost certainly correct. Thus reform of soft money must go hand in hand with reform of issue advocacy. Moreover, reform often produces unexpected consequences—few foresaw the explosion of PACs that resulted from the FECA amendments. It is impossible to manage the flow of political money by legislating once every 25 years—instead it is important that legislation be adapted to changing practices.

Opponents of reform often argue that money, like water, will eventually find a way to overcome all barriers. Given enough time between regulatory efforts, this is almost certainly true. The immense power of slow erosion is most evident in the Grand Canyon, which was carved by water over millions of years. Yet this does not mean that the only alternative is to surrender and drown in the flood. The Dutch have shown that careful planning and hard work can tame the oceans and reclaim dry ground. Given the stakes, reform seems worth that kind of effort.

REFERENCES

Baida, Peter. 1992. "The Legacy of Dollar Mark Hanna." In Stephen Wayne and Clyde Wilcox (eds), *The Quest for National Office*. New York: St. Martins. 16-19.

Caro, Robert. 1982. *The Path to Power*. New York: Alfred Knopf.

Clines, Francis X. 1997. "Most Doubt Resolve to Change Financing System, Poll Finds." *New York Times* April 9, 1997. P A1.

Coleman, John, and Paul Manna. 2000. "Congressional Campaign Spending and the Quality of Democracy." *Journal of Politics* 62: 757-789.

Drew, Elizabeth. 1983. *Politics and Money: The New Road to Corruption*. New York: Macmillan.

Heard, Alexander. 1960. *The Costs of Democracy*. Chapel Hill: University of North Carolina Press.

Lardner, George, and Susan Schmidt. 20002. "Attorneys General Raise Funds for GOP." *The Washington Post*. Thursday, March 30, 2000; Page A01

Overacker, Louise. 1932. *Money in Elections*. New York: Macmillan.

Magleby, David. 2000. "Dictum without Data: The Myth of Issue Advocacy and Party Building." Published by the Center for the Study of Elections and Democracy, Brigham Young University. *http://www.byu.edu/outsidemoney/ dictum/index.html*

Magleby, David, 2001. Election Advocacy: Soft Money and Issue Advocacy in the 2000 Congressional Elections. *http://www.byu.edu/outsidemoney/ 2000general/index.html*

Mann, Thomas. 1999. "The U.S. Campaign Finance System Under Strain." *http://www.brook.edu/views/Articles/Mann/SNP.htm*

Marks, Peter. 2000. "Parties Playing a Larger Role in Election Ads." *The New York Times* September 28, 2000. *http://www.nytimes.com/2000/28/politics/ 28buy.html*

Schmidt, Susan. 2000. "Toricelli's Money Push Also Raises Some Hackles." *The Washington Post* June 17, 2000, A1. *http://www.washingtonpost.com/wp-dyn/ articles/A9919-2000Jun16.html*

Slass, Lorie. 2001. "Spending on Issue Advocacy in the 2000 Cycle." Annenberg Public Policy Center.

Sorauf, Frank J. *Inside Campaign Finance* New Haven: Yale University Press.

Van Natta, Don, Jr., and John M Broder. 2000. "The Few, the Rich, the Rewarded Donate the Bulk of GOP Gifts." *The New York Times on the Web*, August 2, 2000.

ARTICLE 9

A LOOK AT LIBERALISMS'S TRANSFORMATION: THE RISE OF POWERFUL AND WELL-FINANCED CITIZEN LOBBIES

Jeffrey M. Berry

One of the accepted truisms about American politics is that liberalism is dead. Labor unions are weak; the welfare state has collapsed; conservatives were beginning to dominate Congress even before the Republicans formally took control in 1995; and Bill Clinton won re-election in 1996 only by running on Republican issues. Liberals are seen as a sad lot, still trying to figure out what happened.

But liberalism is not dead. Indeed, it's thriving. It has, however, changed its stripes. The old liberalism of FDR and LBJ, with its emphasis on economic equality, social welfare and labor union issues, has withered. A new liberalism, born of affluence, has arisen over the past three decades and has become remarkably powerful, especially on Capitol Hill. Unlike traditional liberalism, the new liberalism is not aimed at improving the material well-being of Americans. It is centered on quality-of-life issues such as environmentalism, consumer affairs, good government and group rights.

Citizen lobbying groups have been the driving force behind this modern liberalism. Their impact is difficult to discern because this disparate set of groups lacks the coherence and visibility of a political party. As a result, the new liberalism in America is often confused with the decaying liberalism of an earlier time. Nevertheless, these well-financed citizen groups have become a lobbying power second in influence only to corporate lobbyists, who once enjoyed unparalleled access to Congress.

Conservative citizen groups abound, too, and they have their own set of quality-of-life concerns, predominantly abortion and other family values issues. For all the attention they receive, however, research shows that the conservative groups are far less effective when it comes to enacting or blocking legislation. It is the liberal citizen groups that have most changed the way things are done in Washington and, especially, in Congress.

My conclusion is based on a detailed analysis of what Congress actually works on and what is passed into law. I examined all the major domestic social and domestic economic legislation that came before House and Senate committees in several different years, beginning with the 1963 session. In 1963, a typical bill was something like the Domestic Cotton-Price Equalization Act, which required members of Congress to determine acreage allotments. Two-thirds of the bills before committee's that year required legislators to reconsider how the economic pie was carved up, or to try to devise ways to expand that pie. Only a third of the bills dealt with quality-of-life issues such as consumer or environmental concerns.

By 1991, the pattern was reversed. Seventy-one percent of all congressional hearings that year took up legislation that had quality-of-life concerns at the center of the policies being debated, while just 29 percent of the domestic legislation involved exclusively economic issues.

Analysis of each bill revealed that groups such as the Wilderness Society, the Sierra Club, the Consumer Federation of America and the Ralph Nader organizations often pushed the legislation forward. The lobby that showed up most often in the 1991 session of Congress was not the Business Roundtable or the Chamber of Commerce, but the Natural Resources Defense Council. More often that not, the legislation pushed by liberal citizen lobbies put business groups on the defensive.

A key test of the liberal citizen groups' power came when the Republicans took control of Congress in 1995. The liberal citizen lobbies lost much of their influence over what bills gain hearing in Congress. Conversely, conservative citizen lobbies now had their friends in charge. At the beginning of the 104th Congress, the Christian Coalition proposed its own agenda, the Contract With the American Family. The group's director at the time, Ralph Reed, asked the Republican leadership to act on it as soon as the GOP's Contract With America passed the House.

But the conservative electoral revolution did not translate into a legislative one, largely because the conservative citizen groups had nowhere near the clout of their liberal counterparts. For liberal groups, the most serious threat came from the alliance of business lobbies and sympathetic Republican House members, who worked together to fashion far-reaching regulatory reform measures. The heart of is effort was the Job Creation and Wage Enhancement Act, part of the Contract With America. This sweeping legislation would have required the government to use cost-benefit analysis to justify policies and regulations. The Newt Gingrich-led House passed the bill, but the outcry from environmentalists forced Bob Dole, Senate Majority leader at the time, to beat a hasty retreat. He never even brought the bill up for a vote.

Business lobbies were equally enthusiastic about a rewrite of the Clean Water Act, but when environmentalists started to call it the "dirty water bill," Dole ran from that, too. The environmental groups easily defeated efforts to rewrite the Superfund act and the endangered species laws.

Meanwhile, the Christian Coalition stumbled with its Contract With the American Family. House Majority Leader Dick Armey summarily dismissed the group's agenda, and only bits and pieces of it made their way into law. Few would have guessed at the outset of the 104th Congress that its biggest winners would be the environmental lobbies and its biggest loser would be the Christian Coalition.

When I began this research six years ago, I expected to find that both liberal and conservative citizen groups were gaining influence. Conservative citizen groups such as Focus on the Family, the Family Research Council, the Eagle Forum, and the Christian Coalition are well-known advocates of family values issues. Yet in 1991, conservative citizen groups actively lobbied on just 4.5 percent of the primary domestic legislation before Congress that year. Liberal citizen groups lobbied on 66 percent of the same set of bills. The conservative groups seem to be AWOL, while the liberal groups lobby across almost the entire range of domestic legislation that Congress takes up.

What explains the liberal groups' strength? One advantage they have over the conservative groups is that their issues are increasingly perceived as more mainstream. When the Audubon Society talks about the environment or the Center for Science in the Public Interest talks about carcinogens in food, or the Center for Auto Safety talks about design flaws in minivans, they don't seem like radicals promoting left-wing causes. Such concerns contrast sharply with the agenda of conservative citizen groups, whose hot-button issues such as abortion and school prayer strike many Americans as ideologically right of center.

Surprisingly, many of the liberal lobbies active on Capitol Hill are larger and richer in resources than conservative citizen groups. A number of environmental groups have more than half a million members and annual budgets in the tens of millions of dollars. The liberal groups have large staffs characterized by lawyers, PhDs and assorted policy works. The expertise of these staffers pays handsome dividends because it gives their organizations more credibility. Information still equals power, at least on Capitol Hill and for much of the media.

Over the years, the leaders of the liberal groups, have been willing to make costly commitments to the long-term lobbying that is necessary to push issues on to the agenda of Congress. It is mundane work, which begins with publicizing research and working with committee staffers, but it eventually can culminate in legislators taking up the issue. Mother was right: Hard work pays off. The numbers indicate that conservative citizen groups don't put nearly as much energy or money into lobbying the Hill or hiring policy experts.

Liberals speak in terror of the resources available to the groups on the right. Yet my measurements of the three most precious resources for interest groups—visibility, credibility and funding—indicate that the liberal lobbies are far better off than the conservative groups.

The greater visibility and credibility of the liberal groups can be explained by the large bureaucracies they have build, the policy experts they employ, the research they fund and the long-term stability of their organizations. Their superior funding over conservative groups in largely explained by the underlying class difference among donors. The liberal groups appeal to the upper-middle-class suburban constituency, while the Christian right groups appeal primarily to the population of more modest means.

Most conservative groups rely heavily on direct mail, which means that a $25 donation might cost them $24. They consistently overfish their fund-raising waters, and sometimes find that they are spending $27 to raise that $25 donation. This is why once-prominent groups with substantial memberships, such as the Moral Majority and the National Conservative Political Action Committee (NCPAC), can end up bankrupt and out of business.

Liberal citizen groups use direct mail, too, but get a higher return on their investment because their contributors can afford to give more. They also receive more of their funds from other sources, such as large individual gifts, foundations grants and government support. Business remains the best-funded and most powerful interest group sector. But citizen groups, with their expanding resources, are becoming increasingly effective when they compete directly against business lobbies in the Congress.

The growing prosperity of citizen groups representing the new liberalism contrasts sharply with the decline of labor unions, the heart and soul of traditional liberalism. Unions still have access to very large sums of money, but their most precious resource—their membership—has declined sharply. As a percentage of the work force, union membership has dropped to about half of what it was in 1950, from about one in three workers to about one in six. Interest group influence has never been strictly a function of the number of members or constituents, but the diminishing size of labor unions has been too visible and too dramatic not to alter the way that politicians view them.

As liberal citizen groups mobilized their followers in the 1960s and '70s, Ralph Nader liberalism began to eclipse Hubert Humphrey liberalism. Not surprisingly, the liberal citizen lobbies represent those who were already well represented in American politics: wealthy, well-educated suburbanites. Yet these people have been organized in new ways, and their lobbies in Washington have done an impressive job of raising new issues. At the same time, the success of those groups has pushed traditional liberal concerns for the poor and disadvantaged further to the margins of American politics.

The same trend is evident in Democratic Party politics. Often accused of not having any firm principles, President Clinton has turned out to be steadfast in his support of women's rights, environmental protection, education and consumer protection—all central concerns of the new liberalism. At the same time, Clinton turned away from the traditional liberal constituencies with his support of welfare reform and NAFTA. The previous Democratic president, Jimmy Carter, never would have signed the welfare bill. He also felt indebted to labor for the help some unions gave him in his race for the Democratic nomination in 1976. It was Clinton who saw the fork in the road. Embarking on his campaign for president, Vice President Gore's signature issue is environmental protection. As the Democrats enter the twenty-first century, the new liberals seem firmly in control of the party once ruled by Franklin Roosevelt and Lyndon Johnson.

MEDIA AND
PUBLIC OPINION

The media are an all-pervasive influence in modern American life. Although various forms of media have been influential throughout our history, the rapid-paced news environment of today is a relatively recent development brought about by the rise of the Internet and other forms of "new media." Political scientist John Anthony Maltese studied the impact of the new media environment on the evolution of the story of the Clinton-Lewinsky scandal in 1998 and 1999. As Maltese shows, much of the coverage of the presidential scandal was driven by new media sources, particularly the Internet. Traditional news sourcing practices were routinely violated in the interest of getting the story first. The presidential spin team had to be geared up constantly for responses to rumors, allegations, and other new developments that were driving the news. Yet despite all of the changes that created this fast-paced media environment, Maltese shows that the "old media" did not wane in influence, as many predicted would eventually be the case. Indeed, the Clinton White House made the serious error initially of trying to circumvent the traditional White House press corps and found itself eventually having to make amends with reporters who had turned sour on the Clinton presidency. Today, therefore, the new media and the old compete side-by-side and presidential management of the news has become more complicated than ever.

Scholar Herbert J. Gans challenges the accuracy of the journalistic theory of democracy—a theory that presumes the role of the journalist is to inform the public and therefore make democratic citizens more interested and willing to participate in politics. He questions whether journalists indeed fulfill their role in maximizing democracy and in fact finds that today's reporting does little to enhance citizen participation in politics. Much of what journalists report about governmental decision-making—the internal debates in Congress over budget priorities, for example—is outside the realm of direct citizen participation. Gans suggests that as long as reporters operate under the illusion that their work contributes to democratic participation, they will never truly enhance the democratic process in the U.S. He recommends a more realistic theory and some fundamental changes in the ways that journalists report and analyze contemporary political debates.

Scholar Michael Schudson's essay lends strong credibility to Gans's view of an electorate not sufficiently informed by today's journalistic practices. Recent polling data show that Americans know remarkably little about their history and contemporary issues and political leaders. He asks the key question: "How can the United States claim to be a model democracy if its citizens know so little about public life?" Indeed, studies show that political knowledge in the United States has not improved significantly in the past half century, despite more widely available education and more media sources of information. What can be done to overcome this long trend of ignorant voters? There is no simple solution. There is no one policy reform that will turn around the cultural tendency in the U.S. to place little importance on knowledge of political life. Schudson is encouraged by the prospects for a greater emphasis on civic education. Political change that was brought about by mass movements too has been shown to increase public awareness of issues more generally. Nonetheless, it is hard to think of any changes that will fundamentally alter the long-standing lack of political knowledge within the electorate.

ARTICLE 10

THE NEW MEDIA AND THE LURE OF THE CLINTON SCANDAL

John Anthony Maltese

On January 17, 1998, President Clinton videotaped a deposition for the Paula Jones sexual harassment lawsuit against him. The next day, former White House adviser George Stephanopoulos appeared on the Sunday morning ABC News program "This Week." Discussion turned to the Jones lawsuit, and Stephanopoulos confidently predicted that Clinton would win in court. ABC correspondent Sam Donaldson asked why the president did not settle out of court with Jones to avoid damaging revelations at the trial. "But Sam," Stephanopoulos replied incredulously, "What worse can come out than already has been out? . . . What else can come out?"[1]

Three days later, America woke up to startling reports that the president had had an affair with a 24-year-old White House intern, had lied about it under oath the previous Saturday, and had urged her to lie about it as well. *Newsweek* reporter Mike Isikoff had been investigating the Lewinsky story for a year and had been on the verge of publishing it the weekend of the president's deposition. Over Isikoff's objections, *Newsweek* editors chose not to run the story, in part because Kenneth Starr, the independent counsel investigating the president, had asked them not to.[2] But gossip columnist Matt Drudge posted details of the story on his Internet site, which, in turn, prompted the *Washington Post* to run the story in its Wednesday morning edition (preceded by an early-morning posting on its Web site).[3] Sources also revealed that the president—contrary to his previous denials—had admitted in his deposition to having an affair with Gennifer Flowers.

Reprinted with the permission of Georgetown University Press

At 9:45 A.M., Press Secretary Mike McCurry sat down for his daily off-camera session with reporters in his office. In a rare move, he read a two-sentence statement carefully crafted by aides in the early morning hours: "The president is outraged by these allegations. He's never had any improper relationship with this woman and he's made clear from the very beginning that he wants people to tell the truth in all matters." McCurry's daily on-camera briefing was scheduled for 1:00 P.M., but he did not appear until 1:24 P.M. Mindful of the president's history of evasive answers, reporters asked over and over again what the White House meant by an improper relationship. . . . Why didn't the White House say that there was no sexual relationship? McCurry refused to elaborate: "I'm not going to parse the statement. You all got the statement I made earlier . . . so, I'm not going to parse the statement."[4]

At 3:15 P.M., President Clinton sat down for a previously scheduled interview with Jim Lehrer for the PBS news program *The News Hour with Jim Lehrer.* Questioning began with the allegations:

JIM LEHRER: The news of this day is that Kenneth Starr, the independent counsel, is investigating allegations that you suborned perjury by encouraging a 24-year-old woman, a former White House intern, to lie under oath in a civil deposition about her having had an affair with you. Mr. President, is that true?

PRESIDENT CLINTON: That is not true. That is not true. I did not ask anyone to tell anything other than the truth. There is no improper relationship. And I intend to cooperate with this inquiry. But that is not true.

JIM LEHRER: No improper relationship. Define what you mean by that.

PRESIDENT CLINTON: Well, I think you know what it means. It means that there is not a sexual relationship, an improper sexual relationship, or any other kind of improper relationship.

JIM LEHRER: You had no sexual relationship with this young woman?

PRESIDENT CLINTON: There is not a sexual relationship. That is accurate.[5]

Reporters immediately pounced on the president's use of the present tense: there *is* no sexual relationship. As Mara Liasson of National Public Radio put it the next day: "Everybody thought, oh, he's pulling a Clinton. He's saying there was one but there isn't now."[6] Later in the day, *Roll Call* magazine interviewed the president. This time he did not rely on the present tense. When asked, "What exactly was the nature of your relationship with her?" the president responded, "The relationship was not improper and I think that is important enough to say." Then he added what appeared to be a more categorical denial: "The relationship was not sexual."[7]

Even that did not satisfy reporters. Recorded telephone conversations between Lewinsky and Linda Tripp suggested that the president drew a distinction between oral sex and adultery, and Lewinsky said on the tapes that there had been only oral sex. Chris Bury reported on ABC's "Nightline" that "such distinctions may prove important in the context of what constitutes an improper relationship."[8] To illustrate why such careful parsing was necessary, Bury ran a segment showing Clinton responding to charges in 1992 that he had had a twelve-year affair with Gennifer Flowers. Asked in 1992 about the story alleging the affair, Clinton said: "I read the story. It isn't true. It isn't a true story."

That was the line that Clinton maintained for the next six years. He admitted in a famous 1992 interview with his wife on CBS's "60 Minutes" that he had caused pain in his marriage, but when asked during the same interview whether the supermarket tabloid story of a twelve-year affair was true, Clinton again responded, "That allegation is false." Six years later, in his January 17,1998, Paula Jones deposition, Clinton finally admitted to an affair with Flowers. As Bury told his television audience, "That precise allegation, a *twelve-year* affair, may indeed have been false. But [prior to the deposition] Bill Clinton carefully avoided answering or denying the fundamental question, did he have an affair with Gennifer Flowers."

Bury then played excerpts of a tape of a telephone conversation between Clinton and Flowers that Flowers had released after the 1992 "60 Minutes" interview. In it, Clinton appeared to coach Flowers on what to say if asked about the affair: "If they hit you with it, just say no and go on. There's nothing they can do. If all the people who are named deny it, that's all. I mean I expect them to come look into it and interview you and everything, but I just think if everybody's on record denying it, you've got no problems."[9] Finally, Bury showed Press Secretary McCurry's response to a question about the contradiction between Clinton's 1992 public statements that the Gennifer Flowers story was not true and his 1998 admission under oath that he did have an affair with Flowers. McCurry said, "The president knows that he told the truth in 1992 when he was asked about that relationship and he knows that he testified truthfully on Saturday, and he knows his answers are not at odds."[10]

In the ensuing firestorm of media coverage, many media commentators predicted that Clinton would be forced to resign or would be impeached. Even Stephanopoulos publicly predicted resignation or impeachment if the story proved to be true.[11] Clinton stonewalled, convinced (reportedly with the help of polls from his former adviser Dick Morris) that he could not survive if he told the truth about his relationship with Lewinsky. On January 25, a Fox network television reporter asked White House Communications Director Ann Lewis point blank whether it was true that the president did not consider oral sex to be a "sexual relationship." Lewis responded categorically: "No. Sex is sex."[12] Clinton did not correct her. The next day, Clinton made his famous finger-wagging statement: "I did not have sexual relations with that woman, Miss Lewinsky."

CLINTON AND THE NEW MEDIA

The New Media (the Internet, cable, satellite technology, and the like) played an important role in shaping the Lewinsky story. The Internet broke the story and then propelled it in the coming months. As one commentator wrote shortly after the Lewinsky scandal broke, "the Web was not simply a convenient conduit for releasing an exclusive story—it was the entity that was driving the media frenzy about the alleged presidential sex scandal."[13] Even Clinton's relationship with the White House press corps had been shaped, in part, by the president's attitude toward the New Media.

Just as Franklin Roosevelt mastered the use of radio and John F. Kennedy mastered the use of television, Bill Clinton came to office expecting to master the use of the New Media. Advances in technology had dramatically changed the nature of communication by 1992. Cable, satellite technology, and the Internet all provided an unparalleled opportunity for direct communication with the American people. In the 1992 presidential campaign, Clinton had effectively followed a strategy of "narrowcasting"—using media outlets like MTV, "Arsenio Hall Show," "Phil Donahue," and Don Imus's radio talk show to transmit direct, targeted messages to particular constituencies.[14]

Once Clinton was elected, his advisers planned to expand their use of the New Media to bypass the critical filter of the White House press corps. Sidney Blumenthal, who later joined the White House as a communication strategist, touted such possibilities for unmediated communication in an article in the *New Yorker.* There he wrote that the "Old Media," such as the three big network news shows, were "anachronistic" and were "no more likely to return than are the big bands."[15] The White House seemed to agree. It created a White House Web site, making it possible for virtually anyone with a computer to download the text of Clinton's public remarks, his daily schedule, White House press briefings, and even photographs. This electronic channel bypassed the filter of reporters who used to be the only source for transmitting such material.[16] White House Media Affairs Director Jeff Eller also spoke, only partly in jest, of creating what he called "BC-TV"—the Bill Clinton Television Network—to broadcast White House events unedited.[17]

Cable outlets, talk radio, and local media also provided ways for Clinton to bypass the White House press corps. During his first two months in office, President Clinton did not even hold a full-scale press conference for the White House press corps. He did, however, hold some twenty-five sessions with representatives of local media as part of an effort to target messages to specific media markets.[18] The first lady followed a similar strategy; by mid-April of 1993, she had granted interviews to nineteen local television news anchors, but had granted only three interviews to the White House press corps.[19] Ann Compton of ABC News said that of the five presidents that she had covered, Clinton was the only one who "did everything in his power to go around, under, and away from the White House press corps."[20]

It soon became evident, however, that the White House was not the only one who could use such tactics of circumvention. Administration opponents also used the New Media to spread charges of presidential scandal and ineptitude. Talk radio, which Clinton had used so effectively in the 1992 presidential campaign, came back to haunt him as president. By 1997, news/talk was the most popular radio format in America, carried by 1,330 commercial-radio stations (up from only 308 in 1989).[21] The growth was spurred by the 1987 repeal of the Fairness Doctrine, and conservative shows dominated the airwaves. Soon they became a powerful vehicle for criticizing Clinton and spreading stories about White House scandals. Some, including the mainstream media, blamed talk radio for helping to fan the opposition that ultimately doomed Clinton's nomination of Zoe Baird for U.S. Attorney General in 1993.[22] Democrats blamed talk radio for contributing to their disastrous showing in the 1994 midterm elections, when they lost control of both houses of Congress to the Republicans.[23] President Clinton publicly suggested in 1995 that conservative talk radio had fanned the flames of societal unrest that led to the Oklahoma City bombing.[24] And Hillary Clinton dismissed the Lewinsky story in early 1998 as part of a "right-wing conspiracy," of which talk radio was a part.[25]

Likewise, the Internet altered the way that the Old Media responded to breaking news stories. The Old Media had served not only as a filter of White House news but also as a more general gatekeeper of other news. With the Internet, however, virtually anyone could post a story. Not only did the "Drudge Report" on the Internet break the Lewinsky story, but the Internet came to shape the way the media covered the scandal. Before the Lewinsky scandal most major media outlets followed an unwritten rule that they would not use their web site to break a story; instead, web sites contained information that had already been reported in other venues.[26] This changed with the Lewinsky scandal. As competing news organizations struggled to stay one step ahead of the competition, web sites became important. The first mainstream coverage of the Lewinsky scandal appeared on the *Washington Post* web site, prompting *Newsweek* to follow suit. In the drive to scoop the competition, errors were made. The *Dallas Morning Herald,* for example, posted an erroneous story on its web site that a secret service agent was an eyewitness to a presidential tryst. The editors subsequently pulled the story, but not before other news outlets, such as ABC, had reported it.[27]

Such situations prompted Cable News Network (CNN) senior analyst Jeff Greenfield to worry about what he called an "echo effect"—news organizations picking up and repeating without independent corroboration a story from a single source. Regardless of the story's reliability, the simple act of repetition by different news venues made the story seem more credible.[28] The incessant chatter of talking heads on twenty-four-hour cable news networks like CNBC, MSNBC, and Fox News further enforced the echo effect. There the story seemed to be "All-Monica, All-the-Time," with pundits endlessly repeating and analyzing the story—even if they had no particular expertise on the matter.[29] MSNBC created a nightly show called "The White House in Crisis" to discuss the scandal—even when there was nothing new to discuss.

Fox and MSNBC, both of whom joined the cable news lineup in 1996, relied heavily on talk shows to fill their air time. Talk is easy and talk is cheap, and the proliferation of these shows led to saturation coverage of the Lewinsky story.[30] They also led to high ratings. And although many of these talk shows aired on "news" networks, their approach often descended into gossip. Indeed, a Committee of Concerned Journalists issued the results of a study in October 1998 suggesting that the talking heads on these shows were responsible for the most blatant errors and distortions in the coverage of the Lewinsky scandal. For example, rumors of Clinton liaisons with other interns that would have never merited coverage by a responsible news organization were fair game for the talking heads.[31] Ironically, this saturation coverage may have ultimately helped Clinton. By the time impeachment hearings rolled around in the fall of 1998, many Americans just wanted the story to go away.

Quite simply, the New Media were changing how news was released and the rules of the game by which news organizations played. Both the Web and twenty-four-hour cable news networks quickened the pace of news reporting and increased the sheer volume of coverage of the story.

CLINTON AND THE OLD MEDIA

Even if the scandal stories were driven by the New Media, the Old Media proved to be harsh critics of the president in the early days of the Lewinsky scandal. There is no doubt that the Lewinsky story would have created a furor under any circumstances, but the president's sour relationship with the White House press corps had festered since the earliest days of the administration and did nothing to discourage coverage of the scandal.

Problems of arrogance and inexperience badly damaged Clinton's relations with the White House press corps in the early days of his first term. Those wounds never completely healed. The Clinton White House began its first term by turning a cold shoulder, both substantively and symbolically, to the White House press corps. When Clinton took office, the West Wing of the White House was transformed overnight from a place where President George Bush had enforced a dress code (men had to wear ties, women skirts) to one where almost anything went. Those in power were young and inexperienced. As Tom Rosenstiel has noted, Director of Satellite Services David Anderson was twenty-three years old, had spiked hair, wore all black, and had not yet finished college (he was working at night after work to finish up his degree at Oberlin). The director of Ratio Operations, Richard Strauss, also twenty-three, was finishing up his degree at UCLA at night by correspondence. Rosenstiel added that sixty-three out of the roughly 450 people who were full-time White House staffers were under the age of twenty-four. Communications Director George Stephanopoulos had reached the ripe old age of thirty-two.[32] Veteran White House reporters experienced a generation gap. Faced with gum-chewing male aides with earrings who blared rock and roll from their offices, the staid, sixty-three-year-old David Broder of the *Washington Post* said that covering the new White House was like "coming home and finding your kids got into the liquor cabinet."[33]

The extent to which these new kids on the block wanted to control the news and put veteran reporters at bay stunned the press corps. One of Communications Director Stephanopoulos's first decisions was to close off access to the upstairs foyer in the West Wing where Stephanopoulos and White House Press Secretary Dee Dee Meyers had their offices. For more than twenty years, reporters had been free to wander that foyer in search of news. They could chat informally with communications officials or poke their heads into the press secretary's office to get a quick answer to a question. It was a clear sign that reporters and officials were on an equal playing field. Now, as Ann Compton put it, the foyer was a "no-fly zone" symbolizing the hierarchical relationship between reporters and officials.[34] In the new arrangement, reporters had to wait to be spoon-fed—and the White House appeared to be making only minimal efforts to do even that. Calls from downstairs were not returned in time for reporters to meet their deadlines, and some reporters felt that even when Stephanopoulos did invite them upstairs, he did not treat them with respect.[35]

The press corps reacted with fury. Stephanopoulos, who seemed surprised by the reaction, refused to rescind his decision to shut off the upstairs foyer. He did try to increase access elsewhere, however. He assigned two communications staffers, Lorrain Voles and Arthur Jones, to the lower press room on a permanent basis to handle reporters' queries.[36] He also added an extra press briefing each day. In addition to Stephanopoulos's own midday briefing, Press Secretary Myers began briefing the press at both 9:15 A.M. and 5:00 P.M.[37] But the new measures did nothing to calm the irate press corps. They had lost their space and, with it, a kind of access that was irreplaceable. In turn, the White House lost the goodwill of reporters. "Put it this way," said Karen Hosler, Washington correspondent for the *Baltimore Sun* and president of the White House Correspondents Association, "We're not going to cut them any breaks."[38]

Early on, the Clinton White House felt that it could get away with this kind of treatment. What the White House failed to realize was that the Old Media still mattered. A 1998 Gallup Poll showed that Americans continued to get most of their news from the Old Media and, even more importantly, *trusted* the Old Media more than the New.[39] Despite all the new sources of news, Americans embraced the gate-keeping role of the Old Media because they trusted it. In the new environment, narrowcasting and circumvention of the White House press corps had its place. But the symbiotic relationship between the White House and the Old Media continued to exist, and that worked only if the White House courted the press corps and fed it information instead of snubbing it. The White House learned that lesson too late.

A study by the Center for the Media and Public Affairs showed that only one-third of the stories aired on the three major television networks about Clinton in his first six months in office were positive (former President George Bush, in comparison, received 55 percent positive stories in his first year in office in 1989).[40] Public opinion polls were also troubling. Clinton pollster Stan Greenberg found that 70 percent of the American people rated Clinton in the poor or fair categories, while only 28 percent chose the excellent or good categories.[41]

By the spring of 1993, the White House had significantly revamped its communications operation. The president moved Stephanopoulos out of the communications director post (replaced by Mark Gearan) and brought in David Gergen (communications director for Republican presidents Gerald Ford and Ronald Reagan) as counselor to the President in charge of communications. Gergen reopened the upstairs foyer in the West Wing, saw to it that reporters' calls were returned before deadline, held backgrounders, and quickly arranged for the president to hold a press conference. In July 1993, a month after Gergen took over, network news coverage was 40 percent positive (up from 27 percent positive in May).[42]

Still, Gergen could not get the White House to fashion a consistent media message. Part of this reflected internal White House splits, such as the one between Gergen, who wanted Clinton to move toward the political center, and Stephanopoulos (now senior advisor to the President for policy and strategy), who wanted Clinton to articulate a more liberal message. But it also reflected Clinton's own lack of discipline in communicating. Howard Kurtz has noted that the president was "unfocused and error-prone" in his dealings with reporters and "seemed unable to leave any question unanswered, even one on MTV about his underwear."[43]

Clinton further compounded the problem. On occasion, he openly treated reporters with contempt. Like Richard Nixon before him, Clinton seemed to feel that the press were conspiring to undo him. Kurtz has written that Clinton's staff felt that if the president had an Achilles' heel, "it was his tendency to go off half-cocked about the press."[44] At times unable to control his temper in front of reporters who antagonized him, Clinton further damaged his relationship with the press corps and fostered the image that he was petty.

Out of necessity, Clinton reached out to reporters after the disastrous 1994 midterm elections and sought to mend fences.[45] The president now asked for their forgiveness. He opened up to them at informal bagel breakfasts, cultivated ties with influential opinion makers like E.J. Dionne, and scrupulously practiced his answers to questions in formal sessions with his staff before any encounter with reporters. Known as the "pre-brief," these sessions focused the president's responses, but White House aides also used them to limit public displays of Clinton's temper by allowing him to vent privately before meeting with the press.[46]

By the time Clinton won reelection in 1996, he was more focused and disciplined in his relationship with the press. He enjoyed high public approval ratings and had the potential for a successful second term. But the never ending stream of scandals would not go away. Travelgate, Filegate, Whitewater, allegations of fundraising abuses, and the Paula Jones sexual harassment suit all dogged him. And the White House press corps remained suspicious. From their years of covering Clinton, they had concluded that he was the master of what was known in the Watergate days as the "non-denial denial"—evasive answers that skirted the truth. Privately they continued to rail at his lack of candor and their belief that Clinton arrogantly felt that he could get away with anything.[47]

That pent-up hostility may have fueled the media firestorm that erupted when the Lewinsky story broke in January 1998. When the president wagged his finger and denied sexual relations with Monica Lewinsky, reporters were not convinced. Nor were they predisposed to come to the president's defense. Only when it became clear that a majority of the American people were not as concerned about the scandal as the reporters seemed to be did the Old Media reflect on their frenzy and temper coverage.

COORDINATING THE MESSAGE

Planning and distributing the White House message is now the job of many White House staffers and of several distinct staff units.[48] During the Lewinsky scandal, such units included the White House Press Office and the White House Office of Communications, both of which deal directly with media relations. But staff also included a wide array of other staff units ranging from an ad hoc group set up specifically to deal with damage control associated with the scandal to the Office of Congressional Relations, which worked closely with Democrats on Capitol Hill during the House impeachment debate and subsequent Senate trial.

The development of these many staff units is a relatively recent phenomenon that corresponds with the enormous growth in presidential staff over the last seventy years. During Franklin Roosevelt's first term, the entire White House staff numbered only forty-seven. By 1974, it had grown to over five hundred. If you include the Executive Office of the President, created in 1939 to give the president ongoing expert advice on a variety of topics ranging from national security to economics, presidential staff has numbered over five thousand.[49] The purpose of this staff is to help the president. But the tremendous growth of staff has also posed some problems. As it multiplied, duplication and overlap sometimes undermined its effectiveness. Internal power struggles became more likely. The chain of command became less clear. Public statements from different officials were more likely to conflict. And the media, whose penchant for dramatic stories leads to a preoccupation with conflict, were eager to focus on any apparent dissension within the ranks.[50] Such stories only increase the tensions between those at odds and make the president look like a poor manager.[51]

The president's personal staff in the White House all have a vested interest in the president's success. Yet different staff units within the White House often split badly over how to further the president's "best interest." This was apparent during the Lewinsky scandal in the split between President Clinton's legal advisers and his political advisers over how to respond publicly to the accusations. Likewise, officials from different parts of the administration represent different constituencies and may take positions that conflict. As the Lewinsky scandal unfolded, for example, the public statements of FBI Director Louis Freeh conflicted with those of the White House. Inevitably, Attorney General Janet Reno distanced herself from White House communications strategies. Clearly, the interest in maintaining the legitimacy of her office required a different communications strategy than one designed to keep Bill Clinton in office.

From the start of his presidency, Clinton had a tendency to supplement the advice of formal staff units with informal advice from a variety of sources. In the area of communications, Clinton has set up several ad hoc staff units and relied on the advice of an array of special White House counselors (ranging from David Gergen to Dick Morris), as well as former Clinton advisers and other individuals outside of the administration (such as James Carville and former White House chief of staff Leon Panetta). With so many different individuals and staff units sharing similar functions, personality splits, policy differences, and other self-interested motivations ultimately pulled at the fabric of a seamless communications strategy. These divisions contributed to Clinton's lack of focus in his first term.

The Clinton administration's initial response to the Lewinsky story again reflected a divided set of advisers who were working with incomplete information. In an attempt to coordinate a response, the White House created a special communications team to deal specifically with the Lewinsky story. That reflected the seriousness of the story, but it also reflected the White House desire to put the story on a "separate track"—to have the rest of the White House go on with business as usual. At the same time, the Democratic National Committee established an office led by Karen Hancox to help coordinate damage control.[52] Hancox worked closely with White House communications director Ann Lewis. As impeachment drew near, they coordinated public statements from a wide array of pro-Clinton spokespersons, suggesting, for example, that Ken Starr was a sex-obsessed Republican zealot and that Republicans in the House of Representatives were unfair in their partisan maneuvers to impeach the president. The coordinated line was clearly on display on December 19, 1998, the day the full House voted to impeach the president. In a morning statement to reporters, White House press secretary Joe Lockhart three times decried "the politics of personal destruction." House minority leader Richard Gephardt repeated the line that morning in a speech on the floor of the House. So, too, did the president in his Rose Garden speech after the impeachment vote.

Often, though, the president's communications advisers seemed adrift. White House press secretary Mike McCurry later admitted that he purposely stayed out of the loop so that he could truthfully respond that he did not know the answers when questioned by reporters. After leaving his office, McCurry suggested that the alternative to being out of the loop would have been to "disseminate erroneous information, because the president was obviously in denial and concealing his affair."[53] Meanwhile, the president's legal advisers were said to have stymied attempts to have the president admit his guilt and offer a full apology. And, as the impeachment process proceeded, events sometimes unfolded beyond White House control. At times the president seemed to be aided by luck as much as by any systematic strategy for coping with the scandal.

Most importantly, the president was buoyed throughout the scandal and the impeachment trial by high public opinion polls. Indeed, scandal stories only seemed to drive the president's approval ratings higher. A week after the scandal broke, President Clinton's approval rating reached 67 percent—up from 59 percent before the story broke and the highest approval rating of his presidency.[54] A surging economy no doubt helped to bolster the president's approval ratings. But there may have been more to it than that. "Just maybe," Samuel Kernell has suggested, "survey respondents discriminate between the president as a public and private person."[55] Whatever the reason for the polls results, the White House took them seriously and effectively used them in its campaign to suggest that impeachment was simply a partisan maneuver.

Throughout his presidency, Clinton has been described as a president driven by polls.[56] Some White House advisers later speculated to members of the press that the president's high approval ratings had actually lulled them into a false sense of security—especially after the November 1998 midterm elections, when Democrats did far better than expected. How, they had thought, could the House of Representatives vote to impeach in the face of such strong public opinion? But impeach it did, and, even then, the president's approval ratings just went higher. By at least one poll, it reached its highest point to date (73 percent approval) immediately after the full House voted to impeach.[57] When Clinton delivered his

1999 State of the Union address in the midst of the Senate impeachment trial, an ABC News survey showed that 77 percent approved of the speech.[58] When the Senate finally voted to acquit, it must have been mindful of the polls.

CONCLUSIONS

This brief overview of the Lewinsky scandal and the Clinton communications strategies suggests several things about the Old and New Media. First, the New Media has significantly altered the way news is reported. It has undermined the gate-keeping function of the Old Media by allowing virtually anyone to post information, speeding up the pace with which news is reported, and contributing to saturation coverage of high-visibility stories. Second, despite these developments, the Old Media is alive and well. It remains the news source that most Americans trust and that most Americans continue to rely on. Although certainly influenced by the pressures of the New Media, the Old Media has not been shunted aside. Third, the Clinton White House underestimated this continued importance of the Old Media. The White House squandered its opportunity to forge a close working bond with the White House press corps in the early days of the administration.

All of this serves as a reminder that presidents must engage in a balanced approach to communications. They cannot afford to ignore the Old Media any more than they can afford to ignore the opportunities of the New Media. Although the gate-keeping function of the Old Media may sometimes seem to be a hindrance to White House communications, presidents should remember that this gate-keeping function can also help them—and the American people—by filtering out rumor and unsubstantiated stories and serving as a tempering influence on the news.

NOTES

1 ABC News, "This Week," 18 January 1998, transcript no. 98011805–jl2.

2 Howard Kurtz, *Spin Cycle: How the White House and the Media Manipulate the News* (New York: Touchstone, 1998), 291.

3 Susan Schmidt, Peter Baker, and Toni Locy, "Clinton Accused of Urging Aide to Lie," *Washington Post,* 21 January 1998, A1.

4 ABC News, "Nightline," 21 January 1998, transcript no. 98012101–jO7.

5 ABC News, "ABC Special Report," 21 January 1998, transcript no. 98012101-jl4. The PBS interview was carried live on ABC television and was also published in "Clinton: 'There Is No Improper Relationship'," *Washington Post,* 22 January 1998, A13.

6 ABC News, "Nightline," 22 January 1998, transcript no. 98012201–jO7.

7 "Clinton: 'There Is No Improper Relationship'."

8 ABC News, "Nightline," 22 January 1998.

9 Clinton's aides suggested that this tape was doctored.

10 ABC News, "Nightline," 22 January 1998.

11 ABC News, "Good Morning America," 22 January 1998, transcript no. 98012217–jl4.

12 Kathy Kiely, "Defenders Work the Talk Shows; Blue Subject Spurs Red-Hot Language," *New York Daily News,* 26 January 1998, 7.

13 David Noack, "Clinton Sex Story Forces Print Media Changes," *Editor & Publisher Magazine,* 31 January 1998, 30.

14 Tom Rosenstiel, *The Beat Goes On: President Clinton's First Year with the Media* (New York: Twentieth Century Fun, 1994), 7.

15 Sidney Blumenthal, "The Syndicated Presidency," *The New Yorker,* 5 April 1993, 42–47.

16 Richard L. Berke, "'Hey Prez!': Computers Offer New Line to Clinton," *New York Times,* 5 April 1993, Al.

17 Blumenthal, "The Syndicated Presidency," 44.

18 Ibid., 42. Clinton's first formal televised news conference came on March 23, 1993, three months into his administration.

19 Rosenstiel, *The Beat Goes On,* 8.

20 Rita K. Whillock, "The Compromising Clinton: Images of Failure, A Record of Success," in *The Clinton Presidency: Images, Issues, and Communication Strategies,* ed. Robert E. Denton Jr. and Rachel L. Holloway (Westport, Conn.: Praeger, 1996),126.

21 "Talking the Talk," *Insight on the News,* 9 February 1998, 9.

22 Randall Bloomquist, "The Word According to Talk," *Adweek,* 3 May 1993, 1.

23 Mark Hudis and Cheryl Heuton, "Talk Ratings Are Stronger than Ever," *Mediaweek,* 8 April 1996, 4.

24 Laura Rich, "Liberals in the Land of Limbaugh," *Inside Media,* 7 June 1995, 1.

25 Ivo Dawnay, "Fightback at the White House: The Saving of a President," *Washington Post,* 1 February 1998, 22.

26 Noack, "Clinton Sex Story Forces Print Media Changes," 30.

27 Dan Trigoboff, "The 'Source' Heard Round the World," *Broadcasting & Cable,* 2 February 1998, 62.

28 Ibid., 62.

29 Robin Pogrebin, "Lewinsky Story Feeds Cable News Networks," *New York Times,* 8 August 1998, A10.

30 Alicia C. Shepard, "White Noise," *American Journalism Review,* January/February 1999, 20.

31 Ibid., 20.

32 Rosenstiel, *The Beat Goes On,* 8.

33 Ibid., 9.

34 Burt Solomon, "How a Leak-Loathing White House Is Putting the Press in Its Place," *National Journal,* 13 February 1993, 416.

35 Rosenstiel, *The Beat Goes On,* 10.

36 Leslie Kaufman, "The Young and the Relentless," *American Journalism Review,* March 1993, 30.

37 Solomon, "How a Leak-Loathing White House," 417.

38 Kaufman, "The Young and the Relentless," 30.

39 Frank Newport and Lydia Saad, "A Matter of Trust," *American Journalism Review,* July/August 1998, 30.

40 Rosenstiel, *The Beat Goes On,* 21.

41 Bob Woodward, *The Agenda: Inside the Clinton White House* (New York: Simon & Schuster, 1994), 226.

42 Rosenstiel, *The Beat Goes On,* 19–21.

43 Kurtz, *Spin Cycle,* xiv.

44 Ibid., 69.

45 Ibid., 73–74.

46 Kurtz, "White House at War," *Vanity Fair,* January 1999, 40.

47 White House reporters, interview by author, tape recording, Washington, D.C., 29 August 1997. See also, Kurtz, "White House at War," 40.

48 See, for example, Michael Baruch Grossman and Martha Joynt Kumar, *Portraying the President* (Baltimore: Johns Hopkins University Press, 1981), and John Anthony Maltese, *Spin Control: The White House Office of Communications and the Management of Presidential News,* 2d ed. (Chapel Hill: University of North Carolina Press, 1995).

49 Gary King and Lynn Ragsdale, eds., *The Elusive Executive* (Washington, D.C.; CQ Press, 1988), 205, 208. For some of the problems associated with counting the number of staff in the White House office, see John Hart, *The Presidential Branch,* 2d ed. (Chatham, N.J.: Chatham House, 1995), 112–25.

50 David L. Paeltz and Robert M. Entman, *Media Power Politics* (New York: Free Press, 1981), 16.

51 Robert M. Entman, "The Imperial Media," in *Politics and the Oval Office,* ed. Arnold J. Meltsner (San Francisco: Institute for Contemporary Studies, 1981), 89.

52 John F. Harris, "Office of Damage Control: DNC Operation to Counter Negative Publicity," *Washington Post,* 31 January 1998, Al.

53 John Kennedy, "Mike McCurry's About-Face," *George,* March 1999, 78.

54 Frank Newport and Alec Gallup, "Clinton's Popularity Paradox," *Gallup Monthly Poll,* January 1998, 14.

55 Samuel Kernell, "The Challenge Ahead for Explaining President Clinton's Public Support," *PRG Report,* spring 1999, 3.

56 Carl M. Cannon, "Hooked on Polls," *National Journal,* 17 October 1998, 2438ff.

57 Judy Keen and Richard Benedetto, "Clinton Poll Ratings Surge," *USA Today,* 21 December 1998, IA.

58 Jack W. Germond and Jules Witcover, "The Defendant Gave a Boffo Speech," *National Journal,* 23 January 1999, 226.

ARTICLE 11

WHAT CAN JOURNALISTS ACTUALLY
DO FOR AMERICAN DEMOCRACY?

Herbert J. Gans

However cynical American journalists may sometimes be, they are dedicated to strengthening the country's democracy. But they do not always think as clearly as they could about how to do it. Although other professions can be accused of the same failing, part of the journalists' fault can be found in the shortcomings of what might be called the journalistic theory of democracy.

THE JOURNALISTIC THEORY OF DEMOCRACY

The theory remains unwritten, but since it seems to have widespread acceptance in the profession, it can be teased out from the spoken and written comments of journalists. Stated most simply, the theory has three parts: (1) The journalist's democratic role is to inform citizens; (2) the more informed these citizens are, the more likely they are to participate politically; and (3) the more they participate, the more democratic the country is apt to be.

By "democracy," journalists presumably mean America's representative form of democracy, but the theory assigns citizens, once informed, a more central part than most thinkers about democracy do. James McCartney, a retired Knight Ridder columnist, goes so far as to claim that "the Constitution of the United States created a governmental process reliant on an informed citizenry"—although the Constitution did little more than spell out that citizens (white male citizens originally) could vote. *Washington Post* columnist E.J. Dionne, writing about journalism's "primary purpose," sees it as "helping . . . citizens make informed decisions and encouraging a

Reprinted from the Harvard International Journal of Press/Politics 3(4): 6–12 wide-ranging democratic debate." However, the theory never spells out how the debate takes place or how it affects either government or politics.

By emphasizing the informed citizen, the theory assigns journalists a central role in maximizing democracy, yet it asks nothing of journalists other than what they already do to get their paychecks. Since the theory does not prescribe how citizens are to be informed or even what kinds of news they need to be offered, journalists can continue to do what they do now, supplying whatever news they consider to be newsworthy. When journalists do their regular job, the theory assumes, citizens will be informed or will inform themselves.

The consequences laid out in the remaining two parts of the theory are not up to the journalists, however, since the theory implies that they will occur automatically. Once citizens have been informed, they will debate and vote, and the country will become democratic.

THE THEORY'S SHORTCOMINGS

Unfortunately, the theory has a number of shortcomings. The first part simply states what journalists should do—to inform citizens—but it does not ask journalists to produce informed citizens. The question of whether supplying the news informs citizens sufficiently to perform their democratic responsibilities is still being debated. A number of studies report what people, including news audiences, *know* about American government and politics, but the more relevant question, whether that knowledge makes them able—or willing—to participate, needs further study.

The second part of the theory is inaccurate. Although most audience studies indicate that better-informed people are more active politically, the cause is not their being informed, but their high level of education and socioeconomic class, which in turn cause their being more informed. Nonetheless, uninformed citizens often become politically active, at least temporarily, when they are angry enough. Lack of information is not, nor has it ever been, an obstacle to participation. And if angry people, informed or uninformed, want to believe something badly enough, they do not allow either the facts or the journalists bearing them to get in the way of what they do as a result. For example, taxpayers' anger at the poor produced a number of false beliefs about their behavior that helped end the federal-welfare program.

The third part of the theory is even more questionable, for citizen activity per se does not produce democracy. The history of America's rural and urban political machines and of the congressional seniority system, to mention just two examples, suggests that if and when powerful individuals and interest groups control the strategic levers of politics and government, citizen activity alone will not necessarily reduce their power.

This is even more the case if citizens limit their participation to the debates that are so important in the journalistic theory of democracy. Aside from the already noted fact that no visible citizen debates ever take place, the theory implies that these debates, and the formal and informal discussions among citizens that surely do take place, can somehow overcome differences of interests and values; resolve other differences produced by class, religion, race, and other dividing lines in America; and result in the compromises necessary to democracy. Partly as a result, journalists are sometimes blind to the difficulty that many Americans have in compromising and to their choosing instead to nurture grievances and blame those differing with them for whatever is wrong, including the news media.

Nevertheless, the underlying shortcoming of the theory is its implication that democracy is the outcome, of the information journalists supply to citizens. This proposition assumes that information is power, which sometimes encourages journalists to claim to be able to "empower" their readers, viewers, and listeners. In reality, however, the reverse is true: Power is needed to obtain access to the right information. People in high places can identify the information that is relevant to participating in governmental decision making, the sources from which it can be obtained, and how those sources can be accessed. Conversely, ordinary people, and news buffs especially, may wind up with a bad case of information overload without ever learning what they need to know to get close to the circles where power and politically relevant information are passed out.

THE THEORY—AND JOURNALISTIC PRACTICE

The question of whether and to what extent journalists consciously apply the journalistic theory in their everyday practice requires a study of newsroom decision making, which I have not done. Still, there are certain parallels between theory and practice that suggest that the theory may in fact influence what journalists do and do not do in covering the news.

For example, the journalistic theory of democracy virtually shuns the notion of power, since its conception of participation is limited to debate and voting. This shows up in journalistic practice. Although journalists do report the exercise of power by the White House and a few other national politicians, political news coverage is dominated by presidential and other election campaigns and, to a lesser degree, congressional debates and voting.

However, journalistic theory has nothing to say about how informed citizens can affect government policy between elections. Journalists do report a limited number of major legislative, budget, and policy disputes and decisions that they consider newsworthy, but these disputes and decisions often take place at governmental levels that are more or less insulated from citizen participation. In any case, normal news coverage has as little relevance to democracy between elections as does the journalistic theory; it is only sufficient to enable the news audience to "keep up with the news" until the next election.

The shortage of between-election news does not prevent interested citizens from participating, however—as letter writers, members of citizen lobbies, funders of pressure groups, and even as Marchers on Washington. But the news is rarely detailed enough to supply them the information they need to participate. Consequently, citizen lobbies and other participatory groups in which citizens can take an active role all develop newsletters and other supplementary news media, including telephone chains, e-mail, and Web pages, to supply their members with the detailed and often time-bound news they need to participate, whether it is information for writing their representatives or news about the Washington demonstration in which they will march.

Moreover, the journalistic theory helps to create a misleading depiction of democracy. The theory implies that once citizens are sufficiently informed, American democracy will operate on the basis of majority rule and the one-citizen-one-vote principle. The political news that journalists report constantly says otherwise. For example, journalists have long written about the political influence of economically powerful organizations and their dollars. Although well-funded candidates usually beat poorly funded ones and corporate and other lobbyists constantly buy "access" to politicians at all levels of government, journalistic theory nevertheless continues to assume that democracy can be preserved as long as journalists do their best to keep citizens informed.

Indeed, the theory discourages journalists from reporting—or even asking themselves—what needs to be done to preserve democracy. At present, much of the news journalists actually report is about powerful officials making decisions and engaging in partisan squabbling. This could easily give citizens the impression that politicians are not very interested in their problems and that there is little reason to become informed.

Conversely, journalists rarely report instances of active citizen participation, except perhaps when the activity involves protest or demonstration. Then, however, stories deal more with whether the participation was accompanied by violence or how it might affect some politician's future electoral chances than with whether it achieved the citizens' stated aims. Current conceptions of objectivity prevent journalists from supplying news audiences with information about how they can participate in political meetings and demonstrations.

The theory's shortcomings also hurt journalists directly. Its superficiality helps to trivialize journalistic self-criticism and self-examination. Strengthening American democracy cannot be achieved by reducing the number of journalist-celebrities and overpaid journalist-lecturers or by increasing the length of politician sound bites on television news. Nor can it be achieved if citizens pay more attention to the news, especially foreign news, as if their news consumption could alter what is happening in countries like Bosnia or Congo.

In addition, the theory blinds journalists to the forces and institutions that limit democracy. The ability of multinational corporations to ignore national boundaries and the power of large organizations to persuade elected officials to meet behind closed doors to rewrite regulations in their favor are a bigger threat to democracy than the amount of "infotainment" in the news.

A BETTER THEORY OF DEMOCRACY?

In effect, journalists need a better theory of democracy, one that reflects the government and political system that they actually cover every day. That theory should correct the current inaccuracies about the informed citizenry, but it must also say something about how and why citizens participate (or do not) and what news they need to participate—that is, what makes for an informed and participating citizen.

Such a theory also needs at least two other sets of propositions. One set should help journalists understand the political and especially the nonpolitical institutions that help democracy and most often endanger it. The other set should spell out journalists' roles in democracy and the limits to what journalists can do.

What Else Can Journalists Do?

Above all, however, a better theory ought to provide journalists with guidance for better practice: for what else they can do to strengthen democracy. This is a task for journalists, but I can make a handful of illustrative suggestions.

User-Friendly News for Potential Participants Journalists need to find ways of reporting how citizens participate on issues; in what groups; how and why they succeed and fail; and to the extent that objectivity permits, how they can participate more easily and more often. Above all, news coverage of an issue must include what potential participants, citizens not now involved, need to know about the issues and the politics in which they are embedded. Features and analytic stories should also report on participation sui generis, informing news audiences on how and why citizens participate and how and why they do not. At election times, such stories should explore a now poorly covered topic: the nonvoter. Reporting who did not vote and why will complement the picture of people's feelings about government and politics obtained from voters and the polls.

More News on Policies Journalists spend so much energy on politics, especially the "horse-race" elements of electoral politics, that they do not devote enough attention to what interests their audiences the most, the governmental policies and other actions that actually affect their everyday lives. Who benefits from and pays for new tax proposals and environmental reforms is often well reported, but that coverage should be extended to include the benefits and costs of less dramatic new policies and the implementation of older ones. Then citizens might have more to participate about.

Deeper Coverage of Politics Partly because of their preoccupation with politics, journalists do not report enough the activities of the lobbies and other organizations that seek to influence government or those that "mark up" legislation or shape it in other, frequently not very visible, ways. Currently, who pays for election campaigns is big news, but the kinds of access to government officials and the drafting of government policies that this money provides, if any, is too rarely traced.

Even more important, journalists need to expand their narrow focus beyond government and politics and report how the larger society and the economy affect these subjects—*and* democracy. For example, journalists must learn to cover the citizen's and the worker's end of the economy as comprehensively as they now cover the investor's and the banker's. The Dow Jones Industrials or the monthly unemployment rate are insufficient to keep track of that multifaceted and multilayered set of regional, national, and multinational institutions too often described falsely as *the* economy. Instead, journalists must keep track of the actual economics in which their audiences work and live.

In addition, journalists need to pay more attention to the ways in which people's political behavior and attitudes are almost always influenced by what else is bothering them. The current distrust of government, the decrease in voting, and even the hostility toward illegal immigrants and the poor can be traced in part to the continuing job and economic insecurity and income inequality that many citizens feel. Nonetheless, politics also includes the religious and cultural battles in an America that has become so diverse that there may no longer be a single American Dream.

More Fundamental Changes

These suggestions, and others like them, imply more fundamental changes in journalism and especially in the division of labor among news media. The daily event-centered reportage that confronts the news audience with a continually repeated potpourri of unrelated stories should be reduced and replaced by more topic-centered features, especially in the news media that can accommodate longer stories. Audiences do not need or want daily updates of who did what to whom in Congress, but they might pay more intense attention to thoughtful periodic summaries of what Congress is or is not doing for them and for the country as a whole, particularly about the problems that worry them.

Topic-centered coverage calls for more active reporting and less reactive and passive dependence on what is offered by the White House or the other major sources of national political news. It also requires more *analytic* stories. If journalists really want to encourage citizen participation, citizens must know more about how and why the events and trends that most affect them are taking place. Analytic stories can help people understand which institutions and individuals are especially responsible and can enable them to take the appropriate political actions. At present, the analytic vacuum in daily and weekly news is too often filled only with book-writing journalists such as E.J. Dionne or William Greider, but most of the news audience never sees their books.

Needless to say, topic-centered features and analytic stories require that reporters have more time for reporting and analysis. In some cases, new beats may be needed, as well as additional training for reporters, editors, and producers to cover those beats and to write about them in audience-friendly ways. All of this equals more costly news coverage, which may be economically feasible only for national media that can recoup some of their costs through syndication, at least as long as corporate news firms expect to make as much profit as entertainment enterprises.

Improving the journalistic role in strengthening democracy will not be cheap or easy. However, the global and domestic complexities that America will likely face in the twenty-first century will, in any case, require the modernization of twentieth-century journalism.

BIOGRAPHICAL NOTE

Herbert J. Gans is the Robert S. Lynd Professor of Sociology at Columbia University. This article is based on a presentation to the Fellows' Seminar of the Freedom Forum's Media Studies Center, where the author was a Senior Fellow in 1996–97.

A R T I C L E   12

AMERICA'S IGNORANT VOTERS

Michael Schudson

Every week, the *Tonight Show's* Jay Leno takes to the streets of
Los Angeles to quiz innocent passersby with some simple
questions: On what bay is San Francisco located? Who was
president of the United States during World War II? The audience
roars as Leno's hapless victims fumble for answers. Was it Lincoln?
Carter?

No pollster, let alone a college or high school history teacher,
would be surprised by the poor showing of Leno's sample citizens.
In a national assessment test in the late 1980s, only a third of American 17-year-olds could correctly locate the Civil War in the period
1850–1900; more than a quarter placed it in the 18th century. Two-
thirds knew that Abraham Lincoln wrote the Emancipation Proclamation, which seems a respectable showing, but what about the 14
percent who said that Lincoln wrote the Bill of Rights, the 10 percent who checked the Missouri Compromise, and the nine percent
who awarded Lincoln royalties for *Uncle Tom's Cabin*?

Asking questions about contemporary affairs doesn't yield any
more encouraging results. In a 1996 national public opinion poll,
only 10 percent of American adults could identify William Rehnquist as the chief justice of the Supreme Court. In the same survey,
conducted at the height of Newt Gingrich's celebrity as Speaker of
the House, only 59 percent could identify the job he held. Americans
sometimes demonstrate deeper knowledge about a major issue before the nation, such as the Vietnam War, but most could not
describe the thrust of the Clinton health care plan or tell whether the

"America's Ignorant Voters" (as appeared in *Wilson Quarterly,* Spring 2000, Vol. 24,
pp. 16–22). Reprinted with permission of the author.

Reagan administration supported the Sandinistas or the contras during the conflict in Nicaragua (and only a third could place that country in Central America).

It can be misleading to make direct comparisons with other countries, but the general level of political awareness in leading liberal democracies overseas does seem to be much higher. While 58 percent of the Germans surveyed, 32 percent of the French, and 22 percent of the British were able to identify Boutros Boutros-Ghali as secretary general of the United Nations in 1994, only 13 percent of Americans could do so. Nearly all Germans polled could name Boris Yeltsin as Russia's leader, as could 63 percent of the British, 61 percent of the French, but only 50 percent of the Americans.

How can the United States claim to be a model democracy if its citizens know so little about political life? That question has aroused political reformers and preoccupied many political scientists since the early 20th century. It can't be answered without some historical perspective.

Today's mantra that the "informed citizen" is the foundation of effective democracy was not a central part of the nation's founding vision. It is largely the creation of late-19th-century Mugwump and Progressive reformers, who recoiled from the spectacle of powerful political parties using government as a job bank for their friends and a cornucopia of contracts for their relatives. (In those days before the National Endowment for the Arts, Nathaniel Hawthorne, Herman Melville, and Walt Whitman all subsidized their writing by holding down federal patronage appointments.) Voter turnout in the late 19th century was extraordinarily high by today's standards, routinely over 70 percent in presidential elections, and there is no doubt that parades, free whiskey, free-floating money, patronage jobs, and the pleasures of fraternity all played a big part in the political enthusiasm of ordinary Americans.

The reformers saw this kind of politics as a betrayal of democratic ideals. A democratic public, they believed, must reason together. That ideal was threatened by mindless enthusiasm, the wily maneuvers of political machines, and the vulnerability of the new immigrant masses in the nation's big cities, woefully ignorant of Anglo-Saxon traditions, to manipulation by party hacks. E. L. Godkin, founding editor of the *Nation* and a leading reformer, argued that "there is no corner of our system in which the hastily made and ignorant foreign voter may not be found eating away the political structure, like a white ant, with a group of natives standing over him and encouraging him."

This was in 1893, by which point a whole set of reforms had been put in place. Civil service reform reduced patronage. Ballot reform irrevocably altered the act of voting itself. For most of the 19th century, parties distributed at the polls their own "tickets," listing only their own candidates for office. A voter simply took a ticket from a party worker and deposited it in the ballot box, without needing to read it or mark it in any way. Voting was thus a public act of party affiliation. Beginning in 1888, however, and spreading across the country by 1896, this system was replaced with government-printed ballots that listed all the candidates from each eligible party. The voter marked the ballot in secret as we do today, in an act that affirmed voting as an individual choice rather than a social act of party loyalty. Political parades and other public spectacles increasingly gave way to pamphlets in what reformers dubbed "educational" political campaigns. Leading newspapers, once little more than organs of the political parties, began to declare their independence and to portray themselves as nonpartisan commercial institutions of public enlightenment and public-minded criticism. Public secondary education began to spread.

These and other reforms enshrined the informed citizen as the foundation of democracy, but at a tremendous cost: Voter turnout plummeted. In the presidential election of 1920, it dropped to 49 percent, its lowest point in the 20th century—until it was matched in 1996. Ever since, political scientists and others have been plumbing the mystery created by the new model of an informed citizenry: How can so many, knowing so little, and voting in such small numbers, build a democracy that appears to be (relatively) successful?

There are several responses to that question. The first is that a certain amount of political ignorance is an inevitable byproduct of America's unique political environment. One reason Americans have so much difficulty grasping the political facts of life is that their political system is the world's most complex. Ask the next political science Ph.D. you meet to explain what government agencies at what level—federal, state, county, or city—take responsibility for the homeless. Or whom he or she voted for in the last election for municipal judge. The answers might make Jay Leno's victims seem less ridiculous. No European country has as many elections, as many elected offices, as complex a maze of overlapping governmental jurisdictions, as the American system. It is simply harder to "read" U.S. politics than the politics of most nations.

The hurdle of political comprehension is raised a notch higher by the ideological inconsistencies of American political parties. In Britain, a voter can confidently cast a vote without knowing a great deal about the particular candidates on the ballot. The Labor candidate generally can be counted on to follow the Labor line, the Conservative to follow the Tory line. An American voter casting a ballot for a Democrat or Republican has no such assurance. Citizens in other countries need only dog paddle to be in the political swim; in the United States they need the skills of a scuba diver.

If the complexity of U.S. political institutions helps explain American ignorance of domestic politics, geopolitical factors help explain American backwardness in foreign affairs. There is a kind of ecology of political ignorance at work. The United States is far from Europe and borders only two other countries. With a vast domestic market, most of its producers have relatively few dealings with customers in other countries, globalization notwithstanding. Americans, lacking the parliamentary form of government that prevails in most other democracies, are also likely to find much of what they read or hear about the wider world politically opaque. And the simple fact of America's political and cultural superpower status naturally limits citizens' political awareness. Just as employees gossip more about the boss than the boss gossips about them, so Italians and Brazilians know more about the United States than Americans know about their countries.

Consider a thought experiment. Imagine what would happen if you transported those relatively well-informed Germans or Britons to the United States with their cultural heritage, schools, and news media intact. If you checked on them again about a generation later, after long exposure to the distinctive American political environment—its geographic isolation, superpower status, complex political system, and weak parties—would they have the political knowledge levels of Europeans or Americans? Most likely, I think, they would have developed typically American levels of political ignorance.

Lending support to this notion of an ecology of political knowledge is the stability of American political ignorance over time. Since the 1940s, when social scientists began measuring it, political ignorance has remained virtually unchanged. It is hard to gauge the extent of political knowledge before that time, but there is little to suggest that there is some lost golden age in U.S. history. The storied 1858 debates between Senator Stephen Douglas and Abraham Lincoln, for example, though undoubtedly a high point in the nation's public discourse, were also an anomaly. Public debates were rare in 19th-century political campaigns, and campaign rhetoric was generally overblown and aggressively partisan.

Modern measurements of Americans' historical and political knowledge go back at least to 1943, when the *New York Times* surveyed college freshmen and found "a striking ignorance of even the most elementary aspects of United States history." Reviewing nearly a half-century of data (1945–89) in *What Americans Know about Politics and Why It Matters* (1996), political scientists Michael Delli Carpini and Scott Keeter conclude that, on balance, there has been a slight gain in Americans' political knowledge, but one so modest that it makes more sense to speak of a remarkable stability. In 1945, for example, 43 percent of a national sample could name neither of their U.S. senators; in 1989, the figure was essentially unchanged at 45 percent. In 1952, 67 percent could name the vice president; in 1989, 74 percent could do so. In 1945, 92 percent of Gallup poll respondents knew that the term of the president is four years, compared with 96 percent in 1989. Whatever the explanations for dwindling voter turnout since 1960 may be, rising ignorance is not one of them.*

As Delli Carpini and Keeter suggest, there are two ways to view their findings. The optimist's view is that political ignorance has grown no worse despite the spread of television and video games, the decline of political parties, and a variety of other negative developments. The pessimist asks why so little has improved despite the vast increase in formal education during those years. But the main conclusion remains: no notable change over as long a period as data are available.

Low as American levels of political knowledge may be, a generally tolerable, sometimes admirable, political democracy survives. How? One explanation is provided by a school of political science that goes under the banner of "political heuristics." Public opinion polls and paper-and-pencil tests of political knowledge, argue researchers such as Arthur Lupia, Samuel Popkin, Paul Sniderman, and Philip Teflock, presume that citizens require more knowledge than they actually need in order to cast votes that accurately reflect their preferences. People can and do get by with relatively little political information. What Popkin calls "low-information rationality" is sufficient for citizens to vote intelligently.

This works in two ways. First, people can use cognitive cues, or "heuristics." Instead of learning each of a candidate's issue positions, the voter may simply rely on the candidate's party affiliation as a cue. This works better in Europe than in America, but it still works reasonably well. Endorsements are another useful shortcut. A thumbs-up for a candidate from the Christian Coalition or Ralph

---

*There is no happy explanation for low voter turnout. "Voter fatigue" is not as silly an explanation as it may seem: Americans have more frequent elections for more offices than any other democracy. It is also true that the more-or-less steady drop in turnout starting in about 1960 coincided with the beginning of a broad expansion of nonelectoral politics that may have drained political energies away from the polling places: the civil rights movement the antiwar demonstrations of the Vietnam years, the women's movement, and the emergence of the religious Right. The decline in turnout may signify in part that Americans are disengaged from public life, but it may also suggest that they judge electoral politics to be disengaged from public issues that deeply concern them.

Nader or the National Association for the Advancement of Colored People or the American Association of Retired Persons frequently provides enough information to enable one to cast a reasonable vote.

Second, as political scientist Milton Lodge points out, people often process information on the fly, without retaining details in memory. If you watch a debate on TV—and 46 million did watch the first presidential debate between President Bill Clinton and Robert Dole in 1996—you may learn enough about the candidates' ideas and personal styles to come to a judgment about each one. A month later, on election day, you may not be able to answer a pollster's detailed questions about where they stood on the issues, but you will remember which one you liked best—and that is enough information to let you vote intelligently.

The realism of the political heuristics school is an indispensable corrective to unwarranted bashing of the general public. Americans are not the political dolts they sometimes seem to be. Still, the political heuristics approach has a potentially fatal flaw: It subtly substitutes *voting* for *citizenship*. Cognitive shortcuts have their place, but what if a citizen wants to persuade someone else to vote for his or her chosen candidate? What may be sufficient in the voting booth is inadequate in the wider world of the democratic process: discussion, deliberation, and persuasion. It is possible to vote and still be disenfranchised.

Yet another response to the riddle of voter ignorance takes its cue from the Founders and other 18th-century political thinkers who emphasized the importance of a morally virtuous citizenry. Effective democracy, in this view, depends more on the "democratic character" of citizens than on their aptitude for quiz show knowledge of political facts. Character, in this sense, is demonstrated all the time in everyday life, not in the voting booth every two years. From Amitai Etzioni, William Galston, and Michael Sandel on the liberal side of the political spectrum to William J. Bennett and James Q. Wilson on the conservative side, these writers emphasize the importance of what Alexis de Tocqueville called "habits of the heart." These theorists, along with politicians of every stripe, point to the importance of civil society as a foundation of democracy. They emphasize instilling moral virtue through families and civic participation through churches and other voluntary associations; they stress the necessity for civility and democratic behavior in daily life. They would not deny that it is important for citizens to be informed, but neither would they put information at the center of their vision of what makes democracy tick.

Brown University's Nancy Rosenblum, for example, lists two essential traits of democratic character. "Easy spontaneity" is the disposition to treat others identically, without deference, and with an easy grace. This capacity to act as if many social differences are of no account in public settings is one of the things that make democracy happen on the streets. This is the disposition that foreign visitors have regularly labeled "American" for 200 years, at least since 1818, when the British reformer and journalist William Cobbett remarked upon Americans' "universal civility." Tocqueville observed in 1840 that strangers in America who meet "find neither danger nor advantage in telling each other freely what they think. Meeting by chance, they neither seek nor avoid each other. Their manner is therefore natural, frank, and open."

Rosenblum's second trait is "speaking up," which she describes as "a willingness to respond at least minimally to ordinary injustice." This does not involve anything so impressive as organizing a demonstration, but something more like objecting when an adult cuts ahead of a kid in a line at a movie theater, or politely rebuking a coworker who slurs a racial or religious group. It is hard to define "speaking up" precisely, but we all recognize it, without necessarily giving it the honor it deserves as an element of self-government.

We need not necessarily accept Rosenblum's chosen pair of moral virtues. Indeed a Japanese or Swedish democrat might object that they look suspiciously like distinctively American traits rather than distinctively democratic ones. They almost evoke Huckleberry Finn. But turning our attention to democratic character reminds us that being well informed is just one of the requirements of democratic citizenship.

The Founding Fathers were certainly more concerned about instilling moral virtues than disseminating information about candidates and issues. Although they valued civic engagement more than their contemporaries in Europe did, and cared enough about promoting the wide circulation of ideas to establish a post office and adopt the First Amendment, they were ambivalent about, even suspicious of, a politically savvy populace. They did not urge voters to "know the issues"; at most they hoped that voters would choose wise and prudent legislators to consider issues on their behalf. On the one hand, they agreed that "the diffusion of knowledge is productive of virtue, and the best security for our civil rights," as a North Carolina congressman put it in 1792. On the other hand, as George Washington cautioned, "however necessary it may be to keep a watchful eye over public servants and public measures, yet there ought to be limits to it, for suspicions unfounded and jealousies too lively are irritating to honest feelings, and oftentimes are productive of more evil than good."

If men were angels, well and good—but they were not, and few of the Founders were as extravagant as Benjamin Rush in his rather scary vision of an education that would "convert men into republican machines." In theory, many shared Rush's emphasis on education; in practice, the states made little provision for public schooling in the early years of the Republic. Where schools did develop, they were defended more as tutors of obedience and organs of national unity than as means to create a watchful citizenry. The Founders placed their trust less in education than in a political system designed to insulate decision making in the legislatures from the direct influence of the emotional, fractious, and too easily swayed electorate.

All of these arguments—about America's political environment, the value of political heuristics, and civil society—do not add up to a prescription for resignation or complacency about civic education. Nothing I have said suggests that the League of Women Voters should shut its doors or that newspaper editors should stop putting politics on page one. People may be able to vote intelligently with very little information—even well-educated people do exactly that on most of the ballot issues they face—but democratic citizenship means more than voting. It means discussing and debating the questions before the political community and sometimes raising new questions. Without a framework of information in which to place them, it is hard to understand even the simple slogans and catchwords of the day. People with scant political knowledge, as research by political scientists Samuel Popkin and Michael Dimock suggests, have more difficulty than others in perceiving differences between candidates and parties. Ignorance also tends to breed more ignorance; it inhibits people from venturing into situations that make them feel uncomfortable or inadequate, from the voting booth to the community forum to the town hall.

What is to be done? First, it is important to put the problem in perspective. American political ignorance is not growing worse. There is even an "up" side to Americans' relative indifference to political and historical facts: their characteristic openness to experiment, their pragmatic willingness to judge ideas and practices by their results rather than their pedigree.

Second, it pays to examine more closely the ways in which people do get measurably more knowledgeable. One of the greatest changes Delli Carpini and Keeter found in their study, for example, was in the percentage of Americans who could identify the first 10 amendments to the Constitution as the Bill of Rights. In 1954, the year the U.S. Supreme Court declared school segregation unconstitutional in *Brown* v. *Board of Education,* only 31 percent of Americans could do so. In 1989, the number had moved up to 46 percent.

Why the change? I think the answer is clear: The civil rights movement, along with the rights-oriented Warren Court, helped bring rights to the forefront of the American political agenda and thus to public consciousness. Because they dominated the political agenda, rights became a familiar topic in the press and on TV dramas, sitcoms, and talk shows, also finding their way into school curricula and textbooks. Political change, this experience shows, can influence public knowledge.

This is not to say that only a social revolution can bring about such an improvement. A lot of revolutions are small, one person at a time, one classroom at a time. But it does mean that there is no magic bullet. Indeed, imparting political knowledge has only become more difficult as the dimensions of what is considered political have expanded into what were once nonpolitical domains (such as gender relations and tobacco use), as one historical narrative has become many, each of them contentious, and as the relatively simple framework of world politics (the Cold War) has disappeared.

In this world, the ability to name the three branches of government or describe the New Deal does not make a citizen, but it is at least a token of membership in a society dedicated to the ideal of self-government. Civic education is an imperative we must pursue with the full recognition that a high level of ignorance is likely to prevail—even if that fact does not flatter our faith in rationalism, our pleasure in moralizing, or our confidence in reform.

PART 4

DOMESTIC AND FOREIGN POLICY ISSUES

Issues of federalism have been at the core of political debates in the United States since the founding era. The constitutional framers labored over the issue of the extent of the federal government's responsibilities and how much power should be reserved for the states. Presidents and congresses of the modern era still grapple with this issue. Former president Bill Clinton appropriately spoke on the topic of federalism in late 1999 in Canada. Our nation's neighbor to the north indeed has had to contend with highly controversial federalism issues, as many residents of the Quebec province continue to push for independence from the nation altogether. Clinton's speech addressed his philosophy of the appropriate role of the federal government in modern times. The former president argued that the model given to us by the eighteenth century founders is inadequate in modern times and that the federal government increasingly has to take the lead over states and localities in insuring the rights of citizens, preserving of land, and preventing crime. Clinton outlined his specific disagreements with Republicans who articulated a different view—one in which more power resides with states and localities and the federal government plays a smaller role in making policy.

In November 1999, the then-Texas governor and presidential aspirant, George W. Bush, made a speech on foreign policy at the Ronald Reagan Library in California. As a governor Bush had a distinct interest in outlining his foreign policy vision, as governors are susceptible to criticism for not having sufficient experience abroad to be effective in the presidency. Bush articulated the view that the United States must continue to have a strong internationalist role as well as a realistic sense of our own priorities in the world. He argued that national interests must be the guiding principles in the establishment of U.S. foreign policy and that protecting such interests requires first and foremost a strong national defense. Bush examined many of the major challenges facing the U.S. in light of the end of the Cold War and the rise of what he calls "Eurasia's greatest powers"—Russia and China.

Government runs on the people's money. Consequently, federal tax policy dominates many of the debates of contemporary Washington. A popular Republican proposal is the flat-tax: an across-the-board single tax rate for all Americans, regardless of income level (though in some variations of the flat-tax the lowest income Americans are exempt from federal taxes altogether). GOP House Majority Leader Richard Armey (TX) argues that the flat-tax is the most simple and fair means of assessing federal taxes. Such a policy would eliminate the complexity of the tax system and, he argues, generate stronger revenues for the federal government even while providing for tax relief for most Americans. To the contrary, Brookings Institution economist William G. Gale argues that the current tax structure, with its varied tax rate levels and deductions, is a reflection of the normal political pressures rendered on a democratic system. Differential tax rates exist because Americans want fairness, deductions are enacted because certain groups or industries argue that such benefits are necessary to achieve some important societal end. It is hard to imagine, Gale argues, that once adopted, the flat-tax would not succumb to the same democratic pressures and eventually the tax code would end up looking like the current system.

Local property taxes largely fund the U.S. system of education. Once again, fairness issues arise because of the vast differences in the quality of education in communities throughout the country depending on the tax base: wealthier communities simply have better schools, more resources, and their students are better educated on the whole than those from less affluent and poor communities. Education experts differ strongly as to what should be done to both improve education and provide more fairness in the system. One prominent proposal is for a system of education vouchers. There are a variety of voucher proposals but what they all have in common is the belief that parents should have the freedom to use the portion of property taxes that they pay for either public or private education. Conservative Clint Bolick likes the voucher idea because, in his view, it gives more autonomy to parents over their children's educations and it provides a market-oriented solution to the problem of poor quality education in many schools. Under the voucher plan, parents choose where to educate their children and schools that cannot compete effectively for vouchers will have to either increase quality to draw a clientele or close. Barbara Miner opposes the voucher concept as potentially contributing to a dual system of education in the U.S.: one for the wealthy and one for everyone else. She raises constitutional issues that confront the public funding of private schools, especially ones with a religious orientation. Furthermore, Minor argues that public schools are the hallmark of a fair and inclusive system of education that is available to all and does not favor any one class of citizens.

To what extent should the federal government play a role in influencing the personal choices of citizens, particularly in those cases where such choices are damaging to individuals? Is it government's job to save people from themselves? Or, should people be free to make whatever choices they like for themselves, as long as those choices do not harm the community? These questions are at the core of modern debates over regulating tobacco. But the issue is even more complicated due to conflict over the issue of second hand smoke. If indeed the evidence of second hand smoke being dangerous is true, then it stands to reason that the choice to smoke tobacco affects more than just the individual. And what about the cost to society of many Americans suffering the health consequences of their choices to smoke? No one argues any more that tobacco may not be harmful, as a number of tobacco company executives did in the 1980s in their testimonies before Congress. The issue is whether the government should regulate this product, and if so, how? Steven F. Goldstone of RJR Nabisco and John R. Garrison of the American Lung Association offer different views of what government's role should be with regard to regulating tobacco.

On September 11, 2001 terrorist attacks against the United States changed the fabric of public life in the nation. Suddenly many contentious policy debates in Congress did not seem at all important. President George W. Bush declared the fight against terrorism as the necessary focus of his young administration. On September 20, 2001 the president spoke to the nation before a joint session of Congress. His words reassured a troubled nation of his administration's resolve to defeat international terrorism.

Article 13

FEDERALISM

Bill Clinton

October 8, 1999

Thank you. Thank you so much. Prime Minister Chretien; to the Prime Minister of Saint Kitts and Nevis, Denzil Douglas; Premier Bouchard; cochairs of this conference, Bob Rae and Henning Voscherau; to distinguished visitors; Governors—I think the lieutenant governor of South Dakota, Carole Hillard, is here—and to all of you: I think it is quite an interesting thing that we have this impressive array of people to come to a conference on federalism, a topic that probably 10 or 20 years ago would have been viewed as a substitute for a sleeping pill.

But in the aftermath of the conflicts in the former Yugoslavia; the interesting debates—at least I can say this from the point of view as your neighbor—that has gone on in Quebec; the deepening, troubling efforts to reconcile different tribes who occupy nations with boundaries they did not draw in Africa; and any number of other issues, this topic of federalism has become very, very important.

It is fitting that the first global conference would be held here in North America, because federalism began here—a founding principle forged in the crucible of revolution, enshrined in the Constitution of the United States, shared today by all three nations on our continent, as I'm sure President Zedillo said.

It is also especially fitting that this conference be held in Canada. A land larger than China, spanning 5 times zones and 10

In an Oct. 8 address at the Forum of Federations Conference, Pres. Clinton discusses the importance of the relationship between a people and their federal government, explaining the reforms made by his administration in order to improve that relationship in the United States.

distinct provinces, it has shown the world how people of different cultures and languages can live in peace, prosperity, and mutual respect.

In the United States, we have valued our relationship with a strong and united Canada. We look to you; we learn from you. The partnership you have built between people of diverse backgrounds and governments at all levels is what this conference is about and, ultimately, what democracy must be about, as people all over the world move around more, mix with each other more, live in close proximity more.

Today I would like to talk briefly about the ways we in the United States are working to renew and redefine federalism for the twenty-first century; then, how I see the whole concept of federalism emerging internationally; and finally, how we—how I think, anyway—we should judge the competing claims of federalism and independence in different contexts around the world.

First let me say we are 84 days, now, from a new century and a new millennium. The currents of change in how we work and live and relate to each other, and relate to people far across the world, are changing very rapidly.

President Franklin Roosevelt once said that new conditions impose new requirements upon government and those who conduct government. We know this to be the case not only in the United States and Canada, Great Britain and Germany, Italy and France, Mexico and Brazil, but indeed, in all the countries of the world. But in all these places there is a federalist system of some form or another. We look for ways to imbue old values with new life and old institutions with new meaning.

In 1992, when I ran for President, there was a growing sense in the United States that the compact between the people and their government, and between the states and the federal government, was in severe disrepair. This was driven largely by the fact that our federal government had quadrupled the national debt in 12 years, and that had led to enormous interest rates, slow growth, and grave difficulties on all the states of our land which they were powerless to overcome.

So when the Vice President and I ran for national office, we had no debate from people who said, "Look, this is a national priority, and you have to deal with it." But we talked a lot to governors and others about the necessity to create again what our Founding Fathers called the laboratories of democracy. We, frankly, admitted that no one knew all the answers to America's large welfare caseload, to America's enormous crime rate, to America's incredible diversity of children and challenges in our schools. And so we said we would try to give new direction to the nation and deal with plainly national problems, but we would also try to build a new partnership that would make all of our states feel more a part of our union and more empowered in determining their own destiny.

Now, people develop this federalist system for different reasons. It came naturally to the United States because Great Britain set up colonies here as separate entities. And the states of our country actually created the national government. So we always had a sense that there were some things the states were supposed to do and some things the federal government were supposed to do.

Our Founding Fathers gave us some indication in the Constitution, but the history of the United States Supreme Court is full of cases trying to resolve the whole question of what is the role and the power of the states as opposed to what is the role and the power of the national government in ever new circumstances.

There are different examples elsewhere. For example, in the former Yugoslavia when it existed before, federalism was at least set up to give the appearance that all the different ethnic groups could be fairly treated and could have their voices heard.

So in 1992 it appeared that the major crisis in federalism was that the states had been disempowered from doing their jobs because the national economy was so weak and the fabric of the national society was fraying in America. But underneath that I knew that once we began to build things again we would have to resolve some very substantial questions, some of which may be present in your countries, as well.

As we set about to work, the Vice President and I, in an effort that I put him in charge of, made an attempt to redefine the mission of the federal government. And we told the people of the United States that we actually thought the federal government was too large in size, that it should be smaller but more active, and that we should do more in partnerships with state and local governments and the private sector, with the ultimate goal of empowering the American people to solve their own problems in whatever unit was most appropriate, whether it was an individual citizen, the family, the community, the state, or the nation.

And we have worked at that quite steadily. Like Canada, we turned our deficit around and produced a surplus. We also shrank the size of the federal government. The size of the United States federal government today is the same as it was in 1962, when John Kennedy was President, and our country was much, much smaller.

In the economic expansion we have been enjoying since 1993, the overwhelming majority of the jobs that were created were created in the private sector. It's the largest percentage of private sector job creation of any economic expansion in America since the end of World War II.

Meanwhile, many of our state and local governments have continued to grow in size, to meet the day-to-day demands of a lot of the domestic issues that we face in our country. And I think that is a good thing.

In addition to shrinking the size of government, we've tried to empower the states to make more of their own decisions. For example, the Department of Education has gotten rid of two-thirds of the rules that it imposed on states and school districts when I became President. Instead, we say, "Here are our national objectives; here is the money you can have; you have to make a report on the progress at meeting these national objectives, but we're not going to tell you how to do it anymore." And it's amazing what you can do if you get people to buy into national objectives with which they agree, and you stop trying to micromanage every instance of their lives and their daily activities. So we found some good success there.

We've also tried to give the states just blanket freedom to try more new ideas in areas where we think we don't have all the answers now, from health policy to welfare reform to education to fighting crime.

We have always felt this has been easy in the United States, though, compared to a lot of places because we've had this history of believing from the time of our Founders that the national government would never have all the answers, and that the states should be seen as our friends and our partners because they could be laboratories of democracy. They could always be out there pushing the envelope of change. And certain things would be possible politically in some places that would not be possible in others.

And we have been very well served by that. It has encouraged a lot of innovation and experimentation. Here is the problem we have with the basic business of government and federalism today. In the twenty-first century world, when we find an answer to a problem, very often we don't have time to wait for every state to agree that that's the answer. So we try to jumpstart the federalist experience by looking for ideas that are working and then embodying them in federal legislation and giving all the states the funds and other support they need to do it.

Why do we do this? Well, let me give you one example. In 1787, in the United States, the Founding Fathers declared that all the new territories would have to set aside land for public schools, and then gave the responsibility for public education to the states. Now, then, in the next few years, a handful of states mandated education. But it took more than 100 years for all of our states to mandate free public education for all of our children. That was nineteenth century pace of change. It's inadequate in the twenty-first century.

So I have tried to do what I did as a governor. If something is working in a state, I try to steal it, put it into federal law, and at least give all the states the opportunity and the money necessary to implement the same change. But it's very, very important.

Since our Ambassador is a native of Georgia, I'll give you one example. One of my goals is to make universal access to colleges and universities in America, and we now have something called the HOPE scholarship, modeled on Ambassador Giffin's home state program, which gives all students enough of a tax subsidy to at least afford the first 2 years of college in America, because we found in a census that no matter where you come from in the United States, people with at least 2 years of education after high school tended to get jobs where their incomes grew and they did better. People with less than that tended to get jobs where their incomes stayed level or declined in the global economy.

Now, we've also tried to make dealing with Washington less of a problem. We've ended something that was very controversial, at least prospectively, called unfunded mandates, where the federal government would tell the states they had to do something and give them about 5 percent of the money it cost to do it. That, I think, is a problem in every national federal system. We continue to give the states greater freedom and flexibility. And this summer I signed a new Executive order on federalism which would reaffirm in very specific ways how we would work in partnership and greater consultation with state and local officials.

Federalism is not a fixed system; it, by definition, has to be an evolving system. For more than 200 years, the pendulum of powers have swung back and forth one way or the other. And I do want to say—for those of you who may be looking outside in, thinking the Americans could never understand our problems, they don't have any problems like this—it is true that, by and large, in our state units we don't have people who are of just one racial or ethnic or religious groups. But to be sure, we have some of that. I'll give you one example that we're dealing with today.

The United States Supreme Court has to decide a case from the State of Hawaii in which the state has given native Hawaiians, Pacific Islanders, the right to vote in a certain kind of election—and only native Hawaiians. And someone in Hawaii has sued them, saying that violates the equal protection clause of the United States Constitution. We disagree because of the purpose of the election.

But you can see this is a federalist issue. We basically said the national government would give that to the states, the states want to do it this way; then a citizen says, "No, you can't do that under national law."

Another example that causes us a lot of problems in the West—what happens when the federal government actually owns a lot of the land and the resources of a state? The national government is most unpopular in America in states like Wyoming or Idaho, where there aren't very many people; there's a lot of natural resources. Cattlemen, ranchers have to use land that belongs to the federal government, and we feel that we have to protect the land for multiple uses, including environmental preservation as well as grazing or mining or whatever. And so it's an impossible situation.

It's very funny—in these states, when we started, the federal government was most popular in the areas where we own most of the land, because we built dams and channeled rivers and provided land for people to graze their cattle. And within 50 years, the federal government has become the most unpopular thing imaginable. Now, I used to go to Wyoming on vacation just to listen to people tell me how terrible the job I had was. But it's a problem we have to face.

And let me say one other thing I think might be interesting to you is that the Democratic Party and the Republican Party in the United States tend to have different ideas about federalism depending on what the issue is, which is why it's always good to have a dynamic system.

For example, we Democrats, once we find something working at the local level that advances our social policy, or our economic policy, we want to at least make it a national option, if not a national mandate. When I became President, crime was going up, but there were cities where crime was going down. I went there and found out why it was going down. And it was obvious to me we didn't have enough police officers preventing crime in the first place, so I said we're going to create 100,000 police at the national level and give them to the cities.

The conservatives were against that. They said, "You're interfering with state and local rights, telling them how to fight crime." Of course, I wasn't; I was giving them police. They didn't have to take them if they didn't want them. And it turned out they liked it quite well; we have the lowest crime rate in 26 years. But there was a genuine federalism dispute.

Now we're having the same dispute over teachers. We have the largest number of children in our schools in history; lots of evidence that smaller classes in the early grades yield permanent learning gains to children. So I said, now let's put 100,000 teachers out there. And they say I'm trying to impose this terrible burden on state and local governments, sticking my nose in where it doesn't belong.

On the other hand, in the whole history of the country, personal injury law, including economic injuries, commercial law has always been the province of state and local government except for things like securities, stocks, bonds, things that required a national securities market. But many people in the Republican Party believe that since there is essentially a national economy and an international economic environment, that we should take away from the states all their states' rights when it comes to determining the rules under which people can sue businesses. And they really believe it.

And I have agreed with them as it applies to securities litigation because we need a national securities market. But I have disagreed with them as it applies to other areas of tort reform where they think it's a bad thing that there is state rights.

And I say this not to attack the other party, but only to illustrate to all of you that in whatever context you operate, there will always be differences of opinion about what should be done nationally and what should be done at the state level. That cannot be eliminated. The purpose of federalism, it seems to me, is to, number one, take account of the genuinely local feelings which may be, in the United States, a result of economic activities and ties to the land and history; or it may be in another country the result of the general segregation of people of various racial, ethnic, or religious groups into the provinces in the federal system.

So the first process is to give people a sense of their identity and autonomy. And then you have to really try to make good decisions so that the system works. I mean, in the end, all these systems only have integrity if the allocation of decisionmaking authority really produces results that people like living with, so they feel that they can go forward.

Now, let me just discuss a minute what is sort of the underlying tension here that you see all across the world, which is, what is the answer to the fact that on the edge of a new millennium—where we would prefer to talk about the Internet, and the decoding of the human gene, and the discovery of billions of new galaxies in outer space—those of us in politics have to spend so much time talking about the most primitive slaughter of people based on their ethnic or racial or religious differences.

The great irony of the turning of the millennium is that we have more modern options for technology and economic advance than ever before, but our major threat is the most primitive human failing: the fear of the other and the sense that we can only breathe and function and matter if we are somehow free of the necessity to associate with and deal with and maybe even under certain circumstances subordinate our own opinions to, the feelings of them—people who are different from us, a different race, a different religion, a different tribe.

And there is no answer to this that is easy. But let me just ask you to look in the context of the former Yugoslavia, where we are trying to preserve a Bosnian State, Prime Minister Chretien and I and our friends—which serves Croatians and Muslims, after 4 years of horrible slaughter, until we stopped it in 1995. Or in Kosovo, where we're exploring whether Kosovo can continue to be an autonomous part of Serbia, notwithstanding the fact that the Serbs ran all of them out of the country and we had to take them back.

Why did all this happen? Partly because it was an artificially imposed federalism. Marshal Tito was a very smart man who basically said, "I'm going to create federalism out of my own head. I'm going to mandate the participation of all these groups in government. And I'm going to forbid my government from talking about ethnic superiority, or oppression, or problems." He wouldn't even let them discuss the kind of ethnic tensions that are just part of the daily life in most societies in this world. And it all worked until he died. And then it slowly began to unravel.

So one of the reasons you have all these people clamoring for the independence of ever smaller groups is that they had a kind of phony federalism imposed from the top down. So the first lesson I draw from this is every federalist system in the world today—a world in which information is widely shared, economic possibilities are at least—always, to some extent, based on global forces, certainly in terms of how much money you can get into a country—the federalism must be real. There must be some real sense of shared authority. And people must know they have some real range of autonomy for decisions. And it must more or less correspond to what they perceive they need to accomplish.

On the other hand, it seems to me that the suggestion that a people of a given ethnic group or tribal group or religious group can only have a meaningful communal existence if they are an independent nation—not if there is no oppression, not if they have genuine autonomy, but they must be actually independent—is a questionable assertion in a global economy where cooperation pays greater benefits in every area of life than destructive competition.

Consider, for example, the most autonomous societies on Earth, arguably, the tribes still living in the rainforests on the island of New Guinea. There are 6,000 languages still existent in the world today, and 1,000 of them can be found in Papua, New Guinea, and Irian Jaya, where tribes living 10, 20 miles from one another have compete self-determination. Would you like that?

On the other hand, consider the terrible problems of so many African peoples where they're saddled with national borders drawn for them at the Conference of Berlin in 1885, that took no reasonable account of the allocation of the tribes on certain lands and the history of their grazing, their farming, their moving.

So how to work it out? There is no answer. We have to provide a framework in which people can work it out. But the only point I want to make to you today—I don't want to beat this to death, because we could stay here for a week discussing this—is that at the end of World War I, the European powers, I think, and America sort of withdrew, so we have to share part of the blame, but our record is not exactly spotless in how we went about carving up, for example, the aftermath of the Ottoman Empire. And so we have spent much of the twentieth century trying to reconcile President Woodrow Wilson's belief that different nations had the right to be free nations—being people with a common consciousness—had a right to be a state.

And the practical knowledge that we all have that, if every racial and ethnic and religious group that occupies a significant piece of land not occupied by others became a separate nation—we might have 800 countries in the world and have a very difficult time having a functioning economy or a functioning global polity. Maybe we would have 8,000; how low can you go?

So that doesn't answer any specific questions. It just means that I think when a people thinks it should be independent in order to have a meaningful political existence, serious questions should be asked: Is there an abuse of human rights? Is there a way people can get along if they come from different heritages? Are minority rights, as well as majority rights, respected? What is in the long-term economic and security interests of our people? How are we going to cooperate with our neighbors? Will it be better or worse if we are independent, or if we have a federalist system?

I personally believe that you will see more federalism rather than less in the years ahead, and I offer, as exhibit A, the European Union. It's really a new form of federalism, where the states—in this case, the nations of Europe—are far more important and powerful than the federal government, but they are giving enough functions over to the federal government to sort of reinforce their mutual interest in an integrated economy and in some integrated political circumstances.

In a way, we've become more of a federalist world when the United Nations takes a more active role in stopping genocide in places in which it was not involved, and we recognize mutual responsibilities to contribute and pay for those things.

So I believe we will be looking for ways, over and over and over again—the Prime Minister Chretien, Jean and I have endorsed the Free Trade Area of the Americas—we'll be looking for ways to integrate our operations for mutual interest, without giving up our sovereignty. And where there are dissatisfied groups in sections of countries, we should be looking for ways to satisfy anxieties and legitimate complaints without disintegration, I believe.

That's not to say that East Timor was wrong. If you look at what the people in East Timor had been through, if you look at the colonial heritage there, if you look at the fact that the Indonesians offered them a vote, they took it, and nearly 80 percent of them voted for independence—it seems that was the right decision there.

But let us never be under the illusion that those people are going to have an easy path. Assuming that those of us that are trying to support them help them; assuming we can stop all the pro-integrationist militias from oppressing the people, and we can get all the East Timorese back home, and they'll all be safe—there will still be less than a million of them, with a per capita income among the poorest in the world, struggling to make a living for their children in an environment that is not exactly hospitable.

Now, does that mean they were wrong? No. Under the circumstances they faced, they probably made the only decision they could have. But wouldn't it have been better if they could have found their religious, their cultural, their ethnic, and their economic footing—and genuine self-government—in the framework of a larger entity which would also have supported them economically? And reinforced their security instead of undermined it? It didn't happen; it's too bad.

But I say this because I don't think there are any general rules, but I think that, at the end of World War I, when President Wilson spoke, there was a general assumption, because we were seeing empires break up the Ottoman Empire, the Austro-Hungarian Empire; there was the memory of the Russian Empire; British colonialism was still alive in Africa, and so was French colonialism—at that time, we all assumed, and the rhetoric of the time imposed the idea that the only way for people to feel any sovereignty or meaning was if they were independent.

And I think we've spent a lot of the twentieth century minimizing the prospects of federalism. We all have recoiled, now, so much at the abuse of people because of their tribal, racial, and religious characteristics, that we tend immediately to think that the only answer is independence.

But we must think of how we will live after the shooting stops, after the smoke clears, over the long run. And I can only say this, in closing: I think the United States and Canada are among the most fortunate countries in the world because we have such diversity; sometimes concentrated, like the Inuits in the north; sometimes widely dispersed within a certain area, like the diversity of Vancouver. We are fortunate because life is more interesting and fun when there are different people who look differently and think differently and find their way to God differently. It's an interesting time. And because we all have to grow and learn when we confront people who are different than we are, and instead of looking at them in fear and hatred and dehumanization, we look at them and see a mirror of ourselves and our common humanity.

I think if we will keep this in mind—what is most likely to advance our common humanity in a smaller world; and what is the arrangement of government most likely to give us the best of all worlds—the integrity we need, the self-government we need, the self-advancement we need—without pretending that we can cut all the cords that bind us to the rest of humanity—I think more and more and more people will say, "This federalism, it's not such a bad idea."

Thank you very much.

NOTE: The President spoke at 2:25 p.m. in the Chateau Mont-Tremblant. In his remarks, he referred to Prime Minister Jean Chretien of Canada; Premier Lucien Bouchard of Quebec; President Ernesto Zedillo of Mexico; and U.S. Ambassador to Canada Gordon Giffin. The President also referred to Executive Order 13132-Federalism, published in the Federal Register on August 10, 1999. This item was not received in time for publication in the appropriate issue.

A DISTINCTLY AMERICAN INTERNATIONALISM

George W. Bush

It is an honor to be with you at the Reagan Library. Thank you Secretary Shultz for your decades of service to America—and for your kindness and counsel over the last several months. And thank you Mrs. Reagan for this invitation—and for your example of loyalty and love and courage.

My wife Laura says that behind every great man there is a surprised woman. But, Mrs. Reagan, you were never surprised by the greatness of your husband. You believed it from the start. And now the rest of the world sees him as you always have—as a hero in the American story. A story in which a single individual can shape history. A story in which evil is real, but courage and decency triumph.

We live in the nation President Reagan restored, and the world he helped to save. A world of nations reunited and tyrants humbled. A world of prisoners released and exiles come home. And today there is a prayer shared by free people everywhere: God bless you, Ronald Reagan.

Two months ago at the Citadel in South Carolina I talked about American defense. This must be the first focus of a President, because it is his first duty to the Constitution. Even in this time of pride and promise, America has determined enemies who hate our values and resent our success—terrorists and crime syndicates and drug cartels and unbalanced dictators. The Empire has passed, but evil remains. We must protect our homeland and our allies against missiles and terror and blackmail.

Foreign Policy Remarks At The Reagan Library, Simi Valley, California, November 19, 1999

We must restore the morale of our military—squandered by shrinking resources and multiplying missions—with better training, better treatment and better pay. And we must master the new technology of war—to extend our peaceful influence, not just across the world, but across the years.

In the defense of our nation, a President must be a clear-eyed realist. There are limits to the smiles and scowls of diplomacy. Armies and missiles are not stopped by stiff notes of condemnation. They are held in check by strength and purpose and the promise of swift punishment.

But there is more to say, because military power is not the final measure of might. Our realism must make a place for the human spirit. This spirit, in our time, has caused dictators to fear and empires to fall. And it has left an honor roll of courage and idealism: Scharansky, Havel, Walesa, Mandela. The most powerful force in the world is not a weapon or a nation but a truth: that we are spiritual beings, and that freedom is "the soul's right to breathe."

In the dark days of 1941—the low point of our modern epic—there were about a dozen democracies left on the planet. Entering a new century, there are nearly 120. There is a direction in events, a current in our times. "Depend on it," said Edmund Burke. "The lovers of freedom will be free."

America cherishes that freedom, but we do not own it. We value the elegant structures of our own democracy—but realize that, in other societies, the architecture will vary. We propose our principles, we must not impose our culture.

Yet the basic principles of human freedom and dignity are universal. People should be able to say what they think. Worship as they wish. Elect those who govern them. These ideals have proven their power on every continent. In former colonies—and the nations that ruled them. Among the allies of World War II—and the countries they vanquished. And these ideals are equally valid north of the 38th parallel. They are just as true in the Pearl River Delta. They remain true 90 miles from our shores, on an island prison, ruled by a revolutionary relic.

Some have tried to pose a choice between American ideals and American interests—between who we are and how we act. But the choice is false. America, by decision and destiny, promotes political freedom—and gains the most when democracy advances. America believes in free markets and free trade—and benefits most when markets are opened. America is a peaceful power—and gains the greatest dividend from democratic stability.

Precisely because we have no territorial objectives, our gains are not measured in the losses of others. They are counted in the conflicts we avert, the prosperity we share and the peace we extend.

Sometimes this balance takes time to achieve—and requires us to deal with nations that do not share our values. Sometimes the defenders of freedom must show patience as well as resolution. But that patience comes of confidence, not compromise. We believe, with George Washington, that "Liberty, when it begins to take root, is a plant of rapid growth." And we firmly believe our nation is on the right side of history—the side of man's dignity and God's justice.

Few nations have been given the advantages and opportunities of our own. Few have been more powerful as a country, or more successful as a cause. But there are risks, even for the powerful. "I have many reasons to be optimistic," said Pericles in the golden age of Athens. "Indeed, I am more afraid of our own blunders than of the enemy's devices."

America's first temptation is withdrawal—to build a proud tower of protectionism and isolation. In a world that depends on America to reconcile old rivals and balance ancient ambitions, this is the shortcut to chaos. It is an approach that abandons our allies, and our ideals. The vacuum left by America's retreat would invite challenges to our power. And the result, in the long run, would be a stagnant America and a savage world.

American foreign policy cannot be founded on fear. Fear that American workers can't compete. Fear that America will corrupt the world—or be corrupted by it. This fear has no place in the party of Reagan, or in the party of Truman. In times of peril, our nation did not shrink from leadership. At this moment of opportunity, I have no intention of betraying American interests, American obligations and American honor.

America's second temptation is drift—for our nation to move from crisis to crisis like a cork in a current.

Unless a President sets his own priorities, his priorities will be set by others—by adversaries, or the crisis of the moment, live on CNN. American policy can become random and reactive—untethered to the interests of our country.

America must be involved in the world. But that does not mean our military is the answer to every difficult foreign policy situation—a substitute for strategy. American internationalism should not mean action without vision, activity without priority, and missions without end—an approach that squanders American will and drains American energy.

American foreign policy must be more than the management of crisis. It must have a great and guiding goal: to turn this time of American influence into generations of democratic peace. This is accomplished by concentrating on enduring national interests. And these are my priorities.

An American President should work with our strong democratic allies in Europe and Asia to extend the peace. He should promote a fully democratic Western Hemisphere, bound together by free trade. He should defend America's interests in the Persian Gulf and advance peace in the Middle East, based upon a secure Israel. He must check the contagious spread of weapons of mass destruction, and the means to deliver them. He must lead toward a world that trades in freedom. And he must pursue all these goals with focus, patience and strength.

I will address these responsibilities as this campaign continues. To each, I bring the same approach: A distinctly American internationalism. Idealism, without illusions. Confidence, without conceit. Realism, in the service of American ideals.

Today I want to talk about Europe and Asia . . . the world's strategic heartland . . . our greatest priority. Home of long-time allies, and looming rivals. Behind the United States, Eurasia has the next six largest economies. The next six largest military budgets.

The Eurasian landmass, in our century, has seen the indignities of colonialism and the excesses of nationalism. Its people have been sacrificed to brutal wars and totalitarian ambitions. America has discovered, again and again, that our history is inseparable from their tragedy. And we are rediscovering that our interests are served by their success.

In this immense region, we are guided, not by an ambition, but by a vision. A vision in which no great power, or coalition of great powers, dominates or endangers our friends. In which America encourages stability from a position of strength. A vision in which people and capital and information can move freely, creating bonds of progress, ties of culture and momentum toward democracy.

This is different from the trumpet call of the Cold War. We are no longer fighting a great enemy, we are asserting a great principle: that the talents and dreams of average people—their warm human hopes and loves—should be rewarded by freedom and protected by peace. We are defending the nobility of normal lives, lived in obedience to God and conscience, not to government.

The challenge comes because two of Eurasia's greatest powers—China and Russia—are powers in transition. And it is difficult to know their intentions when they do not know their own futures. If they become America's friends, that friendship will steady the world. But if not, the peace we seek may not be found.

China, in particular, has taken different shapes in different eyes at different times. An empire to be divided. A door to be opened. A model of collective conformity. A diplomatic card to be played. One year, it is said to be run by "the butchers of Beijing." A few years later, the same administration pronounces it a "strategic partner."

We must see China clearly—not through the filters of posturing and partisanship. China is rising, and that is inevitable. Here, our interests are plain: We welcome a free and prosperous China. We predict no conflict. We intend no threat. And there are areas where we must try to cooperate: preventing the spread of weapons of mass destruction . . . attaining peace on the Korean peninsula.

Yet the conduct of China's government can be alarming abroad, and appalling at home. Beijing has been investing its growing wealth in strategic nuclear weapons . . . new ballistic missiles . . . a blue-water navy and a long-range airforce. It is an espionage threat to our country. Meanwhile, the State Department has reported that "all public dissent against the party and government [has been] effectively silenced"—a tragic achievement in a nation of 1.2 billion people. China's government is an enemy of religious freedom and a sponsor of forced abortion—policies without reason and without mercy.

All of these facts must be squarely faced. China is a competitor, not a strategic partner. We must deal with China without ill-will—but without illusions. By the same token, that regime must have no illusions about American power and purpose. As Dean Rusk observed during the Cold War, "It is not healthy for a regime . . . to incur, by their lawlessness and aggressive conduct, the implacable opposition of the American people."

We must show American power and purpose in strong support for our Asian friends and allies—for democratic South Korea across the Yellow Sea . . . for democratic Japan and the Philippines across the China seas . . . for democratic Australia and Thailand. This means keeping our pledge to deter aggression against the Republic of Korea, and strengthening security ties with Japan. This means expanding theater missile defenses among our allies.

And this means honoring our promises to the people of Taiwan. We do not deny there is one China. But we deny the right of Beijing to impose their rule on a free people. As I've said before, we will help Taiwan to defend itself.

The greatest threats to peace come when democratic forces are weak and disunited. Right now, America has many important bilateral alliances in Asia. We should work toward a day when the fellowship of free Pacific nations is as strong and united as our Atlantic Partnership. If I am President, China will find itself respected as a great power, but in a region of strong democratic alliances. It will be unthreatened, but not unchecked.

China will find in America a confident and willing trade partner. And with trade comes our standing invitation into the world of economic freedom. China's entry into the World Trade Organization is welcome, and this should open the door for Taiwan as well. But given China's poor record in honoring agreements, it will take a strong administration to hold them to their word.

If I am President, China will know that America's values are always part of America's agenda. Our advocacy of human freedom is not a formality of diplomacy, it is a fundamental commitment of our country. It is the source of our confidence that communism, in every form, has seen its day.

And I view free trade as an important ally in what Ronald Reagan called "a forward strategy for freedom." The case for trade is not just monetary, but moral. Economic freedom creates habits of liberty. And habits of liberty create expectations of democracy. There are no guarantees, but there are good examples, from Chile to Taiwan. Trade freely with China, and time is on our side.

Russia stands as another reminder that a world increasingly at peace is also a world in transition. Here, too, patience is needed— patience, consistency, and a principled reliance on democratic forces.

In the breadth of its land, the talent and courage of its people, the wealth of its resources, and the reach of its weapons, Russia is a great power, and must always be treated as such. Few people have suffered more in this century. And though we trust the worst is behind them, their troubles are not over. This past decade, for Russia, has been an epic of deliverance and disappointment.

Our first order of business is the national security of our nation—and here both Russia and the United States face a changed world. Instead of confronting each other, we confront the legacy of a dead ideological rivalry—thousands of nuclear weapons, which, in the case of Russia, may not be secure. And together we also face an emerging threat—from rogue nations, nuclear theft and accidental launch. All this requires nothing short of a new strategic relationship to protect the peace of the world.

We can hope that the new Russian Duma will ratify START II, as we have done. But this is not our most pressing challenge. The greater problem was first addressed in 1991 by Senator Lugar and Senator Sam Nunn. In an act of foresight and statesmanship, they realized that existing Russian nuclear facilities were in danger of being compromised. Under the Nunn-Lugar program, security at many Russian nuclear facilities has been improved and warheads have been destroyed.

Even so, the Energy Department warns us that our estimates of Russian nuclear stockpiles could be off by as much as 30 percent. In other words, a great deal of Russian nuclear material cannot be accounted for. The next president must press for an accurate inventory of all this material. And we must do more. I'll ask the Congress to increase substantially our assistance to dismantle as many of Russia's weapons as quickly as possible.

We will still, however, need missile defense systems—both theater and national. If I am Commander-in-Chief, we will develop and deploy them.

Under the mutual threat of rogue nations, there is a real possibility the Russians could join with us and our friends and allies to cooperate on missile defense systems. But there is a condition. Russia must break its dangerous habit of proliferation. In the hard work of halting proliferation, the Comprehensive Test Ban Treaty is not the answer.

I've said that our nation should continue its moratorium on testing. Yet far more important is to constrict the supply of nuclear materials and the means to deliver them—by making this a priority with Russia and China. Our nation must cut off the demand for nuclear weapons—by addressing the security concerns of those who renounce these weapons. And our nation must diminish the evil attraction of these weapons for rogue states—by rendering them useless with missile defense. The Comprehensive Test Ban Treaty does nothing to gain these goals. It does not stop proliferation, especially to renegade regimes. It is not verifiable. It is not enforceable. And it would stop us from ensuring the safety and reliability of our nation's deterrent, should the need arise. On these crucial matters, it offers only words and false hopes and high intentions—with no guarantees whatever. We can fight the spread of nuclear weapons, but we cannot wish them away with unwise treaties.

Dealing with Russia on essential issues will be far easier if we are dealing with a democratic and free Russia. Our goal is to promote, not only the appearance of democracy in Russia, but the structures, spirit, and reality of democracy.

This is clearly not done by focusing our aid and attention on a corrupt and favored elite. Real change in Russia—as in China—will come not from above, but from below. From a rising class of entrepreneurs and business people. From new leaders in Russia's regions who will build a new Russian state, where power is shared, not controlled. Our assistance, investments and loans should go directly to the Russian people, not to enrich the bank accounts of corrupt officials.

America should reach out to a new generation of Russians through educational exchanges and programs to support the rule of law and a civil society. And the Russian people, next month, must be given a free and fair choice in their election. We cannot buy reform for Russia, but we can be Russia's ally in self-reform.

Even as we support Russian reform, we cannot excuse Russian brutality. When the Russian government attacks civilians—killing women and children, leaving orphans and refugees—it can no longer expect aid from international lending institutions. The

Russian government will discover that it cannot build a stable and unified nation on the ruins of human rights. That it cannot learn the lessons of democracy from the textbook of tyranny. We want to co-operate with Russia on its concern with terrorism, but that is impossible unless Moscow operates with civilized self-restraint.

Just as we do not want Russia to descend into cruelty, we do not want it to return to imperialism. Russia does have interests with its newly independent neighbors. But those interests must be expressed in commerce and diplomacy—not coercion and domination. A return to Russian imperialism would endanger both Russian democracy and the states on Russia's borders. The United States should actively support the nations of the Baltics, the Caucasus and Central Asia, along with Ukraine, by promoting regional peace and economic development, and opening links to the wider world.

Often overlooked in our strategic calculations is that great land that rests at the south of Eurasia. This coming century will see democratic India's arrival as a force in the world. A vast population, before long the world's most populous nation. A changing economy, in which 3 of its 5 wealthiest citizens are software entrepreneurs.

India is now debating its future and its strategic path, and the United States must pay it more attention. We should establish more trade and investment with India as it opens to the world. And we should work with the Indian government, ensuring it is a force for stability and security in Asia. This should not undermine our longstanding relationship with Pakistan, which remains crucial to the peace of the region.

All our goals in Eurasia will depend on America strengthening the alliances that sustain our influence—in Europe and East Asia and the Middle East. Alliances are not just for crises—summoned into action when the fire bell sounds. They are sustained by contact and trust. The Gulf War coalition, for example, was raised on the foundation of a President's vision and effort and integrity. Never again should an American President spend nine days in China and not even bother to stop in Tokyo or Seoul or Manila. Never again should an American President fall silent when China criticizes our security ties with Japan.

For NATO to be strong, cohesive and active, the President must give it consistent direction: on the alliance's purpose; on Europe's need to invest more in defense capabilities; and, when necessary, in military conflict. To be relied upon when they are needed, our allies must be respected when they are not.

We have partners, not satellites. Our goal is a fellowship of strong, not weak, nations. And this requires both more American consultation and more American leadership. The United States needs its European allies, as well as friends in other regions, to help us with security challenges as they arise. For our allies, sharing the enormous opportunities of Eurasia also means sharing the burdens and risks of sustaining the peace. The support of friends allows America to reserve its power and will for the vital interests we share.

Likewise, international organizations can serve the cause of peace. I will never place U.S. troops under U.N. command—but the U.N. can help in weapons inspections, peacekeeping and humanitarian efforts. If I am President, America will pay its dues—but only if the U.N.'s bureaucracy is reformed, and our disproportionate share of its costs is reduced.

There must also be reform of international financial institutions —the World Bank and the IMF. They can be a source of stability in economic crisis. But they should not impose austerity, bailing out bankers while impoverishing a middle class. They should not prop up failed and corrupt financial systems. These organizations should encourage the basics of economic growth and free markets. Spreading the rule of law and wise budget practices.

Promoting sound banking laws and accounting rules. Most of all, these institutions themselves must be more transparent and accountable.

All the aims I've described today are important. But they are not imperial. America has never been an empire. We may be the only great power in history that had the chance, and refused—preferring greatness to power and justice to glory.

We are a nation that helped defeat Germany in 1945—which had launched a war costing 55 million lives. Less than five years later we launched an airlift to save the people of Berlin from starvation and tyranny. And a generation of Germans remember the "raisin bombers" that dropped candy and raisins for children.

We are a nation that defeated Japan—then distributed food, wrote a constitution, encouraged labor unions and gave women the right to vote. Japanese who expected retribution received mercy instead. Over the entrance of one American army camp, there was a banner that read, "Be neat. Be soldierly. Be proud. Behave. Be American."

No one questioned what those words meant: "Be American." They meant we were humble in victory. That we were liberators, not conquerors. And when American soldiers hugged the survivors of death camps, and shared their tears, and welcomed them back from a nightmare world, our country was confirmed in its calling.

The duties of our day are different. But the values of our nation do not change. Let us reject the blinders of isolationism, just as we refuse the crown of empire. Let us not dominate others with our power—or betray them with our indifference. And let us have an

American foreign policy that reflects American character. The modesty of true strength. The humility of real greatness. This is the strong heart of America. And this will be the spirit of my administration. I believe this kind of foreign policy will inspire our people and restore the bipartisanship so necessary to our peace and security.

Many years ago, Alexander Solzhenitzyn challenged American politicians. "Perhaps," he said, "some of you still feel yourselves just as representatives of your state or party. We do not perceive these differences. We do not look on you as Democrats or Republicans, not as representatives of the East or West Coast or the Midwest. . . . Upon [you] depends whether the course of world history will tend to tragedy or salvation."

That is still our challenge. And that is still our choice.

Thank you.

AFTER YEARS OF ABUSE, AMERICANS DESERVE A FLAT-TAX BREAK TODAY

Richard K. Armey

Americans are crying out for relief from the current oppressive federal tax code. It's easy to see why: We have a system that's too complicated, unfair and hinders economic growth.

The tax code is so complex that when *Money* magazine asked 45 tax professionals to prepare a return for a fictional family, no two came up with the same tax total.

This complicated code fosters not only resentment toward the government, but toward our fellow citizens. One reason is that our nation's capital is dominated by 67,000 lobbyists who seek to advance the agenda of special interests rather than the broader public interest. Not surprisingly, more lobbyists work on taxes than any other issue.

The result is that each year, Americans spend more than 5.4 billion hours complying with the tax code—that's more time than it takes to make every car, truck and van in the United States.

Taxpayers are fed up. Two out of three Americans say that overhauling the nation's tax system is very important to them, according to a recent *Washington Post* poll.

Republican Richard K. Armey of Texas is the majority leader of the U.S. House of Representatives.

Insight on the News, Aug. 17, 1998. Vol. 14, No. 30, p. 29(1)

"After Years of Abuse, Americans Deserve a Flat-Tax Break Today" (as appeared in *21 Debated: Issues in American Politics,* 2000, p. 195–197). Reprinted by permission granted by Prentice Hall Publishing.

The Republican Party is responding. We've been leading the charge on fundamental tax reform, which is the best issue conservatives have had since the Reagan tax revolution of 1981. The tax-reform movement is sweeping the nation.

Republican Rep. Billy Tauzin of Louisiana and I have been traveling the country since last October to make our case for comprehensive tax reform and debate the merits of Tauzin's national sales tax and my 17 percent flat-rate income tax. On Aug. 18, we will bring the "scrap the code" tour to Kansas City and Chicago, marking our 30th public debate. The response has been stunning.

In Atlanta, for example, one of the tour's first stops, the 1,000 seat auditorium and the overflow room were filled to capacity. Hundreds more spilled over into the convention-center foyer to view the debate on closed-circuit television. At an impromptu rally after the debate, hundreds of emotionally charged taxpayers shouted their support for our reform efforts. The mood was electric. Jim Miller, former Reagan budget director and counselor for the Citizens for a Sound Economy Foundation, the sponsor of the tax tour, remarked, "I haven't witnessed such a display of enthusiasm over a public-policy issue since my days with Reagan."

Atlanta is not unique. In cities and towns all across America, taxpayers no longer accept today's corrupt, destructive tax code. They are demanding that their leaders scrap it and replace it with a code that is simple and fair. That's why my flat-tax legislation is so popular. It would scrap the current tax code and replace it with a 17 percent tax on all income. You could file your return on a 10-line postcard. There are no loopholes or tax breaks for special interests. And it would lead to an economic boom and higher wages. In coffee shops, around kitchen tables across America and on the Internet— my flat-tax World Wide Web site (www.flattax.gov) receives about 100,000 hits each month—people enthusiastically are embracing the tax-reform movement.

So powerful, in fact, is the growing tax-reform movement that many reform opponents find they no longer can defend the status quo and are discovering creative ways to jump on the tax-reform bandwagon. For example, following last fall's Senate hearings that exposed an IRS run amok, President Clinton went from an unapologetic defender of the status quo to a reluctant supporter of the Republican-led, bipartisan IRS reform legislation. According to the *New York Times,* Clinton was prodded into reversing course out of fear that Republicans could use the issue against Democrats in the 1998 elections to gain the upper hand on an array of tax-related issues.

Public discontent with the current tax code has made possible what was before unthinkable—a Clinton signature on a real IRS reform bill. As a result, the American people will have some measure of protection against tax-collection abuses until we can pass comprehensive tax reform.

In addition, just a few weeks ago, the House of Representatives passed a revolutionary bill that would terminate the current IRS code by 2002. Such measures, although destined for a Clinton veto, help to elevate the tax-reform debate which pits reformers against the defenders of the status quo. As a result, I strongly believe that all serious candidates for the GOP presidential nomination in 2000 will have to make tax reform a centerpiece of their campaign.

Now more than ever, comprehensive tax reform is a realistic and achievable goal. When I began drafting flat-tax legislation in 1994, I wanted a bill that was radical enough to yank the entire tax debate away from half-measures and tinkering.

I knew that there would be ferocious opposition from the establishment, For example, Washington's $8.4 billion lobbying industry employs more than 67,000 people. Many of these people make very good livings securing and defending special tax breaks and loopholes for their powerful clients. Then there is the Clinton administration and its class warriors and income redistributors at the Treasury Department. I knew that they would oppose any tax plan that treats all taxpayers the same. (There is no gentle way to scrap the tax code and shift power from Washington to Main Street without angering those who are wedded to the status quo.)

In 1994, I said that the flat tax would be enacted into law when America beat Washington. At that time I believed that passing the flat tax would be a 10-year project. But today I believe that it can be achieved sooner.

Like any campaign of this magnitude, the opposition will be fierce and there will be many obstacles to success. But when the dust settles, it will be the flat tax that comes out on top.

SIMPLE, EFFICIENT, FAIR. OR IS IT?

William G. Gale

The U.S. tax system remains continually, and deservedly, under attack. Many people find taxes too complex. Analysts blame the tax system for depressing saving, entrepreneurship, and economic growth. Few people believe it to be entirely fair or transparent.

Members of both political parties have put forth plans to overhaul the current tax system. The best known is the "flat tax." Conceived by Stanford economist Robert Hall and political scientist Alvin Rabushka in the early 1980s, the flat tax has been given legislative form in the past few years by Rep. Richard Armey (R-TX) and Sen. Richard Shelby (R-AL).

The flat tax would replace taxes on personal and corporate income and estates. Households would pay taxes on wages and pension income in excess of substantial personal and child allowances. Businesses would pay taxes on their sales less their wage and pension payments, input costs, and capital purchases. No other income would be taxed, no other deductions allowed. Businesses and individuals would face the same flat tax rate.

Proponents have made strong claims for the flat tax. It would be so simple that the tax form could fit on a postcard; it would take tax considerations out of people's economic decisionmaking, thereby

William G. Gale is a senior fellow in the Brookings Economic Studies program. He is the author, with Henry J. Aaron, of a forthcoming Brookings book on tax policy.

Reprinted by permission. *Brookings Review,* Summer 1998. Vol. 16, Issue 3, p. 40, 5p.

"Simple, Efficient, Fair. Or Is It?" (as appeared in *21 Debated: Issues in American Politics,* 2000, pp. 197–204). Reprinted by permission granted by Prentice Hall Publishing.

increasing efficiency and revitalizing the economy; it is a fair and airtight system.

In theory, the flat tax is, indeed, a clever, principled approach to changing the nature of federal taxation. Whether it could satisfactorily meet the competing demands placed on the tax system—fairness, simplicity, growth—and the transition to the real world is an open question.

JUST WHAT IS THE FLAT TAX??

The flat tax is not an income tax, but a consumption tax. The simplest form of consumption tax is a tax on retail sales. If we switch to a consumption tax, why not just adopt the simplest?

Implementing a national retail sales tax would be problematic for several reasons. First, it would be regressive. Poor households consume a much greater share of their income than do other households. Taxing their total consumption would be a large burden, especially compared with the current income tax system, which channels money to many poor working households via the earned income tax credit. In addition, as the sales taxes that now exist in 45 states have shown, it is often hard to distinguish business-to-business sales from business-to-household sales. But if each sale from business to business is taxed, the eventual product is taxed several times, resulting in "cascading," a problem that encourages firms to integrate vertically and also creates capricious redistributions of tax-burdens across goods and people. Most important, though, a retail sales tax with a rate high enough—well over 30 percent—to replace existing federal taxes would be very hard to enforce. European countries that have tried to raise significant revenue by retail sales taxes have found that they become unadministrable at rates as low as 10–12 percent. They have therefore shifted to a different form of consumption tax, a value-added tax (VAT).

A sales tax and a VAT differ in the point at which they are exacted: a sales tax, on the final sale price, a VAT, at each stage of production. Under a VAT, each business pays a tax on the difference between gross revenues from all sales (including business-to-business sales) and the cost of materials, including capital goods. Thus it pays taxes on wages, interest, and profits, the sum of which represents the value added by the firm in providing goods and services.

The VAT avoids cascading because sales between businesses wash out. The baker who sells bread to the grocer pays VAT on the sale, but the grocer deducts the purchase in calculating his VAT. The VAT is also easier to enforce. One reason is that the seller, in trying to decide whether to report a transaction to the tax authorities, knows that the buyer will file the transaction with the tax authorities to claim the deduction for funds spent.

Like the sales tax, however, the VAT is regressive. Governments can address that problem by exempting from taxation, say, the first $20,000 of consumption by sending each family a check for $5,000 (assuming a 25 percent tax rate). But financing such transfers requires higher tax rates. Targeting the transfers to the poor would mean that rates would not have to be raised as much, but it would require all households to file information on income, thus sacrificing some of the simplicity gain.

The flat tax is a VAT, with two adjustments that help address the regressivity problem. First, businesses deduct wages and pensions, along with materials costs and capital investments. Second, the wages and pensions that businesses deduct are taxed at the individual (or household) level above a specified exemption. Dividing the VAT into two parts, one for businesses and one for households, makes possible the family exemptions that can case the burden of the consumption tax for lower-income households.

HOW DOES THE FLAT TAX DIFFER FROM THE CURRENT SYSTEM?

Today's federal "income" tax is actually a hybrid between an income and a consumption tax. A pure income tax would tax all labor earnings and capital income, whether realized in cash, in kind, or accrued. But the current system does not tax certain forms of income, such as employer-provided health insurance or accrued gains on unsold assets. And it taxes some income more than once: in the case of corporate earnings, once at the corporate level and again at the individual level when distributed as dividends. It also taxes some items not properly considered income, such as the inflationary components of interest payments and realized capital gains. The flat tax would not tax capital income—such as interest, dividends, and capital gains—at the household level, or financial flows at any level. On the other hand, most saving—in pensions, IRAs, and so forth—is already taxed as it would be under a consumption tax.

Unlike the flat tax, the current income tax also permits dozens of allowances, credits, exclusions, and deductions. Taken together these "loopholes" reduced personal tax collections by some $1.3 trillion in 1993, about 50 percent of the actual tax base. Eliminating them all would make it possible to reduce tax rates across the board, or set rates as low as 13.5 percent.

The income tax is graduated: its six rates—0, 15, 28, 31, 36, and 39.6 percent—rise with taxable income. Multiple tax rates increase progressivity, but raise compliance and administrative costs and the importance of the deductions. A deduction that matters little when the tax rate is 10 percent is of much more consequence when the rate is 40 percent.

But the biggest differences between the existing system and the flat tax arise not because of large inherent differences in the underlying tax base. In fact, if the flat tax allowed firms to deduct investment expenditures over time, in accordance with the economic depreciation of their assets, instead of allowing them to deduct all investment expenses the year they are made, the flat tax would then be a flat income tax.

Rather, the key point is that the differences arise because, in response to a variety of political pressures, the existing tax system has strayed from a pure income tax structure. Indeed, perhaps the crucial question about the flat tax is how it would respond to those same pressures if it were to move from idea to reality.

The Armey-Shelby flat tax proposal features a $31,400 exemption for a family of four and a 20 percent tax rate. After two years the exemption would rise to $33,300 and the rate would fall to 17 percent. (The low tax rate is possible because the proposal is not "revenue neutral"; that is, it combines tax reform with a tax cut.)

But in recent years, different variants of the flat tax have begun to take on some features of today's income tax. Sen. Arlen Spector's (R-PA) proposal would reinstate the mortgage and charity deductions. So would Pat Buchanan's, which would also tax at least some capital income at the household level. The Kemp Commission favored deductions for payroll taxes and for mortgage interest and charity. Robert Dole voiced a wish to protect deductions for mortgages, charity, and state and local taxes.

These cracks in the flat tax armor, appearing long before serious legislative action takes place, suggest that the pressures that led to an impure income tax are likely to affect the flat tax as well.

POLITICAL AND ECONOMIC DILEMMAS TAX REFORM

Richard Armey, like some other advocates of the flat tax, candidly links his proposal to big tax cuts (although he does not specify how he would cut government spending to make up for the lost revenue). Because it is misleading to compare a plan that simultaneously reforms the tax structure and cuts taxes with the existing system, I will lay out the issues raised by the flat tax without the confounding effects of tax reduction.

Tax reform that collects the same amount of revenue in a new way will necessarily redistribute tax burdens among taxpayers. Those who stand to lose often try to prevent reform or to secure "transition relief" to avoid or delay the full brunt of the new law. The flat tax embodies this problem in stark form, because it proposes a single rate on businesses and on household money wages above a threshold, with no deductions and no transition relief.

The biggest transition problem for the flat tax involves business. Under the current system, businesses may deduct depreciation, the loss of value of capital assets over their useful lives, in computing taxable business income. Under the flat tax, businesses can deduct the full value of the asset the year it is purchased. The practical, problem is what to do about assets that have not been fully depreciated when the new tax takes effect.

The pure flat tax would allow no deductions for depreciation on existing assets. But companies that lose their existing depreciation deductions will claim unfair treatment. And the stakes are high. In 1993, corporations claimed $363 billion in depreciation deductions, unincorporated businesses about one-third that.

Similarly, under the current system many businesses have net operating losses that they can carry forward as offsets against future profits. And businesses' interest payments are deductible because they are a cost of earning income. The flat tax would disallow both the carryforwards and the deduction for interest payments. Firms that depend an those provisions will press for transition relief under the flat tax.

Flat tax advocates have already acknowledged the need for transition relief. The Kemp Commission, for example, recommended that policymakers "take care to protect the existing savings, investment, and other assets" during a transition to a new tax system. But these political concessions carry a big price tag. Transition relief will reduce the size of the tax base and therefore require higher tax rates on the rest of the base. Policymakers will have to choose: the more transitional relief they provide, the less efficient the new tax system.

WHAT ABOUT THE EXISTING DEDUCTIONS?

Many prominent features of the income tax have long been a part of American economic life. The original (1913) income tax allowed deductions for mortgage interest and for state and local income and property taxes. Deductions for charity and employer-financed health insurance followed by 1918.

A pure flat tax would scrap these longstanding provisions. Without question, doing so would hurt the affected sectors of the economy. That, after all, is one of the points of tax reform: using the tax code to subsidize these sectors has channeled too many of society's resources to them. Removing the subsidy would make for a more efficient overall allocation of resources across sectors. But the affected groups are not likely to see things that way.

Under current tax law, for example, owner-occupied housing enjoys big advantages over other investments.

Homeowners may deduct mortgage interest and property taxes without being required to report the imputed rental income they receive as owners. These deductions increase demand for owner-occupied housing and boost the price of housing and land. By treating owner-occupied housing and other assets alike, the flat tax would reduce the relative price of housing. Estimates of how much range widely, but even declines as low as 5–10 percent would hurt homeowners and could affect lending institutions through increased defaults.

Confronted with these realities, is Congress likely to end the tax advantages of owner-occupied housing? Perhaps not. But retaining the mortgage interest deduction means that tax rates would have to be higher to replace revenue lost from the deduction.

The same story would unfold with each of the other long-standing deductions. Under the flat tax, health insurance would no longer be deductible by businesses and would become taxable at the flat tax rate. Jonathan Gruber and James Poterba calculate that the change would boost the price of health insurance by an average of 21 percent and reduce the number of people who are insured by between 5.5 million and 14.3 million people. Pressure to keep the deduction would be strong. But if Congress were to retain it, the flat tax base would shrink, and rates would have to rise to maintain revenues.

Likewise, terminating the charitable contributions deduction would reduce charitable giving—and at a time when cuts in government spending are being justified on the grounds that private philanthropy should pick up the slack. But retaining the deduction means a higher tax rate to maintain revenues.

FLAT TAX TRADE-OFFS: HOW MUCH?

In short, the flat tax is unlikely to be adopted in its pure form. What are the budget implications of various policy changes to the pure flat tax structure?

By my calculations, the Armey-Shelby plan with a 17 percent rate would have raised $138 billion less in 1996 than the current system. Even a 20 percent rate, which Jack Kemp referred to as the maximum acceptable flat tax rate in press conferences after the Kemp Commission report was released, would result in a shortfall of $29 billion. Allowing businesses to grandfather existing depreciation deductions—one form of transition relief—would raise the required rate to 23.1 percent. Allowing deductions for mortgage interest payments, as well as transition relief, would raise the required rate to 24.4 percent. If the deduction for employer-provided health insurance were also retained, the rate would rise to 26.5 percent. Adding in deductions for charitable contributions, individual deductions of state and local income and property tax payments, and the earned income tax credit would raise the rate to 29 percent. With all these adjustments, a tax rate of 20 percent would generate a revenue loss of well over $200 billion. Even with a flat tax rate of 25 percent, the revenue loss would be just over $100 billion.

Finally, retaining current payroll tax deductions for businesses would raise the required rate to 32 percent. The revenue shortfall, at a 20 percent tax rate, would be a whopping $280 billion a year. Even at a 25 percent tax rate, the revenue shortfall would be about $163 billion.

Politicians might find it hard to support a flat tax with these rates, since more than three-quarters of taxpayers now face a marginal tax rate of 15 percent or less, and less than 4 percent pay more than 28 percent on the margin. On the other hand, capping the rate at 20 percent or 25 percent would generate large losses in tax revenues that might also be hard to support.

One thing is clear. The flat tax is considered a simple tax with a relatively low rate in large part because it eliminates, on paper, deductions and exclusions that no Congress has dared touch.

THE FLAT TAX AND ECONOMIC GROWTH

Retaining existing deductions and providing transition relief will also eat into the economic growth that flat tax advocates claim the tax will spur.

The most complete economic model that generates realistic estimates of the impact of the flat tax on growth, developed by Alan Auerbach of the University of California, Laurence Kotlikoff of Boston University, and several other economists, finds that moving from the current system to a pure, flat rate, consumption tax, with no exemptions, no deductions, and no transition relief or other adjustments, would raise output, relative to what it would have been under the income tax, by 6.9 percent after the first 2 years, 9 percent after 9 years, and almost 11 percent in the long run. These are remarkably large gains, but they vanish as the tax plan becomes more realistic.

For example, if the personal exemption is set at $9,000, somewhat less than the $11,000 personal exemption in the Armey-Shelby plan, and transition relief is provided for existing depreciation deductions, the economy would grow by only 0.6 percent over 2 years, 1.8 percent after 10 years, and 3.6 percent in the long run. Adding exemptions for children (which the Armey plan now provides) would drive these estimates to zero. Adding transition relief for interest deductions and retaining the earned income credit and deductions for mortgages, health insurance, taxes paid, and charity would reduce growth further. Thus, implementing realistic versions of the flat tax could even slow economic growth.

TAX REFORM IN THE REAL WORLD

Good tax reform requires discipline. It is not hard to look at the U.S. tax code and see the need for a simpler, cleaner tax. But it is hard to look at the 1997 Taxpayer Relief Act, passed by Congress and signed by the president, and believe that the political system has the discipline to pass broad-based fundamental reform. After all, there is nothing—other than political forces and views of social equity—stopping our political leaders right now, or in any other year, from passing legislation that would broaden the tax base, close loopholes, and reduce tax rates. Those political forces and views of social equity will not vanish when the flat tax is passed. As one congressman noted, "You can't repeal politics."

The flat tax is a simple and thoughtful response to many of the problems in today's tax system. But tax reform is not a free lunch: we can't get everything we might want.

There are two ways out of this quandary. One would start with the flat tax proposals and make them less pure. For example, holding personal exemptions at about their current level would generate added revenue. And coupling the lower exemption levels with a two-tier tax rate system (similar to the 15 percent and 28 percent brackets that now apply to the vast majority of taxpayers) would raise revenue, enhance progressivity, and maintain many benefits of the flat tax.

The less radical alternative would be to start with the existing income tax system and simplify, streamlining the tax treatment of capital income, reducing the use of the tax code to run social policy, and reducing and flattening the rates. That would be an extension of the principles developed in the Tax Reform Act of 1986. Either alternative would place the resulting system somewhere between the current tax system and the flat tax on simplicity, efficiency, and equity—the three primary issues under debate.

The flat tax is an important advance in tax policy thinking and represents a thoughtful approach to several problems in the tax code and the economy. But removing the entire body of income tax law and starting over with a whole new system is a monumental task. We should approach the issue with our eyes open concerning the likely benefits, costs, and practical issues that would arise in adopting a flat tax.

WHY I DON'T VOUCH FOR VOUCHERS

Barbara Miner

S upporters tout vouchers as the solution to school accountability problems. Yet voucher proposals raise disturbing questions about public information, equity, segregation, and the separation of church and state.

The principal was being fired, teachers were leaving, the school was in upheaval. At the time, I was a reporter for the *Milwaukee Journal,* covering a parents' meeting on the controversy.

I never made it to the meeting. Lawyers stood in my way. They said it was a private school and reporters were not welcome. End of discussion. I was angry but found out the lawyers were right. Shutting a reporter out of a parents' meeting is illegal in Milwaukee public schools. But private schools operate by different rules.

I was reminded of the incident when the Wisconsin Supreme Court ruled last June that Milwaukee's voucher program does not violate the constitutional separation of church and state. For now, low-income students in Milwaukee will be able to use public vouchers to attend private and religious schools.

End of discussion? Not this time. The court decision has not resolved the controversy over vouchers. It has merely opened up a Pandora's box of new issues.

Barbara Miner is Managing Editor of *Rethinking Schools* newspaper and coeditor of *Selling Out Our schools: Vouchers, Markets, and the Future of Public Education.*

Reprinted by permission. *Educational Leadership,* Oct. 1998, Vol. 56, Issue 2, p. 40.

"Why I Don't Vouch for Vouchers" (as appeared in *21 Debated: Issues in American Politics,* 2000, pp. 256–259). Reprinted by permission granted by Prentice Hall Publishing.

PROBLEMATIC POLICY

Milwaukee began providing vouchers for private schools in 1990. The program initially was limited to a small number of low-income children at a handful of nonreligious schools. The court ruling allows the program to expand to as many as 15,000 children attending private and religious schools. Cleveland has a similar program.

Although still small in size, voucher programs are becoming the educational buzz of the day. On the federal level, the rhetoric of vouchers has been used to justify such initiatives as tuition tax credits. In addition, there are several privately funded voucher programs. If a voucher proposal is not yet available in your state, just wait. Vouchers are coming your way.

Everyone knows there are problems with achievement and accountability in our public schools. But the best response is to make the public schools more accountable, not to use tax dollars to subsidize private schools with minimal public accountability. Do we really want to set up two separate school systems, one private and one public, yet both supported by tax dollars?

The U.S. Supreme Court must ultimately decide whether public vouchers for religious schools violate the separation of church and state. Constitutional issues aside, voucher proposals raise important questions. Here are just a few.

Just because something is legal, is it good public policy?

It's not mere coincidence that the term *private* is so often followed by the phrase *Keep Out!* Private schools, like private roads, private beaches, and private country clubs, don't have to answer to the public.

What does it mean when private schools that get public dollars don't have to follow the same rules as public schools? The answer is particularly important in Milwaukee because 100 percent of a voucher school can be funded by vouchers—the schools aren't required to have a single student who privately pays tuition—and the school still gets to call itself "private." Under Milwaukee's voucher program, participating schools

♦ Do not have to obey the state's open meetings and records laws.
♦ Do not have to hire certified teachers—or even to require a college degree.
♦ Do not have to release information on employee wages or benefits.
♦ Do not have to administer the statewide tests required of public schools.
♦ Do not have to publicly release data such as test scores, attendance figures, or suspension and drop-out rates. The only requirement is a "financial and performance evaluation audit" of the entire voucher program to be submitted to the legislature in the year 2000.

Will vouchers be used to further segregate our schools?

Families send their children to private schools for many reasons. But one of Milwaukee's dirty little secrets is that some white parents use private schools to get around desegregation efforts. In Milwaukee, the public schools are approximately 60 percent African American. At Divine Savior/Holy Angels and Pius XIth High Schools, only 3 percent of the students are African American. At Milwaukee's most elite religious high school, Marquette University High School, 5 percent of the students are African American. Some religious elementary schools in Milwaukee do not have any African American students. The issue also goes beyond race. Will vouchers further stratify our schools along religious lines?

Will private schools weed out "undesirable" students?

Private schools can control whom they accept and the terms upon which students stay enrolled. The Milwaukee program, which is far better than most voucher proposals, has two safeguards: The schools are to select voucher students on a random basis, and they may not discriminate on the basis of race, color, or national origin. One problem, however, is enforcement. Who ensures that the rules are followed? More important, controversy has erupted over whether the voucher schools must follow other requirements of Wisconsin public schools—for example, that they not discriminate on the basis of gender or sexual orientation. One of the most contentious issues in Milwaukee involves students with special educational needs, who account for about 15 percent of public school students. Voucher proponents argue that the private schools don't have the money for special education students, thus the Milwaukee Public Schools must serve them.

Milwaukee voucher schools have also used more subtle means to select their students. Some set parental involvement requirements, for instance. Perhaps most important, private schools can expel students, for both academic and discipline reasons, without adhering to the rights of due process. Will voucher schools be able to do likewise?

In one telling incident in Milwaukee in 1995, an African American student was asked not to return to the elite and private University School after she criticized the school as racist in a speech before her English class. She filed suit on grounds of freedom of speech. She lost. Federal judge Terrence Evans wrote,

> It is an elementary principle of constitutional law that the protections afforded by the Bill of Rights do not apply to private actors such as the University School. Generally, restrictions on constitutional rights that would be protected at a public high school . . . , need not be honored at a private high school.

How can the public oversee religious schools without stepping on religious principles?

Under the First Amendment, the government is not to "entangle" itself in the running of religious institutions. As a result, however, religious schools can fire teachers who violate deeply held religious principles—such as a gay teacher or a teacher who supports the right to abortion. What will happen with religious schools that receive public vouchers? Will they be able to teach that homosexuality is a sin, that creationism is superior to the theory of evolution, that corporal punishment keeps children in line, that birth control violates the law of God, that the Jews killed Christ, or that there is no God but Allah?

Can the marketplace solve the problems of our public schools?

Some voucher supporters are guided by the admirable desire to provide individual opportunities for low-income children in urban areas. The moving forces behind vouchers, however, have a more specific ideological agenda. In essence, voucher proposals assume that privatization and the marketplace—in other words, the dismantling of the institution of public education—hold the key to education reform.

But in what other social arena—whether health care, housing, food, or jobs—has the marketplace equitably and adequately provided services? We live in the bastion of free enterprise, the richest, most powerful country in the world. Yet one quarter of our nation's young children live in poverty, and millions go hungry and homeless.

Under the rules of the marketplace, some people live in cardboard boxes and some people have vacation homes on Cape Cod. Some take the bus, some drive brand new BMWs. In the marketplace, money doesn't talk. It shouts. Is that our vision for public education?

Further the marketplace values individual choice and decision making over collective responsibility for the common good. If we look to private schools and parental choice to solve complicated problems of school reform, we distort the purpose of public education. We are "saving" a few children while giving up on the majority who will remain in public schools.

Up to 15,000 children will be allowed to use public money to attend private and religious schools in Milwaukee this year. With the voucher worth almost $5,000 a pupil, as much as $75 million in taxpayers, money will be taken from the Milwaukee Public Schools and given to private schools—with minimal public accountability. It may be legal. But is it a good idea?

ARTICLE 18

BLOCKING THE EXITS

Clint Bolick

Libertarian opposition to school vouchers is an attack on freedom.

What do many thoughtful, committed libertarians and Sandra Feldman of the American Federation of Teachers union have in common? Almost nothing—except their opposition to school choice. Answering the concerns of these libertarians is essential to defeating the reactionary likes of Feldman and realizing the potential of school choice.

School vouchers empower parents to spend their public education funds in public, private, or religious schools. The cause of choice unites conservatives, most libertarians, and growing numbers of centrists and even liberals. It brings together disparate reformers because all at once it expands parental autonomy, increases competition, promotes educational equity, and addresses the greatest challenge facing America today: ensuring educational opportunities for low-income children in the inner cities.

Some libertarians fear, however, that school vouchers will not expand freedom, but will instead turn the private schools that serve roughly 11 percent of America's youngsters into clones of failed

Clint Bolick is the vice president and the director of litigation of the Institute for Justice, a public-interest law firm based in Washington, D. C. This article is adapted from a debate at The Heritage Foundation.

Reprinted by permission. *Policy Review,* May/June, 1998, Issue 89, p. 42.

"Blocking the Exits" (as appeared in *21 Debated: Issues in American Politics,* 2000, pp. 260–264). Reprinted by permission granted by Prentice Hall Publishing.

government schools. That price, they argue, is too high, even for the sake of expanding the private sector in education and improving opportunities for millions of youngsters who desperately need them.

I wish the school-choice naysayers could have shared my experiences with the public-school monopoly and the choice alternative. My original career aspiration was classroom teaching; remarkably, upon my graduation from college, the New Jersey education cartel conferred upon me life time teacher certification. But my experiences as a student teacher left me convinced that our system of public K-12 education desperately needed fundamental change. I concluded, first, that parents, not bureaucrats, should control essential education decisions; and second, that a system of parental choice should replace the command-and-control system of public education in America.

For a long time school choice held only academic interest for me, but I became downright militant about the issue in 1990, when I had the honor of defending the constitutionality of the nation's first school-choice program, in Milwaukee. I walked the hallways of the schools that 1,000 economically disadvantaged children were able to attend for the first time. I talked to their parents, most of whom were themselves poorly educated yet keenly understood that this was a chance—perhaps the only chance—for their children to have a better life. And I saw the beaming faces of children—beacons of pride, self-discipline, and hope. That's when school choice became a matter of heart and soul as well as mind.

The nation's second school-choice program, launched in Cleveland in 1995, had an equally profound effect on me. It has permanently etched the figure "one in 14" in my memory. You see, children in the Cleveland Public Schools have a one-in-14 chance of graduating on schedule with senior-level proficiency. They also have a one-in-14 chance, each year, of being victimized by crime in their school. When a school district can offer its children no greater chance of learning the skills they need to become responsible citizens than of being victimized by crime during the school day, we are in serious jeopardy.

THE SPECTER OF REGULATION

I do not mean to diminish the ever-present specter of government regulation of private schools. When it was enacted in 1990, Milwaukee's school-choice program was not only challenged in court, but also sentenced to death by bureaucratic strangulation. The education establishment insisted that private schools meet all state and federal regulations applicable to public schools. Not surprisingly, every single private school refused to participate under those conditions. We fought these regulations in court even as we were defending the program's constitutionality.

The regulatory threat from federal school-choice proposals is even more ominous. For example, when some members of Congress proposed parental-choice legislation for the District of Columbia last year, we found ourselves battling to head off all manner of federal regulations on participating private schools.

Though we won both these skirmishes, we know the regulatory threat is serious. But these episodes suggest caution, not abandonment, of this freedom enterprise. The position of school-choice critics is akin to resisting the demise of communism because the free markets that would emerge might be subjected to government regulation. This is hardly a Hobson's choice.

Virtually all libertarian arguments against parental choice are grounded in hypothetical speculation. And the greatest antidote to speculation is reality. But even the critics' worst case does not trump the value of choice. The critics of choice point to the example of American higher education as the ultimate horror story of government control. In the 1980s, the U.S. Supreme Court ruled that postsecondary institutions that accept any federal funds—even student loan guarantees—must also submit to federal regulation. So federal regulators have now ensnared all but a handful of fiercely independent private colleges.

But from the standpoint of our current system of elementary and secondary education, this so-called nightmare looks more like a dream. Libertarian alarmists warn that vouchers will lead to a system of primary and secondary schools under monolithic government control. But that's exactly what we have already! Only 11 percent of America's children attend independent elementary and secondary schools, while 89 percent attend government schools. Moreover, private schools already are subject to regulations concerning health and safety, nondiscrimination, the length of the school year, curriculum content, and the like.

In my view, our overwhelming concern should be for those children who are already captive of the educational standards and ideological dogma of the public-school monolith. Surely any reform that diminishes the near-monopoly status of government schooling—even at the cost of greater regulation of private schools—will still yield a net increase in freedom. We should be particularly confident of that outcome when the mechanism of reform is a transfer of power over educational decisions from bureaucrats to parents.

Moreover, the regulatory threat to private-school independence is simply not illuminated by reference to higher education. In that instance, federal oversight entered an arena of vibrant competition between a vigorous and effective public sector and a vigorous and effective private sector. The horizons for elementary and secondary schools, by contrast, are limited by a dominant, overregulated, and ineffective public sector. The likely main outcome of expanding access to the highly effective, lightly regulated private sector will be to deregulate the public sector.

And that is exactly what we are seeing. The mere prospect of school choice has already sparked deregulation of public schools. In Milwaukee, efforts to increase regulation of private schools have failed, while the public sector has responded to choice by allowing more flexibility in the management of public schools and passing two charter-school statutes. In Arizona, a 1994 parental choice proposal in the state legislature failed by just a few votes, but a "compromise" produced the nation's most ambitious charter-school legislation. Today, one-sixth of public schools in Arizona are charter schools, many of which are operated by private nonprofit and for-profit entities.

THE MARKETPLACE MEETS THE CLASSROOM

Parental choice is the cornerstone of market oriented education reforms. If we liberate public education funding from the grip of school districts and let children take it wherever they go, we will create a dynamic educational marketplace. I predict that, if we expand these reforms across the nation, then public schools will quickly lose their eight-to-one advantage in enrollment. Instead we will enjoy a system of choice among government schools, quasi-public charter schools, quasi-private charter schools, and private schools; in sum, a system far more free than the command-and-control system to which the overwhelming majority of America's children are confined today.

I would remind critics of choice that other safeguards support a firewall against excessive regulation. First, private schools can decide for themselves whether to accept choice funding from the government. In Milwaukee, when choice was expanded to religious schools, they were all forced to think long and hard about participating and accepting the modest regulations imposed by the program. In the end, more than 100 of 122 private schools in the city agreed to participate. Critics worry that schools may be unwisely tempted by the prospect of funding, or that they will tolerate rising regulation after becoming dependent on the funding. For the many inner-city schools that are approaching insolvency, this may not be a bad deal. But that is a choice that the schools should be trusted to make on their own—and anti-voucher libertarians who argue otherwise are indulging in uncharacteristic paternalism.

Some schools will exercise their fundamental right not to participate. At the elementary and secondary level, many families can afford the median private tuition of $2,500 to $3,500. We always will have private schools that thrive outside of a choice system, and we should vigorously protect those schools. But that is not a sound basis for denying opportunity to children who cannot afford a private-school education but desperately need it.

A second safeguard is the U.S. Constitution itself. First Amendment precedents forbid "excessive entanglement" between the state and religious schools. If regulations supplant essential school autonomy, they will be struck down.

Perhaps most important, the power of the education establishment will diminish in exact proportion to the power gained by parents. The education establishment fights every meaningful parental choice proposal as if its very survival depends on it—because it does.

The more zealous and irresponsible libertarian critics oppose vouchers because they wish to see the system of government-run schools collapse altogether. The reality is that the public funding of education enjoys nearly unanimous public support. The most extreme libertarians are missing—indeed, helping to defeat—the chance to end the government-school monopoly and to allow public education to take place outside the public sector.

For some of the kids involved, getting out of inner-city public schools is literally a matter of life and death. Many of my libertarian opponents on this issue are people of enormous good will, but when I see them blocking the exits for these children, I cannot look upon them with affection. I understand, even share, their concerns about government's destructive power. But I do not understand why they fail to see where the interests of freedom lie in this fight.

To them I say: When you actively oppose parental choice, please know what you are doing. You are aiding and abetting the most reactionary forces in American society. They trot you out and use you to preserve the status quo. It is a perverse spectacle.

Ted Kennedy . . . Jesse Jackson . . . Kweisi Mfume . . . Eleanor Holmes Norton . . . Norman Lear . . . Bill Clinton . . . Richard Riley . . . Keith Geiger . . . Sandra Feldman . . . Bob Chase. Among those enemies of change, my fellow libertarians do not belong, for they want what I want: freedom. I believe that a system of parental choice would mark the greatest domestic expansion of freedom in this century.

Friends, come over to the freedom side.

THE FAILURE OF THE TOBACCO LEGISLATION: WHERE IS THE POLITICAL LEADERSHIP?

Steven F. Goldstone

Thank you. I appreciate the opportunity to be here today; to give you a personal perspective on the ongoing national debate affecting one of RJR Nabisco's companies—the Reynolds Tobacco Company in Winston Salem, North Carolina.

It is perhaps not an everyday occurrence when the future of a $60 billion industry, in this case the tobacco industry, becomes the focus of almost every single one of the nation's politicians.

And while there is no question that the issues presented by tobacco regulation in the country may be unique and difficult, I still think it edifying for all of us to step back and review the recent events in Washington.

There's an important lesson to be learned about the quality of political leadership in the White House and the Capitol, and it should not be a comforting one, for anybody.

Let me give you some of the background.

I became Chairman of RJR Nabisco two years ago. The company is the sixth largest consumer products company in the world. The companies we own have developed some of the greatest brands in history, such as Oreos, Ritz Crackers, Planters Nuts, and Winston and Camel.

Steven F. Goldstone is Chairman and CEO of RJR Nabisco. He delivered this article in a speech to The City Club of Cleveland, Cleveland, OH, on July 31, 1998.

Reprinted by permission. *Vital Speeches of the Day,* Oct. 1, 1998, Vol. 64, Issue 24, p. 760.

"The Failure of the Tobacco Legislation: Where Is the Political Leadership?" (as appeared in *21 Debated: Issues in American Politics,* 2000, pp. 267–274). Reprinted by permission granted by Prentice Hall Publishing.

As Chairman, I am accountable, in the ways familiar to you, to thousands of employees, shareholders and customers all over the world.

I came to RJR Nabisco with the firm belief that tobacco companies can and should be able to offer their products to adult customers. The most recent national polls confirm that this belief is shared by the vast majority of Americans.

At the same time, the tobacco industry and the country both share a paramount interest in a sound, advanced, national policy that educates people about all the public health issues concerning tobacco products.

In my early months as chief executive, I thought long and hard about how to balance this belief with my responsibilities to thousands of shareholders, as well as my obligations to 80,000 employees and thousands of retirees.

I also had to consider the important interests of all the other participants in this business: important businesses like Hollin Oil, Fuelmart and BP and the thousands of smaller, independent neighborhood stores all of which take part in the business of distributing tobacco products in the United States today.

I believed all these interests, those of the participants in the industry and of the country in general, were not incompatible.

But when I arrived at RJR Nabisco, I realized that things were not so simple. I was confronted for the first time with the institutional anti-tobacco forces—what Myron Levin of the *Los Angeles Times* has called the "growth industry of sophisticated professionals who are supported by governmental contracts and foundation grants," and who are devoted to the absolutist advocacy of a single cause—the eradication of tobacco. I was amazed at the intensity of the emotion, the constant attacks, the charges and counter-charges, the harsh rhetoric—a general lack of civility and endless litigation.

I also found it impossible to plan for the future when one of our companies was portrayed as outside the mainstream of commerce absorbed in massive litigation, under regulatory, and political attack, with no normal working relationship with federal or state governments.

It was clear to me that the 40 years of litigation, in which the industry never lost a case, was not providing an answer. Further escalation of the war, even with more courtroom victories, would not change anything for the better and would not address the problem that many Americans wanted addressed, that is, how to curtail the number of underage teenagers who use tobacco products in the United States today.

Forty years of successful litigation had avoided courtroom defeats, but had not prevented the industry from becoming isolated and demonized by its professional attackers.

Perhaps of even more immediate concern, the industry was also becoming the object of an unprecedented litigation assault, not by private citizens, but by state governments.

Let me remind you what happened here, because it bears remembering.

Some local and state politicians, combining forces with the powerful plaintiffs' bar, came up with a new way to target this disfavored industry. The states, which for years had approved tobacco as a legal product and taxed it to the point of no return, would now sue for the alleged health care costs caused by the use of the products by adult consumers.

The possibility of literally billions of dollars in legal fees attracted the titans of tort lawyers, and the politician plaintiffs were off to the races.

As Paul Gigot said in the *Wall Street Journal,* it was a "Trend explained by opportunity and ambition, fueled by governments political marriage with the plaintiffs' bar."

The politics of demonization, combined with the potential for a huge payday, proved irresistible. More states joined in. Some states like Florida even went so far as to rewrite their tort law, specifically to facilitate victory in the courtroom against tobacco.

Here is just one example from a state law recently introduced in the Vermont legislature, which is typical, of others. It creates a new claim for money damages on behalf of the state, specifically against the targeted tobacco companies. And it goes on:

"In any [such] action, all principles of common law and equity regarding affirmative defenses normally available to a defendant are hereby abrogated to ensure full recovery." In other words, the government simply strips the targeted industry of all the legal rights and defenses afforded to every other defendant, to make sure the state wins and tobacco loses. In any event, by 1997, the industry was facing this kind of confiscatory litigation in states all across the country, with states essentially using their local courts as new tax agencies and changing the rules as they went along to make it easier to collect.

It's a disturbing trend not necessarily limited only to tobacco products, and some governments have recently expanded it to go after gun manufacturers for the health damages inflicted by their legal products. The next logical candidates are obvious. One health advocate at Yale University recently opined that Ronald McDonald was more evil (and perhaps more suable) than Joe Camel.

But for tobacco, the trend only guaranteed that the future of the industry, and the millions of people whose jobs depend on it, would be dictated by bet-your-company litigation results, not by a free and open policy debate. There would be no constructive dialog about the public health issues or how to solve them. It was hard to see, from any rational perspective, how anyone—in the industry, in government or the public health community—would really be satisfied with the prospect of decades of more litigation with no thoughtful resolution of the underlying issues in sight.

So we in the industry sat down and tried to come up with a solution that literally could reverse the course of history.

We asked, what could the world look like if we put on the table our traditional rights and freedoms as a company in a free enterprise system—many of which are protected by the Constitution—in order to address dramatically the real national concern about children's smoking?

What if we were willing to give up marketing freedoms—especially critical to Reynolds, trying as it is to reverse a long-term decline in its competitive position?

Yet, we ultimately did put these freedoms on the negotiating table in an effort to get to a comprehensive resolution of the tobacco controversy.

Even further, what would the world look like if we agreed to pay unprecedented amounts of money, forever, to end finally the years of litigation? There is no question there would be a serious negative impact on Reynolds' earnings.

Yet, we ultimately ended up putting these sums of money on the negotiating table. We sat down at a table with our adversaries to try to produce a better result for everyone. Three months of intense negotiations led to a remarkable, comprehensive agreement, tougher and more wide-ranging than any of us had expected, that would have settled the bulk of the litigation and fundamentally changed the way tobacco products are regulated, marketed and sold in this country.

In so doing, experts thought it would have done more to reduce youth smoking than anything anyone had previously proposed.

There has been a lot of water over the dam since that agreement, almost exactly one year ago. But let me remind you what a few people said at that time about the June 20th settlement last year.

The *New York Times* said: "Tobacco negotiators announced a historic settlement proposal today that, if ratified, promises to change forever the way cigarettes are marketed in the United States, to provide billions of dollars in compensation to states and to permanently alter the nation's legal, regulatory and public health landscape."

One attorney general, who had participated, said: "This is the biggest public health achievement and corporate settlement in the history of this country."

A leading anti-tobacco advocate, Matt Myers of the National Center for Tobacco free Kids, said: "This plan offers the best hope for protecting our children." He called it "the single most fundamental change in the history of tobacco control, in the history of the world."

What happened next, though, is by now painfully familiar to everyone, instead of embracing the achievement, Washington destroyed it.

Our national leaders prevaricated and played politics with it.

Leadership was nowhere to be found.

And into that vacuum of leadership rushed politicians on a political goldrush, along with activists bent on destruction of the tobacco industry.

In the end, we witnessed a sorry spectacle of politicians trying to tax a legal industry and 47 million American smokers into oblivion, all under the guise of protecting the nation's youth. When the Senate bill finally collapsed in June of its own weight, one editorial writer called it "a distressing example of Congress' finest product—an unrecognizable mess, confusing in content, plastered with special interest favors, stripped of its original intent."

You have to ask yourself, how could this happen? Why did it happen?

Well, I've been asking myself that question a lot, and I have two answers—one obvious, one perhaps more surprising.

First, the obvious one. We have today in Washington an Administration without the will, or the courage, to lead. After actively encouraging the tobacco companies and the attorneys general, at meetings in the White House, to risk an unprecedented compromise, the Administration opted for partisan positioning instead of bold political leadership.

We learned the wisdom of Churchill's comment that: "nothing is more dangerous . . . than to live in the temperamental atmosphere of a Gallup poll, always feeling one's pulse and taking one's temperature."

But that's the political dance the country got from a White House unwilling to seize ownership of a historic opportunity presented on a silver platter.

More surprising is what was revealed by this vacuum of political leadership, and that is this: We learned that the essential premise of our attempted resolution—that the public health leaders of our country, would support a comprehensive resolution if it provided for real public health advances—was simply not true.

The June 20th agreement gave them a public health advocate's dream come true, but they would not take "yes" for an answer.

Into the vacuum of political leadership marched the professional advocates of an absolutist cause.

And so it is that the public health activists became the greatest single impediment to a remarkable public health advance for the country.

The self-appointed leaders of our public health community, to whom the politicians ceded their responsibility of office, turn out to have an agenda which excludes mutual resolution, at any cost, whatever the public health consequences.

The evidence of this emerged as events played out after June 20th last year. Before the ink was dry, the anti-tobacco lobby turned on the attorneys general and other negotiators, and did everything they could think of to destroy the economic viability of the industry.

Here's what happened: The anti-tobacco lobby didn't concentrate at all on the public health provisions of the agreement. They focused instead on the money—on radically increasing the already punishing financial burdens on the companies and their consumers.

First, they claimed that financial penalties of up to billions of dollars assessed yearly against the industry if youth smoking rates did not drastically decline were not severe enough. No reason why . . . just not sufficiently harsh. This, despite the fact that no one in the history of this country had ever previously proposed, much less agreed to, a penalty on an industry for consumer conduct that it couldn't control.

How did the politicians respond? They obediently tripled the penalties, thereby assuring bankrupting fines for conduct that the companies could not prevent.

Then, the public health advocates took on another new expertise. They became experts on litigation against the industry, arguing that the public health of the nation depended on class action lawsuits and punitive damage awards.

Any settlement of litigation, no matter at what price, was quote "immunity" unquote for the industry, which could not be tolerated under any circumstances.

How did the politicians respond? They dutifully dismantled the litigation settlement contained in the agreement.

And finally, the anti-tobacco advocates came up with the ultimate weapon to achieve the destruction they desired. Changing their tune after years of criticizing industry advertising and marketing practices, they argued that to really stop kids from smoking, the only viable approach was to raise prices through the roof to all adult consumers.

There was never any real evidence to support this idea that skyhigh prices would have anything like the claimed effect on underage smoking choices. In fact, you'll remember that just two years ago, the Clinton Administration, and its FDA Commissioner David Kessler, announced FDA regulations which they claimed would reduce youth smoking in half over seven years, all without a penny in new taxes or price increases.

For some mysterious reason, now two years later, the only approach that would work was price increases that would make noncontraband tobacco prohibitively expensive for most adult smokers, and thereby threaten the economic viability of the industry.

Why would people who call themselves advocates for the public health do this? Why would they make financial arguments and legal arguments one after the other—in an effort to destroy a compromise which might resolve issues and move the country forward in a sensible, balanced way?

David Kessler gave us the answer a few weeks ago, in an article in the *New York Times*. He's got a different agenda: "I don't want to live in peace with these (tobacco) guys. If they cared at all for the public health, they wouldn't be in this business in the first place. All this talk about it being a legal business is euphemism. There's no reason to allow them to conduct business . . ." Dr. Koop's zeal on tobacco also allows no room for compromise. In the same article, he called it "evil" for companies to produce these products, despite the fact that our society has deemed them to be legal adult products for over 200 years. "There shall be no compromise," he decreed. "No bill is better than a compromise bill," proclaimed Dr. Kessler.

Don't get me wrong. I'm not quarreling with their right to hold these opinions. All Americans have a right to voice their opinions. But most Americans reject such unbending commands not to compromise—and would choose not to sail away on the Pequod under these kinds of orders.

Most Americans accept that tobacco is a legal business and want to find reasonable solutions to the issues presented by the product.

Dr. Koop has devoted much of his career to improving the nation's health, and for that I have the utmost personal respect. His anti-smoking message is worthy of respect when delivered individually and persuasively to his patients, or even publicly as part of an educational campaign. But it should become a cause of concern when he has it legislatively imposed on free people who have the right as individuals to reject even Dr. Koop's expert advice.

What's wrong here is how some of our political leaders, whose job it is to seek balanced and practical solutions to the nation's problems, can so easily be persuaded to default on their responsibility in favor of a single, absolutist and ultimately undemocratic point of view. This default guarantees no consensus will be reached.

It guarantees no balance will be struck.

It guarantees no real progress.

In this case, the anti-tobacco activists, in their effort to eradicate a legal industry, led the Senators into what one commentator called "The most purely punitive piece of legislation in history,"

One whose aim was not to address youth smoking, but to control adult behavior . . . to punish the industry and the 47 million adult Americans who choose to use tobacco products and to coerce them to change their ways, for their own good.

Others are now finally realizing that this was the agenda all along, and that it doomed any cooperative effort to failure.

Senator McCain, who allowed himself to be led by them, says: "No matter what we put in this legislation, it has never been enough for them . . . Now I know why they haven't gotten anything accomplished in 40 years."

Mike Moore, the leading negotiator for the attorneys general in the June 20th agreement, says: "The public health people overreached."

Richard Kluger, noted author on tobacco said in the *New York Times*: "They should have understood that regulating tobacco, not punishing the industry, was the primary goal . . . their self-righteous view missed the larger point."

The country rightly should expect its elected leaders to protect us from the overreaching of professional, single-issue activists, and the well-meaning absolutists like Dr. Kessler and Dr. Koop, who have held progress and resolution of tobacco issues hostage to their own personal prescriptions of what is in our best interest. Instead, our leaderless politicians have let them snatch defeat from the jaws of victory.

Where does Washington's failure leave us today? It is wrong to say last month's event was a victory for tobacco companies. We tried last year, with the June 20th agreement that we signed with the attorney general, to chart a new course; and that effort has completely failed. Last month only proved that.

We are left right where we were when I began speaking out a couple of months ago. I pledged then that my company was going to take the debate out of the broken-down process in Washington, and engage the American people in a public policy discussion. I have told my shareholders that I see this as an important part of my job for them, as the future of their company and the industry in which it operates is truly at stake. That is what we have been doing these last two months, and that is what we are going to continue to do.

And we are going to do everything we can to bring reason and common sense back to the discussion, until Washington gets real on tobacco.

I believe that ultimately, the people will make the politicians lead, and force them to focus on goals the country wants to achieve:

Do we want to punish tobacco companies, or do we want to create reasonable and responsible rules for the future of 7 million American adult smokers, or do we want to do something effective at actually reducing underage use of tobacco products?

Do we want to promote another generation of litigation in the courts, or do we want to settle the controversies and move on?

Do we want government to coerce the legal behavior of adult Americans who choose to smoke, or do we want a balanced compromise that embraces free, informed choice and that values personal responsibility?

If there is any silver lining for the country, perhaps the events in Washington last month will finally make our leaders focus on the issues Americans want addressed.

I continue to think that a balanced, comprehensive approach, along the lines of the June 20th agreement, would do the most to resolve the controversies and move the country forward to a new era of responsible tobacco regulation.

But if that is not possible, we at RJR Nabisco remain committed to working and cooperating with responsible efforts to address parents' well-founded concerns about their teenagers.

We have a responsibility to do that, and we will do that. But only when our leaders provide a balance against zealotry and embrace consensus, can the real work begin.

ARTICLE 20

FACT SHEET: SMOKING

John R. Garrison

Smoking-related diseases claim an estimated 430,700 American lives each year, including those affected indirectly, such as babies born prematurely due to prenatal maternal smoking and some of the victims of "secondhand" exposure to tobacco's carcinogens. First-hand smoking alone costs the United States approximately $97.2 billion each year in health-care costs and lost productivity.

Cigarettes contain at least 43 distinct cancer-causing chemicals. Smoking is directly responsible for 87 percent of lung cancer cases and causes most cases of emphysema and chronic bronchitis. Smoking is also a major factor in coronary heart disease and stroke; may be causally related to malignancies in other parts of the body; and has been linked to a variety of other conditions and disorders, including slowed healing of wounds, infertility, and peptic ulcer disease.

Smoking in pregnancy accounts for an estimated 20 to 30 percent of low-birth weight babies, up to 14 percent of preterm deliveries, and some 10 percent of all infant deaths. Even apparently healthy, full-term babies of smokers have been found to be born with narrowed airways and curtailed lung function. Only about 30 percent of women who smoke stop smoking when they find they

John R. Garrison is the CEO of the American Lung Association. This article was delivered in a speech on November 20, 1998.

Reprinted by permission. The American Lung Association, www.lungusa.org

are pregnant; the proportion of quitters is highest among married women and women with higher levels of educational attainment. In 1995, 14 percent of women who gave birth smoked during pregnancy.

Smoking by parents is also associated with a wide range of adverse effects in their children, including exacerbation of asthma, increased frequency of colds and ear infections, and sudden infant death syndrome. An estimated 150,000 to 300,000 cases of lower respiratory tract infections in children less than 18 months of age, resulting in 7,500 to 15,000 annual hospitalizations, are caused by secondhand smoke. A 1992 study of the urine analysis of several hundred children exposed to smoke revealed significant levels of cotinine, the major metabolite of nicotine.

Secondhand smoke involuntarily inhaled by nonsmokers from other people's cigarettes is classified by the U.S. Environmental Protection Agency as a known human (Group A) carcinogen, responsible for approximately 3,000 lung cancer deaths annually in U.S. nonsmokers.

More than 22 million American women are smokers. Current female smokers aged 35 years or older are 12 times more likely to die prematurely from lung cancer than nonsmoking females. More American women die annually from lung cancer than any other type of cancer; for example, lung cancer will cause an estimated 67,000 female deaths in 1998, compared with 43,500 estimated female deaths caused by breast cancer.

As smoking has declined among the white non-Hispanic population, tobacco companies have targeted both African Americans and Hispanics with intensive merchandising, which includes billboards, advertising in media targeted to those communities, and sponsorship of civic groups and athletic, cultural, and entertainment events.

The prevalence of smoking is highest among Native Americans/ Alaskan Natives (36.2 percent), next highest among African Americans (25.8 percent) and whites (25.6 percent), and lowest among Asians and Pacific Islanders (16.6 percent). Hispanics (18.3 percent) are less likely to be smokers than non-Hispanic blacks and whites.

Tobacco advertising plays an important role in encouraging young people to begin a lifelong addiction to smoking before they are old enough to fully understand its long-term health risk. It is estimated that at least 4 million U.S. teenagers are cigarette smokers; 24.6 percent of high school seniors smoke on a daily basis. Approximately 90 percent of smokers begin smoking before the age of 21.

The American Lung Association coordinates the Smoke-Free Class of 2000 in response to former Surgeon General C. Everett Koop's call for a smoke-free society by the Year 2000. We are focusing on the three million children who entered the first grade in

1988, to increase students' awareness and education, to focus media attention on a tobacco-free society, and to place tobacco-use prevention education programs in school health curricula. These students are now in high school and the focus is on empowering them to become peer educators on the dangers of tobacco and tobacco control advocates in their communities.

Workplaces nationwide are going smoke-free to provide clean indoor air and protect employees from the life-threatening effects of secondhand smoke. According to a 1992 Gallup poll, 94 percent of Americans now believe companies should either ban smoking totally in the workplace or restrict it to designated areas.

Employers have a legal right to restrict smoking in the workplace, or implement a totally smoke-free workplace policy. Exceptions may arise in the case of collective bargaining agreements with unions.

Nicotine is an addictive drug, which when inhaled in cigarette smoke reaches the brain faster than drugs that enter the body intravenously. Smokers become not only physically addicted to nicotine; they also link smoking with many social activities, making smoking a difficult habit to break.

In 1995, an estimated 44.3 million adults were former smokers. Of the current 47 million smokers, more than 31 million persons reported they wanted to quit smoking completely. Currently, both nicotine patches and nicotine gum are available over-the-counter, and a nicotine nasal spray and inhaler, as well as a non-nicotine pill, are currently available by prescription; all help relieve withdrawal symptoms people experience when they quit smoking. Nicotine replacement therapies are helpful in quitting when combined with a behavior change program such as the American Lung Association's Freedom From Smoking® (FFS), which addresses psychological and behavioral addictions to smoking and strategies for coping with urges to smoke.

For more information call the American Lung Association at 1-800-LUNG-USA (1-800-586-4872), or visit our Web site at http://www.lung-usa.org.

LUNG ASSOCIATION DISAPPOINTED AS STATES APPROVE TOBACCO DEAL (STATEMENT OF JOHN R. GARRISON, CEO, AMERICAN LUNG ASSOCIATION, NOVEMBER 20, 1998)

The American Lung Association is disappointed that the states have settled with the tobacco industry. The deal concedes far too much to Big Tobacco and provides far too little to protect public health.

Fortunately, the war against the disease and death caused by tobacco use is not over. Skirmishes continue on battlefields all across the nation. From state house to courthouse, from city hall to the halls of Congress, we have the tobacco industry on the run. The industry still faces lawsuits from health insurance providers, labor union health plans, class actions brought by injured smokers, and thousands of individual cases. Local ordinances to provide smoke-free environments were only dreams a decade ago but are becoming the norms today. Earlier this month, voters in Oregon and Maine reaffirmed their smoke-free laws despite an onslaught of tobacco industry cash that funded their opposition. The Minnesota settlement forced the release of thousands of documents that have detailed a decades-long trail of deceit by the tobacco industry. And, despite a multi-million-dollar misinformation campaign by the tobacco industry, California voted to increase its cigarette excise tax by 50 cents.

There also is growing recognition that Congress can no longer ignore a product that kills more than 420,000 Americans and millions more around the globe each year.

These successes energize the American Lung Association and its allies as we pursue aggressive action at the state and local levels. The American Lung Association will continue to lead this fight. We will work to ensure that the Medicaid dollars the states recover through the settlement are invested in protecting the public health and eliminating tobacco use.

It is unfortunate that the states have decided not to confront the tobacco industry in the courts. But the American Lung Association will continue its fight on the local, state and national levels to protect our children from the deadly lure of tobacco.

The American Lung Association has been fighting lung disease for more than 90 years. With the generous support of the public and the help of our volunteers, we have seen many advances against lung disease. However, our work is not finished. As we look forward to our second century, we will continue to strive to make breathing easier for everyone. Along with our medical section, the American Thoracic Society, we provide programs of education, community service, advocacy and research. The American Lung Association's activities are supported by donations to Christmas Seals® and other voluntary contributions. You may obtain additional information via our America Online site, keyword: ALA, or our Web site at: http://www.lungusa.org.

ARTICLE 21

FREEDOM AT WAR WITH FEAR

George W. Bush

September 20, 2001

Mr. Speaker, Mr. President Pro Tempore, members of Congress, and fellow Americans:

In the normal course of events, Presidents come to this chamber to report on the state of the Union. Tonight, no such report is needed. It has already been delivered by the American people.

We have seen it in the courage of passengers, who rushed terrorists to save others on the ground—passengers like an exceptional man named Todd Beamer. And would you please help me to welcome his wife, Lisa Beamer, here tonight.

We have seen the state of our Union in the endurance of rescuers, working past exhaustion. We have seen the unfurling of flags, the lighting of candles, the giving of blood, the saying of prayers—in English, Hebrew, and Arabic. We have seen the decency of a loving and giving people who have made the grief of strangers their own.

My fellow citizens, for the last nine days, the entire world has seen for itself the state of our Union—and it is strong.

Tonight we are a country awakened to danger and called to defend freedom. Our grief has turned to anger, and anger to resolution. Whether we bring our enemies to justice, or bring justice to our enemies, justice will be done.

I thank the Congress for its leadership at such an important time. All of America was touched on the evening of the tragedy to see Republicans and Democrats joined together on the steps of this

---

Address to a Joint Session of Congress and the American People, United States Capitol, Washington, D.C.

Capitol, singing "God Bless America." And you did more than sing; you acted, by delivering $40 billion to rebuild our communities and meet the needs of our military.

Speaker Hastert, Minority Leader Gephardt, Majority Leader Daschle and Senator Lott, I thank you for your friendship, for your leadership and for your service to our country.

And on behalf of the American people, I thank the world for its outpouring of support. America will never forget the sounds of our National Anthem playing at Buckingham Palace, on the streets of Paris, and at Berlin's Brandenburg Gate.

We will not forget South Korean children gathering to pray outside our embassy in Seoul, or the prayers of sympathy offered at a mosque in Cairo. We will not forget moments of silence and days of mourning in Australia and Africa and Latin America.

Nor will we forget the citizens of 80 other nations who died with our own: dozens of Pakistanis; more than 130 Israelis; more than 250 citizens of India; men and women from El Salvador, Iran, Mexico and Japan; and hundreds of British citizens. America has no truer friend than Great Britain. Once again, we are joined together in a great cause—so honored the British Prime Minister has crossed an ocean to show his unity of purpose with America. Thank you for coming, friend.

On September the 11th, enemies of freedom committed an act of war against our country. Americans have known wars—but for the past 136 years, they have been wars on foreign soil, except for one Sunday in 1941. Americans have known the casualties of war—but not at the center of a great city on a peaceful morning. Americans have known surprise attacks—but never before on thousands of civilians. All of this was brought upon us in a single day—and night fell on a different world, a world where freedom itself is under attack.

Americans have many questions tonight. Americans are asking: Who attacked our country? The evidence we have gathered all points to a collection of loosely affiliated terrorist organizations known as al-Qa'eda. They are the same murderers indicted for bombing American embassies in Tanzania and Kenya, and responsible for bombing the USS Cole.

Al-Qa'eda is to terror what the mafia is to crime. But its goal is not making money; its goal is remaking the world—and imposing its radical beliefs on people everywhere.

The terrorists practice a fringe form of Islamic extremism that has been rejected by Muslim scholars and the vast majority of Muslim clerics—a fringe movement that perverts the peaceful teachings of Islam. The terrorists' directive commands them to kill Christians and Jews, to kill all Americans, and make no distinction among military and civilians, including women and children.

This group and its leader—a person named Osama bin Laden— are linked to many other organizations in different countries, including the Egyptian Islamic Jihad and the Islamic Movement of Uzbekistan. There are thousands of these terrorists in more than 60 countries. They are recruited from their own nations and neighborhoods and brought to camps in places like Afghanistan, where they are trained in the tactics of terror. They are sent back to their homes or sent to hide in countries around the world to plot evil and destruction.

The leadership of al-Qa'eda has great influence in Afghanistan and supports the Taliban regime in controlling most of that country. In Afghanistan, we see al-Qa'eda's vision for the world.

Afghanistan's people have been brutalized—many are starving and many have fled. Women are not allowed to attend school. You can be jailed for owning a television. Religion can be practiced only as their leaders dictate. A man can be jailed in Afghanistan if his beard is not long enough.

The United States respects the people of Afghanistan—after all, we are currently its largest source of humanitarian aid—but we condemn the Taliban regime. It is not only repressing its own people, it is threatening people everywhere by sponsoring and sheltering and supplying terrorists. By aiding and abetting murder, the Taliban regime is committing murder.

And tonight, the United States of America makes the following demands on the Taliban: Deliver to United States authorities all the leaders of al-Qa'eda who hide in your land. Release all foreign nationals, including American citizens, you have unjustly imprisoned. Protect foreign journalists, diplomats and aid workers in your country. Close immediately and permanently every terrorist training camp in Afghanistan, and hand over every terrorist, and every person in their support structure, to appropriate authorities. Give the United States full access to terrorist training camps, so we can make sure they are no longer operating.

These demands are not open to negotiation or discussion. The Taliban must act, and act immediately. They will hand over the terrorists, or they will share in their fate.

I also want to speak tonight directly to Muslims throughout the world. We respect your faith. It's practiced freely by many millions of Americans, and by millions more in countries that America counts as friends. Its teachings are good and peaceful, and those who commit evil in the name of Allah blaspheme the name of Allah. The terrorists are traitors to their own faith, trying, in effect, to hijack Islam itself. The enemy of America is not our many Muslim friends; it is not our many Arab friends. Our enemy is a radical network of terrorists, and every government that supports them.

Our war on terror begins with al-Qa'eda, but it does not end there. It will not end until every terrorist group of global reach has been found, stopped and defeated.

Americans are asking, why do they hate us? They hate what we see right here in this chamber—a democratically elected government. Their leaders are self-appointed. They hate our freedoms—our freedom of religion, our freedom of speech, our freedom to vote and assemble and disagree with each other.

They want to overthrow existing governments in many Muslim countries, such as Egypt, Saudi Arabia, and Jordan. They want to drive Israel out of the Middle East. They want to drive Christians and Jews out of vast regions of Asia and Africa.

These terrorists kill not merely to end lives, but to disrupt and end a way of life. With every atrocity, they hope that America grows fearful, retreating from the world and forsaking our friends. They stand against us, because we stand in their way.

We are not deceived by their pretenses to piety. We have seen their kind before. They are the heirs of all the murderous ideologies of the 20th century. By sacrificing human life to serve their radical visions—by abandoning every value except the will to power—they follow in the path of fascism, and Nazism, and totalitarianism. And they will follow that path all the way, to where it ends: in history's unmarked grave of discarded lies.

Americans are asking: How will we fight and win this war? We will direct every resource at our command—every means of diplomacy, every tool of intelligence, every instrument of law enforcement, every financial influence, and every necessary weapon of war—to the disruption and to the defeat of the global terror network.

This war will not be like the war against Iraq a decade ago, with a decisive liberation of territory and a swift conclusion. It will not look like the air war above Kosovo two years ago, where no ground troops were used and not a single American was lost in combat.

Our response involves far more than instant retaliation and isolated strikes. Americans should not expect one battle, but a lengthy campaign, unlike any other we have ever seen. It may include dramatic strikes, visible on TV, and covert operations, secret even in success. We will starve terrorists of funding, turn them one against another, drive them from place to place, until there is no refuge or no rest. And we will pursue nations that provide aid or safe haven to terrorism. Every nation, in every region, now has a decision to make. Either you are with us, or you are with the terrorists. From this day forward, any nation that continues to harbor or support terrorism will be regarded by the United States as a hostile regime.

Our nation has been put on notice: We are not immune from attack. We will take defensive measures against terrorism to protect

Americans. Today, dozens of federal departments and agencies, as well as state and local governments, have responsibilities affecting homeland security. These efforts must be coordinated at the highest level. So tonight I announce the creation of a Cabinet-level position reporting directly to me—the Office of Homeland Security.

And tonight I also announce a distinguished American to lead this effort, to strengthen American security: a military veteran, an effective governor, a true patriot, a trusted friend—Pennsylvania's Tom Ridge. He will lead, oversee and coordinate a comprehensive national strategy to safeguard our country against terrorism, and respond to any attacks that may come.

These measures are essential. But the only way to defeat terrorism as a threat to our way of life is to stop it, eliminate it, and destroy it where it grows.

Many will be involved in this effort, from FBI agents to intelligence operatives to the reservists we have called to active duty. All deserve our thanks, and all have our prayers. And tonight, a few miles from the damaged Pentagon, I have a message for our military: Be ready. I've called the Armed Forces to alert, and there is a reason. The hour is coming when America will act, and you will make us proud.

This is not, however, just America's fight. And what is at stake is not just America's freedom. This is the world's fight. This is civilization's fight. This is the fight of all who believe in progress and pluralism, tolerance and freedom.

We ask every nation to join us. We will ask, and we will need, the help of police forces, intelligence services, and banking systems around the world. The United States is grateful that many nations and many international organizations have already responded—with sympathy and with support. Nations from Latin America, to Asia, to Africa, to Europe, to the Islamic world. Perhaps the NATO Charter reflects best the attitude of the world: An attack on one is an attack on all.

The civilized world is rallying to America's side. They understand that if this terror goes unpunished, their own cities, their own citizens may be next. Terror, unanswered, can not only bring down buildings, it can threaten the stability of legitimate governments. And you know what—we're not going to allow it.

Americans are asking: What is expected of us? I ask you to live your lives, and hug your children. I know many citizens have fears tonight, and I ask you to be calm and resolute, even in the face of a continuing threat.

I ask you to uphold the values of America, and remember why so many have come here. We are in a fight for our principles, and our first responsibility is to live by them. No one should be singled out for unfair treatment or unkind words because of their ethnic background or religious faith.

I ask you to continue to support the victims of this tragedy with your contributions. Those who want to give can go to a central source of information, libertyunites.org, to find the names of groups providing direct help in New York, Pennsylvania, and Virginia.

The thousands of FBI agents who are now at work in this investigation may need your cooperation, and I ask you to give it.

I ask for your patience, with the delays and inconveniences that may accompany tighter security; and for your patience in what will be a long struggle.

I ask your continued participation and confidence in the American economy. Terrorists attacked a symbol of American prosperity. They did not touch its source. America is successful because of the hard work, and creativity, and enterprise of our people. These were the true strengths of our economy before September 11th, and they are our strengths today.

And, finally, please continue praying for the victims of terror and their families, for those in uniform, and for our great country. Prayer has comforted us in sorrow, and will help strengthen us for the journey ahead.

Tonight I thank my fellow Americans for what you have already done and for what you will do. And ladies and gentlemen of the Congress, I thank you, their representatives, for what you have already done and for what we will do together.

Tonight, we face new and sudden national challenges. We will come together to improve air safety, to dramatically expand the number of air marshals on domestic flights, and take new measures to prevent hijacking. We will come together to promote stability and keep our airlines flying, with direct assistance during this emergency.

We will come together to give law enforcement the additional tools it needs to track down terror here at home. We will come together to strengthen our intelligence capabilities to know the plans of terrorists before they act, and find them before they strike.

We will come together to take active steps that strengthen America's economy, and put our people back to work.

Tonight we welcome two leaders who embody the extraordinary spirit of all New Yorkers: Governor George Pataki, and Mayor Rudolph Giuliani. As a symbol of America's resolve, my administration will work with Congress, and these two leaders, to show the world that we will rebuild New York City.

After all that has just passed—all the lives taken, and all the possibilities and hopes that died with them—it is natural to wonder if America's future is one of fear. Some speak of an age of terror. I know there are struggles ahead, and dangers to face. But this country will define our times, not be defined by them. As long as the United States of America is determined and strong, this will not be an age of terror; this will be an age of liberty, here and across the world.

Great harm has been done to us. We have suffered great loss. And in our grief and anger we have found our mission and our moment. Freedom and fear are at war. The advance of human freedom—the great achievement of our time, and the great hope of every time—now depends on us. Our nation—this generation—will lift a dark threat of violence from our people and our future. We will rally the world to this cause by our efforts, by our courage. We will not tire, we will not falter, and we will not fail.

It is my hope that in the months and years ahead, life will return almost to normal. We'll go back to our lives and routines, and that is good. Even grief recedes with time and grace. But our resolve must not pass. Each of us will remember what happened that day, and to whom it happened. We'll remember the moment the news came—where we were and what we were doing. Some will remember an image of a fire, or a story of rescue. Some will carry memories of a face and a voice gone forever.

And I will carry this: It is the police shield of a man named George Howard, who died at the World Trade Center trying to save others. It was given to me by his mom, Arlene, as a proud memorial to her son. This is my reminder of lives that ended, and a task that does not end.

I will not forget this wound to our country or those who inflicted it. I will not yield; I will not rest; I will not relent in waging this struggle for freedom and security for the American people.

The course of this conflict is not known, yet its outcome is certain. Freedom and fear, justice and cruelty, have always been at war, and we know that God is not neutral between them.

Fellow citizens, we'll meet violence with patient justice—assured of the rightness of our cause, and confident of the victories to come. In all that lies before us, may God grant us wisdom, and may He watch over the United States of America.

Thank you.

P A R T 5

CULTURE AND POLITICS

I n 2000 many leading political observers boldly predicted an easy presidential victory for Vice President Al Gore solely on the basis of a strong economy. Forecasting models developed by political scientists suggested that a strong economy so much favors the party in the White House that Gore would not only win, but that he would win big.

Campaign predictions based on economic circumstances are bound to fail when voters factor other issues in their decisions. Political scientist John C. Green examines the "culture clashes" that characterized the political debates of campaign 2000, and he finds that George W. Bush's use of social issues enabled him to significantly overcome Vice President Gore's advantages from the strong economy. Although the nation was economically strong by election time, the public was deeply concerned about the moral climate, particularly given the scandals of the Clinton years and widespread reporting of Gore's tendency to embellish stories of his own background. Green observes that Bush benefited from the public's concern with character in public office because of the combination of the election being at the end of the Clinton era and the closeness of the Bush-Gore race. It is therefore difficult to conclude that moral and cultural issues will always be so important to presidential elections outcomes.

Sociologist James Davidson Hunter writes more broadly of the "culture wars" that are indeed such a prominent fixture of contemporary American politics. Different systems of moral understanding create conflict not only over religion, but also politics and society. This conflict is more deeply rooted than the usual political debates in America because moral principles are at the core of peoples' beliefs and of how they view their role in this world. Consequently, such principles do not easily lend themselves to compromise. Passionate differences over moral principles therefore translate into deeply divisive cultural clashes.

President Clinton's administration was at the core of many of the cultural conflicts of the 1990s. These conflicts still resonate loudly today, as the scandals and cultural battles of the Clinton era continue. Clinton was a president who attracted both an intensely loyal following of supporters and an especially intense opposition from detractors. The scandals and culture clashes of the Clinton years have had a long-lasting impact and, as "The Two Sides of the Clinton Legacy" shows, have created significant challenges for President George W. Bush. Although President Bush has expressed a desire to create a new spirit of bipartisanship and cooperation in Washington, D.C., he is finding that the scars of the Clinton era battles remain.

Cultural clashes in America are frequently imbued with debates over group "rights." Mary Ann Glendon discusses the implications for our democracy of the heavy emphasis by groups on "rights." Our constitutional tradition is one of promoting the welfare of society and the liberties of individuals. Contemporary politics emphasizes the unique rights of specific groups in the electorate, often to the exclusion of the general welfare. Glendon expresses the hope that an enlightened political leadership can renew the rhetoric of moderation and inclusiveness to enable the nation to move beyond its current infatuation with rights-based language.

CULTURE CLASH: SOCIAL ISSUES AND THE 2000 PRESIDENTIAL VOTE

John C. Green

The 2000 presidential election was one of the closest in American history and many observers believe social issues had a major impact on the outcome. For example, journalist Thomas Edsall found that traditional measures of economic status, such as income and education, were less important than "more subtle social and moral matters" in explaining support for Vice President Al Gore and Texas Governor George W. Bush. Republican pollster William McInturff agreed: "We have two massive, colliding forces: One rural, Christian, religiously conservative, with guns at home, terribly unhappy with Clinton's behavior . . . And we have a second America that is socially tolerant, pro-choice, secular, living in New England and the Pacific coast, and in affluent suburbs." Democratic pollster Geoff Garin elaborated: "You can't just look at someone's demographics anymore and understand them politically. You have to understand their belief structure."[1]

This "culture clash" surprised observers accustomed to the dominance of economic issues in presidential campaigns.[2] Social issues allowed Governor Bush to blunt Vice President Gore's advantages stemming from a strong economy. Indeed, if the campaign had been waged substantially on economic issues, history strongly suggests that Gore would have been the undisputed winner. Concern with the nation's moral climate, President Clinton's scandals, and the candidates' characters were especially important in this regard. In addition, a series of specific social policy disputes, including abortion, gay rights and school vouchers, divided the electorate and undergirded the presidential vote. However, most Americans were not deeply polarized on all of these issues, with only a minority of voters gave top priority to social issues. Overall, 2000 campaign was characterized by a series of cultural "shouting matches," sometimes approaching the rhetoric, but not the reality, of cultural "wars."

CONTEMPORARY CULTURAL CONFLICT

By "social," "cultural," or "moral" issues most observers mean political controversies based on the ethics of personal behavior. Thus defined, social issues cover a wide range of topics. One useful distinction is the breadth or specificity of the issues. At the broadest level are general assessments of the moral climate of the country, such as a sense that the nation has lost its "moral compass." Of somewhat greater specificity are disagreements over the institutions that create and maintain social order, from families to the government. The character and qualities of public officials, especially the president, are central to such concerns. At the most specific level are disputes over the government regulation of individual behavior, such as whether and when abortions should be legal.

Another useful way to look at social issues is by subject matter. One important area involves sexual behavior and its consequences; here disputes over abortion and gay rights are especially prominent. Related matters include women's rights, family structure, and the raising of children. In this regard, education, popular culture, and the public role of religion are also salient concerns. Other matters of public order, such as gun control, crime, and substance abuse are perennial topics of concern, as are questions of personal honesty, respect, and tolerance for others. Racial issues are also a mainstay of cultural conflict, although their politics are so distinctive that scholars regularly treat them separately from other social issues.

Despite this complexity, social issues are commonly distinguished from economic ones, which generally include the performance of the economy, the government's economic role, and the provision of specific governmental benefits. This distinction arises in large measure because social issues are believed to be especially divisive. As political scientist Theodore Lowi notes, the politics of social issues tends to be "more ideological, more moral, more directly derived from fundamental values, more intense, less utilitarian, more polarized, and less prone to compromise."[3] Simply put, this kind of politics does not lend itself easily to resolution. If taken to its logical conclusion, such divisiveness can produce a polarized public, gridlock in government, rejection of the political process, and even violence.

In fact, the intensity of social issue conflicts in the last decades of the twentieth century has prompted some to declare that America is in the throes of "culture wars." The best known example was conservative commentator Patrick Buchanan's proclamation of a "culture war" at the 1992 Republican National Convention. He declared that "Clinton and Clinton" (Bill and Hillary—and by implication their ally, Al Gore) were "on one side" of such a war and then-President George H. W. Bush (the father of George W. Bush) was on "our side." Ironically, some prominent liberals then attacked Buchanan, helping to fulfill his prophecy.[4]

At about the same time, sociologist James Davison Hunter offered a more systematic analysis of this prospect in his book Culture Wars.[5] To Hunter, American politics was increasingly dominated by two rival coalitions, the "orthodox" and the "progressive." The former were characterized by traditional moral and religious beliefs, while the latter were defined by modern, relativistic views on personal behavior and religion. In principle, these rivals disagreed on the full range of issues, including the economy, but the battle lines were mostly fiercely drawn on specific social policies. Both Buchanan and Hunter allege something like "two massive colliding forces" based on rival "belief structures" characterize American politics.

Many observers have found the culture war metaphor to be a cogent description of the "new politics of old values."[6] Certainly, scores of zealous political activists regularly confront one another across the cultural landscape. For instance, "religious right," pro-life, and gun owner organizations regularly square off against their opposites among gays rights, pro-choice, and gun control groups.[7] These "cultural warriors" have helped the major political parties deploy "wedge issues" in elections. Republicans have promoted "family values" to pull working-class evangelical Protestants and Catholics away from the Democrats. And to a lesser extent, Democrats have used women's rights and social tolerance to attract support from suburban Republican women.[8]

Other observers are quite skeptical of the culture wars metaphor, however.[9] While not doubting the importance of social issues for some people on some occasions, they believe that the intensity of cultural conflict in the mass public has been greatly exaggerated. To begin with, cultural issues are typically salient to only a minority of citizens, with economic and social welfare issues attracting much more attention.

The American public is basically moderate even on social issues, these critics argue, and thus not deeply polarized. Historian Leo Ribuffo sums up this point view by noting that the United States is in the throes of cultural "shouting matches" rather than "culture wars."[10]

What impact did social issues have on the 2000 election? Did they reflect "two massive colliding forces" rooted in rival "belief structures"? Was social issue conflict best characterized as cultural "wars" or "shouting matches"? We can address these questions by means of public opinion surveys taken during the 2000 campaign.[11]

Survey results must be viewed with some caution, of course, because they are at best snapshots of public opinion at a particular point in time. But taken together, Tables 1 to 5 illustrate the impact of social issues on the presidential vote, beginning with broad assessments of the nation's situation and ending with specific social policy disputes.

MORAL AND ECONOMIC ASSESSMENTS

A good place to begin is with general assessments of the nation's well-being, reported in Table 1. The first item asked if the "moral condition" of the country was on the "right track." Just two-fifths of likely voters agreed, while the remaining three-fifths felt the country was on the "wrong track." (Here, as in the remaining tables, the first column reports the distribution of opinion in the electorate as a whole—the **bold entries** add to 100 percent down the page. Respondents without opinions were excluded for ease of presentation.)

This moral assessment was strongly related to vote choice: nearly three-quarters of respondents who thought the country was on the "right track" supported Gore. In contrast, two-thirds of the "wrong track" voters backed Bush. (Here, as in the remaining tables, the second and third columns report the support of the respondents for the major party candidates—the *italic entries* add to 100 percent across the page. We report just the two-party vote for ease of presentation.)

The second item in Table 1 helps put this moral assessment in context. Respondents were asked if the country as a whole was on the "right track," a question that tends to reflect economic well being. Here better than two-thirds of voters answered in the affirmative, and they strongly backed Gore. The remaining one-third felt the country was on the "wrong track" overall, and they strongly supported Bush.

Put another way, three-fourths of Bush voters had a negative view of the nation's moral health, while four-fifths of Gore voters had a positive view of the nation's economic performance. The source of these rival assessments are illuminated by next two items in Table 1. The third item asked if the government should promote "moral values." Three-fifths of the respondents said agreed and the remaining two-fifths did not. Note, however, that these attitudes were not as clearly linked to the presidential vote as the moral assessment: only slightly more than one-half of the "moralizers" voted for Bush, while about the same, small proportion of the "nonmoralizers" voted for Gore. This finding suggests that the moral assessment was less based on rival views of the government's role promoting values than on dismay over recent events, from sexual scandals to school shootings.

TABLE 1

MORAL AND ECONOMIC ASSESSMENTS AND THE 2000 PRESIDENTIAL VOTE

	PERCENT OF VOTERS	PERCENT FOR GORE	PERCENT FOR BUSH	
Country's moral condition is:*				
On the right track	40	72	28	100%
On the wrong track	60	35	65	100%
	100%			
Overall, country is:*				
On the right track	68	63	37	100%
On the wrong track	32	21	79	100%
	100%			
Government should promote moral values:**				
Yes	60	47	53	100%
No	40	56	44	100%
	100%			
Government should improve standard of living:**				
Yes	61	70	30	100%
No	39	25	75	100%
	100%			
Top Priority:**				
Social Issues	19	18	82	100%
Other Issues	81	58	42	100%
	100%			

*2000 Exit Poll, Voter News Service
**2000 Moral Values Survey, Washington Post/Kaiser Foundation/Harvard University

The fourth item in Table 1 asked respondents if the government should work to improve people's standard of living. Three-fifths of the electorate said yes and two-fifths said no. These attitudes were associated with stark divisions in the 2000 vote: almost three-quarters of the former voters backed Gore, while three-quarters of the latter supported Bush. Unlike the moral assessment, this pattern suggests that the economic assessment was connected to fundamental differences over the government's role in the economy rather than just the recent prosperity.

To what extent did these general assessments reflect voter's issue priorities? The final item in Table 1 shows that about one-fifth of likely voters claimed that social issues were their top priority in the 2000 election, with four-fifths naming some other issue. Overall, education received the top mention, with two-fifths of the respondents, and a number of other issues, such as health care, Social Security, taxes and the general performance of the economy, rated ahead of social issues. So, social issue voters were a minority of the electorate in 2000. To put this number in perspective, all the social issue voters were outnumbered two-to-one by the voters who felt the country was on the "wrong track" morally.

However, social issue priorities were strongly associated with the vote: better than four-fifths of the social issue voters supported Governor Bush and less one-fifth backed Vice President Gore. Thus, social issue voters made up about one-third of Bush's supporters and roughly one-tenth of Gore's backers. These are hardly trivial numbers in a very close election, but more importantly, these "culture warriors" of the right and left played a critical indirect role in the campaign, mobilizing support and getting out the vote for each candidate.

For social issue voters, the choice between Bush and Gore was easy to make—even if the candidate did not completely share their beliefs. But for many other voters, the choice for president was quite difficult. They appreciated the country's strong economy, but were dismayed by the nation's lack of morality. They appreciated Vice President Gore's commitment to "fight" for their interests, but also liked Governor Bush's promise to restore "honor and dignity" to the White House.

QUESTIONS OF CHARACTER

Table 2 reports information on candidate qualities and character, factors critical to many voters. The first item concerns the importance of President Clinton's scandals. The President's affair with Monica Lewinsky and his impeachment by congressional Republicans were backdrops to the 2000 campaign. Vice President Gore struggled to disassociate himself from Clinton's personal problems, while at the same time taking credit for the administration's economic successes. Meanwhile, Governor Bush and the Republicans tried to link Gore to the Clinton scandals without reminding voters of the excesses of the impeachment fight.

The Clinton scandal divided the electorate. On election day, one-quarter of voters claimed the scandals were "very important" to their vote and another one-fifth reported they were "somewhat important." These two groups voted strongly for Bush. On the other side of the ledger, less than one-fifth of voters claimed the scandals were "not too important" to their vote and almost two-fifths maintained they were "not important at all." These voters strongly supported Gore.

TABLE 2

CANDIDATE CHARACTER AND QUALITIES AND THE 2000 PRESIDENTIAL VOTE

	PERCENT OF VOTERS	PERCENT FOR GORE	PERCENT FOR BUSH	
In voting, Clinton scandals:*				
Very important	25	18	82	100%
Somewhat important	20	29	71	100%
Not too important	17	61	39	100%
Not important at all	38	80	20	100%
	100%			
Priority for President:*				
Managing government	63	64	36	100%
Moral leadership	36	28	72	100%
	100%			
Candidate Qualities:*				
Has experience	16	83	17	100%
Understands issues	14	80	20	100%
Cares about people	13	67	33	100%
Good judgement	14	49	51	100%
Likeable	2	39	61	100%
Strong leader	15	35	65	100%
Honest/trustworthy	26	16	84	100%
	100%			
Would Gore say anything to get elected?*				
Yes	76	40	60	100%
No	24	77	23	100%
	100%			
Would Bush say anything to get elected?*				
Yes	59	67	33	100%
No	41	23	77	100%
	100%			

*2000 Exit Poll, Voter News Service

One reason Gore chose Senator Joseph Lieberman as his vice-presidential running mate was to help mitigate the effects of the Clinton scandals and negative moral assessments among moderate voters. Senator Lieberman was one of most vocal Democratic critics of President Clinton in the Lewinsky scandal and was an advocate of traditional postures on some social issues. Surveys suggest that Lieberman did indeed help Gore in this regard, although the historic nature of his nomination (he was the first Jew on a presidential ticket) may have been just as important.[12] The Republican vice-presidential nominee, former Defense Secretary Dick Cheney, may have helped Governor Bush as well by easing concerns over Bush's lack of experience. In addition, Cheney's social issue views were acceptable to GOP conservatives.

What were voters looking for in a president in 2000? The second item in Table 2 asked voters to choose between two roles the president might perform: managing the government or providing moral leadership. Although these options are not mutually exclusive, the voters made a clear choice. Slightly less than two-thirds of voters picked managing the government, and nearly two-thirds of them backed Gore. In contrast, a little more than one-third of the electorate chose moral leadership, and almost three-quarters of them backed Bush. Clearly, many voters were troubled by immorality in the White House, but many fewer wanted the Oval Office to become a bully pulpit.

The third item in Table 2 lists seven candidate qualities voters considered at the ballot box. Two of these qualities easily relate to managing the government: experience and understanding issues. Roughly one-sixth of the respondents named these qualities, and those who did strongly supported Gore. Two other qualities relate easily to moral leadership, being "honest and trustworthy" (which garnered the most support with one-quarter of the respondents) and being a "strong leader" (chosen by about one-sixth). Voters who stressed these factors strongly backed Bush. The other qualities in Table 2 could apply to either role, such as "caring about people" (which benefited Gore), "good judgment" (evenly divided between the candidates), and being "likeable" (which benefited Bush). It is interesting to note that very few voters (two percent) were looking for a likeable candidate, a quality where Bush's easy-going personality contrasted sharply with Gore's stiff personal style.

Candidate honesty was central to the 2000 campaign, partly because of the scandals of the 1990s, but also because of behavior of the candidates themselves. Many people already questioned Gore's credibility because of past misstatements, such as claiming "no controlling legal authority" regarding controversial fundraising in 1996. This perception was reinforced by his much publicized "exaggerations" during the campaign. Bush had similar credibility problems due to unanswered questions about his drinking and carousing as a young man—questions that were brought to the public's attention when a 1976 DUI conviction came to light at the very end of the campaign.

The remaining two items in Table 2 address the question of each candidate's credibility by asking respondents if either would "say anything to get elected president." Given public skepticism toward politicians in general, it would not be surprising if many voters affirmed this statement with regard to both candidates. However, more voters were skeptical of Gore than Bush by 76 to 59 percent. As one might expect, voters who doubted Gore's credibility strongly supported Bush, and vice versa.

Overall, the candidate qualities and questions of character reinforced voter's general assessments of the nation's moral and economic climates. Taken together, the information in Tables 1 and 2 help explain the closeness of the 2000 election.

MATTERS OF LIFE—AND DEATH

What impact did specific social policy controversies have on the presidential vote? The 2000 campaign was characterized by an unusual focus on issues: it was largely waged over rival proposals for tax cuts, Social Security reform, and prescription drug benefits for senior citizens. However, there were even larger differences between Gore and Bush on less discussed social issues, the most prominent of which was abortion.

Table 3 covers abortion and other "life" issues. The first item reports opinion on the legality of abortion. About one-quarter of the electorate agreed that abortions "always legal." This pro-choice stance is very similar to Vice President Gore's strong endorsement of a "woman's right to choose." About one-third of the respondents believed that abortions should be "mostly legal." These two groups of voters strongly supported Gore.

In contrast, a little more than one-quarter of the respondents believed that abortions should be "mostly illegal." This position is similar to Governor Bush's position of limiting but not prohibiting all abortions. Finally, about one-sixth of the voters believe that abortions should be "always illegal," the strongest pro-life position. These last two groups strongly backed Bush.

Like most controversies, there are many facets to the abortion debate. Table 3 reviews two that were especially important in the 2000 campaign. One was access to RU-486, a pill produces an abortion in the first trimester of pregnancy. RU-486 was approved by the U.S. Food and Drug Administration in the midst of the 2000 campaign. Gore strongly endorsed this decision, while Bush expressed ambivalence. The electorate was divided on RU-486, with slightly more favoring increased access. Three-fifths of those who favored access to RU-486 voted for Gore, and three-fifths of those opposed it voted for Bush.

Similar divisions occurred over the legality of abortions in the second trimester of pregnancy. Many pro-life activists strongly advocate banning of some such abortions, which they labeled "partial birth abortion." During the 1990s, the Republican controlled Congress passed and President Clinton vetoed such a ban—twice. Governor Bush promised to sign such a ban if he were elected; Vice

TABLE 3			
ABORTION, OTHER "LIFE" ISSUES, AND 2000 PRESIDENTIAL VOTE			
	PERCENT OF VOTERS	PERCENT FOR GORE	PERCENT FOR BUSH
Abortion should be:*			
Always legal	24	74	26	100%
Mostly legal	34	60	40	100%
Mostly illegal	28	30	70	100%
Always illegal	14	23	77	100%
	100%		
Expand access to abortion pill (RU-486):**			
Yes	53	60	40	100%
No	47	40	60	100%
	100%		
Second Trimester abortions should be legal:***			
Yes	35	61	39	100%
No	65	43	57	100%
	100%		
Support doctor-assisted suicide for terminally ill:**			
Yes	54	54	46	100%
No	46	47	53	100%
	100%		
Support the death penalty for convicted murders:**			
Yes	70	41	59	100%
No	30	72	28	100%
	100%		
*2000 Exit Poll, Voter News Service			
**2000 Moral Values Survey, Washington Post/Kaiser Foundation/Harvard University			
***Los Angeles Times Poll #442: Abortion/Gay Rights			

President Gore promised yet another veto. The third item in Table 3 reveals that a little more than one-third of the electorate believed second trimester abortions should be legal, and of these, about three-fifths voted for Gore. In contrast, about two-thirds felt that such abortions should be illegal, and nearly three-fifths voted for Bush.

The final two items in Table 3 deal with other "life" issues. One is doctor-assisted suicide, a controversy that played only a minor role in the 2000 campaign despite some expectations to the contrary. As with RU-486, the public was almost evenly divided; Gore received slightly more support from those who agreed with the practice, and Bush obtained slightly more support from opponents.

The other item is the death penalty for convicted murders. A longstanding controversy, the death penalty attracted new attention in the late 1990s when it was revealed that innocent persons had received capital sentences in several states. Although both Gore and Bush supported the death penalty, Bush presided over several executions during the campaign in his capacity as governor of Texas. In a pattern reminiscent of second trimester abortions, the public strongly supported the death penalty. The pro-capital punishment majority voted for Bush, while the anti-capital punishment minority voted for Gore.

Overall, pro-choice voters make up roughly three-quarters of Gore's supporters, while pro-life voters accounted for three-fifths of Bush's supporters. Thus, abortion undergirded the presidential vote. However, most Americans were not deeply polarized on all aspects of abortion nor on other "life" issues. Indeed, only a minority of voters adopted a "consistent ethic of life," opposing abortion, doctor-assisted suicide, and the death penalty. Instead, most Americans had complex views on these matters.

RIGHTS, GAY AND OTHERWISE

Gay rights was another important issue in the 2000 campaign, and Table 4 reports public opinion on this and other "rights" issues. The first item in Table 4 shows the electorate supported gay rights in general terms, with two-thirds agreeing that "homosexuals should have the same rights as other Americans." This position was consistent with Vice President Gore's support for extending legal protection to gays and lesbians. The remaining one-third of the electorate disagreed with the statement, a position consistent with Governor Bush's opposition to "special rights" for homosexuals. Not surprisingly, the pro-gay rights majority supported Gore and the anti-gay rights minority backed Bush.

A solid majority of the electorate also supported the enactment of "hate crime" laws to protect homosexuals (second item in Table 4). Under such laws, violent crimes carry extra penalties if the victims were singled out because of their sexual orientation. Gore was a vocal proponent of such laws, and received strong support from those who favored them. Meanwhile, opponents of such laws backed Bush, who argued the existing punishments for violent crime were already sufficiently severe and there was no need to take into account the characteristics of the victim.

The question of same-sex marriages appeared in the 2000 campaign largely because the state of Vermont had recognized gay and lesbian "civil unions."[13] Vice President Gore expressed some limited support for such unions (as did the Republican Vice Presidential

TABLE 4

GAY RIGHTS, OTHER RIGHTS ISSUES, AND THE 2000 PRESIDENTIAL VOTE

	PERCENT OF VOTERS	PERCENT FOR GORE	PERCENT FOR BUSH	
Homosexuals should have the same rights as other Americans:**				
Agree	69	57	43	100%
Disagree	31	32	68	100%
	100%			
Support "hate crimes" laws protecting homosexuals:*				
Yes	57	63	37	100%
No	43	34	66	100%
	100%			
Support gay marriage:***				
Yes	35	64	36	100%
No	65	39	61	100%
	100%			
An Equal Rights Amendment is needed to insure women's rights:**				
Agree	76	56	44	100%
Disagree	24	30	70	100%
	100%			
Minorities need governmental assistance to obtain their rightful place in America**				
Agree	51	58	42	100%
Disagree	49	38	61	100%
	100%			

*2000 Moral Values Survey, Washington Post/Kaiser Foundation/Harvard University
**Third National Survey of Religion and Politics, University of Akron, 2000
***Los Angeles Times Poll #442: Abortion/Gay Rights

candidate Dick Cheney, whose daughter is a lesbian); Governor Bush was adamantly opposed. The third item in Table 4 shows that roughly one-third of the electorate supported same-sex marriage, and these individuals backed Gore. However, almost two-thirds of the electorate opposed such unions, and this group backed Bush.

The final two items in Table 4 look at other issues that are often compared to gay rights: women's rights and affirmative action for minorities. Vice President Gore took strong stances in support of both issues, while Governor Bush took more moderate positions, criticizing of the operation of existing programs aimed at protecting such rights.

Overall, three-quarters of the electorate favored an Equal Rights Amendment to the U.S. Constitution, an issue no longer on the public agenda, but still a potent symbol of women's rights; the remaining one-quarter of the electorate opposed this symbol. The pro-ERA majority backed Gore and the anti-ERA minority strongly backed Bush. In contrast, the electorate was much more divided on affirmative action, programs that seek to redress past discrimination against African Americans and other minorities. Here proponents and opponents each made up about one-half of electorate, with the former supporting Gore and the latter backing Bush.

Like abortion, most Americans were not deeply polarized on all aspects of gay rights. Instead, these views were part of a complex web of attitudes regarding personal rights, moral standards, and social justice. On the one hand, voters tended to support the extension of gay rights in general terms, a pattern that resembled support for women's rights. These sorts of concern helped produce a strong "gender gap," with Gore winning the female vote (especially the among younger, single women) and Bush winning the male vote (particularly among older, married men). On the other hand direct recognition of the legitimacy of homosexuality, such as same-sex marriages, was very unpopular. Thus, the overall the impact of gay rights may have resembled the divisions on affirmative action. Indeed, religious and racial divisions were along the sharpest in the electorate.[14]

EDUCATION AND OTHER PUBLIC ORDER ISSUES

As we have seen, education was the top priority of the electorate in 2000. The social policy dimensions of this topic were particularly prominent and Table 5 reports some relevant information. Many religious groups were keenly interested in making public money available to the parents of school-age children in the form of vouchers. Vice President Gore and his allies among public schools teachers were adamantly opposed to vouchers in any form. Governor Bush identified vouchers as a tool of last resort to help reform failing public schools.

The first item in Table 5 concerns the basic concept of vouchers and it reveals an evenly divided electorate. Better than three-fifths of voucher-supporters backed Bush and the same proportion of voucher-opponents backed Gore. However, the next item tells a different story. When asked whether "bad schools" should be fixed with more public money or with vouchers, the public overwhelmingly chose more money. Those who favored more public money to fix "bad schools" on balance backed Gore, while the pro-voucher minority strongly backed Bush.

TABLE 5

EDUCATION, OTHER PUBLIC ORDER ISSUES, AND THE 2000 PRESIDENTIAL VOTE

	PERCENT OF VOTERS	PERCENT FOR GORE	PERCENT FOR BUSH	
Support school vouchers for parents with children in private or parochial schools:**				
Yes	49	37	63	100%
No	51	64	36	100%
	100%			
Solution for bad schools:*				
More public money	83	57	43	100%
School vouchers	17	24	76	100%
	100%			
Support prayer in public school:**				
Yes	74	45	55	100%
No	26	70	30	100%
	100%			
Support more gun regulation:*				
Yes	63	65	35	100%
No	37	24	76	100%
	100%			
Government regulate sex and violence in entertainment:**				
Yes	50	49	51	100%
No	50	53	47	100%
	100%			

*2000 Exit Poll, Voter News Service
**2000 Moral Values Survey, Washington Post/Kaiser Foundation/Harvard University

Many voters were supportive of high standards and character education public schools, issues raised by both candidates, but especially Governor Bush. These matters are frequently related to a perennial issue in American politics, school prayer. Outlawed by the Supreme Court in 1960s, the issue received renewed attention because of the perceived decline of the nation's moral climate. Overall, school prayer remaining quite popular with voters, as can be seen with the third item in Table 5. Almost three-quarters of the electorate approved of school prayer, and more than one-half of this large group supported Bush. In contrast, the one-quarter of the electorate who opposed school prayer strongly backed Gore. It must be noted, however, that most prayer supporters believe in voluntary prayer of one sort or another, not a state-mandated and enforced prayer. Neither presidential candidate endorsed mandatory prayer nor opposed voluntary prayer in public schools.

Americans were also deeply concerned with the safety of public schools in the wake of the fatal shooting in the 1990s, such as at Columbine High School in Colorado. One response was more regulation of guns, an issue that tapped into a longstanding dispute over gun control. Vice President Gore strongly endorsed further restrictions on guns, especially to prevent them from being sold to children. Governor Bush generally opposed new gun regulations, although he did advocate trigger locks to help protect children. As a consequence, gun control and gun owner groups waged a pitch battle in the 2000 campaign. Better than three-fifths of the electorate strongly supported more regulation of guns (fourth item in Table 5), and almost two-thirds of these voters supported Gore. Nearly two-fifths of voters opposed new regulations, and some three-quarters of them backed Bush.

Another issue in the 2000 campaign was limiting sex and violence in the entertainment industry, including movies, television, popular music, and the Internet. Tipper Gore was a champion of this kind of regulation of popular song lyrics in the 1980s, and both Vice President Gore and Senator Lieberman stressed this issue. Although many Republicans also advocated new regulations, Governor Bush was skeptical of government regulation in this area, and contented himself with attacking Gore and Lieberman for taking large sums of campaign funds from the putative objects of such regulations, the entertainment industry. As the final item in Table 5 reveals, the electorate was evenly divided on this issue. Ironically, supporters of such regulation modestly backed Bush and opponents modestly supported Gore.

As with abortion and gay rights, most Americans were not deeply polarized over all the cultural aspects of public education and related public order issues. However, these questions were part of a complicated set of disagreements that undergirded the 2000 presidential vote.

CULTURE CLASH

What do these patterns tell us about the impact on social issues on the 2000 election? As Tom Edsall reported, "more subtle social and moral matters" played an important role in the very close 2000 vote. This culture clash allowed Governor Bush to blunt Vice President Gore's advantage stemming from a strong economy. Concerns about the nation's moral health, President Clinton's scandals, and the candidates' character were especially important in this regard. In addition, a series of specific social policy disputes, including abortion, gay rights, and school vouchers, divided the electorate and under-girded the presidential vote.

Having noted the importance of social issues, two caveats are in order. First, the moral and candidate character assessments seem to reflect distress with recent events rather than fundamental differences about the role of government in promoting values. Scandals in high places and a host of social problems across the social landscape dismayed many voters precisely because their expectations were contradicted. Put bluntly, Americans were less interested in new "moral leadership" from the White House than in having the occupant of the Oval Office behave himself. And by implication, they wanted their neighbors, children—and perhaps even themselves—to behave better as well.

Second, although there were sharp disagreements over what constituted good behavior in many areas, most Americans were not deeply polarized on all such issues. Indeed, only a small minority of voters of gave top priority to social issues. Many of these voters were religious conservatives strongly committed to traditional morality, but others were religious liberals and secular individuals equally committed to progressive values.[15] These "culture warriors" on the right and left were motivated by well-defined and intensely-held "belief structures." They played an important indirect role in the campaign, by mobilizing support and getting out the vote for each candidate. Looked at from this perspective, there may well have been "two colliding forces" in the 2000 campaign, but they were not especially "massive." Thus, the 2000 campaign could be characterized as a series of cultural "shouting matches," sometimes approaching the rhetoric, but not the reality, of cultural "wars."

NOTES

1 These quotes comes from Thomas B. Edsall, "Political Party Is No Longer Dictated By Class Status." *Washington Post* November 9, 2000 A-1.

2 For a good summary of the expected impact of the economy on the 2000 elections, see Robert G. Kaiser, "And the Winner will be . . ." *Washington Post Weekly Edition* June 5, 2000, 6-7. One might argue that Gore's narrow popular vote victory (and his narrow disputed loss in Florida) reveal the political power of the economy. After all, the strong economy allowed Gore to overcome a large, pre-election deficit in the polls rooted in social issues. However, this account still recognizes the importance of social issues in the 2000 election.

3 Theodore J. Lowi, "Foreword: New Dimensions in Policy and Politics," in Raymond Tatalovich and Byron W. Daynes, eds., Moral Controversies in American Politics (Armonk, N.Y.: M.E. Sharpe, 1998), p. xv.

4 For a good discussion of the 1992 campaign see Wilson Carey McWilliams, *Beyond the Politics of Disappointment?* (Chatham, N.J.: Chatham House, 2000), chapter 5.

5 James Davison Hunter, *Culture Wars: The Struggle to Define America* (New York: Basic Books, 1991).

6 See John Kenneth White, *The New Politics of Old Values* (Hanover, N.H.: University Press of New England, 1988).

7 On social issue activists, see Jo Freeman and Victoria Johnson, eds. *Waves of Protest* (Lanham, MD: Rowman & Littlefield, 1999).

8 Ted G. Jelen and Marthe Chandler, "Culture wars in the Trenches: Social issues as Short-Term Forces in Presidential Elections, 1968-1996," *American Review of Politics,* 21(Spring) 2000, pp.69-88.

9 See the essays in Rhys H. Williams, ed. *Culture wars in American Politics* (New York: Aldine De Gruyter, 1997).

10 Comment made at the 2000 Black Point Conference on Religion and Public Life, Black Point Inn, Prouts Neck, ME, June 26-27, sponsored by the Ethics and Public Policy Center, Washington D.C.

11 In the tables that follow, we use the results of four surveys conducted in 2000: 1) National Exit Poll, Voter News Services, November 7, 2000 (N=11,578); 2) 2000 Moral Values Survey, Washington Post/Kaiser Foundation/Harvard University, September 7-17, 2000 (N=1,477); 3) Los Angeles Times Poll #442, Abortion/Gay Rights, June 8=13,2000 (N=2,071); 4) Third National Survey of Religion and Politics, University of Akron, May 2000 (N=4,004). In all cases, the analysis concerned actual voters or likely voters. The author wishes to thank Voter News Services, the *Washington Post,* and the Roper Center for access to these surveys; all interpretations are the responsibility of the authors.

12 The 2000 Moral Values Survey suggests that Lieberman added significant support to the Democratic ticket.

13 The VNS exit poll for Vermont found that 25 percent of the voters were enthusiastic about the civil union law, and 80 percent of them voted for Gore. In contrast, 15 percent of the voters were angry with the law, and 75 percent of them voted for Bush.

14 In fact, racial divisions were among the sharpest in the electorate, with African Americans voting almost nine-to-one in favor of Gore, and Bush winning a majority of the white vote. A similar division occurred among white members of the "religious right," a group that voted four-to-one for Bush.

15 See Andrew Kohut, John C. Green, Scott Keeter, and Robert C. Toth *The Diminishing Divide: Religion's Changing Role in American Politics* (Washington, D.C.: Brookings Institution Press, 2000).

Article 23

CULTURAL CONFLICT IN AMERICA

James Davidson Hunter

NEW LINES OF CONFLICT: THE ARGUMENT IN BRIEF

Let me begin to make sense of the new lines of cultural warfare by first defining what I mean by "cultural conflict." I define cultural conflict very simply as political and social hostility rooted in different systems of moral understanding. The end to which these hostilities tend is the domination of one cultural and moral ethos over all others. Let it be clear, the principles and ideals that mark these competing systems of moral understanding are by no means trifling but always have a character of ultimacy to them. They are not merely attitudes that can change on a whim but basic commitments and beliefs that provide a source of identity, purpose, and togetherness for the people who live by them. It is for precisely this reason that political action rooted in these principles and ideals tends to be so passionate.

So what is new about the contemporary cultural conflict? As we have seen, the cultural hostilities dominant over the better part of American history have taken place *within* the boundaries of a larger biblical culture—among numerous Protestant groups, and Catholics and Jews—over such issues as doctrine, ritual observance, and religious organization. Underlying their disagreements, therefore, were basic agreements about the order of life in community and nation—agreements forged by biblical symbols and imagery. But the old arrangements have been transformed. The older agreements have unraveled. The divisions of political consequence today are not theological and ecclesiastical in character but the result of differing worldviews. That is to say, they no longer revolve around specific doctrinal issues or styles of religious practice and organization but around our most fundamental and cherished assumptions about how to order our lives—our own lives and our lives together in this society. Our most fundamental ideas about who we are as Americans are now at odds.

Because this is a culture war, the nub of political disagreement today on the range of issues debated—whether abortion, child-care, funding for the arts, affirmative action and quotas, gay rights, values in public education, or multiculturalism—can be traced ultimately and finally to the matter of moral authority. By moral authority I mean the basis by which people determine whether something is good or bad, right or wrong, acceptable or unacceptable, and so on. Of course, people often have very different ideas about what criteria to use in making moral judgments, but this is just the point. It is the commitment to different and opposing bases of moral authority and the world views that derive from them that creates the deep cleavages between antagonists in the contemporary culture war. As we will see, this cleavage is so deep that it cuts *across* the old lines of conflict, making the distinctions that long divided Americans—those between Protestants, Catholics, and Jews—virtually irrelevant.

At this point let me introduce a critical word of qualification. Though competing moral visions are at the heart of today's culture war, these do not always take form in coherent, clearly articulated, sharply differentiated world views. Rather, these moral visions take expression as *polarizing impulses* or *tendencies* in American culture. It is important, in this light, to make a distinction between how these moral visions are institutionalized in different organizations and in public rhetoric, and how ordinary Americans relate to them. In truth, most Americans occupy a vast middle ground between the polarizing impulses of American culture. Many will obviously lean toward one side while many others will tilt toward the other. Some Americans may seem altogether oblivious to either. The point is that most Americans, despite their predispositions, would not embrace a particular moral vision wholly or uncritically. Where the polarizing tendencies in American culture tend to be sharpest is in the organizations and spokespeople who have an interest in promoting a particular position on a social issue. It is they who, perhaps unwittingly, give voice to the competing moral visions. (Even then, I might add, the world views articulated are often less than coherent!) These institutions possess tremendous power in the realm of public discourse. They almost seem to have a life of their own: an existence, power, and agenda independent of the people for whom they presumably speak.

Polarizing Impulses: The Orthodox and the Progressive

To come right to the point, the cleavages at the heart of the contemporary culture war are created by what I would like to call *the impulse toward orthodoxy* and *the impulse toward progressivism.* The terms are imperfect, but each aspires to describe in shorthand a particular locus and source of moral truth, the fundamental (though perhaps subconscious) moral allegiances of the actors involved in the culture war as well as their cultural and political dispositions. Though the terms "orthodox" and "progressive" may be familiar to many, they have a particular meaning here that requires some elaboration.

Let me acknowledge, first off, that the words, orthodox and progressive, can describe specific doctrinal creeds or particular religious practices. Take orthodoxy. Within Judaism, orthodoxy is defined mainly by commitment to Torah and the community that upholds it; within Catholicism, orthodoxy is defined largely by loyalty to church teaching—the Roman Magisterium; and within Protestantism, orthodoxy principally means devotion to the complete and final authority of Scripture. Substantively, then, these labels can mean vastly different things within different religious traditions.

But I prefer to use the terms orthodox and progressive as *formal properties* of a belief system or world view. What is common to all three approaches to *orthodoxy,* for example (and what makes orthodoxy more of a formal property), *is the commitment on the part of adherents to an external, definable, and transcendent authority.* Such objective and transcendent authority defines, at least in the abstract, a consistent, unchangeable measure of value, purpose, goodness, and identity, both personal and collective. It tells us what is good, what is true, how we should live, and who we are. It is an authority that is sufficient for all time. Thus, as different as Chuck McIlhenny, Yehuda Levin, and Mae Duggan are in their personal faith commitments, all three believe that moral authority comes from above and for all time. This is seen clearly in Yehuda's statement that what the Torah says about abortion is "the beginning and the end of the subject." Chuck and Mae, in their own ways, would say something similar. This fundamental commitment, then, is what these three share in common and one reason why, in the current climate, their voices tend to resonate with each other.

Within cultural progressivism, by contrast, moral authority tends to be defined by the spirit of the modern age, a spirit of rationalism and subjectivism.[1] Progressivist moral ideals tend, that is, to derive from and embody (though rarely exhaust) that spirit.

From this standpoint, truth tends to be viewed as a process, as a reality that is ever unfolding. There are many distinctions that need to be made here. For example, what about those progressivists who still identify with a particular religious heritage? For them, one may note a strong tendency to translate the moral ideals of a religious tradition so that they conform to and legitimate the contemporary *zeitgeist.* In other words, what all *progressivist* world views share in common *is the tendency to resymbolize historic faiths according to the prevailing assumptions of contemporary life.* This is seen, for example, in Bea Blair's rejection of biblical literalism and her conviction that, as she put it, "people have to interpret the Scripture for themselves." The same theme is illustrated by stories Chuck McIlhenny tells of ministers he has debated, some of whom, Chuck says, reinterpret Scripture to justify homosexuality, while others recognize what the biblical texts say about the immorality of homosexuality but reject its authority over one's life. From Chuck's point of view, progressivist church leaders base their views on the belief that "the Bible is just a human document, no different from any other book." The general point both Bea and Chuck make here is that the traditional sources of moral authority, whether scripture, papal pronouncements, or Jewish law, no longer have an exclusive or even a predominant binding power over their lives. Rather, the binding moral authority tends to reside in personal experience or scientific rationality, or either of these in conversation with particular religious or cultural traditions.

I have been talking about the contemporary cultural divide in the context of religious communities in order to highlight the historical novelty of the contemporary situation. But what about the growing number of "secularists"?[2] These people range from the vaguely religious to the openly agnostic or atheistic. While they would probably claim no affiliation with a church or religious denomination, they nevertheless hold deep humanistic concerns about the welfare of community and nation. Secularists are central to this discussion for the obvious reason that their presence and perspectives have become so prominent in American life. How then do secularists relate to the matter of moral authority?

Like the representatives of religious communities, they too are divided. Yet public opinion surveys show that a decided majority of secularists, are drawn toward the progressivist impulse in American culture.[3] For these people religious tradition has no binding address, no opinion-shaping influence. Some secularists, however, (particularly many secular conservative and neo-conservative intellectuals) are drawn toward the orthodox impulse. For them, a commitment to natural law or to a high view of nature serves as the functional equivalent of the external and transcendent moral authority revered by their religiously orthodox counterparts.

In sum, the contemporary cultural conflict turns upside down (or perhaps inside out) the way cultural conflict has long been waged. Thus, we see those with apparently similar religious or cultural affiliations battling with one another. The culture war encompasses all Americans, religious and "non-religious," in very novel ways.

Political Dispositions: Cultural Conservatives Versus Cultural Progressivist The orthodox and progressivist impulses in American culture, as I have described them, contrast sources of moral truth and also the allegiances by which people, drawn toward one or the other, live and interpret the world. They also express, somewhat imperfectly, the opposing social and political dispositions to which Americans on opposing sides of the cultural divide are drawn. Here, though, a word of elaboration.

It nearly goes without saying that those who embrace the orthodox impulse are almost always cultural conservatives, while those who embrace progressivist moral assumptions tend toward a liberal or libertarian social agenda. Certainly, the associations between foundational moral commitments and social and political agendas is far from absolute; some people and organizations will cross over the lines, taking conservative positions on some issues and liberal views on others. Yet the relationship between foundational moral commitments and social and political agendas is too strong and consistent to be viewed as coincidental. This is true for most Americans (as seen in public opinion surveys), but it is especially true for the organizations engaged in the range of contemporary disputes. For the practical purposes of naming the antagonists in the culture war, then, we can label those on one side cultural conservatives or moral traditionalists, and those on the other side liberals or cultural progressives. These are, after all, the terms that the actors in the culture war use to decribe themselves. The danger of using these "political" labels, however, is that one can easily forget that they trace back to prior moral commitments and more basic moral visions: We subtly slip into thinking of the controversies debated as political rather than cultural in nature. On political matters one can compromise; on matters of ultimate moral truth, one cannot. This is why the full range of issues today seems interminable.

New and Unlikely Alliances The real novelty of the contemporary situation emerges out of the fact that the orthodox and progressivist communities are not fighting isolated battles. Evangelical Protestants, for example, are not locked in an isolated conflict with liberal Protestants. Nor are theologically progressive Catholics struggling in isolation with their theologically conservative counterparts in the Roman hierarchy. The contemporary culture war is much larger and more complicated. *At the heart of the new cultural realignment are the pragmatic alliances being formed, across faith traditions.* Because of common points of vision and concern, the orthodox wings of Protestantism, Catholicism, and Judaism are forming associations with each other, as are the progressive wings of each faith community—and each set of alliances takes form in opposition to the influence the other seeks to exert in public culture.

These institutional alliances, it should be noted, are not always influential in terms of the joint power they hold. Some of the groups, after all, are quite small and have few resources. But these institutional alliances are *culturally* significant, for the simple reason that ideological and organizational associations are being generated among groups that have historically been antagonistic toward one another. Had the disagreements in each religious tradition remained simply theological or ecclesiastical in nature, these alliances would have probably never developed. But since the divisions have extended into the broader realm of public morality, the alliances have become the expedient outcome of common concerns. In other words, although these alliances are historically "unnatural," they have become pragmatically necessary. Traditional religiocultural divisions are superseded—replaced by the overriding differences taking form out of orthodox and progressive moral commitments.

These unlikely alliances are at the center of a fundamental realignment in American culture and, in turn, identify the key actors in an emerging cultural conflict.

Points of Clarification The first mistake we should guard against is to view the culture war as merely the accumulation of social issues debated today (such as abortion, values in schools, homosexuality, or the meaning of Columbus's discovery of America). The culture war encompasses these issues, but the source of the conflict is found in different moral visions. For this reason, it would also be a mistake to view the culture war as merely a social referendum on Ronald Reagan, George Bush, or other presidents and their political legacies. If this were the case, the present conflict would simply be a dispute between political "liberals" and "conservatives." The cleavages run much deeper. For the same reasons, it would be inaccurate to describe this as a collision between "religious liberals" and "religious conservatives."[4] Nor is it a clash between what one scholar described as "New Protestants" and "Old Protestants," "New Catholics" and "Old Catholics," and by extension, "New Jews" and "Old Jews."[5] In a similar vein, it would be wrong to confuse the contemporary culture war with the ambitions of Protestant Fundamentalism and the New Christian Right and the backlash it created among such secular activists as feminists in the National Organization for Women (NOW) or attorneys of the American Civil Liberties Union

(ACLU). It is true that Evangelical and Fundamentalist Protestants are the most vocal and visible actors on the orthodox side of the new cultural divide and that the secular activists of NOW, the ACLU, or the People for the American Way are among the most visible actors on the progressive side of the divide. But to frame the contemporary culture war in this way ignores the central role played by a wide range of other cultural actors on both sides who are neither Fundamentalists on the one hand nor secular activists on the other. Besides, many of the organizations of the New Christian Right (for instance, such as the Moral Majority, Christian Voice, the Religious Roundtable) have either disappeared from public sight or gone out of business. Yet the cultural conflict continues—and it continues without any sign that it will soon abate.

THE STRUGGLE TO DEFINE AMERICA

RANDALL TERRY (spokesman for the pro-life organization Operation Rescue):
The bottom line is that killing children is not what America is all about. We are not here to destroy our offspring.

FAYE WATTLETON (president of Planned Parenthood):
Well, we are also not here to have the government use women's bodies as the instrument of the state, to force women into involuntary servitude—

RANDALL TERRY *(laughing)*:
Oh come on, Faye.

FAYE WATTLETON:
—I think that as Americans celebrate the Fourth of July, our independence, and when we reflect on our personal liberties, this is a very, very somber time, in which the courts have said that the most private aspects of our lives are now . . . not protected by the Bill of Rights and the Constitution. And I believe that that is a time for Americans to reflect on the need to return to the fundamentals, and the fundamentals of personal privacy are really the cornerstones upon which our democracy is built.

RANDALL TERRY:
I think that to assume or even suggest that the founding fathers of this country risked their lives and many of them died so that we can kill our offspring is pathetic.[6]

Although Randall Terry and Faye Wattleton were debating the morality and legality of abortion, what they said goes far beyond the abortion controversy. First, the contemporary culture war is not just an expression of different "opinions" or "attitudes" on this or that issue, like abortion. If this were all there was to it, the conflict I refer to would be, as someone once suggested, the "politics of distraction"—a trivial pursuit that keeps Americans from settling more important matters.[7] No, the conflict is deeper than mere "differences of opinion" and bigger than abortion, and in fact, bigger than the culmination of all the battles being waged. As suggested earlier, the culture war emerges over fundamentally different conceptions of moral authority, over different ideas and beliefs about truth, the good, obligation to one another, the nature of community, and so on. It is, therefore, cultural conflict at its deepest level.

Though the conflict derives from differences in assumptions that are philosophical and even theological in nature, the conflict does not end as a philosophical dispute. This is a conflict over how we are to order our lives together. This means that the conflict is inevitably expressed as a clash over national life itself. Both Randall Terry and Faye Wattleton acknowledge this in their exchange. Hearing them invoke the Bill of Rights, the "founding fathers," "what America is really all about," and so on, we come to see that the contemporary culture war is ultimately a struggle over national identity—*over the meaning of America,* who we have been in the past, who we are now, and perhaps most important, who we, as a nation, will aspire to become in the new millennium. Importantly, Randall Terry and Faye Wattleton are not the only ones who see a larger relationship between a single issue in the culture war and the American character. A well-known photographer whose work has been scrutinized by the FBI claims, "We are not going down without a fight. We're not going to go down without a voice that's saying loudly and clearly, 'this is not what we think America is about.'"[8] A young mother and activist near Sacramento, who protests the content of schoolbooks in California's public schools, said, "The battle we are fighting here is being fought all around the state and around the nation. We as parents get involved because our children are affected but in the end it is our country that is at stake."[9] A video store owner who was prosecuted for violating pornography laws stated, "I feel like I'm fighting for America. I feel like I'm fighting for our rights as Americans. That's what I feel like."[10] And each of the individuals we met in the prologue believes that the battle they wage has consequences for America—its institutions and its ideals. And the list goes on. Arguably, our national identity and purpose has not been more a source of contention since the Civil War.

Though intellectuals and activists of various sorts play a special role in this cultural conflict, it would be very wrong to assume that this conflict is really just the lofty and cerebral machinations of squirrelly academic types who roam the corridors of think tanks and universities. To the contrary, this culture war intersects the lives of most Americans, even those who are or would like to be totally indifferent. This is so because this conflict has an impact on virtually all of the major institutions of American society. As the "stories from the front" suggest, this conflict has a decisive impact on the *family*—not just on the critical issues of reproduction and abortion but on a wide range of other issues such as the limits (if any) of legitimate sexuality, the public and private role of women, questions of child-raising, and even the definition of what constitutes a family in the first place. The cultural conflict concerns the structure and content of public *education*—of how and what American children will learn. Also affected is the content of the popular *media*—from the films that are shown to the television shows that are aired to the books that are read and to the art that is exhibited. It has a critical effect on the conduct of *law*, particularly in the ways in which Americans define rights—who should have them and who should not and with whose interests the state should be aligned. Not least, this cultural clash has tremendous consequences for electoral *politics*, the way in which Americans choose their leaders. The contemporary culture war even has a bearing on the way in which public discussion is carried out—in the way people with opposing ideals and agendas try to resolve their differences in the public forum.

Once again, what seems to be a myriad of self-contained cultural disputes actually amounts to a fairly comprehensive and momentous struggle to define the meaning of America—of how and on what terms will Americans live together, of what comprises the good society.

NOTES

_1_ The term "progressive" is somewhat imprecise but it is suggestive. The word is not totally satisfactory because of its association with the political movement and ideology. It also connotes a positive development which many would find debatable. Yet the search for alternate terms leads to other problems. The antonyms of orthodoxy—heterodoxy or heresy—connote too much. "Revisionism" is problematic, too, as it implies a departure from truth. The problem is not truth versus falsehood but between different interpretations of truth—interpretations that differ because the criteria (or authority) established to measure correct interpretation differ.

_2_ Secularists are represented in such organizations as the American Humanist Association (founded in 1941), the Council for Democratic and Secular Humanism (founded 1980), the National Service Conference of the American Ethical Union (founded 1929), Gay and Lesbian Atheists (founded 1978), Libertarians for Gay and Lesbian Concerns (founded 1981), and the Association of Libertarian Feminists (founded 1975).

3 Their agreement is confirmed in the Religion and Power Survey in James Davison Hunter, John Jarvis, and John Herrmann, "Cultural Elites and Political Values," unpublished paper, University of Virginia, 1988.

4 Robert Wuthnow's book, *The Restructuring of American Religion* (Princeton, N.J.: Princeton University Press, 1988) is the most exhaustive statement on the developments described in this book to date. Those familiar with Wuthnow's treatment should see my book not just as a validation of his general argument but as an extension of it as well. Where Wuthnow focuses upon Protestantism, I focus on the interfaith dimensions of the problems. Where he views the tensions as those that exist between "religious liberals" and "religious conservatives," I view the tensions as both deeper and more significant.

5 See Mark Noll's essay, "The Eclipse of Old Hostilities," in *Uncivil Religion,* ed. Bellah and Greenspahn, p. 99.

6 "The Webster Decision," *Nightline,* ABC-TV broadcast, July 3, 1989.

7 There is little doubt that the controversy over abortion is a central part of the larger conflict. Indeed, it has crystallized the antagonism between the orthodox and progressive as no other issue has. Yet once again, the moral propriety and legality of abortion is just one of many issues over which this war is being fought. David Broder, "Trivial Pursuits," editorial, *Washington Post,* 17 June 1990, p. D7.

8 This comment was made by photographer Jock Sturgis, taken from a transcript of "48 Hours," CBS News, 27 June 1990.

9 Ibid.

10 From an anonymous video store owner interviewed on "48 Hours," ibid.

THE TWO SIDES OF THE CLINTON LEGACY*

Mark J. Rozell

For good or bad, in the modern era the Presidency has become the focus of the nation's attention in American politics. Periods of history are now commonly defined as "the Reagan era", or "the Bush years", or "the Clinton era." Serve one term, it's the "years" and serve two, it's the "era." Some Presidents exit office with the recognition that they have left a major mark on the nation's—perhaps the world's—politics and policies. Others leave office without achieving such recognition.

Not all such characterizations are justified. Former President Ronald Reagan indeed led a major impact presidency. But lately the efforts to memorialize his achievements have gotten badly out of proportion. A massive federal building and a major airport in Washington, D.C. are named for Reagan.[1] Some Republican members of Congress are threatening to withhold federal funding for the Washington, D.C subway system unless the Metro board renames one station after Reagan. The GOP Congress is pressing to suspend the federal policy against creating new national monuments to honor any American hero until 25 years after the person's death. The goal is to erect a major new monument in the city to honor Reagan while he is still alive. A private foundation entitled the Reagan Legacy Project is seeking the creation of a memorial to Reagan to be placed in every county in the U.S. Some have raised money in the hopes of having Reagan's likeness added to Mount Rushmore. At the rate this is going, I almost expect someone to propose renaming the capital city Reaganland. A recent scholars' survey ranking the presidents

---

Revised version of a speech presented at the annual meeting of the British Association of American Studies, April 6–10, 2001, Keele, England.

placed Reagan third greatest, and that was outdone by a popular poll in which the U.S public ranked Reagan the greatest President in history, above Washington and Lincoln.

As absurd as some of the above may seem, there is the serious fact that not only do Presidents care about their legacies, but that the way in which a former Presidency is remembered has important political implications. For those seeking earnestly to memorialize Reagan in every way that they can, there is a clear political agenda at the core of their efforts. Reagan stood for certain things that they believe in and they understand that the symbol of Reagan carries great weight in the U.S. They therefore seek to make the Reagan symbol a pervasive and permanent feature of the U.S. landscape.

Similarly, those who revere the importance of Franklin D. Roosevelt's legacy made certain that a national monument to FDR stands in Washington, D.C., even though the former President himself had once said that he never wanted to be memorialized in such a grand fashion.[2] And advocates of the disabled succeeded in having FDR memorialized seated in a wheelchair, even though FDR would never allow himself to be photographed in the wheelchair. The point is that the monument serves political objectives.

This discussion brings me to the subject of the Clinton legacy—or what I call the "two sides of the Clinton legacy." To be fair, there are two sides to the legacies of all Presidents, even those deemed "great." Roosevelt's internment of the Japanese and Reagan's failed leadership in Iran-Contra each deserves a place in the Presidential hall of shame. Everyone knows that Bill Clinton was both a major impact President and a deeply flawed man who shamed his office. Like all modern Presidents, he cared deeply about his legacy, and yet many of his official actions left most observers wondering how someone who actually cared about history's judgment could have done such foolish things.

It is not possible here to assess history's judgment of Clinton. We are simply too close to the events of the Clinton years to move beyond the partisan battles and personal feelings that many have toward the former President and his policies. It is possible though to examine the current impact of his Presidency and also the likely impact on the future of the institution. I will do so by examining the legacies of both the Clinton scandals and some of his administration's policies.

THE PRESIDENCY OF SCANDAL AND ITS IMPLICATIONS

Long after he left office, the scandals of former President Bill Clinton continued to dominate political discussion and debate in the United States. Indeed, months into George W. Bush's term as President some media content analyses showed that among some of the most prominent news sources, Clinton coverage actually exceeded the attention given to the incumbent administration. Furthermore, the scandals of the Clinton years have left a permanent mark on political Washington and will affect the ability of President Bush to lead, although not necessarily in ways that some leading observers have suggested.

The Clinton era is over, yet because of the former President's controversial last minute pardons, in particular the pardon of fugitive financier Marc Rich, Clinton remains a fixture of the American political debate. As President, Clinton was a powerfully transforming leader and a lightning rod for controversy at the same time. The scandals of his Presidency—from the travel office firings, Whitewater investigation, the Lewinsky episode, to the pardons—affected not only his administration, but also the future of the institution of the Presidency. It is appropriate to therefore identify and analyze some of the implications of the Clinton scandals for present and future Presidential administrations.

First, the culture of scandal, investigations, and deeply personalized politics is now a fixture of U.S. politics. As much as President George W. Bush makes the claim that he can overcome this difficult atmosphere, the reality is that deep scars remain from the political battles of the Clinton years. The incumbent President has made it very clear that he wants the country to move forward and to focus on the new administration's policy agenda. Yet several months into Bush's term key congressional committees were investigating former President Clinton's pardons and there was even talk among some GOP members that new articles of impeachment would be introduced (former Presidents can still be impeached and subsequently denied their government pensions). With these continuing investigations, Bush had some difficulty early in his term in getting the country to pay attention to his agenda rather than Clinton's continuing troubles. At one point Bush even suggested the possibility of a pardon for the former President, but Clinton made it clear that he did not want and would not accept one. In part, Clinton's stand may have been due to the fact that in the U.S. system of justice, acceptance of a pardon is considered the equivalent of an admission of wrongdoing.

In addition to their outrage at the last minute pardons, it is clear that many of Clinton's opponents believe that he was never properly held accountable for his earlier wrongdoing in the Lewinsky controversy. They still have not given up the fight. Furthermore, many Clinton supporters believe that the GOP House dishonored the Constitution by impeaching a President for what many considered merely private indiscretions. The result is that neither side has disarmed from the Clinton era wars, even though the former President is just a private citizen. The anger continues. The old debates persist.

Of course, none of this suggests that President Bush will be subject to the same level of scrutiny from opponents as his predecessor. Bush at least has the present advantage of a GOP-led House of Representatives, meaning that any investigations emanating from that chamber would have to be initiated by his own party—an unthinkable prospect.[3] Furthermore, although there have been past allegations regarding Bush's personal conduct as a young adult, there is not a hint of a suggestion of any official wrongdoing on his part.

Second, another lingering consequence of the Clinton scandals is the persistence of scandal coverage. Many leading and once obscure journalists found their careers catapulted by their coverage of the scandal. Cable television talk shows and talk radio programs had unprecedented ratings. A number of the reporters covering the scandal became regular television pundits, wrote best-selling books, and now command big speaking fees on the lecture circuit. The scandal was simply great business for the media and the lesson is clear: scandals sell, detailed discussions of policy do not.

Tabloid journalism entered the mainstream of political coverage during the Clinton years. Tabloid newspapers that have claimed that John F. Kennedy is still alive and that Ross Perot takes political advice and endorsements from extra-terrestial beings have also broken some of the prominent political scandal stories of the past decade, including the Clinton-Gennifer Flowers affair and some of the details of the Marc Rich pardon. We have witnessed the spectacle of the respectable press chasing the lead of the tabloids and a blending of political coverage that renders the once stodgy news sources increasingly less reputable.

Internet "journalism" also rose to prominence as a result of the Clinton scandals, with many of the most salacious details of Clinton's affair with Lewinsky being first published on Web sites. The *Washington Post* broke the story on its Web site, not in its daily newspaper edition. One of the more disturbing developments is the relaxing of traditional journalistic standards for sourcing information prior to publishing. The Internet "journalists" created a hectic-paced news coverage that placed enormous pressure on mainstream news organizations to "be first", or at least not get left behind the pack. Many reputable news organizations in their quest to keep up with the competition reported false information and seriously damaged their credibility.[4]

To be sure, although the scandals have been good business for the U.S. media, opinion polls make it clear that American journalism has lost a lot of respect because of the perception that news people are obsessed with the personal lives of public people. American public opinion today perceives journalists as no more committed to honor and the truth as the people they investigate. Citizens absorb scandal coverage, but decry its overemphasis at the same time.

Third, the Clinton scandals have profoundly influenced perceptions and even the realities of the powers of the separate branches. For example:

Congress allowed the Independent Counsel Statute to expire and has not come up with an alternative system for having independent, non-partisan investigations of allegations of executive branch wrongdoing. Even with the creation eventually of some alternative (perhaps even similar) system, future investigators are likely to find that their powers are very narrowly limited by statute. Congress may be reluctant ever again to appropriate substantial funding for a Presidential investigation. In effect, this change may actually strengthen the Presidency as Congress weakens the ability of any investigation to proceed with appropriate scope of authority and necessary resources. The cost and extent of former Independent Counsel Kenneth Starr's investigation of Clinton were entirely too large in the public's view.

President Clinton's specious claims of executive privilege (the right of the President to withhold information—documents or testimony usually—from those with compulsory power) have weakened that power for future administrations. Even though federal court decisions on executive privilege claims struck down Clinton's actions repeatedly and yet at the same time affirmed the legitimacy of that power under appropriate circumstances, the former President's actions—like Nixon's actions during Watergate—brought disrepute to the very concept of Presidential secrecy. The taint of Watergate delegitimized executive privilege for years and Clinton's actions in the Lewinsky scandal will likely have the same effect.

Clinton forced the uncomfortable issue of a so-called secret service protective privilege. Because the Starr investigation sought testimony from secret service agents assigned to protect the President, Clinton pushed a legal claim that such agents are immune from having to testify due to their unique responsibilities. With no legal precedent existing for such a privilege, Clinton lost his case and now secret service agents may be compelled to testify anytime there are investigations involving White House activity.

The Lewinsky scandal also opened the Presidency for the first time to private lawsuits. Clinton tried to claim immunity from such suits, but was ultimately repudiated by the Supreme Court. Future Presidents may therefore be subject to all kinds of civil suits that could distract administrations from public leadership and policy.

Many speculate that such suits may become the strategy of political opponents seeking to distract a President from pursuing his agenda.

Finally, there is the issue of impeachment itself. Some observers suggest that the GOP Congress lowered the standard for "high crimes and misdemeanors" and thereby made future impeachments more likely. To the contrary, the strong public rebuke of the impeachment managers and their failure to secure a simple majority in the Senate on any article of impeachment seem more likely to send the message that the impeachment power should be reserved for only the most compelling circumstances. It appears more likely that the future prospects for holding Presidents accountable will suffer because of the likelihood that Congress will shy from using or even threatening the use of the impeachment power.

To what extent will all of these factors influence the current Bush administration? The answer is not so simple. First, it is clear that the culture of investigations and deeply personalized politics persists. Bush wants the emphasis on Clinton's past actions to end and yet he has no power over a GOP-led House committee's decision to investigate. And by pushing his party hard to move beyond Clinton-related issues, he risks alienating much of his core conservative base. Bush cannot win either way.

Second, the media emphasis on scandal and intrigue began before Clinton, but reached a high-point during the Clinton years and shows no sign of abating. As the controversies over the Clinton pardons recede, the media have paid increasing attention to Bush's agenda. And if Bush's administration stays scandal-free, the tone of coverage will have to change (at least until the next Washington scandal).

Third, the Presidency is not necessarily a weaker office as a result of the Clinton scandals, as many scholars suggest. To be sure, executive privilege is weakened by its now negative connotation. But like the post-Watergate Presidencies of Ford, Carter, Reagan, and Bush, the new Bush administration may find other constitutional and statutory bases for exercising secrecy than executive privilege. The lack of an independent counsel and the likelihood that any position created by Congress as a replacement will be a weakened version are encouraging for Bush and future Presidents. And some say that Bush has nothing to worry about regarding the lack of a secret service protective privilege or the possibility of private lawsuits simply because his current personal behavior is unimpeachable. As long as Bush and his administration are ethical, the culture of scandal and personal attacks will somewhat recede—but be certain that Bush can only drive these tendencies underground for now and not eradicate them from Washington forever.

THE IMPACT OF CLINTONISM ON THE BUSH PRESIDENCY

The Clinton Presidency has had other long-lasting implications for the future of American politics. Here I wish to examine how some of Clinton's actions are defining the Presidency of George W. Bush.

First, perhaps the most lasting and beneficial policy impact of the Clinton Presidency was a result of the 1993 budget package that included substantial tax increases and spending reductions. Economists generally regard that bill as the single most important action by the government during the Clinton years that ultimately contributed to current annual budget surpluses. Of course, other factors unrelated to government action and other government policies also had a strong impact on the overall economy of the 1990s. Nonetheless, the economic boom and budget surpluses of the Clinton years have made President George W. Bush's policy options much easier than was the case of his GOP predecessors George Bush and Ronald Reagan, both of whom had to make policy trade-offs due to enormous deficits.

The hallmark of Bush's first year domestic agenda is the passage of federal income tax rate reductions. Without the current budget surplus, the prospects for such a policy would have been unthinkable. On two occasions, the chairman of the Federal Reserve Board publicly lent his support to the general proposition that income tax relief for citizens would be good economic policy given the size of the annual surpluses. Perhaps it is no small irony that Clinton's major domestic success made Bush's first big policy victory possible.

The President also proposed substantial spending increases for defense and even a number of domestic programs traditionally favored by Democrats. Perhaps most conspicuous is Bush's proposal for an 11% increase in one year in federal spending on education. In an address to the Congress, Bush offered substantial spending increases for the environment, national parks, health care and other Democratically-favored programs. Bush may be able to sustain support for some of his policies in part because he is not attacking many of the programs favored by the opposition party and therefore he is not making political enemies in Congress.

Bush therefore had the luxury early in his term to be a Presidential Santa Claus, offering tax relief, more money for defense and domestic programs, and not asking for any major sacrifices from Americans. Nonetheless, the loyal opposition in Congress did not give the President a free ride. There is considerable Democratic-led debate over the wisdom of tax cuts at a time when the government debt still needs to be reduced and the economy has slowed down. Democrats objected to Bush's tax policy on fairness grounds—that it benefits wealthier taxpayers more than the poor or middle class.

Furthermore, budget surpluses may have the affect of making it more difficult for Bush to try to bring some needed fiscal discipline to certain programs. The president may find that his appeals to streamline the military and to bring fiscal order to medicare and social security will fall flat because of a lack of any sense of urgency. Annual budget surpluses may ultimately distract lawmakers from the tasks of making government programs more efficient and cost-effective.

The budget surpluses also allow Bush to appropriate a GOP version of Clinton's famed "triangulation" strategy. Recall that Clinton effectively defined himself as the third force in U.S. politics, standing between the so-called extremism of the GOP and the alleged failures of the old Democratic Party. A part of that successful strategy was "stealing" popular elements of the opposition party's agenda and giving these new initiatives a distinct flavor. So, for example, rather than concede the "values" agenda to the social conservatives in the GOP who favored some unpopular policies, Clinton recognized the appeal of values-oriented issues and promoted instead such popular initiatives as mandatory school uniforms, the V-chip in televisions, regulating popular entertainment programming, regulating tobacco, among others.

President Bush similarly has learned to appropriate the rights-based language of liberalism and also the liberal language of compassion and good government, all the while putting a conservative twist on the policies he promotes. Bush has made a substantially larger commitment to fund education than his predecessors, stealing the Democrats' label of being the most "pro-education," even while he seeks such conservative programs as vouchers. In his first several weeks in office Bush made a number of political gestures to signify his intention to address issues of race, including a promise to end the practice of racial profiling by law enforcement authorities. In so doing, Bush favorably positions himself on traditionally Democratic Party policy territory and softens criticism of his other very conservative programs.

Second, Clinton's personalized Presidency has transformed expectations about the office in ways that are affecting Bush's leadership style. While in the White House, Bush's father refused to communicate to the public through various new media including daytime talk shows because he thought that such a practice was beneath the dignity of the Presidency. When in public he held his emotions in check because that was what he thought Presidents should do. Clinton by contrast did not hesitate to use new means of political communication, even appearing on such television programs as MTV. Early in Clinton's term many commentators decried this practice as undignified, yet by the end of his eight years in the White

House most had accepted Clinton's approach as a leadership necessity and a reflection of contemporary American culture. Clinton did not hesitate to use emotional appeals and gestures that conveyed a new openness for an American President.

No one expects President Bush to appear on MTV, nor especially to talk openly about his preference for certain styles of undergarments. But in many respects, Bush appears more attuned to Clinton's personalized approach to leadership than to his own father's more formal style. As a candidate for office, Bush did not shy from making appearances on daytime talk shows and late night comedic programs. As President, to date he has exhibited an informal style with journalists, even to the point of using endearing nicknames for certain White House reporters. He seems equally comfortable using emotional appeals and gestures. He easily dispenses with criticism and even the mockery of his flawed use of language by poking fun at himself, even to the point of self-parody. On some occasions he has made joking references to Saturday Night Live parodies by using some of the same garbled words and sentences used on the program to mock the President.

In large part, these stylistic changes in the Presidency may be due more to the transformation of the media environment than to Clinton's unique communications skills. Clinton's skills happened to fit the moment, but the reality is that no president can ignore the requirements of the new media environment in the U.S. The challenge for Bush will be to find ways to sustain media relations and communications strategies that will work for a man who is acknowledged to be a somewhat weak communicator. It is hard to imagine Bush ever commanding the national debate through the force of his communications skills the way in which Clinton was able to do so. On the other hand, previously as a candidate Bush was the constant beneficiary of very low expectations. It is conceivable that he can continue to prevail by simply outperforming the low expectations of others.

Third, Clinton's well-known character flaws, scandals, and controversial manner by which he left office, have all enabled Bush to maintain a respectable level of public support simply because he appears honorable by contrast. A substantial amount of negative news coming out of Washington still focuses on Clinton. Bush's "honeymoon" period stood in sharp contrast to Clinton's in 1993 when the President was embroiled in controversies over some of his policies, appointments, and White House hostility toward the press corps. The quantity of the early Bush coverage in the U.S. media was quite small for a new President and stood in very sharp contrast to the media scrutiny of Clinton's 1993 honeymoon period. That situation appeared to favor Bush, as he was somewhat better able to communicate his priorities without any constant drumbeat of criticism from the media. Sometimes in American politics, less news is good news.

CONCLUSION

The Clinton years altered American politics. President George W. Bush cannot escape Clinton's lasting influence, even while he seeks to change the political culture in Washington and to offer his own different programs. Clinton's actions created both opportunities and challenges for the new President. The greatest opportunities are due to the expanding budget surpluses that make policy trade-offs in the Bush administration so much less painful than during the era of annual deficits. The toughest challenges for Bush are to overcome the sharply personal and partisan tone of Washington and to carve out a significant positive legacy of his own.

POSTSCRIPT

The events of September 11, 2001, several months after the completion of this essay, dramatically transformed the Bush presidency. To many observers, the scandals of the Clinton years no longer merit much of the nation's attention as the public unites behind President Bush. At this writing, just a few weeks after the national tragedy, it is difficult to speculate how the terrorist attacks will affect history's judgment of the Clinton legacy. At the moment, some of the former president's critics are suggesting that Clinton had not done enough while in office to combat terrorism. The former president himself has been quick to point out that his administration indeed had effectively taken all reasonable measures to protect the country from terrorism. Whatever the truth may be, the fight against terrorism belongs to the Bush administration.

NOTES

1 Near the date of the renaming of National Airport Reagan's closest political adviser of over forty years Lyn Nofziger gave a guest lecture to my undergraduate American Government class. He decried the renaming of the airport as absurd because Reagan had never once in his life used the airport for travel. Nofziger believed that a massively costly federal building in the nation's capital city was not the best way to honor a president who lambasted federal spending as excessive.

2 Outside the National Archives Building on Pennsylvania Avenue in Washington, D.C. there is a little known, small plaque on the ground honoring Roosevelt. That was all the memorial that FDR desired.

3 At this writing in Summer 2001 the Democrats control the Senate by the slimmest of margins: 50 to 49 (with one independent).

4 See John Anthony Maltese's essay in this volume.

ARTICLE 25

REFINING THE RHETORIC OF RIGHTS

Mary Ann Glendon

Those who won our independence believed that the final end of the
state was to make men free to develop their faculties; and that in its
government the deliberative forces should prevail over the
arbitrary. . . . They believed that . . . the greatest menace to freedom is
an inert people; that public discussion is a political duty; and that this
should be a fundamental principle of the American government.

—Justice Louis D. Brandeis[1]

The strident rights rhetoric that currently dominates American
political discourse poorly serves the strong tradition of protection for individual freedom for which the United States is
justly renowned. Our stark, simple rights dialect puts a damper on
the processes of public justification, communication, and deliberation upon which the continuing vitality of a democratic regime depends. It contributes to the erosion of the habits, practices, and
attitudes of respect for others that are the ultimate and surest
guarantors of human rights. It impedes creative long-range thinking
about our most pressing social problems. Our rights-laden public
discourse easily accommodates the economic, the immediate, and
the personal dimensions of a problem, while it regularly neglects
the moral, the long-term, and the social implications.

Rights talk in its current form has been the thin end of a wedge
that is turning American political discourse into a parody of itself
and challenging the very notion that politics can be conducted

through reasoned discussion and compromise. For the new rhetoric of rights is less about human dignity and freedom than about insistent, unending desires. Its legitimation of individual and group egoism is in flat opposition to the great purposes set forth in the Preamble to the Constitution: "to form a more perfect Union, establish justice, promote the general Welfare, and secure the Blessings of Liberty to ourselves and our Posterity."

Merely refining the rhetoric of rights—if such a thing could be done—would hardly remedy all the ills that currently beset American culture and politics. Yet language, with its powerful channeling effects on thought, is centrally implicated in our dilemma and in our prospects for surmounting it. Political language will be an important determinant of our success or failure in preserving and developing the democratic idea under social and economic conditions that could not have been imagined by the Founders. Unfortunately, American political discourse has become vacuous, hard-edged, and inflexible just when it is called upon to encompass economic, social, and environmental problems of unparalleled difficulty and complexity. To make matters worse, the possibility must be reckoned with that our shallow rights talk is a faithful reflection of what our culture has become. Thus a critique of our current rights talk must at least address some difficult questions whose answers are far from clear. Is our distinctive rights dialect, for better or worse, a mirror of contemporary American society? If not, what indigenous materials, if any, are at hand from which to fashion a more capacious public language? If such materials exist, is there any reason to believe that Americans could or would employ them to change the way we debate public issues?

Even one who wishes to believe that our current political discourse does not do justice to the richness and variety of American moral sentiments must acknowledge that it does grow out of, and reflect, our culture and aspirations in certain unmistakable ways. Our political speech has become as lifeless and cliché-ridden as the generic, popular speech that we use to communicate across most ethnic, economic, and other differences in the course of an average day. Like the basic patter we routinely deploy in dealing with strangers, political speech has to be intelligible to a wide assortment of individuals who increasingly share few referents in the form of common customs, literature, religion, or history. Under these circumstances, it is not surprising that contemporary public figures borrow heavily from a language that takes the individual as the basic social unit, that treats all individuals as presumptively strangers to one another, and that distances itself from moral judgment. The hallmark of legal discourse, whose very symbol from ancient times has been the blind-fold, is to deliberately disregard the particular traits that make one human being different from another.

Our anemic political discourse does help to solve a communications problem arising out of our diversity. But abandoning the effort to inform, explain, justify, and translate has higher costs in the realm of politics than in popular speech. It deprives citizens of the information and reasoned argument they need to hear in order to make intelligent choices among candidates, and to responsibly assess the long-and short-term costs and benefits of proposed programs and policies. When political actors resort to slogans and images rather than information and explanations, they hinder the exercise of citizenship. Leaving so much unsaid, they create a discrepancy between what we officially proclaim and what we need in order to make sense of our lives.[2] The result for many people is a generalized frustration with politics that observers often misdiagnose as civic apathy.

Our careless rights talk is of a piece with another troubling aspect of contemporary American culture. It is a specific instance of the tendency of middle-class Americans, observed by Robert Bellah and his colleagues, to use a "first language" of individualism in speaking of what is most important to them.[3] Bellah's *Habits of the Heart* study suggests, moreover, that the sort of individualism that now pervades American speech and society is different in kind from the older individualisms of the frontier, of early capitalism, and of traditional Protestantism.[4] The current strain is characterized by self-expression and the pursuit of self-gratification, rather than by self-reliance and the cultivation of self-discipline. Rights in the current American dialect are the expression of desires the drafters of the Bill of Rights viewed with suspicion—to be completely free, to possess things totally, to be treated justly without being asked to act justly. Christopher Lasch, in his sombre works of social criticism, makes it seem plausible that our current rights talk tells the whole story. He claims that America has lost its basic stock of patriotic, biblical, and folkloric legends that once provided young people with ideals toward which they might aspire, and with frameworks for endowing their lives with meaning. Without that background, he says,

> the foreground fills the whole picture—an insistent "I want." Wants themselves become formless and unspecifiable. To the question, "What *do* they want, then?" there is only one answer in the case of people whose desires are unformed by the experience of participating in a culture larger than themselves: "Everything. "[5]

The surveys of the political attitudes of young Americans to which I have referred from time to time contain much to support Lasch's pronouncement that "the moral bottom has dropped out of [American] culture."[6] A collective portrait emerges from them of a population of young adults that is indifferent to public affairs and that places its highest value on self-fulfillment.[7]

There is much evidence, however, that cooperative, relational, patterns of living survive in the United States to a greater degree than our individualistic public rhetoric would suggest. Most Americans still live, work, and find meaning within a variety of overlapping small groups that generate, as well as depend on, trust, fairness, and sharing. Around the kitchen table, in the neighborhood, the workplace, in religious groups, and in various other communities of memory and mutual aid, men and women maintain ongoing dialogues about freedom and responsibility, individual and community, present and future. The commonest and most particularistic of these discourses is household table talk with its familiar shorthand expressions born of shared family and, often, ethnic history. To be sure, the language of rights has invaded American homes, but there it is often held in check by recollection and retelling of the family's concrete experiences, and by the household's fund of stories about relationships, obligations, and the long-term consequences of present acts and decisions. Some of every family's talk is intelligible only to its own members, but much is also part of a more widely dispersed American conversation.[8]

Traditionally, it has been women who have taken primary responsibility for the transmission of family lore and for the moral education of children. As mothers and teachers, they have nourished a sense of connectedness between individuals, and an awareness of the linkage among present, past, and future generations. Hence the important role accorded by many feminists to the values of care, relationship, nurture, and contextuality, along with the insistence on rights that the women's movement in general has embraced. Women are still predominant among the country's caretakers and educators, and many are carrying insights gained from these experiences into public life in ways that are potentially transformative. Their vocabularies of caretaking are important sources of correctives to the disdain for dependency and the indifference to social bonds that characterize much of our political speech.

Another indigenous discourse that contains helpful antidotes for some of the extremes of rights talk is one that itself has been a major contributor to those excesses. It is ironic that Americans have saturated their political language with what is only a secondary language of the law. The predilection for exaggeration and absoluteness that all of us often indulge when speaking of rights seems recognizably related to the strategic use of language by courtroom performers, hardball negotiators, takeover artists, and other zealous advocates ready to go to almost any lengths on behalf of a client or a cause. The majority of lawyers in the United States, however, spend most of their working hours engaged in the legal equivalent of preventive medicine.

The rank and file of the legal profession help their clients to plan and maintain relationships that depend on regular and reliable fulfillment of responsibilities. They know that the assertion of rights is usually a sign of breakdown in a relationship. They endeavor to prepare agreements, leases, estate plans, charters, and bylaws, so as to minimize occasions for friction. They are careful—often to a fault—in their use of language. When discord arises, they assist in negotiation and adjustment. Only when something goes drastically wrong is the matter turned over to the litigator, and even then, her initial efforts normally will be directed toward settlement. Most lawyers (like most other people) understand that, over time, selective exaggeration and omission undermine relationships as well as credibility. They, too, tell their children the cautionary tales of Chicken Little and the little boy who cried "Wolf." Abraham Lincoln's exhortation to lawyers to be "peacemakers" still reflects the commonsense ideals, and the way of life, of lawyers engaged in what is still the main business of the profession—helping citizens to live decently together.

> Discourage litigation. Persuade your neighbors to compromise whenever you can. Point out to them how the nominal winner is often a real loser—in fees, expenses, and waste of time. As a peacemaker the lawyer has a superior opportunity of being a good man. There will still be business enough.[9]

Similarly, the uncelebrated majority of American judges are engaged in a kind of work that is characterized by careful distinction and discerning accommodation. Practical reason, not abstract theorizing, dominates the day-to-day activity of the typical American judge. Year in and year out, she weaves back and forth between facts and law, the parts and the whole, the situation at hand and similar situations that have arisen in the past or are likely to arise in the future. She attends carefully to context, she explores analogies and distinctions, the scope and the limits of generalizing principles. She recognizes that neither side has a monopoly on truth and justice. She is neither a mere technician nor a tyrant, but something between an artist and an artisan, practicing what the Romans called the "art of the good and equitable."

Within the legal academy, too, the tolerance for complexity and the sense of proportion that are often lacking in the rights fraternity are still the criteria of scholarship in the less glamorous areas of law—taxation, antitrust, contracts, torts, property, and so on. All in all, the dominant ethos of the legal profession is still one where civility and adequately complex speech are the order of the day, and where nuance and subtlety are expected to the degree required by the subject under discussion.

There is further untapped potential for renewal of political discourse within immigrant groups, in ethnic enclaves, and within religious and other associations. American thinking about the favored
subject of property rights, for example, has been decisively shaped
by an increasingly problematic belief that man can master and sub-
due the natural world. We have much to learn from native Americans who have long known that there is a way in which the land
owns us, even as we pretend to own the land, and that we ignore
that fact at our own peril. Many conservationists are coming to recognize that, where environmental issues are concerned, the biblical
language of stewardship may be more appropriate than endowing
trees with rights, and more conducive to responsible use of resources than vague promises that everyone has a "right" to a healthy
environment.

The greatest hope for renewal, perhaps, lies in the American political tradition itself, in its time-honored ideals of tolerance, respect
for others, public deliberation, individual freedom and responsibility, and the mandate for self-restraint implicit in the rule of law. In a
spirited defense of liberalism "properly understood" against its
communitarian critics, Stephen Macedo has argued that the "moral
core" of our public order is a commitment to public justification, that
is, to an ongoing process of demanding, offering, and testing public
moral arguments and reasons.[10] Such a commitment, it must be acknowledged, assumes that men and women are capable of giving
and accepting the kinds of reasons which are not mere references to
narrow interests, but which can survive critical examination and be
widely seen to be good.[11] But it does not require us to pin all our
hopes on the rational faculties of human beings, or to underestimate
the degree of intractable discord in a large and diverse society. When
we are left with important matters upon which agreement seems, for
the time being, unobtainable, the liberal virtue of moderation suggests that often the best thing to do will be "to moderate our claims
in the face of the reasonable claims of others, to balance, and split at
least some of our differences. "[12]

The United States (more than many other less diverse and more
secularized countries) thus seems endowed with a wide array of cultural resources that could help to temper some of the extravagances
and remedy some of the deficiencies of our rights talk. We do not
lack materials for refining our deliberations concerning such matters
as whether a particular issue is best conceptualized as involving a
right; the relation a given right should have to other rights and interests; the responsibilities, if any, that should be correlative with a
given right; the social costs of rights; and what effects a given right
can be expected to have on the setting of conditions for the durable
protection of freedom and human dignity. The very heterogeneity

that drives us to seek an excessively abstract common language may indeed be one of our most promising resources for enriching it.

But how might this latent cultural energy be released? Could some latter-day Abraham Lincoln find a way to draw on our rich but highly diverse cultural heritage in order to speak to "the better angels of our nature"? Might some new Martin Luther King, Jr., call on the teachings of the world's great religions to reunite our love of individual freedom with our sense of a community for which we accept a common responsibility? A host of daunting obstacles make it increasingly difficult for ideas and arguments possessing any degree of complexity to break into a public conversation that is kept simple by habit and technology. Rights language not only seems to filter out other discourses; it simultaneously infiltrates them. (What parent has not heard about children's rights in the midst of an argument over mittens, manners, or spinach?)

Moreover, the men and women who wield the most influence in our society, and enjoy the greatest access to the public forum, are often the most remote from alternative American discourses and the sources from which they spring. To members of the knowledge class that now predominates in government, political parties, corporations, universities, and the mass media, strong ties to persons and places, religious beliefs, or attachment to traditions are frequently relatively unimportant, or even counterproductive.[13] Geographically mobile, and deriving prestige, power, and satisfaction from their work, American movers and shakers are often at best indifferent to the "delicate communities on which others depend for practical and emotional support."[14] Their common attitude that the educated are better equipped to govern than the masses finds its institutional expression in a disdain for ordinary politics and the legislative process, and a preference for extending the authority of courts, the branch of government to which they have the easiest access.[15]

Over a century ago, John Stuart Mill warned that a soft form of tyranny was being exercised by untutored majorities and by a vulgar press whose members were "much like" their "mediocre" readers: "the opinions of masses of merely average men are everywhere become or becoming the dominant power."[16] The emerging mass media, he thought, were especially threatening to "exceptional" men and women, intellectuals, and creative persons. In the midst of the rights revolution, however, a new form of soft tyranny has been building. Hyperindividualistic values and language have become pervasive in the education and information industries. Journalism has become one of the professions, leaving what Mill referred to pejoratively as "average" men and women with few spokespersons or outlets for their concerns. A press more preoccupied with celebrities than with the world of work, and often more disposed to entertain than to inform, inevitably loses touch with the daily lives of most Americans. A striking instance of this trend is the virtual disappearance of the once respected "labor beat" from American newspapers, and the scanty coverage accorded by the media generally to workers' issues.[17] A study of labor and the media showed that in 1989 the three network evening news programs devoted only about two percent of their time to all American workplace issues, including child care, the minimum wage, and occupational safety and health. These developments are all the more remarkable when one reflects on the sharp rise in women's labor force participation since the 1960s, and on the steadily increasing importance of paid employment as a determinant of standing and security in American society.[18] Speculating on the reasons for the decline in media attention to issues of vital interest to the 100 million men and women who compose the American labor force, the director of the study, Jonathan Tasini, observed: "There is a growing gap between the experiences of working people in the United States and the individuals who are supposed to report on their lives."

What, then, are the prospects for the sorts of broad-based, free-ranging, reasoned processes of deliberation that our constitutional order both invites and requires? In a landmark free-speech case, from which the epigraph to this chapter is taken, Justice Brandeis asserted that public discussion is indispensable to a regime that purports to be concerned with the free development of the human person. Deliberation, he said, is our best defense against arbitrary rule, and an "inert people" the principal menace to freedom. What Justice Brandeis left out (and what American political actors generally ignore), however, is that supporters of a system that relies so heavily on public deliberation cannot afford to neglect the effective conditions for deliberation. The greatest obstacle to political renewal under present circumstances may not be an "inert people" so much as the failure of persons in positions of leadership to provide models by personal example and to work actively to create opportunities for discussion.

At the most basic level, deliberation requires time, information, and forums where facts, interests, and ideas can be exchanged and debated.[19] It requires vigorous political parties with the ability to articulate programs and attract participation. If deliberation is not to take the form of a mere clash of unyielding interests, and to end in seemingly irreconcilable conflicts, these simple necessary conditions are not sufficient. It is becoming plain that our liberal regime of equality and personal freedom depends, more than most theorists of liberalism have been willing to admit, on the existence and support of certain social assumptions and practices: the belief that each and every human being possesses great and inherent value, the willingness to respect the rights of others even at the cost of some disadvantages to one's self, the ability to defer some immediate benefits for the sake of long-range goals, and a regard for reason-giving and civility in public discourse. It took a Tocqueville—with his peculiar combination of sympathy, curiosity, and ironic distance—to see how essential, and yet how difficult, it would be for democratic regimes to nourish the habits and beliefs on which their ambitious enterprises depend. If participation and deliberation are not to be merely the means of advancing short-term individual and group interests, if they are also to serve as aids to transcending these narrow concerns, political leaders must attend to the social structures where cultural value systems are transmitted, and where civic skills are acquired.

In his 1990 New Year's address, Czechoslovak President Vaclav Havel rhetorically asked a question that is pertinent to our own circumstances: How did a people that to all appearances was beaten down, atomized, cynical, and apathetic find the strength to embark on a great project of social and political renewal?

> [W]e ask where the young people, in particular, who have never known any other system, find the source of their aspirations for truth, freedom of thought, civic courage, and civic foresight? How is it that their parents, the generation which was considered lost, also joined in with them?[20]

Havel's first comment on his own question was that "man is never merely a product of the world around him, he is always capable of striving for something higher."[21] A second factor that helped to regenerate a seemingly moribund political life, according to Havel, was the recovery of the "humanistic and democratic traditions" that "lay dormant somewhere in the subconscious of our nations and national minorities, and were passed on from one generation to the next in order for each [of] us to discover them within us when the time was right."[22] The main carriers of these dormant traditions were the associations of civil society—communities of mutual aid like Solidarity in Poland, and many communities of memory, both ethnic and religious. The slogans that stirred them and that spread like brushfire from country to country were not only about rights. They were about the courage to be honest; about men and women "living in truth"; and about calling "good and evil by name."[23]

With hindsight, it seems that no small part of the great transformations that have taken place in East Central Europe have been powered by the same kinds of forces that still silently support our mature, and relatively complacent, democracies in the West. The East European freedom movements can be and often are described in abstract political language as campaigns for "human rights." But they were also (like the American civil rights movement of the 1950s and 1960s) nourished through their dark days and nights by inspiring religious leaders. Participants in these historic struggles found strength and solace in communities of shared experience and recollection, as well as in their common quest for political and civil liberties.

Here at home, where humanistic and democratic traditions are far from dormant, political life, in theory, should be easier to revive, and its prospects less uncertain. On the political horizon, there are scattered signs that may well favor a revision in the location, terms, and content of political debate, bringing it closer to potential sources of renewal. The Supreme Court seems to be relaxing its hold on some of the issues that it had removed from legislative and local control with little mandate from the design, text, or tradition of the Constitution. This more deferential judicial posture leaves wider scope for democratic processes of bargaining, education, and persuasion to operate. It gives state and local governments more leeway to be "laboratories" where a variety of innovative approaches to vexing social problems (open-air drug markets, child care, drunk driving) can be tested on a limited basis, and their successes or failures assessed. Like muscles long unused, atrophied political processes will move awkwardly at first; they will need exercise before they become healthy and strong. Meanwhile, slowly but irreversibly, African-Americans, Asian-Americans, Hispanics, women, and others who have been underrepresented in politics, are assuming their rightful roles in public life. To what extent their presence will have a transformative effect on the terms and content of public discussion is an open question (transformation works both ways), but some will bring new insights and modes of discourse into the public square.

At the grassroots level, men and women of widely varying beliefs and backgrounds are increasingly manifesting their discontent with what had come to seem an unwritten law that morally or religiously grounded viewpoints are out of bounds in public dialogue.[24] Whether or not this unrest amounts to a full-blown "culture struggle," as some say, it is bringing still more new players onto the political scene. Many of them, like Dr. King, are adept at articulating their perspectives in such a way as to make them accessible to all men and women of good will. Long years of interfaith discussions, begun in an effort to improve relations between Christians and Jews, and among Christian sects, have produced secular side effects as substantial as they were unexpected. In learning, slowly and with great difficulty, to communicate across painful memories and profound differences, members of America's religious groups have made important discoveries. They learned that they could enter into dialogue, find some common ground, and, where common ground did not seem to exist, achieve mutual understanding—all without losing their own religious distinctiveness. Fear, suspicion, divisiveness, and intolerance were lessened, not aggravated, through open exchange. In resolutely seeking out ways to "translate" particular discourses, without sacrificing subtlety and complexity; in finding areas of agreement; and in learning to disagree without losing mutual respect America's religions have helped to model ways of entering into dialogue across deep differences. They have provided challenging and inspiring examples of coexistence in pluralism.

Many devotees of rights talk will find these bits of evidence scattered examples, and suggestive developments unconvincing. Those who hold that only power can check power will be unmoved by a case that pins so many hopes on cogent argument, persuasion, negotiation, and self-restraint. Those who believe that, in many cases, there is no basis whatsoever for communication or mutual understanding between political antagonists will prefer rights in their starker forms, untempered by limits or obligations. Those who count on science to take care of environmental problems, and on economic growth to provide for posterity, will be untroubled by the present-mindedness of rights talk. Those who consider that families, churches, labor unions, and the like are more apt to oppress than to empower individuals, will be content to continue to work out our collective destiny on the individual-state-market grid. Those who have given up on ordinary politics and the legislative process will not be unduly distressed if most important controversies are entrusted to the courts for decision.

Unhappily, there are all too many reasons to give naked force its due, to despair of mediating group conflict, to live for the moment, and to be cynical about politics. Spousal and child abuse in some households, periodic religious scandals, and corrupt leaders in some unions have soured many on the potential of the nation's families, churches, and workers' groups to serve as seedbeds of civic virtue or as buffers between the individual and large organizations. It is an illusion, however, to believe that the "parchment barriers" of legal rights alone can shelter citizens from the arbitrary exercise of public or private power. There should be no mistaking the fact that a conversation carried on in our current American rights dialect is a dialogue of despair, an admission that we have lost the historic wager in *Federalist* No. 1 that our political order need not be determined by force and accident, but can be established through "reflection and choice."

Only time will tell whether the public square can be effectively regained for an ongoing broad-based conversation about the means and ends of government, about what kind of society we are, and about what kind of future we hope to create for our children and for posterity. The very features that have made us different from other advanced welfare democracies may turn out to be the most conducive to the renewal of political discourse: the variety of our racial and ethnic groups, the opportunities for innovation and experimentation inherent in our sort of federalism, our neighborliness, our stubborn religiosity, and even, within bounds, our attachment to a gambling, risk-taking, profit-making economy. There is reason to believe that a significant constituency exists in the United States for candor, moderation, and complexity adequate to the matter at hand. What is less clear is whether Americans in positions of leadership have the will, ability, courage, and imagination necessary to respond to and mobilize such a constituency.

Refining the rhetoric of rights would be but one element in a project of transformative politics. Yet even quite small shifts in circumstances can produce remarkable distant effects in complex systems.[25] The American experiment in ordered liberty has been brought to its present state by a long series of great and small events. Luck and misfortune have played their role, and so have the sheer exertion of force and power. What is of more interest, however, are the shaping effects of the experience, the intelligence, the imagination, the decisions, the sacrifices, and the personal examples of the men and women who have preceded us. Which of these ingredients will predominate in the period of our own stewardship is not within anyone's power to predict. If the ancient practice of politics is in any sense a science, its subject matter is the elusive one of shifting probabilities. Still, politics, as Havel has reminded the world, is not only the art of the possible: "It can also be the art of the impossible, that is, the art of making both ourselves and the world better."[26] While the current state of the art does not exactly provide grounds for optimism, it does leave room for the more sober, responsible, attitude that prophets have called hope.

NOTES

1 *Whitney v. California,* 274 U.S. 357, 375 (1927) (concurring opinion).

2 See Charles Taylor, *Sources of the Self: The Making of the Modern Identity* (Cambridge: Harvard University Press, 1989), 9.

3 Robert N. Bellah et al., *Habits of the Heart: Individualism and Commitment in American Life* (Berkeley: University of California Press, 1985), 20.

4 Ibid., 27–51.

5 Christopher Lasch, "The I's Have It for Another Decade," *New York Times,* 27 December 1989, A23. See, generally, Lasch, *The Culture of Narcissism* (New York: Warner, 1979) and *The Minimal Self* (New York: Norton, 1984).

6 Lasch, "The I's Have It."

7 People for the American Way, *Democracy's Next Generation: A Study of Youth and Teachers* (Washington, D.C.: People for the American Way, 1989), 14–17. A similar national study by the Times Mirror Center is described by Michael Oreskes, "Profiles of Today's Youth: They Couldn't Care Less," *New York Times,* 28 June 1990, A1, D21.

8 See Barbara Whitehead, "Reports from the Kitchen Table: The Family in an Unfriendly Culture," 3 *Family Affairs* 1 (1990).

9 Abraham Lincoln, *Selected Speeches, Messages, and Letters,* ed. T. Harry Williams (New York: Rinehart, 1957), 34.

10 Stephen Macedo, *Liberal Virtues* (Oxford, England: Clarendon Press, 1990), 34, 41.

11 Ibid., 46.

12 Ibid., 71.

13 Wilson Carey McWilliams, "American Pluralism: The Old Order Passeth," in *The Americans,* 1976, ed. Irving Kristol and Paul Weaver (Lexington: D.C. Heath, 1976), 293, 315.

14 Robert E. Rodes, Jr., "Greatness Thrust Upon Them: Class Biases in American Law," 1983 *American Journal of Jurisprudence* 1, 6.

15 Carl E. Schneider, "State-Interest Analysis in Fourteenth Amendment Privacy Law: An Essay on the Constitutionalization of Social Issues," 51 *Law and Contemporary Problems* 79, 109 (1988).

16 John Stuart Mill, "On Liberty," in *Utilitarianism, Liberty, and Representative Government* (New York: E. P. Dutton, 1951), 163–67.

17 The data in this paragraph are from Jonathan Tasini, "Labor and the Media," 3 *Extra!* (Summer 1990), 1–13.

18 Mary Ann Glendon, *The New Family and the New Property* (Toronto: Butterworths, 1981).

19 See Marc K. Landy, Marc J. Roberts, and Stephen R. Thomas, *The Environmental Protection Agency: Asking the Wrong Questions* (New York: Oxford University Press, 1990), 3–17.

20 Vaclav Havel, "New Year's Day Address," Foreign Broadcasting Information Service, Eastern Europe, 90–001, 2 Jan. 1990, 9–10.

21 Ibid., 10.

22 Ibid.

23 Timothy Garton Ash, *The Uses of Adversity: Essays on the Fate of Central Europe* (New York: Random House, 1989), 48, 191, 203.

24 George Weigel, *Catholicism and the Renewal of American Democracy* (New York: Paulist Press, 1989), 5.

25 See James Gleick, *Chaos: The Making of a New Science* (New York: Viking, 1987).

26 Vaclav Havel, "New Year's Day," 10.

INDEX